Chicano
Psychology

Contributors

FRANK X. ACOSTA

RAYMOND BURIEL

ALFREDO CASTAÑEDA

FELIPE G. CASTRO

ROGELIO DIAZ-GUERRERO

EUGENE E. GARCIA

JOHN GARCIA

RAYMOND T. GARZA

SPENCER KAGAN

MIKE LÓPEZ

STEVEN LOPEZ

JOE L. MARTINEZ, JR.

JANE R. MERCER

MANUEL R. MIRANDA

NATHAN MURILLO

ESTEBAN L. OLMEDO

AMADO M. PADILLA

ALBERT RAMIREZ

MANUEL RAMIREZ III

RENE A. RUIZ

MARIA NIETO SENOUR

Chicano
Psychology

Edited by
JOE L. MARTINEZ, JR.

Department of Psychobiology and
Program in Comparative Culture
University of California, Irvine
Irvine, California

ACADEMIC PRESS   New York   San Francisco   London

A Subsidiary of Harcourt Brace Jovanovich, Publishers

Cover design by Manuel Hernandez-Trujillo

ACADEMIC PRESS, INC.
111 Fifth Avenue, New York, New York 10003

United Kingdom Edition published by
ACADEMIC PRESS, INC. (LONDON) LTD.
24/28 Oval Road, London NW1

Library of Congress Cataloging in Publication Data

Main entry under title:

Chicano psychology.

    Bibliography: p.
    1.   Mexican Americans—Psychology—Addresses, essays,
lectures.   2.   Mexican Americans—Mental health—Address-
es, essays, lectures.   3.   Mexican Americans—Education—
Addresses, essays, lectures.   4.   Mexican Americans—
Education—Language arts—Addresses, essays, lectures.
5.   Bilingualism—United States—Addresses, essays, lec-
tures.   I.   Martinez, Joe L.   [1.   Ethnopsychology.
BF731 C532]
E184.M5C45   301.45'16'872073   77-74056
ISBN 0-12-475650-6

*This book is dedicated to
George I. Sánchez, the father of Chicano Psychology.
We can only hope that our work emulates
his level of scholarship and excellence.*

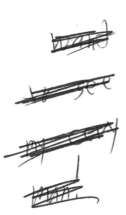

CONTENTS

PART II   BILINGUALISM

PART III   PSYCHOLOGICAL TESTING

LIST OF CONTRIBUTORS

Numbers in parentheses indicate the pages on which the authors' contributions begin.

FRANK X. ACOSTA (215), Department of Psychiatry, University of Southern California, School of Medicine, Los Angeles, California

RAYMOND BURIEL (279), Department of Psychology, University of California, Riverside, Riverside, California

ALFREDO CASTAÑEDA (355), School of Education, Stanford University, Stanford, California

FELIPE G. CASTRO (245), Department of Psychology, University of Washington, Seattle, Washington

ROGELIO DIAZ-GUERRERO (17), National University of Mexico, Georgia No. 123, Mexico 18, DF

EUGENE E. GARCIA (141), Department of Chicano Studies, University of California, Santa Barbara, Santa Barbara, California

JOHN GARCIA (197), Neuropsychiatric Institute, University of California, Los Angeles, Los Angeles, California

RAYMOND T. GARZA (97), Department of Psychology, University of California, Riverside, Riverside, California

SPENCER KAGAN (45, 279), Department of Psychology, University of California, Riverside, Riverside, California

MIKE LÓPEZ (127), Department of Chicano Studies, University of Minnesota, Minneapolis, Minnesota

STEVEN LOPEZ* (263), La Frontera Mental Health Center, Tucson, Arizona

JOE L. MARTINEZ, JR. (11, 29), Department of Psychobiology and Program in Comparative Culture, University of California, Irvine, Irvine, California

JANE R. MERCER (155), Department of Sociology, University of California, Riverside, Riverside, California

MANUEL R. MIRANDA (249), School of Social Work, University of Minnesota, Minneapolis, Minnesota

NATHAN MURILLO (1), Counseling Center, California State University, Northridge, California

ESTEBAN L. OLMEDO (175), Spanish Speaking Mental Health Research Center, University of California, Los Angeles, Los Angeles, California

AMADO M. PADILLA (111), Department of Psychology, University of California, Los Angeles, Los Angeles, California

ALBERT RAMIREZ (87), Department of Psychology, University of Colorado, Boulder, Colorado

MANUEL RAMIREZ III (343), Follow-Through Project, University of California at Santa Cruz, Santa Cruz, California

RENE A. RUIZ (3), Family Studies Center, University of Missouri, Kansas City, Missouri

MARIA NIETO SENOUR (329), Department of Counselor Education, San Diego State University, San Diego, California

*Present address: Spanish Speaking Mental Health Research Center, University of California, Los Angeles, Los Angeles, California

One word has come to symbolize the basic, underlying motivation of the Chicano movement in the United States—justice. Appropriately, one of the major concerns permeating Chicano psychology is the need for social justice, long denied to many Mexican-Americans as the *direct result* of policies and practices developed in American institutions on the basis of ethnocentric interpretations of data related to psychological tests of intelligence and achievement. Concern for social justice for all groups is, in principle, a societal concern in any nation guided by concepts of democracy.

Several of the present contributions emphasize the need for the inclusion and analysis of *sociocultural* variables, particularly in those areas of psychological study where their influence appears most relevant, such as language, cognitive processing, interpersonal relations, and personality. This focus on the part of Chicana and Chicano psychologists not only serves to mute ethnocentric tendencies in interpreting the behavior of Mexican-Americans but also can serve as a heuristic model for approaches to the sociopsychological study of other ethnic populations.

Chicano psychologists are exceedingly few in number and, on the average, only a few years into their postdoctoral careers. Despite these rather modest demographic characteristics, the quality and caliber of conceptualization of research in the area of *biculturality* from the perspective of language, cognition, and personality processes constitute substantial advances in this field.

Chicano Psychology should unequivocally set the record straight as far as what is and what is not intended by the term. Expressions implying "separatism," "exclusivity," "reverse ethnocentrism," are nonexistent, and the contents are clearly of interest to other than Mexican-American psychologists. All psychologists will find this book of value, interest, and importance.

ALFREDO CASTAÑEDA

ACKNOWLEDGMENTS

Most of the articles in this book were presented at the First Symposium on Chicano Psychology held at the University of California, Irvine, in May 1976. The symposium was made possible by a grant from the Ford Foundation, as well as by financial support from the following offices at the University of California, Irvine: the Chancellor, the Vice-Chancellor for Student Affairs, the Affirmative Action Office, the Graduate Division, The Student–Faculty Colloquia Series, The Program in Comparative Culture, and the Minority Programs Committee. We are also grateful to the Ford Foundation for its financial contributions in support of this publication. The editor would like to thank Dr. James L. McGaugh, Vice-Chancellor for Academic Affairs, and Mr. Ramon Curiel, Affirmative Action Officer at the University of California, Irvine; and Mr. Richard Mendoza, Mr. Anthony Zamudio, and Ms. Dolores Muñoz whose help was invaluable in this project.

CHAPTER 1

THE WORKS OF GEORGE I. SÁNCHEZ: AN APPRECIATION

NATHAN MURILLO

California State University, Northridge

It is indeed fitting that the works of Professor Sánchez be reviewed, for his career spans a time during which many events of importance to Chicanos have occurred. Sánchez, virtually alone, stood at the beginning of the present Chicano *movimiento* (movement), and his writings focused on issues of continuing major concern to Chicano psychologists. We can gain strength and further direction for our efforts by looking to the leadership he provided.

George Isidore Sánchez was born in New Mexico in 1906 and died in 1972 during his sixty-sixth year. He began his professional career teaching in a one-room rural school in New Mexico, later becoming a school principal and supervisor, college professor, director of research with the state department of education, and president of the New Mexico Educational Association. He obtained his master's degree from the University of Texas in 1931 and received his doctorate in education from the University of California, Berkeley, in 1934. From 1937 to 1938, Dr. Sánchez served as general technical adviser to the Ministry of Education and as director of the Venezuelan National Pedagogical Institute in Caracas. He returned to the University of New Mexico in 1938 to serve as associate professor of education and as research associate. In 1940, he became professor of Latin American education at the University of Texas in Austin and remained at the University of Texas, filling various posts there until his death. For example, from 1951 to 1959, he was chairman of the Department of History and Philosophy of Education, and from 1963 to 1972, he was director of the Educational Center for International Education.

During his distinguished career, Professor Sánchez served on numerous national and international commissions and boards and worked with many agencies.

1

He was frequently called to Washington to serve as a consultant, especially in the area of Latin American affairs and education. In addition to these activities, he served as an editorial consultant for various journals, writing and contributing his own works as well. He continued to remain close to his people, and from 1941 to 1942 served as national president of the League of United Latin American Citizens.

Although Sánchez devoted his life to helping the lowly and removing the burdens of ignorance, disease, and poverty from the long-suffering, within the Chicano movement he was personally hurt by criticism and rejection (Carter, Note 1). Criticism of Sánchez in more recent years claimed that he was not sufficiently militant in his efforts to achieve changes for Chicanos. Rather than militancy, he advocated persuasive methods and working within and through the system to foster evolutionary changes. He strongly believed in a concept of cultural dualism and accord whereby the Spanish-speaking could share in American society, contribute to it, and obtain its benefits. He always made it clear that the barriers that prevented this from occurring were caused by a failure on the part of the United States government to provide for the special needs of its Spanish-speaking citizens and by the racism of the dominant Anglo society. Perhaps Sánchez's own life serves as the best example of what he expected from the concept of cultural dualism. Nevertheless, his position against a move toward Chicano nationalism was not accepted by some.

Sánchez was a man willing to accept the consequences of expressing his own beliefs. Rejection by some of his own people must have wounded him deeply; yet, viewing his work from the perspective of time and historical setting, one can only admire his deeds while recognizing the personal penalties they incurred. Vaca noted, "And Dr. Sánchez wrote some of his strongest criticisms of the American Educational System vis-à-vis the Mexican-American child in an atmosphere of patent societal and academic hostility" (Vaca, Note 2). Despite his international reputation, there are indications that Sánchez suffered both professionally and monetarily for his outspoken views. In his monograph on the Navajo Indians, published in 1948, a point was made in the foreword that the statements made by Sánchez exaggerate the problems of Navajos and therefore do not reflect the opinion of the United States Indian Service. In the last years of his life, he continued to carry on his numerous activities although his health was poor and he experienced constant and severe physical pain. Thus, given the conditions under which he worked, his accomplishments appear even more remarkable.

According to Thomas Carter (Note 1), who knew him as a former student and later, for many years, as a friend and colleague, Sánchez was modest in his manner of relating to others. He was always patient and understanding, living according to his humanistic beliefs. Thoroughly humanitarian in his outlook, he never ceased to work for the rights of others, no matter what their ethnic, racial, or national identities. Reviewing the writings of Sánchez, one is impressed with the range and depth of his knowledge. His persistence, determination, and courage were also conspicuous. In one instance, his research led him to discover the Mayan numerical concept of zero, a fact that had not been known to scholars in the field.

He published his book on the subject himself in 1961 because he was unable to find a publisher.

Professor Sánchez became an educator because he saw clearly that education is the socializing agent of our society and mirrors its social values. He saw education as the primary vehicle for effecting changes in society and for progressing toward improved conditions for all its members. He devoted his career to making constructive changes in the educational system and to equalizing educational opportunities for every individual. He never ceased to place responsibility for the education of citizens, according to democratic principles, firmly on the government and its leaders, often criticizing government sharply for what he considered to be a default of leadership. His philosophy of education was pragmatic in that he believed education and educational systems should provide people with functional tools. In order to do this, education must remain flexible. He consistently viewed present reality in terms of its future potential and as the basis for effective planning. In this context, he felt that proper educational planning must consider all relevant social science theory and knowledge. Although his writings often presented historical material, he saw history mainly as the source of a necessary perspective to help guide constructive planning and change for the future.

Among the earliest of Dr. Sánchez's published works were articles on the intelligence testing of Spanish-speaking children, a subject that continues to be of major interest to all Chicano psychologists. In an article published in 1932, Sánchez attacked the notion that Spanish-speaking children are inherently intellectually inferior to English-speaking American children, as indicated by differences in IQ scores (1932a). Sánchez made it clear that no such conclusion could legitimately be drawn from the research literature, inasmuch as many studies showed environmental and linguistic factors to be significantly related to IQ scores. He emphasized the particular problems of bilingual children with language expression and language understanding and brought into serious question the interpretation of heredity as the primary basis for observed differences in IQ scores. Sánchez criticized those who accept the IQ test results of Spanish-speaking children without paying attention to data obtained on other groups that showed clearly that factors beyond heredity could influence IQ scores.

In a second article published the same year, Sánchez presented data demonstrating an improvement in the IQ scores of Spanish-speaking children on repeated tests of intelligence (1932b). Sánchez gave parallel forms of the Stanford achievement test and the Haggerty intelligence test to 45 Spanish-speaking children, grades three to eight, in New Mexico public schools. He administered these tests four times at approximately five month intervals from December 1928 to April 1930 and found that although there were marked correlations in all abilities tested, reading correlated most highly with all the other subtests. Reading had the highest correlation to intelligence. Sanchez concluded that environmental factors were significant and must be taken into account when test results of Spanish-speaking children were interpreted. Specifically, he saw English language ability as one of the most important variables resulting in different IQ scores among the Spanish-speaking children.

In 1934, Sánchez published an article strongly criticizing the misuse and mis-application of mental tests in measuring the intelligence of school children (1934a). He directed his attack against those who blindly accepted the doctrine of individual differences and totally disregarded the importance of such fundamental facts as personal, social, cultural, and environmental differences and their effects upon intellectual measurement. He reserved his greatest criticism for those who ignored bilingual and cultural factors in their interpretation of test results. He pointed out many times that the validity of any test was limited to the normative sample on which that test was based and claimed that the facts of genetics and heredity were being "garbled" in order to champion the superiority of one "race" over another. He noted that IQ tests were continuing to be misapplied to bilingual children and that the results were being accepted uncritically. Sánchez argued that the worth of any test instrument lay only in its proper interpretation and the assistance this provided in furthering the educational needs of the pupil: "The IQ only has value when it is used to promote the best educational interests of the child [Sánchez, 1934a]." He criticized the misuse of the Binet tests of vocabulary for bilingual students, indicating how the vocabulary was inappropriate for those students and therefore invalid as a measure of intelligence. He also objected to those who would simply translate a test from English into Spanish and expect it to assess the intelligence of bilingual children accurately. In his writings, he urged an examination of the responsibility of schools toward bilingual children in the achievement of desirable goals. He fostered the position that the school has the responsibility of creating experiences for bilingual children that make the knowledge sampled by an IQ test as common to them as to the Anglo children on whom the norms were based. He felt that only after equal opportunity had been given to bilingual children could failure to score high on an IQ test be considered a failure of the children.

In a second article published in 1934, Sánchez turned his attention to the importance of a basal vocabulary in English for bilingual children before they could actually participate meaningfully in their classrooms (1934b). He also attempted to highlight the significance of language as a problem in the valid assessment of Spanish-speaking children. Using a standard 660 basal vocabulary list of English words, he compared the words to the vocabulary in the Stanford-Binet tests for 3-8-year-olds. In various subtests he found 82 words that did not appear on the criterion list. Since some of these specific words affected as many as six separate subtests, he reasoned that the influence of the "unknown" words was actually much more extensive than it appeared at first. He went on to examine in detail the effect of these words on test-taking and to examine other aspects of vocabulary such as homonyms and word usage. He gave examples of differences in word usage that might be particularly difficult and confusing to a child just acquiring a new vocabulary or new concepts in English. For example, "What do you call yourself?" becomes, "What is your name?"; and, "How many years do you have?" becomes,

"How old are you?" Assuming that the English vocabulary of the Spanish-speaking child upon entering school fell short of the prerequisite basal vocabulary, Sánchez concluded that the Spanish-speaking child had to be properly equipped with at least the rudiments of the English language before progress in school could be expected. He placed the responsibility for this directly on the schools.

Sánchez's concern for improving the educational opportunities of Spanish-speaking children led him to promote bilingual, bicultural educational programs. In the article just discussed, he raised a question about the extent to which the schools build or add on to the experiences and language that Spanish-speaking children bring with them. Sánchez believed curriculum should be determined by what is in the community and that education should begin with the language of the community and the experiences of the children. He noted that for Spanish-speaking children the schools proceeded in the opposite direction, creating innumerable difficulties and all but insurmountable obstacles. Sánchez viewed learning a language as natural. Acquiring a second language became a problem primarily when one language was seen as less valuable than another and this attitude was internalized by the child, causing confusion and conflict. Sánchez reminded us again in 1958 that all language development proceeds from experience. He emphasized that bilingualism should be viewed as a prize, not a problem (Hughes & Sánchez, 1958).

In several writings, Dr. Sánchez evaluated the educational status of the Spanish-speaking in the United States. In these publications, he presented abundant data consistently showing that the schools failed to educate these students. In assessing responsibility for the shocking conditions his investigations and data analysis invariably revealed, Sánchez was forced to conclude that government had failed in its duty to these citizens and to the democratic principle of equal educational opportunity for all. In fact, Sánchez's first major work, his dissertation (1974a),was aimed at evaluating the status of education for children of Spanish descent and educational practices as they affected these children. His study showed that bilingual students warranted special attention because of their unique educational problems. He deplored the common practice of segregating Spanish-speaking children because it is contrary to the aims and ideals of educational theory. In his estimation, this practice limited the educational opportunity for Spanish-speaking students in the New Mexico school system. He attributed the deficiencies he found primarily to an administrative policy that discriminated against children of Mexican-American heritage and to lack of financial support to the predominantly Spanish-speaking schools.

Governmental neglect of the health, educational, and economic needs of the Spanish-speaking people was portrayed by Sánchez most movingly in what is perhaps his best known book, *Forgotten People: A Study of New Mexicans*, first published in 1940. In this work he described the geographical and cultural isolation these people have endured for close to 400 years. He traced the relationship between the United States government and the Spanish-speaking people of New Mexico from the time that land became a territory of the United States.

Sánchez described the Spanish-speaking New Mexican as severely handicapped, both socially and economically because of a gap between the impacted New Mexican's and the Anglo culture that surrounded them. Comparing education in New Mexico with education in other states in terms of economic support and pupil achievement, Sánchez found it third from the bottom. He wrote that the problem of educating a bicultural people was never recognized by the United States government. As a consequence, children were systematically forced out of the schools. He provided figures on expenditures for education in various portions of the state which showed that the areas where most of the Spanish-speaking people lived received far less money than others. He pointed out that even though the United States government provided help to the American Indian, the Indian still lags behind; and yet the Spanish-speaking New Mexican, also in desperate need, had received no help whatsoever. He concluded that the inferior status of the New Mexican was caused by the failure of the United States to recognize the special character of the people and their needs when it forced this group into American society. Again, writing in 1941, he emphasized that educational backwardness is not a product of a society's physical or mental constitution but a direct result of the circumstances of a society's history and environment. He believed that the condition of educational backwardness in New Mexico was directly related to the policies of the United States government and wrote, "It is astonishing to have to come to the conclusion that the administration of affairs in New Mexico during the nineteenth century by the United States was lacking in all salient benefits of good, sympathetic, democratic government [1941, p. 65]." He noted that between 1846 and 1910, the statistics on education in New Mexico clearly showed the limited educational opportunities. For him, these statistics also eloquently symbolized the cultural deterioration which he saw as the inevitable result of that condition.

Sánchez was not content merely to criticize. At every opportunity, he provided programs, made recommendations, and discussed problems directed toward ameliorating conditions and improving the educational system to meet the needs of the people. For example, in 1939 he published a detailed discussion of the issues and problems, as he saw them, involved in planning the distribution of state school funds. His purpose was to insure the equalization of educational opportunity for the educationally disadvantaged. At that time the state legislatures and the federal government were developing plans for the appropriation of school funds. Sánchez insisted that there had to be some relationship between educational theory and the financial formula adopted. In other words, he wanted to insure that the way the funds were spent would actually improve the educational system in accordance with sound educational theory. He wrote that educational need should be measured by standards that take into consideration the absence of educational opportunity indicated by such conditions as illiteracy, unsatisfactory health status, nonattendance in school, and child labor. Recognizing the enormity of the problem and concerned that local and state governments might not be strong enough to accomplish equalization, Sánchez wrote:

Furthermore, the standard financial pattern and the measures of educational need utilized in an equalization plan must be such that, when applied to a given community, they will reveal the degree to which the educational situation in that community is in conformity with the total situation symbolized by the standard. In addition, the remedial nature of equalization forces us to recognize that its primary purpose is not served until the equalization funds are applied to overcome education handicap upon which need has been determined. To the extent that this application will not result without implementation within the plan itself, to that extent an equalization law must be made compulsory rather than permissive — to that extent is central control essential to the very function of the law whose ultimate purpose is the equalization of educational opportunity [Sánchez, 1939, pp. 26-27].

Sánchez believed equal distribution of money raised in different communities to be politically justified when it is recognized that education is both a duty and a right of government.

In his proposals for educational reform in New Mexico (1940), Sánchez suggested broad remedial measures. He established as a first priority that citizens be provided with a satisfactory livelihood in the form of food and economic security. To this end, he proposed a plan whereby the government would develop an economic base, purchasing land and establishing a land-use management program. His second priority was establishing a cultural balance through education which, he emphasized, would have to be more than "routine." The educational program he proposed had to be identified with the needs of the people and the setting from which it operated. For example, the programs for reading and writing could not be disassociated from poor health, civic ineffectiveness, and inefficient farming methods. The educational program he proposed was action oriented, designed to overcome existing deficiencies in the social and economic life of the people. In order to do this, the program would require adaptation to the customs and traditions, to the language and historical background of the people. He called for a pooling of resources and cooperative efforts across all agencies and all levels of government. It was his contention that major problems could be solved if every element of government would put forth the necessary effort.

In stressing the responsibility of government to provide educational opportunity to the New Mexican, Sánchez wanted to insure that this group of people could make their proper contribution to the larger society. Although his humanitarian nature caused him to be concerned primarily with alleviation of human misery, he also recognized the loss to the country of human resources in terms of cultural enrichment, loyalty of the citizens, and other potential losses that were a consequence of the government's failure to provide for the educational needs of a significant number of its citizens.

Sánchez did not overlook the issue of segregation in the schools, and he made strong, forceful arguments against such practices and the racism behind them. For example, Sánchez wrote in defense of the Mexican-American Pachuco youths who were being condemned on all sides after the "zoot-suiter" riots in Los Angeles in 1943. He turned the tables on white society which was complaining that it had been victimized by Pachucos: "The crimes of youth should be punished, yes, but what of the society which is an accessory before and after the fact? [Sánchez, 1943, p. 13] ." Continuing, he wrote:

> The frequent prostitution of democratic ideals to the cause of expediency, politic vested interests, ignorance, class and "race" prejudice, and to indifference and inefficiency is a sad commentary on the intelligence and justice of a society that makes claim to those very progressive democratic ideals. The dual system of education presented in "Mexican" and "White" schools, the family system of contract labor, social and economic discrimination, educational negligence on the part of state and local authorities, "homogeneous groupings" to mask professional inefficiency — all point to the need for greater insight into a problem which is inherent in a "melting pot" society. The progress of our country is dependent upon the most efficient utilization of the heterogeneous masses which constitute its population — the degree to which two million or more Spanish-speaking people, and their increment, are permitted to develop is the extent to which a nation should expect returns from that section of its public [Sánchez, 1943, p. 13].

He castigated investigations on the causes of the Mexican-American youth riots as going off "on a tangent witch hunting in anthropological antecedents for causes which lie under their noses." His fear that the real causes of the rioting would be missed was confirmed when the Los Angeles city council failed to confront the issue of negligence by public service agencies to the needs of the Mexican-American community and, instead, spent time deliberating over a city ordinance that would outlaw zoot suits.

Sánchez pointed out many examples of racism against Mexican-Americans in the Southwest. Regarding segregated schools, he perceived that although they were ostensibly established for pedagogical reasons, such schools did not conform to any sound philosophy of education. He observed that only pseudopedagogical reasons would call for shorter school terms, ramshackle school buildings, and poorly paid and untrained teachers for "Mexican" schools and criticized the argument that segregated schools were justified because the Spanish-speaking children suffered under a language handicap. He stated explicitly that the "Mexican problem" was not a Mexican problem, but an American problem "made in the USA."

Writing in 1943, Sánchez foresaw that the racist social attitudes evident in this country would create crime, disease, ignorance, internal discord, and international animosity. He saw the Pachuco as a symbol of a cancerous growth within the majority group gnawing at the core of democracy and the American way of life.

Returning to the subject of segregation in a later article published in 1951, Sánchez made a careful legal case review and analysis of segregated classes and schools. He showed conclusively that such practices were illegal. Further, he put forward practical suggestions for optimal classroom learning when both Spanish-speaking and English-speaking children are together. He concluded, "the 'pedagogical' reasons usually offered to justify segregation are not supported by competent authority; and those reasons must be regarded either as professional blunders, or worse still, as evidence that educational principle is being prostituted to racialism [Sánchez, 1974b, p. 58] ."

About a year before he died, Sánchez participated in a symposium on Mexican-Americans and educational change. He summarized his views in this way:

> While I have championed the cause of educational change for American children
> of Mexican descent for more than 45 years, and while I have seen some changes
> and improvements in this long-standing dismal picture, I cannot, in conscience
> or as a professional educator, take any satisfaction in those developments. The
> picture is a shameful and an embarrassing one [Sánchez, 1974c, p. 14].

Perhaps Chicano psychologists will be wise enough to learn from George I. Sánchez, the man and the teacher. It is not enough to recognize that this dedicated Chicano was perhaps more responsible than any other for laying the foundation of present-day Headstart, and bilingual-bicultural educational programs. If we are to follow his direction, we must assume greater responsibility and continue to develop a more forceful leadership role within our profession and across the country by using our specialized knowledge and research skills with greater discernment and increasing effect. We must press government harder at all levels for positive programs devoted to research, education, and health improvement and take an active part in the development of such programs, insisting that they be guided by empirical information gathered on Chicanos rather than by myths, stereotypes, or warped ideology. Within the profession of psychology, our task is both immediate and great. The Chicano psychologist continues to be almost completely ignored by the American Psychological Association, not to mention state and local organizations. Despite all evidence, which consistently shows the desperate need for Chicano psychologists, neither the professional organizations nor recognized training centers have taken any significant step toward encouraging Chicanos into the profession. The equalization of educational opportunity for Chicano psychologists, beyond financial support, entails dual cultural psychological training to make the program more meaningful and relevant to students who want to work for the improvement of their people.

Psychological training in graduate schools has been Anglo oriented and Anglo dominated. As Sánchez pointed out regarding the education of the Spanish-speaking child, all group and ethnic differences generally have been ignored, with no attention paid to resultant differences in psychological orientation, cognition, attitudes, or patterns of behavior. This has been especially detrimental in the area of mental health, where such factors are most important in that they frequently provide a basis for what is considered "normal" or "abnormal." At present, Chicano psychotherapists must become qualified, according to Anglo criteria, in order to work with Anglo clients. Yet Anglo therapists frequently assume they are already adequately qualified to work with Chicanos, especially if they have some knowledge of Spanish, even though there may be vast cultural differences between them and their clients. As in the field of education where bilingual, bicultural specialization is important, a recognized specialization probably should be developed for psychotherapists who choose to provide services to Latinos.

REFERENCE NOTES

1.   Carter, T. Personal communication, March 1976.
2.   Vaca, N.C. George I. Sánchez memorial lecture (unpublished). University of California, Berkeley, 1972.

REFERENCES

Hughes, M.M., & Sánchez, G.I. *Learning a new language*. 1957-58 General Service Bulletin 101, Washington, D.C.:, Association for Childhood Education International, 1958.

Sánchez, G.I. Group differences and Spanish-speaking children – A critical review. *Journal of Applied Psychology*, 1932, *16*, 549-558. (a)

Sánchez, G.I. Scores of Spanish-speaking children on repeated tests. *Journal of Genetic Psychology*, 1932, *40*, 223-231. (b)

Sánchez, G.I. Bilingualism and mental measures: A word of caution. *Journal of Applied Psychology*, 1934, *18*, 765-772. (a)

Sánchez, G.I. The implications of a basal vocabulary to the measurement of the abilities of bilingual children. *Journal of Social Psychology*, 1934, *5*, 395-402. (b)

Sánchez, George I. The equalization of educational opportunity – Some issues and problems. The University of New Mexico Bulletin, 1939, *10*, 3-47.

Sánchez, G.I. New Mexicans and acculturation. *New Mexico Quarterly Review*, 1941, *11*, 61-68.

Sánchez, G.I. Pachucos in the making. *Common Ground*, 1943, *4*, 13-20.

Sánchez, G.I. *The people: A study of the Navajos*. Washington, D.C.: United States Indian Service, 1948.

Sánchez, G.I. *Forgotten people: A study of New Mexicans*. Albuquerque, N.M.: Calvin Horn, Publishers, 1967.

Sánchez, G.I. The education of bilinguals in a state school system (Doctoral dissertation, University of California, 1934). In *Education and the Mexican American*. New York: Arno Press, 1974. (a)

Sánchez, G.I. Concerning segregation of Spanish-speaking children in the public schools (University of Texas, Austin, 1951).In *Education and the Mexican American*, New York: Arno Press, 1974. (b)

Sánchez, G.I. Educational change in historical perspective. In A Castañeda (ed.), *Mexican Americans and educational change*. New York: Arno Press, 1974. (c)

CHAPTER 2

INTRODUCTION

JOE L. MARTINEZ, JR.

University of California, Irvine

Chicano psychology is a subdiscipline of psychology. This volume assumes that the scientific method is one of the proper ways to gather empirical information on the behavior of Chicanos within the current milieu of the larger Anglo society. However, this approach makes one further important assumption. Human behavior can be understood only if it is viewed within the cultural context in which it occurs. We might call this approach cultural relativism. Psychological formulations that adequately explain the behavior of Anglos within the Anglo culture may not necessarily explain the behavior of Chicanos within the Chicano culture. Thus, a situation exists where improperly applied explanations of the behavior of Chicanos may actually do them harm. For example, the work of Mercer in this volume clearly shows that the "IQ gap" between Chicanos and Anglos may be accounted for by the acculturation level of the Chicano. Therefore, a large number of Chicanos that are classified as feebleminded and so labeled for the rest of their lives may not be feebleminded at all. If this were even a remote possibility, it would be an unconscionable act for the profession of psychology to continue this practice without an immediate moratorium on all psychological testing, and the launching of an in-depth investigation. The work of Olmedo in this volume shows that the American Psychological Association is insensitive to the problem. Moreover, standardized IQ tests are used daily in our schools to assess the intellectual functioning of Chicano children. Therefore, the need and the justification of a Chicano psychology was born out of the moral vacuum of the science and profession of psychology.

This volume is the first comprehensive collection of the work of active Chicano psychologists and others doing research about Chicanos. It summarizes much past research and lays down guidelines for future empirical investigation. The proper subject matter for Chicano psychology seems to encompass four broad areas. The first is social psychology. Evidence is presented in this book which indicates that Chicanos are more cooperative than Anglos (Kagan), that important words such as father and mother have different meanings for Chicanos (Martinez), that the locus of control scale may have a different factor analytic structure within the Chicano as compared to the Anglo culture (Garza), and that Chicanos themselves may have internalized some of the prejudice that exists because they view Anglo professionals as more credible than Chicano professionals (A. Ramirez). In this section, Diaz-Guerrero also makes a cogent plea for cultural relativism by examining data gathered on Mexicans within the Mexican culture.

The second area is psychological testing. Mercer traces the historical origins of the practice of anglicazation within the American school system and demonstrates how acculturation may be viewed as a psychological variable to produce more valid estimates of the intellectual functioning of Chicano school children. Olmedo examines many of the theoretical problems inherent in test construction and suggests ways that psychological tests may be made more fair for minority groups. John Garcia attacks the notion of heredibility and argues strongly that IQ tests are by definition norm-referenced, and appropriate comparisons can only be made within groups. Thus, it is improper to compare Chicanos and Anglos on IQ tests as they are presently constructed. In the beginning of this book the work of George I. Sánchez is reviewed by Nathan Murillo. Sánchez showed more than 40 years ago that IQ tests were probably not valid when used with the Chicano population. Unfortunately, his work went largely unnoticed for those 40 years.

The third area is bilingualism. In this section Padilla, E. Garcia, and Lopez all note that knowing two languages is not detrimental. In fact Padilla argues strongly that it is probably an asset. Much evidence is reviewed that contrary to some psychological opinion, knowing two languages may lead to a greater cognitive complexity. Thus, it is possible that bilingual Chicano children possess an asset that is not being properly developed because of a cultural insensitivity that may be due at least in part to the science of psychology.

The fourth area is that of mental health and psychotherapy. Evidence is presented that mental health facilities are underutilized by Chicanos (Ruiz, Acosta), even though one would expect the opposite based on stress factors that exist within the Chicano community. Moreover, Miranda and Castro present data that show that acculturated Chicanos may benefit more from traditional psychotherapy than unacculturated Chicanos. Both Ruiz and Acosta present recommendations for future mental health intervention strategies. Lopez presents data that shows that psychotherapists themselves may be guilty of harboring stereotypes about Chicanos.

In the last section of this book, *Foundations for a Chicano Psychology*, Kagan and Buriel present extensive evidence that the concept of field independence — dependence may have been improperly applied to Chicanos and that many of the negative personality traits that are associated with being field-dependent and Chicano are due to the fact that the original and subsequent formulations of the construct are ethnocentric and value laden. Manuel Ramirez presents a theoretical formulation of personality structure that is based in cultural relativism and accentuates the positive aspects of being multicultural. Castañeda explores the philosophical implications inherent in explaining the behavior of a people whose culture was based in a traditional value framework (Chicanos) as compared to the behavior of a people whose culture was based in modernism (Anglos). Finally, Senour presents the first comprehensive statement on what traditional psychology has to say about Mexican American women.

This book will be of interest to people working in the areas of cross-cultural psychology, race relations, psychological anthropology, Chicano studies, and bilingual education. Both the scientist and the student should find material of interest in this volume. The articles are comprehensive enough that it may be used as a reference work. Moreover, this book outlines the current frontier of psychological knowledge about the Chicano so that future investigations may be developed by having a working knowledge of its contents.

Even though this volume was born out of neglect by the profession of psychology, it need not end here. The Chicano people, being part of the richest nation on earth, have the potential to develop a truly American psychology that would encompass all peoples of the Americas, both North and South. Diaz-Guerrero noted that we are leading a revolution in psychology, the implications of which are probably international.

PART I
Social Psychology

CHAPTER 3

A SOCIOCULTURAL PSYCHOLOGY?[1]

ROGELIO DIAZ-GUERRERO[2]

National University of Mexico

Introduction

Since Wundt, American and European systems of psychology have labored under the basic assumption that behavior is best explained by variables within individuals. The fundamental objective of this chapter is to show that this assumption is wrong. A more scientific, parsimonious, as well as useful and universal psychology is a sociocultural psychology.

Social psychologists and other behavioral scientists have shown that humans are fundamentally social creatures. Men and women have functioned within groups since their appearance on earth. It is a clear historical fact that groups became societies and societies became nations. It is obvious to anyone who has read a newspaper that the complex historic-sociocultural evolution of our world has produced a large number of different social and individual lifestyles. Still, most psychologists have continued to believe that we shall eventually understand all behavior by concentrating on individual psychological processes such as perceiving, learning, thinking, or, at most, daring to accept the existence of psychodynamic processes that envisage intra- as well as interpersonal interactions.

[1]Paper presented at the First Symposium on Chicano Psychology, May 15-16, 1976, University of California, Irvine.

[2]Research Professor in Psychology, Facultad de Psicologia, U.N.A.M., and President, INCCAPAC.

Although we can discuss the problem of the egg and the chicken forever, the only parsimoniously acceptable position to a scientific psychology is to admit that, beyond whatever genetics (a species more than an individual determinant)[3] does to humans, culture is the other major determinant of human behavior. A climate appears to exist today for the acceptance of a systematic sociocultural psychology. A perusal of the contents of the last six issues of the *American Psychologist* illustrates that consciousness of the relevance of a sociocultural psychology is growing.

There is indeed a defined and increasing concern for topics that either are directly related to such a systematic position or deal with important collateral issues. Papers dealing with ethnic minorities, the role of women, interdisciplinary concerns, public policy, and community services often appear. Noteworthy are the following: (*a*) Allan R. Buss (1975) who expressed concern about the sociology of psychological knowledge; (*b*) Charles A. Kiesler[4] (1976) who underlined in the second from among six points concerning the editorial policy of the *American Psychologist* that "Cultural influences on the development of the science and practice of psychology, merit analysis and discussion. Psychology is partially a product of its history, its times, its expectations, and of random events [p. 103]"; (*c*) the president of the American Psychological Association, Donald T. Campbell (1975), who dealt imaginatively with the conflicts created for human behavior throughout the world by biological determinants versus social preachings — certainly was concerned with several basic social dynamics that would have to be explored thoroughly in the context of a historic-bio-psycho-sociocultural psychology; (*d*) Seymour B. Sarason (1975) stated, "We have been molded by a culture that, because it always does its job well, gives us a selective view of the present and a distorted view of the past [p. 1072]"; (*e*) although Sarason also referred to Vico and his impact upon Lenin, and subsequently upon the behavior of millions of modern Soviets, Murray Levine (1976) who dealt critically with "The academic achievement test, its historical context and social functions," cited a historian, Benjamin Farrington (1949), who stated, "History is the most fundamental science, for there is no human knowledge which cannot lose its scientific character when men forget the conditions under which it originated, the questions which it answered, and the function it was created to serve [p. 173]."

To get even closer to home, thoughtful books like *Explorations in Cross Cultural Psychology* by Douglass Price-Williams (1975) and challenging books like *Cultural Democracy Bicognitive Development and Education* by Manuel Ramirez and Alfredo Castañeda (1974), and this volume, *Chicano Psychology*, edited by Joe L. Martinez, Jr., emphasize the need for the acceptance by psychology of a sociocultural approach and the urgent need for its systematic development.

[3]The difference between humans and any other species is far greater than any difference between human individuals.
[4]The new Executive Officer of the American Psychological Association.

Problems of a Sociocultural Psychology

All of the previous enthusiasm is good, but a sociocultural psychology is not a simple matter, as Price-Williams (1975) ably pointed out. All behavioral scientists will have to tax their ingenuity to the utmost to establish beachheads from which useful inroads into this complex matter may be made. I have established a small beachhead, utilizing both a systematic approach to culture and the methodology of psychology.

One of the first obstacles in the road toward a sociocultural psychology is the problem of creating a useful definition of culture. In previous writings, Diaz-Guerrero (1967, 1972b, 1976, and in press), and Holtzman, Diaz-Guerrero, Swartz *et al.* (1975) have taken up a number of aspects of this problem, taking advantage of the work done by anthropologists, sociologists, and cross-cultural psychologists.

Let me say, for the objectives of this chapter, that the best of culture as we know it will be found in everyday statements about which most people of a given group or culture agree, expressions that embody their intimate views about how life should be lived, the roles that the different individuals in the family and the society should play, the reciprocal obligations between them and the ways to deal with these reciprocal obligations, and the manner of coping with the problems set by life. These statements, which include proverbs and the preachings and commandments to which Campbell (1975) referred, are natural language expressions of people. I call them historic-sociocultural premises (HSCPs). HSCPs are natural language statements embodying a philosophy of life held by an operationally defined majority of the members of a given group, society, culture, or nation. This concept of culture is closely related to the concept of history. Culture at a given time is the result of history; it is actually, in a sense, history at that time.

In order to address directly the question of "the chicken and the egg," I developed a "time-binding" approach (Diaz-Guerrero, in press) in a previous paper. What is pertinent here is that culture, as defined above, can be studied by behavioral science methodologies and can be shown to be related to remote historical antecedents, as well as to actual human personality at a given time.

In short, this approach had to define a method for the study of culture, select that part of "culture" that appeared most meaningful to people, define operational units (the HSCPs), and develop instruments to measure culture. Finally, particularly for the purposes of this paper, it had to be shown that these measurements are related to the aspects of personality measured by psychologists.

Culture and Personality

In order to function as a valid concept, sociocultural psychology must demonstrate that it is possible to relate culture to personality. It should also demonstrate that one can relate culture to the individual psychological processes of perception, learning, and thinking. A number of cross-cultural psychologists have already shown that it is possible to relate cultural, sociological, and socioecological factors to perceptual and cognitive processes. The problem of personality has been more complex, since both the definition of culture and the definition of personality have traditionally been controversial. However, while the controversy raged, clinical practitioners had to deal with human personality and resolve concrete problems at concrete times, and concomitantly psychology was invaded by a large number of theories of personality that often conspicuously displayed characterologies to classify human beings.

In dealing with personality, our only alternatives today are either to accept intuitive and complex systems that always assume universal validity or to demonstrate that culture, operationally defined and reliably measured, can correlate both with personality and with cognitive variables, as they are measured by such rigorous methods as psychometric tests.

In what follows I will report some of the highlights of this approach to a sociocultural psychology of personality, which I believe may in time psychologically liberate ethnic groups in the United States and people of nations with different historic-sociocultural traditions from melting pot Americans and Western Europeans. It might even liberate Americans and Europeans from the grip of intuitive psychological systems, such as orthodox psychoanalytic approaches, or any other approaches that blindly follow the specific premises of the founders. Much in psychodynamic, cognitive, and learning processes is useful; but, in the often personal premises of the founders, little can have adequate validity.

It is, of course, extremely difficult not to project oneself into one's own theories and hypotheses. One of the successful ways of maintaining the battle against subjectivity that every scientist to some extent must undertake, is to try continuously to correct the personal point of view on the basis of observations of and the systematic data obtained from people themselves. A start in this direction was to construct questionnaires of sociocultural premises that approached the natural language of the people as closely as possible.

The Historic-Sociocultural Premises of the Mexican Family

To provide one of two illustrations selected for this chapter, the Mexican family within Mexico was selected as a primary source of information in determining the cultural characteristics of the Mexican. A series of studies measuring intracultural variation led to the factorial scale of HSCPs for the Mexican family (Diaz-Guerrero, 1972a). The scale contains 22 items selected from an earlier questionnaire containing 123. Those showing the greatest number of statistically significant differences between different groups were selected. Items that loaded highest on this scale were "A son should always obey his parents," "A person should always obey his parents," and "The word of a father should never be questioned." There were also substantial loadings from statements such as "The place for women is in the home," "Men should wear the pants in the family," and "The mother is the dearest person in existence." The scale is fundamentally a measure of affilia-tive obedience and a number of traditional attitudes linked to it.

That this approach may contribute to an understanding of the relationship between culture and personality is shown in Table 1. This simple HSCPs scale maintains logical relationships to dimensions within the realm of personality and cognition, as well as with measures of socioeconomic level and parental attitudes. It also shows interesting cross-validating correlations with factors 1 and 2 of the Filosofia de Vida (Philosophy of Life), another scale of sociocultural premises. Although the groups were relatively small, the children had been previously exa-mined every year for five years with a battery of individually applied tests, and from the results reported by Holtzman *et al.* (1975), their willingness and sincerity cannot be doubted.

TABLE 1

Correlations between the Factorial Scale of Historic-Sociocultural Premises (HSCPs) of the Mexican Family and Cognitive, Perceptual, Personality, Parental Attitudinal, and Socioecono-mic Level Variables[a]

	Age I = 12 N = 37-39	Age II = 15 N = 42-48	Age III = 18 N = 34-43
Anxiety (HIT)			-.35*
Penetration (HIT)	-.34*		
Picture completion (WISC)		-.40**	
Block design (WISC)		-.38**	
Human figure drawing (Harris)		-.33*	
Time estimation delay		-.30*	
Picture maturity test	.33*		
Autonomy (PRF)	-.34*		-.55***
Harm avoidance (PRF)			.31*
Impulsivity		-.31*	-.34*
Order (PRF)		.36*	.36*
Social recognition (PRF)			.47**
Infrequency (PRF)		.36*	
Mother's expectation of achievement in the child		-.39*	
Socioeconomic level	.33*		
Parental attitude survey Factor II, sophisticated acceptance			-.39*
Reading vocabulary (Manuel)		-.37**	
Reading speed (Manuel)		-.45**	
Reading comprehension (Manuel)		-.38**	
Factor I, Active self-assertion	-.47**	-.69**	-.65***
Factor II, Active internal control	.46**		

*p<.05   **p<.01   ***p<.001

[a]Translated from Diaz-Guerrero (1976).

One of the most interesting findings in Table 1 is the negative correlation obser-ved at age 15 between the HSCPs and picture completion and block design of the WISC and the Harris human figure drawing score. Besides the fact that these three measures of performance ability were found to be reliable with Mexican children, in the Holtzman *et al.* (1975) study they were also found to correlate highly with Witkin's embedded figures test, which measures cognitive style as well as a type of cognitive development. At this same age (15), one must also pay attention to the moderate negative correlations with reading vocabulary, reading speed, and reading comprehension. These results tend to show that the higher the score of 15-year-old Mexican children from two social classes in Mexico City on this scale (affiliative obedience), the lower their cognitive intellectual development. It is also clear that these 15-year-old Mexicans are less impulsive and more orderly than their peers, two characteristics that were found in the Holtzman *et al.* (1975) study, that uniformly favored Mexican children over American.[5] However, probably because of their reading difficulties, they misread more items from Jackson's personality research form (PRF) (a positive correlation with the infrequency score). The most pathetic finding about these 15-year-old Mexican children is that their mothers — who have apparently succeeded in making them more obedient than their peers — do not expect them to do well at school.

A brief clinical description of those Mexican adolescents that scored higher on the affiliative obedient dimension than their peers, even at 18 years of age, indicates that these children have considerably less need autonomy, are significantly less impulsive, more orderly, and more "harm avoidant" than their peers and have a substantially greater need for social recognition. These apparently rather meek and complacent individuals also showed less symbolic anxiety than their peers in the Holtzman inkblot test (HIT). To make matters worse, their parents are less acceptant of these children, an observation which clinically agrees with the fact that they have such a high need for social recognition. As expected, these children also showed a much lower active self-assertion than their peers. Clinically, one would predict trouble for these individuals if they should suddenly have to stand on their own feet, deprived of the strong support of their families. I understand why, after the earthquakes in Guatemala, the newspapers reported a number of suicides among individuals who had lost their families.

This glimpse at a socioculturally based clinical understanding of personality functioning does not stop here. To be significantly more affiliative obedient than a peer at age 18 is apparently not very good from the point of view of mental health, even in Mexico. To be affiliative obedient at 12 is not only normal for a Mexican but is also a better sign of mental health among children of this age than less affiliative obedience or frank self-assertiveness. The negative correlation with penetration and the positive correlation with factor 2, active internal control, indicate, in good Freudian terms, the foundations of a good ego structure. The results of the picture maturity test also indicate that their perception is maturer than that of their peers. Finally, these children seem to have less need autonomy than their peers, and it is clear that the lower the class, the greater the affiliative

[5]Mexican children, regardless of age, sex, or social class, obtained higher scores in order and lower scores in impulsiveness of the PRF than their American counterparts.

obedience among Mexican 12-year-olds. Finally, for children from three different age groups, there are from substantial to moderately high negative correlations with factor 1 of the Filosofia de Vida that measures active self-assertion, a dimension fundamentally the opposite of affiliative obedience.

Filosofia de Vida

Those interested in further information about the Filosofia de Vida (views of life questionnaire or FV), may refer to previous papers (Diaz-Guerrero, 1973, 1976). Briefly, it is a forced choice instrument with 60 pairs of statements intended to measure coping style. It was hypothesized initially (Diaz-Guerrero, 1965, 1967) that people in all cultures have to deal with problems and that there are different styles of coping with problems. It was felt that the traditional Mexican culture encourages a passive coping style and the traditional North American culture an active coping style. Individuals utilize an active coping style when facing problems if they try to solve them by actively modifying their physical, interpersonal, or social environments. Individuals utilize a passive coping style if they try to solve the problems by accepting or enduring them, often implying active self-modification. A well-based and conservative factor analysis of the results obtained for the Mexican subjects in Table 1 yielded 4 factors.

In this chapter, I will report only the data connected with the second of these factors, active internal control versus passive external control.[6] Items characterizing this factor include statements such as "When I do well on a test in school it is usually because I studied for the test," and also "A person should be respected for what he has done." For this factor there are a good number of correlations at both 12 and 18 years of age.

As presented in Table 2, at age 12 children who obtained high scores on this factor tended to be less aggressive and impulsive, more orderly, and they accurately answered the PRF. They also obtained higher scores in reading vocabulary, speed and comprehension than their peers. They tended not to be as passive-cautious as others, and it is interesting to note that they scored high on affiliative obedience. These results appear to indicate that like any other culture, Mexican culture can produce excellent children who will possess many of the positive Mexican national characteristics together with good cognitive development. Actually, an optimistic, intelligent, honest, upright, well behaved, nonaggressive, orderly, affectionate, obedient, complacent, and happy 12-year-old is undoubtedly the prevalent Mexican stereotype of an ideal 12-year-old. In addition, there is no evidence that this type of personality, at this or later ages, appears with greater frequency in the upper classes rather than the lower or in either sex.

[6] Results in cross-cultural studies and in Mexican children for other factors are reported elsewhere (Holtzman *et al.*, 1975; Diaz-Guerrero, 1973, 1976).

TABLE 2

Correlations of Factor 2 of the Filosofia de Vida (Active Internal Control) and Cognitive, Cognitive Perceptual, Personality, and Parental Attitudinal Variables[a]

	Age I = 12 N = 38 to 44	Age II = 15 N = 48 to 56	Age III = 18 N = 35 to 44
Form appropriateness (HIT)		.37**	
Animal (HIT)		-.32*	
Anxiety (HIT)			-.48**
Lie (TASC)			-.30*
Defensiveness score (TASC)		-.29*	
Aggression (PRF)	-.31*		
Autonomy (PRF)			-.31*
Impulsivity (PRF)	-.30*		
Order (PRF)	.31*	.32*	
Infrequency (PRF)	-.41**		-.36*
Mother's satisfaction with the progress of the child	.40**		
Reading vocabulary (Manuel)	.48**		.48**
Reading speed (Manuel)	.41**		
Reading comprehension (Manuel)	.36*		.36*
Factor I, active self-assertion		-.32*	
Factor III, passive cautiousness	-.34*		
HSCP	.46**		

*p<.05   **p<.01

[a]Translated from Diaz-Guerrero (1976).

In popular articles on a Mexican typology, I pointed out, however, that the social ecology of high schools in Mexico, with too many students and too few teachers and with many opportunities for the blatant expression of several of the most negative aspects of the Mexican culture — including the rawest forms of machismo and a rampant antiintellectualism — is probably not very good for these interesting representatives of Mexican culture. I believe that this is one of the reasons why the picture for this type of child at age 15 is not as clear as at age 12 or 18.

At 18 years of age, when these students enter their professional careers at the university, the violent aspects of machismo have diminished, and studies are taken more seriously. This type of Mexican apparently has a better chance to flourish. At this age, these adolescents score no higher on affiliative obedience than their peers, but continue to have what may be called positive characteristics, particularly in Mexico, with less symbolic anxiety in their responses to the Holtzman inkblot test, less tendency to be defensive with respect to test anxiety, and less need of autonomy than their companions. They continue to be careful and clear about answering the PRF and still have a significant edge over their contemporaries in reading vocabulary and comprehension.

Clinically, it appears that developing this type of active internal control is optimal for Mexican society, permitting the child to be affiliative obedient and complacent when need be and constructive and actively self-assertive when it is necessary to achieve.

Socioculturally Derived versus Intuitive Characterologies

I feel obliged to compare these glimpses at an understanding of personality functioning (for the purpose of a clinical approach) with the results obtained when Fromm and Maccoby (1970) applied the Frommian characterology to Mexican peasants.

To understand personalities as they function in their own sociocultural context it is not enough to be perceptive, intelligent, and have experience in clinical psychology. There is insufficient time or space here to go into a detailed critical analysis of Fromm and Maccoby's study, but a few examples may suffice. In their chapter, "Sex and Character," Fromm and Maccoby produce a mixture of Frommian and Freudian doctrine with anthropological cultural concepts and economic factors — the type of eclecticism Fromm so strongly criticized in his introduction to Oedipus:Myth and Complex (Mullahy, 1948).

It is not sadomasochism intertwined in an asystematic fashion with matriarchy and patriarchy that parsimoniously explains "sex and character" or sexual roles within the Mexican socioculture. It is simply that the Mexican socioculture prescribes, on the one hand, that "the mother is the dearest person in existence" and on the other that "the father must wear the pants in the family." Men, by cultural prescription, are given all the power, and women are given all the love. Under the normal social pattern, the fundamental access to power for women is through their loving behavior. When the man or woman is unable to live up to the expectations and/or demands of the culture or when either or both rebel against these demands, many of the patterns of interaction of men, women, and families can be parsimoniously explained in terms of HSCPs and other explicit and implicit beliefs basic to the culture. In general, individuals may accept, not accept, partially accept, or maximally rebel against the sociocultural premises.[7] Campbell (1975) developed a model for a similar type of sociocultural dynamic.

It is therefore not surprising that when Fromm and Maccoby speak about the character of the villagers, combining the dominant and the secondary modes of relation among them, they find that 82% of the males' and 57% of the females' modes of relationship are either Narcissism I or Narcissism II. Since the rest of the modes of relation, with a 1% exception, are either sadism, masochism, destructiveness, indulgent love or conditional love, 99% of the villagers should be suffering from neurosis at least. If you visit the village in question, you will find, as in almost all the other villages in Mexico, pleasant, complacent people who appear less tense and happier as individuals than the residents of a comparable Anglo-American village would be. It is therefore far from parsimonious to give adjectives and assign roles, from personal characterologies, to people who do not even participate in the sociocultural traditions of the characterologists.

---

[7]Although we consider HSCPs basic in the understanding of personality in action, we realize that other variables intervene (Diaz-Guerrero, 1972b).

A Sociocultural Psychology of Personality

I hope it has become evident that it is possible to have a sociocultural psychology, particularly one dealing with the problems connected with personality function. I must warn you, paraphrasing Winston Churchill, that we are only approaching the end of the beginning. I urge young Chicano psychologists to look carefully and critically into this way of thinking and attempt to develop the kind of questionnaires that will help us understand the sociocultural premises of Chicanos, which in part should be similar to those held by the Mexicans, in part unique to their historical circumstance and goals, and in part, perhaps, similar to those held by the Anglo-Americans. At any rate, citizens of the United States of Mexican descent need their own sociocultural psychology to help their optimum development and to increase their contribution, as an important and capable ethnic minority, to themselves and to the entire society of the United States of Mesonorthamerica.

REFERENCES

Buss, A.R., The emerging field of the sociology of psychological knowledge. *American Psychologist*, 1975, *10*, 988-1002.

Campbell, D.T. On the conflicts between biological and social evolution and between psychology and moral tradition. *American Psychologist*, 1975, *30*, 1103-1104.

Diaz-Guerrero, R. Socio-cultural and psycho-dynamic processes in adolescent transition and mental health. In Sherif & Sherif (Eds.), *Problems of youth*. Chicago, Ill.: Aldine Publishing Co., 1965, 129-152.

Diaz-Guerrero, R. Sociocultural premises, attitudes and cross-cultural research. *International Journal of Psychology*, 1967, *2*, 79-87.

Diaz-Guerrero, R. Una escala factorial de premisas historico-socioculturales de la familia Mexicana. *Revista Interamericana de Psicologia*, 1972, *6*, 235-244. (a)

Diaz-Guerrero, R. *Hacia una teoria historico – biopsico – socio-cultural del comportamiento humano*. Mexico: F. Trillas, 1972. (b)

Diaz-Guerrero, R. Interpreting coping styles across nations from sex and social class differences. *International Journal of Psychology*, 1973, *8*, 193-203.

Diaz-Guerrero, R. Culture and personality revisited. *Conference on issues in cross cultural research*. The New York Academy of Sciences. *Annals of the New York Academy of Sciences*, in press.

Diaz-Guerrero, R. Hacia una psicologia social del tercer mundo. *Cuadernos de humanidades No. 5*, Universidad Nacional Autonoma de Mexico, Mexico, D.F.: 1976.

Farrington, B. *Greek Science. Its moving forces* (Vol. 2), Hammondsworth Middlesex, England: Penguin Books, 1949.

Fromm, E., & Maccoby, M. *Social character in a Mexican village*. Englewood Cliffs, N.J.: Prentice-Hall, 1970.

Holtzman, W.H., Diaz-Guerrero, R., & Swartz, J.D. (in collaboration with L. Lara Tapia, L. Laosa, M.L. Morales, I. R. Lagunes, & D. Witzke). *Personality development in two cultures. A cross cultural longitudinal study of school children in Mexico and the United States*. Austin, Tex.: University of Texas Press, 1975.

Kiesler, C.A., Editorial policy of the *American Psychologist*. *American Psychologist*, 1976, *31*, 103-105.

Levine, M. The academic achievement test, its historical context and social functions. *American Psychologist*, 1976, *31*, 228-238.

Mullahy, P. *Oedipus: Myth and complex*. New York: Hermitage Press, 1948.

Price-Williams, D.R. Explorations in cross cultural psychology. Corte Madera, Calif.: Chandler & Sharp Publishers, 1975.

Ramirez, M. III, & Castañeda, A. Cultural democracy, bicognitive development and education. New York: Academic Press, 1974.

Sarason, S.B. To the Finland station in the heavenly city of the eighteenth century philosophers. *American Psychologist*, 1975, *30*, 1072-1080.

CHAPTER 4

CROSS-CULTURAL COMPARISON OF CHICANOS AND ANGLOS ON THE SEMANTIC DIFFERENTIAL: SOME IMPLICATIONS FOR PSYCHOLOGY

JOE L. MARTINEZ, JR.

Univeristy of California, Irvine

The Semantic Differential

The Osgood semantic differential is a useful tool for comparing affective meaning systems of diverse cultural groups (Osgood, 1964). Osgood and his many co-workers (Osgood, Suci, & Tannenbaum, 1957) argue that there is a universal framework underlying the connotative aspects of language. They believe that this is true across languages that are vastly different, such as Japanese and English (Tanaka, Oyama, & Osgood, 1963) or Spanish and English (Osgood, May, & Miron, 1975). A concept has the same meaning for two individuals or cultural groups when the concept is located in the same position in semantic space (Osgood, 1964). It is proposed that semantic space is "a region of some unknown dimensionality and Euclidean in character. Each semantic scale, defined by a pair of polar (opposite-in-meaning) adjectives, is assumed to represent a straight line function that passes through the origin of this space, and a sample of such scales then represents a multidimensional space [Osgood *et al.*, 1957, p. 25]." Three factors define this universal framework of meaning and reappear in different cultures, and even among diverse groups such as Republicans and Democrats and schizo-phrenics and normals (Osgood *et al.*, 1975). These three factors are first *evaluation*, represented by adjectives like good-bad, kind-cruel; second *potency*, represented by adjectives like strong-weak, hard-soft; and third *activity* represented by such adjectives as fast-slow, excitable-calm. If one assumes that these dimensions repre-sent axes and that they are orthogonal, then a concept rated on these three fac-tors could be plotted in three dimensional space, allowing these points to be com-pared across individuals or cultural groups. Thus it is possible to compare the meaning of certain concepts across language groups (Suci, 1960) or to compare different cultural groups, such as Chicanos and Anglos, who speak the same lan-guage (Martinez, Martinez, & Olmedo, 1975).

The Mexican-American Family Structure

A great deal has been written about both the Mexican family (Diaz-Guerrero, 1955; Ramirez & Parres, 1957) and about the Mexican-American (Chicano) family (Murillo, 1971; Peñalosa, 1968). Most believe that in order to understand the Mexican-American you must understand the culture of Mexico, to which Mexican-Americans are still closely related. Peñalosa (1968) stated some years ago that neither empirical data nor an adequate theoretical framework exists for the analy-sis of Mexican-American family structure. This remains true today. Acculturation pressures have probably forced the Mexican-American family away from the Mexican prototype. Murillo stated: "There is no Mexican-American family type. In-stead there are literally thousands of Mexican-American families, all differing signi-ficantly from one another along a variety of dimensions [Murillo, 1971, p. 97] ."

Is it possible then to define empirically the characteristics of Mexican-Ameri-can family structure that significantly differentiate it from its Anglo counterpart? Ramirez and Castañeda (1974) believe that "status and role definition in family and community" is a basic sociocultural premise to understanding how Mexican-Americans think, feel, and act. There is also empirical evidence to support this notion. For example, Derbyshire (1968) administered the semantic differential to adolescents living in East Los Angeles and asked his subjects to rate the concepts of self, mother, and father. He found that girls identified more closely with the Anglo female and mother roles. Girls saw self and mother similarly, except that mother was seen as braver, more beautiful, and wiser than self. Males, on the other hand, identified more closely with "machismo" and husband roles. Males viewed self and father similarly, except they saw father as more active and harder than self. It seems clear that sex role differentiation exists among most Mexican-Ameri-cans (Staples, 1971) even though there is evidence (Ramirez, 1967, 1969) that young Mexican-Americans are beginning to reject these traditional roles (Padilla & Ruiz, 1973).

By utilizing the apparent adherence of Mexican-Americans to traditional family roles one may begin to develop distinctions between Mexican-American and Anglo-American family structure that should lead to a better understanding of how acculturation forces have changed the Mexican family prototype within the milieu of the current Anglo-American society.

Chicano and Anglo Responses on the Semantic Differential

Martinez *et al.* (1975) investigated the responses of Chicano and Anglo college students on the semantic differential to concepts that should reflect traditional sex role differentiation. The concepts were father, mother, male, female, and self. They found significant differences between Chicanos and Anglos for the distances (Osgood's *D* statistic; Osgood *et al.*, 1957) between (*a*) self-mother, (*b*) father-female, (*c*) self-female, (*d*) self-male, and (*e*) male-female. These differences are presented in Figure 1.

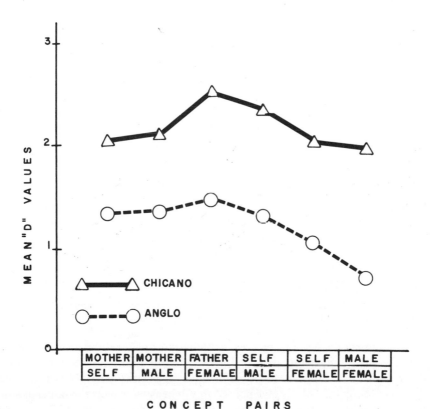

FIGURE 1. Significantly different *D* values between Chicanos and Anglos for the five concept pairs. [Reprinted from Martinez *et al.* (1975) by permission of *Atisbos, Journal of Chicano Research*, Summer 1975, p. 97.]

These results, along with Derbyshire's (1968), suggested that it was indeed feasible to differentiate Chicanos from Anglos in terms of the meanings assigned to culturally sensitive concepts. The data seemed to support the stereotypic notion that differences between male and female roles were more culturally distinct for Chicanos. This is further supported by the fact that the Anglos perceived the pairs of concepts as being much closer in semantic space than did the Chicanos. It is possible, however, that the differences observed were caused by some other cultural variable not necessarily related to sex role differentiation.

Martinez, Martinez, Olmedo, and Goldman (1976) extended the findings of Martinez *et al.* (1975) to high school students' responses on the semantic differential. They found, as before, that Chicano and Anglo responses to the concepts of father, mother, male, female, and self differed significantly. They also found that the loci of Chicano-Anglo differences seemed to be centered on items dealing with potency, and in particular, mother, father, and male potency. Table 1 presents these data. Note the large univariate F-ratios associated with mother, father, and male potency.

TABLE 1
Comparison of Chicanos with Anglos on Semantic Differential Measures[a]

	Variable	Means		Univariate F
		Anglo	Chicano	
1	Mother evaluation	1.479	1.549	<1
2	Mother potency	1.224	.604	32.33***
3	Mother activity	.596	.314	7.70*
4	Father evaluation	1.317	1.187	1.08
5	Father potency	.360	.835	17.83***
6	Father activity	.691	.511	2.74
7	Self-evaluation	1.426	1.267	1.38
8	Self-potency	1.043	.750	7.44*
9	Self-activity	.783	.771	<1
10	Male evaluation	1.658	1.189	12.55**
11	Male potency	- .187	.619	43.69***
12	Male activity	.469	.617	1.63
13	Female evaluation	1.846	1.558	6.81*
14	Female potency	.239	.028	6.18*
15	Female activity	.296	.187	1.19

*p<.01.   **p<.001.   ***p<.0001.

[a] Reprinted from Martinez *et al.* (1976) by permission of Sage Publications, *Journal Cross Cultural Research*, 1976, 7, p. 328.

The presentation in Figure 2 accounts for most of the differences seen in this study. The discriminant functions of Figure 2 can be understood in the following manner. Function 1 appears to be defined, at its positive pole, by male potency and father inactivity. The positive pole of this dimension depicts the father as slow, passive, and calm, whereas the male is strong, hard, and tenacious. Chicano males seem to score high on this dimension, which appears to be consistent with the concept of machismo. Function II seems to be defined, at its positive pole, by male potency and father impotency. This apparent inconsistency describes the male as strong, hard, and tenacious but the father as weak, soft, and yielding. Anglo male subjects scored at the extreme negative pole, indicating that male and father were very different conceptual items for them. Perhaps the most surprising result depicted in Figure 2 is that male Chicanos seemed to be very different from the other three groups, including female Chicanos. On the other hand, at least for the concepts studied, the female Chicano responses were very like the female Anglo responses. This finding agrees with Derbyshire's (1968) earlier study, which reported that female Chicanos identified more closely with the Anglo female and mother roles. However, the results of this study disagree with an earlier study by Vigil (1968) who found that the semantic differential significantly discriminated high school student responses on the concept of mother but not of father.

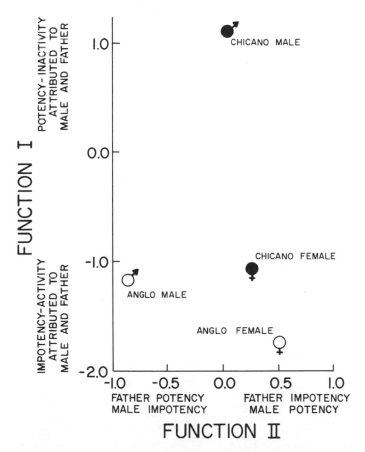

FIGURE 2. Ethnic x sex group centroids in two dimensional space. Function I is defined at its positive pole by male potency and father inactivity. Function II is defined at its positive pole by male potency and father impotency. [Reprinted from Martinez *et al.* (1976) by permission of Sage Publications, Inc., *Journal Cross Cultural Research*, 1976, 7, p. 330.]

Vigil also found that Chicanos in general rated mother as more powerful, more positive, and more active. This apparent discrepancy might be accounted for by the fact that Vigil gathered his data in New Mexico and the present study was conducted in Southern California.

These results can be better understood from an examination of Table 2, which presents data gathered on Chicano and Anglo high school, two-year college, and four-year college students. The table depicts the rank orderings for the five concepts, father, mother, male, female, and self, on the three factors of evaluation, potency, and activity. It is interesting to note first that male Chicanos gave mother the greatest evaluation scores in all three populations. They saw mother as better, kinder, and more beautiful. In contrast, female Chicanos, male Anglos, and female Anglos saw female as being better, kinder, and more beautiful. Second, male Chicanos ranked father highest on the potency dimension. They saw father as strong, hard, tenacious, and severe, whereas female Chicanos and Anglos saw mother as stronger, harder, more tenacious, and more severe. Two of the three male Anglo groups also gave mother the highest potency scores. It seems that the male Chicano was clearly different from the other three groups in the way he perceived the concepts of mother and father. These findings appear to agree with those

TABLE 2

Semantic Differential Responses of High School, Two-Year College, and Four-Year College Students, Rank Ordered for the Three Factors of Evaluation, Potency, and Activity

High School			Two-Year College			Four-Year College		
E	P	A	E	P	A	E	P	A
Male Chicano								
Mother	*Father*	Self	*Mother*	*Father*	Male	*Mother*	*Father*	Self
Self	Male	Male	Father	Male	Self	Father	Mother	Male
Female	Self	Father	Female	Mother	Mother	Female	Male	Mother
Father	Mother	Female	Self	Female	Female	Male	Self	Father
Male	Female	Mother	Male	Self	Father	Self	Female	Female
Female Chicano								
Female	*Mother*	Father	*Female*	*Mother*	Mother	*Female*	*Self*	Self
Male	*Self*	Self	Mother	*Female*	Self	Male	*Mother*	Mother
Mother	*Female*	Male	Male	*Self*	Male	Mother	*Female*	Female
Self	Father	Mother	Father	Father	Father	Father	Male	Female
Father	Male	Female	Self	Male	Female	Self	Father	Male
Male Anglo								
Female	*Mother*	Father	*Female*	*Mother*	Father	*Female*	*Female*	Self
Male	Self	Self	Mother	Father	Self	Male	Self	Male
Father	Father	Mother	Father	Self	Mother	Father	Father	Father
Self	Female	Male	Male	Female	Male	Self	Mother	Mother
Mother	Male	Female	Self	Male	Female	Mother	Male	Female
Female Anglo								
Female	*Mother*	Self	Mother	*Mother*	Self	*Female*	*Mother*	Father
Male	*Self*	Mother	Female	*Self*	Male	Mother	*Self*	Mother
Mother	*Female*	Father	Self	*Female*	Father	Male	*Female*	Self
Self	Male	Male	Male	Male	Female	Self	Father	Male
Father	Father	Female	*Father*	Father	Mother	*Father*	Male	Female

of Diaz-Guerrero (1955) and Ramirez (1967) who found that the majority of Mexican and Mexican-American males agreed with the statement, "Mother is the dearest person in existence."

An examination of the female Chicano and Anglo responses presented in Table 2 reveals another interesting finding. All females gave mother, self, and female the highest potency scores. An interesting contrast is provided by the Chicano males, who clearly gave father the greatest potency scores, and the Anglo males, who gave either mother or female the most potency. It appears that there is less difference between male and female Anglos than there is between male and female Chicanos. These conclusions are supported by the fact that Anglos, both male and female, placed the concept pairs (a) mother-self, (b) mother-male, (c) father-female, (d) self-male, (e) self-female, and (f) male-female closer together in semantic space than did Chicanos (see Figure 1) and by the data presented in Figure 2, which clearly show the Chicano male as the most different. Sex role differentiation was evident among Chicanos but seemed to be less clear among Anglos. Lastly, female Anglos gave father the lowest evaluation ratings and saw him as worse, crueler, uglier, and more unsuccessful than did the other three groups.

Before any of these results can be generally accepted, they must be shown to apply to a diverse population of Chicanos, and socioeconomic and demographic variables must be taken into account. For example, all of the differences reported thus far could result simply from socioeconomic class since most Chicanos occupy lower socioeconomic levels and most Anglos occupy middle ones. To this end, Ramirez, Martinez, Martinez, and Olmedo (Note 1) constructed a scale of bipolar adjectives, highly loaded on the potency dimension, since potency was shown to discriminate well between Chicanos and Anglos (see Table 1) and administered it to three different high school populations that varied in their concentration of Chicano students (10%, 50%, and 70%). It is interesting in this case to note that as the proportion of Chicano students in these high schools varied, the socioeconomic level varied as well. A personal background inventory was also administered that gathered information on head of household's occupation, number of family members, where the head of the household was born and reared, and what language was spoken at home (Mercer, 1972).

Table 3 presents the univariate F-ratios for the adjective pairs that significantly discriminated between Chicanos and Anglos on the four concepts of mother, father, male, and female. It can be seen that most of the significant F-ratios were generated by the concepts of male and father, and to lesser amount by the concept of mother.

In Table 3, the first adjective pair listed under *mother* is hard-soft. The data were based on a 7-point scale that assigned *soft* a value of 1 and *hard* a value of 7. A mean of 4 would indicate that the subjects saw mother as neither hard nor soft. The Chicano mean is 2.87, and the Anglo mean 3.05. Both groups saw mother as more soft than hard, but Chicanos saw her as significantly more soft than did Anglos.

TABLE 3

Comparison of Chicanos and Anglos on the Potency Dimension

Adjective Pair	Univariate F	Means Chicano	Angio
		Mother	
Soft-hard	5.95**	2.87	3.05
Weak-strong	4.47*	4.63	4.55
Lenient-severe	11.16***	2.94	3.29
Beautiful-ugly	4.08*	2.33	3.29
Commonplace-unique	12.17***	4.41	4.96
Simple-complex	23.66****	2.98	3.69
		Father	
Soft-hard	6.38**	4.82	5.09
Lenient-severe	9.83***	3.76	4.20
Yielding-tenacious	9.76***	3.75	4.25
Humorous-serious	4.21*	4.19	3.92
Smooth-rough	9.60**	4.70	5.00
Beautiful-ugly	7.03**	4.70	5.09
Delicate-rugged	29.25****	4.92	5.54
Commonplace-unique	22.74****	4.11	4.95
Simple-complex	15.27***	3.63	4.26
		Male	
Soft-hard	4.50*	4.98	5.21
Lenient-severe	5.64**	3.70	3.99
Humorous-serious	5.65**	4.00	3.60
Smooth-rough	17.87****	4.50	4.95
Delicate-rugged	28.92****	5.01	5.56
Safe-dangerous	9.69**	3.27	3.66
Commonplace-unique	12.34***	4.40	4.91
Simple-complex	20.64****	3.79	4.38
		Female	
Commonplace-unique	26.18****	4.46	5.25
Simple-complex	22.01****	3.18	4.04

$*p < .05.$ $**p < .01.$ $***p < .001.$ $****p < .0001.$

All the data collected in this study were subjected to a multiple regression analysis. Twenty-four variables emerged that significantly discriminated between the groups; they are listed in Table 4. It is not surprising that the variables that discriminated best were questions dealing with language spoken at home. Also high on the list were amount of education of the head of the household and whether the head grew up on a farm.

Many of the significant variables listed in Table 4 were bipolar adjectives associated with the concepts father, male, and mother. It may be asserted that the differences observed between Chicanos and Anglos in these studies were caused, at least in part, by cultural differentiation and not solely by socioeconomic or demographic variables.

It has been shown, then, that the semantic differential and one of its dimensions — potency — can discriminate between Chicanos and Anglos, using high school and college populations. Olmedo, Minor, Martinez, and Martinez (Note 2)

TABLE 4
Variables that Significantly Discriminate between Chicanos and Anglos

Variable	Multiple R
Only English spoken at home	.654
Education of head of household is 0-8 years	.690
Head of the household grew up on the farm	.712
Only Spanish spoken at home	.724
Mostly Spanish spoken at home	.734
The family has 1-5 members	.741
Dangerous-safe for male	.748
Unique-commonplace for father	.754
The family has 6 or more members	.759
The subject has immigrant grandparents	.764
The subject has lived in the U.S. since birth	.767
Ugly-beautiful for father	.769
The head of the household was born in Mexico	.772
The head of the household was born in the U.S.	.775
Tenacious-yielding for father	.778
Rough-smooth for male	.779
Serious-humorous for father	.780
The head of the household has a white collar job	.781
Complex-simple for mother	.781
There are 4-6 sisters in the home	.782
There are 1-3 brothers in the home	.783
The subject is 15 or younger	.783
Severe-lenient for mother	.783
The subject wrote negative comments about the questionnaire	.784

showed that the potency dimension discriminated between Chicano and Anglo junior high school students as well. There happened to be a sizable Mexican population in the school used, so that the responses of Mexicans were compared to those of Chicanos and Anglos. It was found that the potency dimension significantly discriminated among the groups. Figure 3 presents the discriminant functions that describe the differences among the groups on the concept *mother*. It may be seen that Chicano and Anglo ratings of mother were closer to each other than either was to the Mexicans. Chicanos and Anglos saw her as more commonplace and beautiful than did Mexicans. Chicanos also saw her as more violent and stronger than did either Anglos or Mexicans.

Figure 4 presents a similar graph for father, but only one function discriminated significantly between the groups. Again, Chicano and Anglo perceptions were similar; both saw father as harder and more complex. Mexican males, however, saw him as even harder and more complex, but Mexican females saw him as soft and simple.

This study presents perhaps the clearest picture of acculturation. While the previous studies clearly delineate differences between Chicanos and Anglos, the ratings that Mexican junior high school students gave to the concepts of mother and father were much different from those of either Chicanos or Anglos. However,

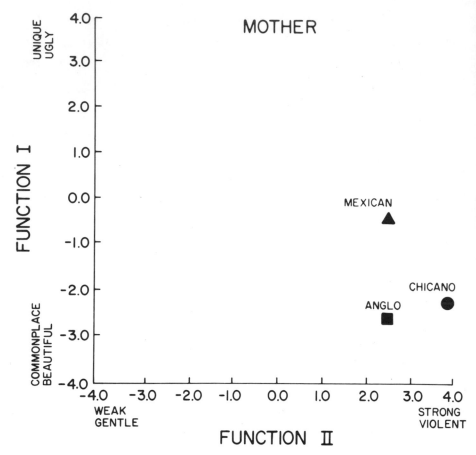

FIGURE 3. A discriminant function for the concept *mother*. The group centroids are plotted in a two dimensional space. Function I is defined at its positive pole by unique and ugly, whereas Function II is defined at its positive pole by strong and violent.

it should be pointed out that the Mexican students' English proficiency was not as great as the other two groups', and words frequently had to be translated into Spanish for the Mexican students.

Implications for Mental Health

Hardy and Cull (1973) commented on "problems" stemming from the effects of differences in understanding language that relate to cultural patterns. They noted that the success of a client-counselor relationship is dependent upon communication. Anglo psychologists should be made aware of sex role differentia-

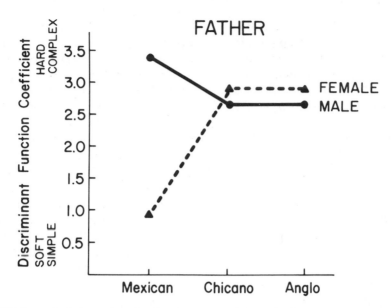

FIGURE 4. A discriminant function for the concept *father*. The function is defined by hard and complex at one pole and simple and soft at the other.

tion in the Chicano family and, in particular, how different a Chicano's perception of father is from an Anglo's.

It also seems clear that the female Chicano is not as unacculturated as the stereotype leads one to believe. She rates the basic concepts that relate to family structure much as the Anglo female. The stereotype that the female is unacculturated may stem from published literature concerning the Mexican family prototype. Diaz-Guerrero (1955) perhaps stated it best. The Mexican family structure is based on clear and rigid sex role differentiation. The father has unquestioned authority in all matters, and the mother must exhibit absolute self-sacrifice.

Acculturation pressures may have pushed the Chicano family away from the Mexican prototype. An Anglo psychologist who read Oscar Lewis (1959) probably would not be much closer to understanding the current problems of a Chicano in Anglo society.

The Development of an Acculturation Scale

It is well known that the Chicano population is not homogeneous (Murillo, 1971). Some Chicanos identify more closely with Mexican culture and some with Anglo culture. It is not surprising that this continuum of acculturation can be considered as a psychological variable and treated as such. Mercer (1972) has most elegantly demonstrated that one's position along this continuum can affect performance on standard psychological measures (see also Chapter 10).

Olmedo, Martinez, and Martinez (Note 3) developed a scale based solely on an empirical discrimination of Chicano and Anglo responses on the potency dimension of the semantic differential and socioeconomic and demographic variables. The variables that discriminate between the two groups were reported in Table 4. Further statistical treatment yielded a scale whose calibration coefficient on the cross-validated sample was highly significant ($r = .7328$, $F = 21.70$, *df* 22, 444, $p < .0001$). The distribution of scores for the predicted Y's for Chicanos and Anglos is presented in Figure 5. The data presented in the figure have some face validity. First, the Anglo population is more homogeneous than the Chicano population. The overlap of the Chicano population into the Anglo distribution is much greater than the converse. Therefore at the extreme negative end of the Chicano distribution, where it might be said that "Chicanoness" is defined, there are no Anglos. Conversely, on the extreme positive side of the Anglo distribution there are few Chicanos. More important, the mean score of Chicanos in the high school with only 10% Chicanos is closer to the Anglo mean than the means of students from the other two high schools where there were greater proportions of Chicanos.

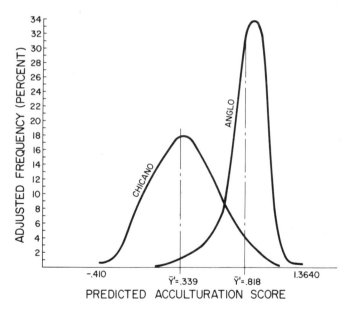

FIGURE 5. A theoretical model of an acculturation scale derived from responses of Chicanos and Anglos on the semantic differential.

Implications for Psychological Testing

The early work of Sánchez (1932a, b, 1934a, b) should have alerted psychologists to the problems associated with using standard psychological tests with the Chicano population. However, his work went largely unnoticed for many years.

Padilla and Ruiz (1973) stated very clearly why most standardized psychological tests are not valid for Chicanos. One very important reason could be that Chicanos are spread out on an acculturation continuum. Mercer (1972) has shown that the IQ of Chicanos rises to the Anglo mean as acculturation variables are taken into account. In other words, the more like a middle-class Anglo a Chicano becomes, the more a Chicano looks like an Anglo on standard psychological measures. An acculturation scale like the one described previously could be used in conjunction with psychological tests as a moderator variable to provide a more valid test assessment of Chicanos.

Conclusions

In summary, several things seem to have emerged from studies investigating Chicano, Anglo, and Mexican responses on the semantic differential to the concepts of mother, father, male, female, and self. First, the concepts clearly have different affective meanings for the three groups. The greatest differences seem to appear in the potency dimension and, in particular, the concept of father. There is greater sex role differentiation among Chicanos than Anglos, and these differences are probably even greater for Mexicans. Chicano and Anglo females seem to be closer in their responses on the semantic differential than do Chicano males and females. In fact, the Chicano males seem the most different. Some of the differences observed in these studies can be attributed to cultural rather than socioeconomic or demographic variables. The semantic differential or the potency dimension of the semantic differential have been administered to a large number of Chicanos and Anglos in a variety of sociocultural environments, and the observed differences appear to be reliable.

It is hoped that the research described in this paper will add to an empirical understanding of Chicano family structure and how it differs from both the Mexican prototype and the Anglo family structure. It should be pointed out that the results described herein are basically monomethod and need to be extended by other means of assessing family roles and patterns before the conclusions are accepted with any generality.

REFERENCE NOTES

1. Ramirez, A., Martinez, J.L., Jr., Martinez, S. & Olmedo, E. A cross-cultural comparison of Chicano and Anglo high school students on the potency dimension of the Semantic Differential, 1976. (Available from A. Ramirez, Psychology Department, University of California, Riverside, CA 92502.)
2. Olmedo, E., Minor, R., & Martinez, J.L., Jr. A comparison of Chicano, Anglo, and Mexican responses of junior high school students on the potency dimension of the Semantic Differential, 1976. (Available from E. Olmedo, Spanish Speaking Mental Health Research Center, University of California, Los Angeles, CA 90024.)

3. Olmedo, E., Martinez, J.L., Jr., & Martinez, S. Development of an acculturation scale for Chicanos, 1976. (Available from E. Olmedo, Spanish Speaking Mental Health Research Center, University of California, Los Angeles, CA 90024.)

REFERENCES

Derbyshire, R. Adolescent identity crisis in urban Mexican Americans in East Los Angeles. In E. Brody (Ed.), *Minority group adolescents in the United States*. Baltimore: The Williams and Wilkens Co., 1968.

Diaz-Guerrero, R. Neurosis and the Mexican family structure. *American Journal Psychiatry*, 1955, *112*, 411-417.

Hardy, R., & Cull, J. Verbal dissimilarity among black and white subjects: A prime consideration in counseling and communication. *Journal Negro Education*, 1973, *42*, 67-70.

Lewis, O. *Five families*. New York: Basic Books, 1959.

Martinez, S., Martinez, J., Jr., & Olmedo, E. Comparative study of Chicano and Anglo values using the Semantic Differential technique. *Atisbos, Journal of Chicano Research*, 1975, *Summer*, 93-98.

Martinez, J., Jr., Martinez, S., Olmedo, E., & Goldman, R. The Semantic Differentail technique: A comparison of Chicano and Anglo high school students. *Journal Cross Cultural Psychology*, 1976, *7*, 325-334.

Mercer, J. I.Q.: The lethal label. *Psychology Today*, 1972, *6*, 44; 46-47; 95-96.

Murillo, N. The Mexican-American family. In C.A. Hernandez, M.J. Haug, & N.N. Wagner (Eds.), *Chicanos: social and psychological perspectives* 2nd ed. Saint Louis: C.V. Mosby, 1971.

Osgood, C. Semantic Differential technique in the comparative study of cultures. *American Anthropologist*, 1964, *66*, 171-200.

Osgood, C., May, W., & Miron, M. *Cross-cultural universals of affective meaning*. Urbana: University of Illinois Press, 1975.

Osgood, C., Suci, G., & Tannenbaum, P. *The measurement of meaning*. Urbana: University of Illinois Press, 1957.

Padilla, A., & Ruiz, R. *Latino mental health*. (Department of Health, Education and Welfare Publication, No. MSM 73-9143). Washington, D.C.: U.S. Government Printing Office, 1973.

Peñalosa, F. Mexican family roles. *Journal Marriage and the Family*, 1968, *30*, 680-689.

Ramirez, M. Identification with Mexican family values and authoritarianism in Mexican Americans. *Journal of Social Psychology*, 1967, *73*, 3-11.

Ramirez, M. Identification with Mexican-American values and psychological adjustment in Mexican-American adolescents. *International Journal Social Psychology*, 1969, *15*, 151-156.

Ramirez, M., & Castañeda, A. *Cultural democracy, bicognitive development, and education*. New York: Academic Press, 1974.

Ramirez, S., & Parres, R. Some dynamic patterns in the organization of the Mexican family. *International Journal Social Psychiatry*, 1957, *3*, 18-21.

Sánchez, G. Group differences in Spanish-speaking children: a critical review. *Journal Applied Psychology*, 1932, *16*, 549-558. (a)

Sánchez, G. Scores of Spanish-speaking children on repeated tests. *Journal Genetic Psychology*, 1932, *40*, 223-231 . (b)

Sánchez, G. Bilingualism and mental measures. *Journal Applied Psychology*, 1934, *18*, 765-772. (a)

Sánchez, G. The implications of a basal vocabulary to the measurement of the abilities of bilingual children. *Journal Social Psychology*, 1934, *5*, 395-402. (b)

Staples, R. The Mexican-American family: Its modifications over time and space. *Phylon*, 1971, *32*, 171-192.

Suci, G. A comparison of semantic structures in American southwest culture groups. *Journal Abnormal Social Psychology*, 1960, *61*, 25-30.

Tanaka, Y., Oyama, T., & Osgood, C. A cross-cultural and cross-concept study of the generality of semantic space. *Journal of Verbal Learning and Verbal Behavior*, 1963, *2*, 392-405.

Vigil, J. A comparison of selected perceptions of Spanish speaking students and non-Spanish speaking students. *Dissertation Abstracts International*, 1968, *29*, 1140A-1141A.

CHAPTER 5

SOCIAL MOTIVES AND BEHAVIORS OF MEXICAN-AMERICAN AND ANGLO-AMERICAN CHILDREN

SPENCER KAGAN[1]

University of California, Riverside

Introduction

Almost half a century ago, the seeds of a classical anthropological debate were planted when Redfield (1930) published his study, *Tepoztlan – A Mexican Village*. Redfield claimed that village life in Mexico was essentially cooperative and Rousseauean, but about 20 years later, Lewis (1951) studied the same village and described in detail the lack of cooperation, tensions among villagers, and pervasive fear and distrust in interpersonal relationships. Since then numerous anthropologists and psychologists have contrasted social motives and behaviors among Mexican and United States groups (Diaz-Guerrero, 1965, 1967; Fromm & Maccoby, 1970; Kagan & Madsen, 1971, 1972a, b; Kluckhohn, 1954; Kluckhohn & Strodtbeck, 1961; Madsen, 1967; Romanucci-Ross, 1973; Whiting & Whiting, 1973).

In spite of the relatively extensive attention given to comparisons between the development of social motives and behaviors in Mexico and the United States, only recently have social scientists begun systematically to investigate the development of social motives and behaviors among Mexican-Americans. Before 1970, there were no published empirical studies that focused directly on the development of social motives among Mexican-Americans. The present chapter, then, is essentially a review and interpretation of work that has been accomplished in the last 6 years.

[1] The author is grateful to Linden Nelson, George Knight, Curt Hoffman, Rick Jacobs, and especially Joe Martinez for their helpful comments on the first draft of this manuscript.

The study of the relationship between Mexican cultural background and the development of social motives and behaviors has been marked by increasing research sophistication with regard to both the definition of cultural background and the definition of social motives and behaviors. Early studies gave little attention to the generation level, economic class, or community characteristics of Mexican-Americans sampled; recent studies are focusing more on those variables. Early studies documented broad behavioral differences which were motivationally ambiguous; recent studies have become more analytic.

This chapter is intended to review the existing literature and provide an explicit conceptual framework within which social motives might be analyzed. Without such a framework the meanings of behavioral differences are difficult to discern, and the relations among studies are difficult to determine. To some extent, such a framework has been implicit in the research to date, but it is set down explicitly as the *social motive matrix* for the first time in this chapter. In the section on motivational analysis of experimental results, the concepts of the social motive matrix are applied in interpreting the existing empirical literature that relates directly to the development of social motives of Mexican-American children. Out of a diversity of samples and methods, a theme emerges: Compared to other children, Mexican-American children are more concerned with certain cooperative motives, especially group enhancement and/or altruism; and when presented with behavioral alternatives in experimental situations, they more often choose alternatives that maximize those cooperative motives rather than alternatives that might satisfy competitive motives. The section on the antecedents of observed differences evaluates some possible causes of the relatively greater development of group enhancement and/or altruism among Mexican-American children. The last section summarizes the findings to date, notes some areas of research that merit further attention, and discusses some implications of the finding that Mexican-American children differ from other United States children in the development of social motives and behaviors.

The Social Motive Matrix

Before we discuss the research relating to the development of social motives and behaviors of Mexican-American children, we must make distinctions among types of social motives, strategies, and social behaviors. These distinctions are essential because the study of cultural differences attempts not only to document how cultures differ in social behaviors, but also to discover the motivational base for those differences. Since social behaviors, social motives, and strategies are highly interrelated, it is necessary to provide a conceptual framework within which social motives can be discussed. The present chapter builds upon yet departs from conceptual frameworks in the experimental game literature (Griesinger & Livingston, 1973; McClintock, Note 1; McClintock, Messick, Kuhlman, & Campos, 1973; Messick & McClintock, 1968; Vinacke, 1969).

It can be argued that motivational constructs such as those proposed in the present chapter are hypothetical constructs with no referents in reality – products of circular reasoning: Motives are inferred from behavior and in turn are used to explain behavior. Even if, phenomenological experience to the contrary, motivational constructs could be demonstrated to be entirely hypothetical, they would nevertheless prove useful in organizing the diverse findings of behavioral studies. The finding that motivational constructs help to explain behavioral data argues that there may be consistent individual and group differences in social motivation. Indeed, recent empirical research indicates that individuals behave as if they differ in their basic social motivations, and knowing these social orientations improves our ability to predict social behavior (Kuhlman & Marshello, 1975; Kuhlman & Wimberly, 1976).

Inferences of motives from behavior are difficult because there is no one-to-one relationship between motives and behavior. The same motive may produce different social behaviors for two individuals or groups because of the different strategies they adopt. That is, they may agree on the goal but disagree on how to get there. For example, in a game of football two teams may both have the same social motive, let us say, each attempting to get more points than the other, but one team may choose a strategy dominated by attempts to minimize the outcomes of the other team while the second may try to win by maximizing its own gains. Thus the same goal may lead to quite different behaviors, depending on considerations of strategy. A related difficulty for those who wish to infer social motives from observable social behaviors arises because different motives may lead to the same social behavior, given the limited opportunities for choice that frequently occur in both experimental and natural settings. For example, a football player may block a player from another team for any combination of the following motives: He wants his team to get more points than the other team (superiority), he wants to hurt the other player (aggression), he wants the crowd to cheer him (individualism), he wants to tie the score (equalitarianism), or he wants to help a teammate complete a pass so the teammate will look good (altruism). Clearly, in many situations a number of motives can all lead to the same behavior, and motives cannot be inferred with any certainty from a limited sample of behavior.

Social motives and behaviors are often expressed in situations of outcome interdependence, situations in which the choices confronting individuals will determine something about their own outcomes and the outcomes of others. There are four types of outcomes about which an individual may be concerned in situations of outcome interdependence: (*a*) absolute outcomes for self; (*b*) absolute outcomes for other; (*c*) relative outcomes for self and other, and (*d*) joint outcomes for self and other. Absolute outcomes refer to the number of gains or losses an individual receives, without regard to the gains or losses of others. Relative outcomes refer to the degree to which the absolute outcomes for an individual exceed or fall short of the absolute outcomes of another (own outcome minus other outcome). A relative gain for one individual, therefore, necessarily implies a relative loss for another. Joint outcomes refer to the number of gains or losses incurred by individuals taken as a group (own outcome plus other outcome). Joint outcomes for self and other are therefore necessarily the same.

Because a relative gain for one person implies a relative loss for the other and a joint gain for one person implies a joint gain for the other, in two-person outcome interdependency situations there is only a limited number of conceptually discrete possible outcomes. The 16 possible outcomes are numbered in the first column of the social motive matrix presented in Figure 1. These behavioral outcomes consist of four absolute outcomes for the self, four absolute outcomes for the other, four relative outcomes for self and other, and four joint outcomes. It is plausible that preferences for some of the outcomes may be motivationally related, and it is useful to distinguish three levels of motivation that might determine choice of a particular outcome; minor motives, major motives, and social orientations.

Behavior that results in one of the 16 behavioral outcomes may at times be the result of a motive for the specific outcome, called a minor motive. The suggested name of the minor motive associated with each of the 16 behavioral outcomes is listed in the second column of the social motive matrix. A minor motive implies only the aim for a specific behavioral outcome. It is important to distinguish minor motives from the behavioral outcomes themselves, for the choice of behavior that results in a certain behavioral outcome can be determined by factors unrelated to a motive for that particular outcome, such as random responding, a right side preference, or satisfaction of some other motive which, in a given situation, happens to be associated with the behavioral outcome in question. When choice of a behavioral outcome does result from a minor motive, that minor motive may be an end in itself, or it may represent a strategy in the service of a more general motive, called a major motive.

Nine such major motives, based on logical combinations of minor motives, can be distinguished. For example, if a person systematically avoids relative losses for himself in a variety of situations, a minor motive to avoid subordination may be inferred. Avoidance of subordination may be an end in itself or may be a strategy in the service of either of two more general, or major motives, as indicated in the social motive matrix. If avoidance of subordination is accompanied by avoidance of dominance, a major motive for equality may be inferred. If, however, avoidance of subordination is accompanied by seeking of dominance, a major motive for superiority may be inferred. Thus the minor motive of avoidance of subordination may be an end in itself or may be a strategy in the service of one of two major motives, equality or superiority. As indicated in the third column of the social motive matrix, only nine major motives can be distinguished: two associated with the absolute outcomes for oneself (individualism versus self-diminution); two with the absolute outcomes of another (altruism versus rivalry); three with relative outcomes (superiority versus equality versus deference); and two with joint outcomes (group enhancement versus group diminution). Three of these major motives (self-diminution, deference, and group diminution) are probably rare, and generally the outcomes they represent are probably valued negatively. Furthermore, two of the major motives (individualism and self-diminution) concern only self-outcomes

Behavioral Outcome	Minor motive	Major motive	Social Orientation
Absolute outcomes for self			
1. Obtain absolute gains for self	Self-gain	Individualism	
2. Avoid absolute losses for self	Self-defense		
3. Obtain absolute losses for self	Self-sacrifice	Self-diminution	
4. Avoid absolute gains for self	Humility		
Absolute outcomes for other			
5. Obtain absolute losses for other	Aggression	Rivalry	Competitive
6. Avoid absolute gains for other	Containment		
7. Obtain absolute gains for other	Helping	Altruism	
8. Avoid absolute losses for other	Protecting		
Relative outcomes (own minus other outcome)			
9. Obtain relative gains for self and relative losses for other	Dominance	Superiority	
10. Avoid relative losses for self and relative gains for other	Avoid subordination		
11. Avoid relative gains for self and relative losses for other	Avoid dominance	Equality	
12. Obtain relative gains for other and relative losses for self	Subordinance	Deference	
Joint outcomes (own plus other outcome)			
13. Obtain joint gains	Group gain	Group enhancement	Cooperative
14. Avoid joint losses	Group defense		
15. Obtain joint losses	Group sacrifice	Group diminution	
16. Avoid joint gains	Group humility		

FIGURE 1. The social motive matrix.

49

and so are not social motives in a formal sense. Thus only five major social motives probably occur with any frequency.

The five major social motives may be subsumed under two even more general social orientations – cooperation and competition. Thus, in terms of the social motive matrix, a cooperative individual prefers the behavioral outcomes comprising altruism, equality, and group enhancement. A competitive individual, in contrast, prefers outcomes that satisfy the motives of rivalry and superiority.

The social motive matrix provides rather precise definitions of cooperative and competitive social orientations in terms of preferences for the variety of behavioral outcomes those social orientations subsume. This approach to defining cooperative and competitive motivation is in contrast to research that has inferred cooperative or competitive motivation from behavior in a single experimental game. The behaviors that have been called cooperative or competitive in various experimental games satisfy different motives, and games often have idiosyncratic strategy characteristics, so inferences about the social motives of individuals or groups based on choices in any one situation can be misleading, as will be demonstrated in the next section of this chapter.

The social motive matrix is only a theoretical framework; the extent to which individuals or groups actually have a consistent cooperative or competitive social orientation must be established empirically. Implicit in the matrix is recognition of the large gulf between behavioral observations and the conclusions that can be drawn about social motivation with any degree of certainty. Moving from left to right in the social motive matrix, from observable behavior that results in certain outcomes for self and other, to the inference of minor motives, major motives, and finally social orientations, necessitates more and more observations to make inferences with any certainty. While the very existence of cooperative and competitive social orientations is questionable, it is useful to apply the social motive matrix to evaluate the results of empirical studies. The matrix not only offers a way to clarify the possible motivational bases of choices in various situations, it also suggests a potentially important research goal. If it could be established that some individuals or groups are truly cooperatively motivated, for example, it would be possible to predict a fair amount about their behavior in a variety of situations.

Before we apply the social motive matrix to the results of empirical research, it will be useful to discuss some of the interrelations among motives as defined by the matrix, the definitions adopted, and some limits and advantages of the matrix.

Interrelations among Motives

The major motives that make up the two social orientations, cooperation and competition, often are not behaviorally independent. For example, if someone has a motive toward rivalry and succeeds in lowering the outcome of someone else, in many but not all situations that person has also succeeded in raising his or her own outcomes relative to the other person. Thus, behavior that satisfies the motive for rivalry often satisfies the motive for superiority as well. In many situations, rivalry and superiority, while conceptually and phenomenologically distinct, lead to the same behavior. Similarly, although the motives toward altruism and group enhancement are conceptually and phenomenologically distinct, in many situations those motives will produce the same behavior. The motives for deference and group diminution are also often satisfied by the same choice.

It is important to note that individualism and self-diminution, as well as deference and group diminution, are not necessarily associated with either a cooperative or competitive social orientation. Individualism and self-diminution involve concern for increasing or decreasing one's own net gains without any necessary regard for the gains of others. Thus in a formal sense, they are not social motives. Individualism, nevertheless, often determines the nature of social behavior, for in some situations behavior that satisfies individualism produces outcomes associated with the cooperative motives, and in other situations behavior that satisfies individualism is associated with the competitive outcomes. Self-diminution, deference, and group diminution all involve some type of loss for oneself or one's group and so are probably negatively valued, except perhaps in persons who might be described as masochistic. A masochistic orientation encompassing self-diminution, deference, and group diminution is conceivable, but unlikely.

DEFINITIONS

In order to clarify the concepts used and to bring the terms into synchrony with dictionary definitions, common usage, and logic, the social motive matrix intentionally deviates in a number of respects from terms used by some investigators to describe social motives.

In the matrix, the term *altruism* does not refer to behavior that helps another at some expense to oneself, but simply to obtaining gains and avoiding losses for others. It is useful to measure willingness to help others in situations where that behavior necessitates some loss to oneself, because the willingness to sacrifice self-gains is an indication of the magnitude of altruistic motivation. However, for several reasons it is not meaningful to define altruistic motivation in terms of a willingness to sacrifice self-gains. First, motives are meaningful only as they indicate the aims or goal states of individuals; they cannot be equated with behaviors. Not all altruistic individuals necessarily have a goal of helping others and simultaneously lowering their own gains. The goal of some individuals is to help others, and sometimes they are willing to make a sacrifice to obtain that goal, but the sacrifice is not part of their goal. Other individuals may be motivated to help others while at the same time incurring some expense to themselves, but their motive is akin to a wish for martyrdom, not to altruism.

In the past some investigators have called the joint gains or group enhancement motive *cooperation*, and the superiority or relative gains motive *competition*. Those definitions are not used in the social motive matrix. The problem with both definitions is similar. Both *cooperation* and *competition* are general terms with broad connotations, and confusions arise if they are used to describe specific motives. For example, an individual might face a choice between (*a*) seven for self and none for other and (*b*) three for self and three for other. A strong joint-gain motive would lead to the selection of alternative (*b*). Calling that behavior *cooperative*, or a reflection of cooperative motivation, however, would be highly confusing, for the behavior does not conform to the accepted definitions of the term. Cooperative motivation probably best refers to the intent to maximize the occurrence of mutually satisfying goals, implying some concern for equality and altruism as well as joint gains. Similarly, *competition* is probably best reserved for a generic description of motives, including rivalry as well as superiority. The introduction of the concept of social orientation thus may prove useful.

By including minor motives, the social motive matrix distinguishes motives that have previously been grouped together and motives which to some extent are phenomenologically and psychologically distinct and may prove to be behaviorally separable as well. For example, previous investigators have used the term *masochism* to refer to the motive to obtain losses for self and avoid gains for self (McClintock, Note 1). In the social motive matrix, the term *self-sacrifice* is reserved for the motive to obtain losses for self; it is distinguished from the motive to avoid gains for self, referred to as *humility*. Similar distinctions are made between aggression and containment, helping and protecting, and self-gain and self-defense. That previous investigators have grouped those pairs of motives reflects an earlier tendency to work with motives at the major motive level. Whether the introduction of minor motives will prove to be useful can only be determined by empirical research. Certainly humility and self-sacrifice, for example, are phenomenologically quite different.

It is important to note that the matrix does not differentiate all possible motives. For example, obtaining a relative gain for oneself and a relative loss for another are conceptually and phenomenologically distinct, and perhaps might be called self-exaltation and other subordination. Nevertheless, because behavior that obtains a relative gain for oneself also necessarily obtains a relative loss for another, such behavior is represented in the social motive matrix by only one minor motive, *dominance*. The matrix only distinguishes motives that have separate behavioral referents.

LIMITS OF THE SOCIAL MOTIVE MATRIX

The matrix has a number of important limits. It does not deal with complex motives, like martyrdom, that may be some combination of helping and self-sacrifice (see McClintock, Note 1). Furthermore, it does not define which behaviors a given individual might experience as a gain or a loss (an individualist's gains might be a masochist's losses). Nor does it dictate how motives might be measured or quantified.

Perhaps the most important limit to the matrix is that it does not allow inferences of motives from behaviors with any certainty — it indicates possibilities but not certainties. For example, individuals sometimes lower their own outcomes relative to others not because they have deference, but because they want to hurt the others by inducing guilt (Menninger, 1938). Even for the behaviors associated with the common major motives, there is no one-to-one relationship with motives. For example, individuals who have, or perceive themselves to have, less than others may seek relative gains for self and relative losses for others, not because of a motive for superiority but because of a motive for equality. The problem of inferring motives from behavior thus becomes especially difficult in situations where the actors have a complicated history of interaction, for example, in experimental games where both subjects make choices over extended trials.

ADVANTAGES OF THE SOCIAL MOTIVE MATRIX

Although the matrix is a limited conceptual framework, it may prove useful in explaining experimental findings. For example, it has been established that avoiding a relative loss is generally more powerful than obtaining a relative gain (Kagan & Madsen, 1972b; Messick & Thorngate, 1967). A glance at the matrix indicates one possible explanation: Avoiding a relative loss appears as behavior associated with both equality and superiority, the two likely relative outcome motives. Obtaining a relative gain, in contrast, is associated only with superiority.

Through the social motive matrix it becomes clear that the motivational basis for behavior is best interpreted in the context of a variety of behaviors. As noted, the behaviors associated with the minor motive called *avoiding subordination* assume a quite different meaning if they occur in the context of behaviors that avoid dominance than if they are associated with behaviors that satisfy the dominance motive. As indicated in the matrix, avoiding subordination in the first case is an expression of a motive for equality, but in the latter case the same behavior may be an expression of a motive for superiority.

There are some interesting relations between social motives as conceptualized in the social motive matrix and social motives as defined by McClelland, Atkinson, and others (Atkinson, 1958) who defined three social motives in terms of a preoccupation with three different goal states: need for *achievement* (excellence); need for *affiliation* (friendship); and need for *power* (influence). At first glance, need for achievement might be thought to relate most to individualism; need for power to superiority; and need for affiliation to the cooperative motives. In fact, however, such motives do not fit neatly into the matrix. The division of behavior into absolute, relative, and joint outcomes suggests that the needs for affiliation, power, and achievement may exist in relation to each type of outcome. Although this hypothesis has not been tested systematically for each motive, Veroff (1969) presented a strong case that need for achievement may be divided into at least two types: autonomous achievement motivation and social achievement motivation. These two types correspond to an absolute and a relative outcome orientation. Further, as will be discussed, Ramirez and Price-Williams (1976) presented evidence that need for achievement may be divided into individual achievement and achievement for the family, corresponding to absolute and joint outcomes. These findings suggested a need for the more analytic motivational constructs presented in the social motive matrix.

Perhaps the most important advantage of the matrix is that it provides a conceptual framework to summarize, interpret, and analyze empirical research. As will be seen in the following section, the social motive matrix points to some limits as well as to some unifying themes that run through the empirical literature regarding the development of social motives among Mexican-American children.

Motivational Analysis of Experimental Results

To date, almost 20 experimental studies have been conducted that provide direct information about the development of social motives and behaviors among Mexican-Americans. These studies have two general aims: (*a*) to understand the nature of social motives and behaviors; and (*b*) to understand the correlates of cultural differences in social motive development. In general, the social motive matrix provides a framework within which these studies may be evaluated and suggests some relationships among these studies that might not otherwise be obvious.

THE NATURE OF SOCIAL MOTIVES AMONG MEXICAN-AMERICANS

Most of the published work on the development of social motives among Mexican-Americans has attempted to determine the nature of differences between Mexican-Americans and other groups. It is in this research area that the social motive matrix is most easily and directly applied. Interpretation of the findings in terms of the matrix both clarifies the possible motivational bases for the observed behavior and indicates some of the limits inherent in the studies themselves. Documentation of the nature of the development of social motives and behavior among Mexican-Americans has taken four forms: (*a*) experimental game studies, (*b*) content analysis of projective material, (*c*) content analysis of role plays, and (*d*) analysis of verbal questions.

Experimental Game Studies

Six major studies have used the experimental game methodology to analyze the nature of social motives and behaviors among Mexican-American children (Madsen & Shapira, 1970; Kagan & Madsen, 1971; McClintock, 1974; Avellar & Kagan, 1976; Kagan, Zahn, & Gealy, 1977; Knight & Kagan, in press).

The studies divide neatly into two groups. The earliest three studies used complex game methodologies in which individualism and cooperation were confounded in such a way that children could get the most for themselves only by cooperating. Because of this and because the games are complex enough to elicit a variety of strategies, the early studies cannot support motivational interpretations with any degree of confidence. In response to these problems, the more recent three studies used simpler games and either controlled or directly measured individualism, so that interpretations about cooperative and competitive motivation could be supported.

None of the games used negative outcomes. The games offered choices between alternatives that provided more or fewer rewards for self and other. The games did allow children to choose alternatives that provided a loss relative to the other alternative, but they did not deal with losses in the absolute sense. A number of the minor motives therefore cannot be assessed. In spite of this limit in the empirical studies, for ease of presentation the possible motivational bases for choices will be interpreted at the major motive and social orientation levels. It should be noted at the outset, however, that inconsistent results in future research that allows negative outcomes might necessitate a reinterpretation of the motivational bases for choices. That is, if future research that does provide negative outcomes demonstrates, for example, that children who avoid absolute gains for others do not also obtain absolute losses for others, then it would be more meaningful to discuss the motivational bases for choice at the minor motive level rather than the major motive level, as in the following presentation.

The Cooperation Board. The first study of cooperative and competitive behaviors to involve Mexican-American children was designed by Madsen and Shapira (1970). The study contrasted the behavior of Afro-American, Anglo-American, Mexican-American, and rural Mexican children, using a behavioral game called the cooperation board. The cooperation board, pictured in Figure 2, consists of a board 18 inches square with an eyelet screwed into each corner.

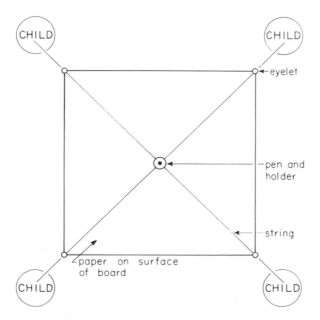

FIGURE 2. The cooperation board.

A string connected to a handle on the outside of the board and a pen holder in the center passes through each eyelet. Thus, the board is constructed so that coordinated movement of the pen demands cooperative behavior (taking turns pulling and releasing the strings). Competitive behavior (pulling against each other) leads to uncoordinated movement of the pen.

Madsen and Shapira (1970) conducted three experiments using the board with Mexican-Americans. In the first experiment, groups of four same-sex, same-ethnic group children from the three United States samples were seated around the cooperation board and were told they could receive prizes by playing a game. The experimenter demonstrated how the pen holder held a pen and how pulling a string could make the pen mark on a paper taped to the board. The experimenter then indicated four circles located between the subjects and told them that they would each receive a reward each time the marker passed through all four circles during a one-minute period. After each one-minute trial, children chose their rewards. After the third trial, the instructions were changed so that children were rewarded individually. That is, the experimenter wrote a child's name in each circle and explained that each had his or her own circle and would receive one prize each time the pen crossed the circle. Children then played three more trials.

Results of the first experiment indicated that all children pulled the marker together to receive an increasing number of toys during the first three group-reward trials, but introduction of the individual-reward condition following the third trial led all children except Mexican-American boys to pull the strings toward themselves. While all other children began to pull against each other on the fourth trial, Mexican-American boys continued to move the marker around the board, crossing circles. They received as many rewards in the individual-reward condition as in the group-reward condition. Mexican-American boys received significantly more rewards in the individual reward trials than did Anglo-American and Afro-American boys. Mexican-American children as a group, however, did not receive significantly more rewards, for Mexican-American girls did not differ significantly from the other girls in the study.

The almost complete cooperative behavior in the initial group reward trials is explained by reference to the social motive matrix. Because children could obtain rewards only as a group, there was no possibility of obtaining superiority. Thus, the motives that would be satisfied by competitive behavior in group reward situations are rivalry, self-diminution, and group diminution. Since self and group diminution are almost certainly negatively valued by most children, and rivalry is probably almost always a weak motive compared to individualism and the three cooperative motives, we might expect almost universally cooperative behavior in group reward situations. And this is what is observed (Madsen, 1967; Madsen & Shapira, 1970; Nelson & Madsen, 1969; Shapira & Madsen, 1969).

Interpreting the results of the individual reward trials, however, is more difficult. Because competitive behavior on the cooperation board leads to no toys for anyone, individualism can actually be satisfied only by cooperation. Thus, in terms of actual outcomes obtained, Mexican-American boys appear more cooperative and/or individualistic. Their behavior best satisfies the motives for altruism, group enhancement, and individualism, in contrast to that of the other children who obtained outcomes associated with rivalry, self-diminution, and group diminution.

The cooperation board, however, involves rather complex behaviors, and there is possibly little correspondence between the outcomes obtained and those children actually desire. Unambiguous motivational interpretations in such situations are not possible. For example, although individualism can only be satisfied by cooperative behavior, children may believe individualism can be satisfied by competitive behavior; that is, they may believe they can get toys for themselves by pulling the string toward themselves against others. Placing the children's names on the circles in front of them probably intensifies this individualistic set, at least for some children. Thus the powerful motive for own gain, individualism, may lead to cooperative or competitive behavior, depending on the beliefs children have about the structure of the game and the strategies they adopt. Similarly, some children may believe that by competing they can obtain superiority, but other children may realize that competitive behavior will lead to no rewards for anyone. Given these ambiguities, the motivational meaning of the observed cultural differences cannot be clarified.

In the second experiment (Madsen & Shapira, 1970) the same subjects were studied, but the reward contingencies were changed. Circles were drawn so that they were directly in front of the eyelets. In this situation, competition might be adaptive, in that a strong child could overpower his peers and receive a reward. The results indicated that there were no significant differences among the children; all behaved competitively, pulling against each other. There was some tendency, however, for Mexican-American children to behave somewhat less competitively; they crossed an average of 1.7 circles compared to 0.7 for both the Anglo-American and Afro-American children. Motivationally, the second experiment establishes little more than the first. Mexican-American children may have been somewhat more motivated toward altruism, group enhancement, or individualism, less competitively motivated, or again they may have been more able to see the futility of pulling against each other, differing primarily in the strategy they adopted.

In the final experiment, new samples of Anglo-American, Afro-American, Mexican-American, and rural Mexican children played four trials of the individual-reward condition on the cooperation board. The results indicated that Mexican-American children were the only United States group to obtain more toys as trials progressed. Rural Mexican children, however, obtained far more toys than any of the United States samples. Motivationally, the third study is as ambiguous as the first two.

The Circle Matrix Board. In part to investigate the effects of an individualistic versus a group set further, Kagan and Madsen (1971) conducted the second experiment to investigate the development of social motives and behaviors among

Spencer Kagan

Mexican-American children. The study contrasted Mexican-American children with Anglo-American and rural Mexican children of two ages using a new task, the circle matrix board, and several instructional sets designed to determine the influence of an individualistic versus a group orientation upon behavior in an individual-reward situation. The circle matrix board was designed to quantify the within-trial behavior of children because this is not easily accomplished with the cooperation board. The circle matrix board is pictured in Figure 3.

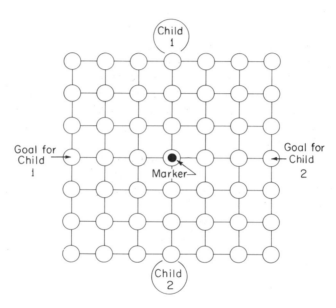

FIGURE 3. The circle matrix board.

Children sat on opposite sides of the matrix board and took turns moving a chip one circle at a time along the lines. The first child to reach his own goal received a reward. The goals were on opposite sides of the board. The chip was placed in the center of the board at the beginning of play. As with the cooperation board, competitive behavior (each child moving only toward his own goal) was nonadaptive because children could receive rewards only by cooperative behavior (moving toward only one goal per trial and taking turns moving toward each goal).

If children moved the marker only toward their own goals, they would use up the 20 allotted moves, neither would reach a goal, and neither would receive a toy. Children played the game under one of three verbal sets, the "I" set, in which the children were spoken to individually and in which the goals were described as belonging to the subjects; the "we" set, in which the children were told as a pair that "if we move the marker to this circle, we can give the toy to (subject's name)"; and the neutral set, which attempted to make a more neutral description of the reward contingencies. A fourth set, which contrasted behavioral and verbal instructions, the I-we set, was also included. In all conditions, the reward contingencies were exactly the same; only the method of describing the contingencies varied, with the aim of creating either an individualistic, neutral, or group orientation set.

The results indicated that Mexican-American children aged 7 to 9 made significantly fewer conflict moves per trial, took fewer moves to reach their goals, and earned more toys than Anglo-American children. Anglo-American and Mexican-American children did not differ at ages 4 to 5, Mexican-American children earned more toys than Anglo-American children, but they did not earn as many toys as rural Mexican children. Cultural differences in both the verbal and behavioral set conditions were relatively small. The instructional sets tended to push behavior in one direction or the other, minimizing cultural differences that appeared in the more neutral condition.

The most interesting differences were revealed in the within-trial patterns of moves that emerged. On each trial, the children's moves were classified into one of six types of behavior, including all cooperative behavior (coordinated movement of both children to the goal of one in the minimum number of moves possible) and partial conflict behavior (which contained at least one instance of a child moving the marker back into the circle from which another child had just moved). Younger children displayed little conflict behavior and mostly cooperative behavior. Older children differed as a function of ethnic group. Mexican-American children displayed cooperative behavior on 29% of the trials, in contrast to Anglo-American (10%) and rural Mexican children (63%). Similarly, Mexican-American children displayed some conflict moves on 50% of their trials, in contrast to both Anglo-American children (73%) and rural Mexican children (12%). Clearly, in terms of behavior the Mexican-American children were far more cooperative than the Anglo-American children and far more competitive than the rural Mexican children.

The instructional sets provide some help in interpreting the possible motivational basis for the observed behavioral differences. In the neutral condition, Mexican-American and rural Mexican children behaved quite as they did in the "we" condition; Anglo-American children, in contrast, behaved more as they did in the "I" condition. To some extent, the neutral condition allowed subjects to structure the game in accordance with their motives. In the neutral condition, Mexican and Mexican-American children behaved as if they spontaneously created a "we" set or group enhancement orientation to the experimental situation; in contrast, the Anglo-American children behaved as if they created an "I" set or individualistic orientation.

This interpretation, however, cannot be made with certainty, for the more cooperative behavior of Mexican and Mexican-American children conceivably could be attributed to a greater major motive toward altruism or group enhancement; and the greater competitiveness of Anglo-American children could be attributed to a stronger motive toward superiority or rivalry. Further, it is possible that children of Mexican cultural background were quicker to realize the futility of competitive behavior in a situation where moving against each other resulted in no progress for anyone.

The Maximizing Difference Game. In an attempt to clarify the development of social motives among Mexican-American children, McClintock (1974) had second, fourth, and sixth grade Mexican-American and Anglo-American children play a matrix game. The Anglo-American children were all males, and the Mexican-American children were males and females who played in same-sex groups. In this case, unlike the previous two studies, socioeconomic class was not controlled. The Anglo-American children came from middle-class backgrounds, and the Mexican-Americans came from lower and lower middle-class backgrounds. Further, the task was more complex than the previous tasks, and some subjects who could not understand the instructions were eliminated.

The task, called a maximizing difference game, is played by two children who simultaneously choose between two alternatives, 1 and 2, so that four possible outcomes can result. That is, the first child (A) can choose A_1 or A_2 and the second child (B) can choose B_1 or B_2, resulting in the following possible outcomes: A_1B_1, A_1B_2, A_2B_1, and A_2B_2. Each outcome is associated with some reward for each child, as follows: A_1B_1 means 6 points each; A_1B_2 means B receives 5, A receives 0; A_2B_1 means A receives 5, B receives 0; and A_2B_2 means both receive 0.

The game is called a maximizing difference game because a concern for obtaining more than another (maximizing the difference between own and other gains), a superiority motive, will tempt individuals to defect from a cooperative sequence of play (choose 2) in hopes of obtaining more than the other. Thus, investigators have used defection in the maximizing difference game as a measure of concern for relative gains.

The results of the McClintock (1974) study indicated that at all three ages, Mexican-American boys and Mexican-American girls defected (chose 2) less often than the Anglo-American boys. All children tended to defect more often with increased age and as trials progressed, but the increase in defection after the first 10 trials was less for Mexican-American than for Anglo-American children. It may be that Mexican-American children were less willing than Anglo-American children to forego the A_1B_1 alternative, which would potentially maximize individualism and the three cooperative motives, or that they were more aware that competitive behavior would often lead to no rewards for either themselves or the other child.

Motivational interpretations of the maximizing difference game cannot be made with any degree of confidence; the game is by far the most motivationally ambiguous of those used to date for the study of Mexican-American children. Because the game is so complex, defection may result from any of the major motives. For example, let us imagine two players who begin with a cooperative outcome, A_1B_1. On the next trial, however, player A defects, producing A_2B_1, or five points for A and none for B. At that point many possible motives might determine a defection by B. B might defect in the service of motives for (*a*) equality: Finding himself five points behind, B might wish to catch up and so might choose B_2 in order to try for A_1B_2; (*b*) rivalry: B, in response to A's defection, may try to lower the overall outcomes of A or prevent gains of A by producing outcomes A_1B_2 or A_2B_2; (*c*) superiority: B may wish to obtain more points than A and try A_1B_2 outcomes; (*d*) individualism, altruism, equality, or group enhancement: B may want an A_1B_1 outcome, but may choose B_2 because he believes A will persist in choosing A_2 unless that choice is made unattractive to A. The defection choice that is interpreted as a reflection of concern for relative gains may be motivated by any of the major motives listed in the social motive matrix. Strategy concerns make behavior in complex games motivationally ambiguous. Actually, it is possible to imagine two players, both motivated by cooperative motives, playing the maximizing difference game and repeatedly defecting in attempts to force the other player back into cooperation. Thus, interpretations of the McClintock (1974) study must be guarded.

Conclusions from the McClintock (1974) study must be tempered by two additional considerations. First, the Anglo-American and Mexican-American children came from different economic classes; and so the observed differences, as McClintock notes, might be due to economic class, not culture per se. As will be indicated in the Knight and Kagan (in press) study, lower income children are substantially more cooperative than middle-income children. Second, the task was designed to elicit competition by a display of the cumulative outcomes of each player after each choice on a digital display system ("comparable to a basketball game scoreboard"). This type of display focused the attention of players upon relative outcomes and tended to increase competitive behavior (Messick & Thorngate, 1967). Further, in contrast to the previous studies, the points accumulated in the maximizing difference game were not rewarded with toys. Playing a game for points rather than toys in the context of a display of relative outcomes might well elicit a set to obtain more points than another, a motive for superiority that might not exist in other situations. Thus, the greater competitiveness of Anglo-American children might be a manifestation of an important general difference or might represent only a response to what they would be likely to perceive as a competitive game.

The effect of trials on the cultural difference also merits analysis. Anglo-American and Mexican-American children did not differ in the first 10 trials; both groups averaged about 50% defection. The ethnic difference emerged and increased only after the first 10 trials; Anglo-American children showed a marked increase in rate of defection for the first 30 trials, while Mexican-American children did not. Mexican-American children did not begin to markedly increase their defection rate until after 40 trials. Their defection rate then increased even more rapidly than that of the Anglo-American group, so that during the last 10 of the 100 trials, Mexican-American children were defecting about 70% of the time, just slightly less often than Anglo-Americans, who defected about 75% of the time.

One interpretation of these results is particularly interesting. It may be that there was no cultural difference in the first trials and that the greatest amount of cooperative responding occurred in those trials because individualism was a salient motive in the first trials for both groups. That is, a cooperative choice could produce the most points (six), and since no points had yet been accumulated during the first trials, points were quite attractive. As trials wore on, however, points accumulated, and so the reward value of six additional points became less. As the accumulation of absolute gains continued, the reward value of additional absolute gains dropped below the reward value of relative gains, and children began to defect more often. Consistent with this interpretation is research indicating that concern for relative gains, for superiority, increases as absolute gains are accumulated (Kagan & Madsen, 1972b; Messick & Thorngate, 1967). What is most interesting is that Anglo-American children shifted to defection earlier than Mexican-American children. This pattern would be observed either if the motive for superiority among Anglo-American children is greater or if the motive for individualism is greater among Mexican-Americans. Interpretations, however, cannot be made with certainty, for (as indicated) strategy concerns make the defection choice motivationally ambiguous.

Rivalry-Altruism Choice Cards. To clarify the motivational differences between Anglo-American and Mexican-American children and to insure that they might not be attributable to economic class differences, Avellar and Kagan (1976) conducted the fourth experimental game study of social motives and behaviors of Mexican-American children.

A previous study by Kagan and Madsen (1972b) employed two-person choice cards to analyze the competitive social motives of Anglo-American and rural Mexican children, but that study did not include a Mexican-American sample. The study indicated that Anglo-American children were willing to sacrifice their own gains to satisfy motives for superiority or rivalry. Some of the spontaneous comments of the children indicated rivalrous motivation; Anglo-American children sometimes expressed a desire to minimize the outcomes of the other ("Giving Jerry only one"), and it appeared that Anglo-American children were willing to sacrifice own gains to satisfy rivalrous motivation. In the Kagan and Madsen cards, however, rivalry and superiority were confounded so that children may have been sacrificing their toys to satisfy motives for superiority, not rivalry.

To pursue and clarify that result, six choice cards were designed, varying in the behavioral outcomes associated with the alternative that would satisfy the motive for rivalry. Valuable toys were offered in exchange for chips on the choice cards. The cards are pictured in Figure 4. Children faced each other with a choice card between them. The chooser's outcomes are represented on the six choice cards shown in Figure 4, and the rivalrous alternative appears on the right. For example, in card 1 a child could choose either to take three for himself and give one to his peer or to take two and give two. Card 1 tests the willingness of children to sacrifice individualism in order to satisfy the cooperative motives of equality and altruism. Cards 2 and 3 control the individualism dimension by providing the same number of rewards to the chooser with both alternatives. In card 2 altruism is associated with deference and rivalry with equality. Card 3 presents a choice between an outcome satisfying the three cooperative motives (altruism, equality, and group enhancement) and an outcome satisfying the two competitive motives (rivalry and superiority), with individualism controlled. Cards 4, 5, and 6 were designed to test the willingness of children to sacrifice their own gains to be rivalrous when rivalry is not the only alternative associated with superiority. Thus, in those cards individualism is associated with altruism and rivalry is never the only alternative associated with superiority.

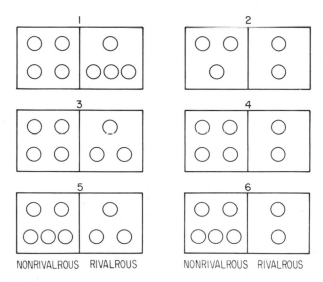

FIGURE 4. The rivalry-altruism choice cards.

The cards were presented to 5-6- and 7-9-year-old Anglo-American and Mexican-American children in similar semirural, low-income communities. The results are presented in Figure 5. For both cultural groups, individualism was clearly the overriding motive. When individualism was associated with rivalry (card 1), Mexican-American and Anglo-American children were almost all always rivalrous, when individualism was associated with altruism (cards 4, 5, and 6), almost all children of both cultural groups were almost always altruistic. There was no evidence that Anglo-American children were willing to sacrifice valued toys to satisfy a rivalry motive when rivalry was not the only alternative associated with superiority.

Culture and age differences emerged only in response to cards 2 and 3, in which individualism was controlled. Under those conditions, with increased age, Anglo-American and Mexican-American children decreasingly chose the alternatives that offered altruism and group enhancement in favor of alternatives that offered rivalry and superior relative outcomes. With increasing age, however, Mexican-American children maintained cooperative behavior more often than Anglo-American children. The two cultural groups did not differ markedly at 5-6 years, but by 7-9, Mexican-American children chose the altruism-group enhancement alternatives on about 25% more trials than Anglo-American children in both cards 2 and 3, as shown in Figure 5.

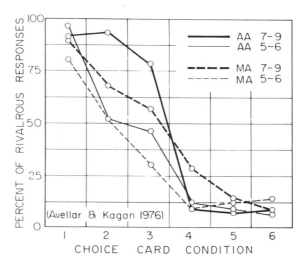

FIGURE 5. Percentage of rivalrous responses on the rivalry-altruism choice cards (Culture x Age x Card, sex collapsed). AA indicates Anglo-American; MA indicates Mexican-American. [From Avellar & Kagan, 1976.]

Interpretation of the motivational bases of the observed differences is fairly unambiguous. Since equality appears on the rivalrous side in card 2 and on the altruism-group enhancement side in card 3, that motive does not appear to explain the more frequent choice of the altruism-group enhancement alternatives by Mexican-American as compared to Anglo-American children in both cards. The only other motives that might explain the observed differences are a greater concern with altruism and/or group enhancement among Mexican-Americans or a greater concern with rivalry and/or superiority among Anglo-Americans. Since the motives for rivalry and superiority cannot be separated in outcome-interdependence situations that control individualism (the choice that maximizes rivalry will also maximize superiority), and since altruism and group enhancement cannot be separated in these situations (the choice that increases altruism will also increase group enhancement), the choice cards in the Avellar and Kagan (1976) study analyzed the nature of the social motive differences between Anglo-American and Mexican-American children into the smallest units possible in a two-person outcome interdependence situation. To conclude, Mexican-American children more frequently choose behavioral outcomes that satisfy motives for altruism and/or group enhancement. In contrast, Anglo-American children more often choose outcomes that satisfy motives for rivalry and/or superiority.

Cooperation-Competition-Individualism Choice Cards. In the fifth experimental game study involving Mexican-American children, Kagan *et al.* (in press) used a new set of six two-alternative choice cards. The cards were administered individually to children who made the choices to obtain rewards for themselves and an absent classmate. Administering the cards individually to children made it possible to determine responses without the possible influences of social interaction and thus probably measured social motivation more directly than previously. The cards were administered to two classrooms of children in each of the following grades: K, 1-2 combination, 4, and 6. The children were approximately equally divided between Anglo-American and Mexican-American cultural backgrounds at each grade level. Unlike previous studies, this study used Anglo-American and Mexican-American children from the same school who were residents of the same neighborhood.

The choice cards used are pictured in Figure 6. The B cards were designed to provide a measure of cooperative versus competitive behavior with individualism controlled; the A and C cards measure the willingness of children to sacrifice individualism for cooperation (A cards) and to sacrifice individualism for competition (C cards). Further, when the percentage of individualistic choices in the A and C cards are summed, a measure of individualism is possible with cooperative and competitive behaviors counterbalanced. That measure varies between 100% for an exclusively individualistic child and 50% for children who were either exclusively rivalrous or exclusively altruistic.

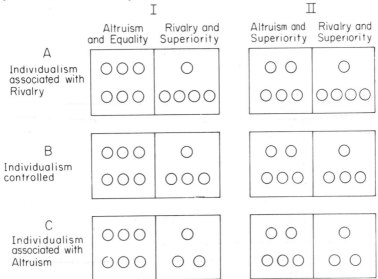

FIGURE 6. The cooperation-competition-individualism choice cards.

The choice cards in card set I measure preference for alternatives that satisfy motives for altruism, equality, and group enhancement in contrast to rivalry, superiority, and group diminution. The choice cards in card set II are similar to those in card set I except that superiority is offered with both alternatives. In fact, the children did not significantly discriminate card sets I and II, so the results are presented with the two card sets collapsed, as pictured in Figure 7. The results indicated that Mexican-American children preferred the cooperative alternatives more than did Anglo-American children at all ages on all games (with the exception of the fourth-grade children in the B games). The size of the cultural difference was smaller than that observed in previous experiments, indicating that when Mexican-American and Anglo-American children are sampled from the same school and come from the same neighborhood, marked differences in social motives are not likely. It is of interest that the children came from a stable community, and many of the Anglo-American and Mexican-American sixth-grade children attended school together from kindergarten. Thus, although the observed differences are not great, they appear quite stable, in that they do not decrease significantly as children interact during the primary school age range.

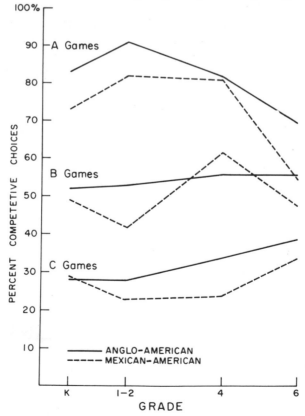

FIGURE 7. Percentage of competitive choices on the cooperation-competition-individualism choice cards (Culture x Game x Grade, sex collapsed).

The individualism measure indicated that there were no significant cultural differences, as pictured in Figure 8. Only a significant effect of age was observed, indicating that children of both cultural groups became more individualistic from grades K through 2, after which they become less so. This finding is consistent with research indicating that children tend to be egocentric until about age 7, after which decentration becomes increasingly marked.

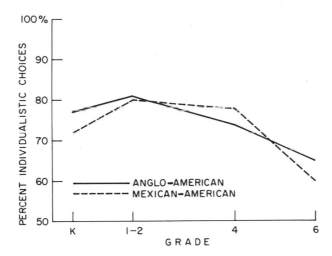

FIGURE 8. Percentage of individualistic choices on the cooperation-competition-individualism choice cards (Culture x Sex x Grade).

The Social Behavior Scale. In order to validate an individual measure of concern for altruism, equality, superiority, and rivalry, Knight and Kagan (in press) developed a four-choice card called the social behavior scale, pictured in Figure 9. The card controls for individualism in that all choices give the same number of absolute gains; the choices differ, however, in the social motives they satisfy. The choice on the right satisfies altruism and group enhancement; the next, equality; the next, superiority; and the far left choice, superiority and rivalry.

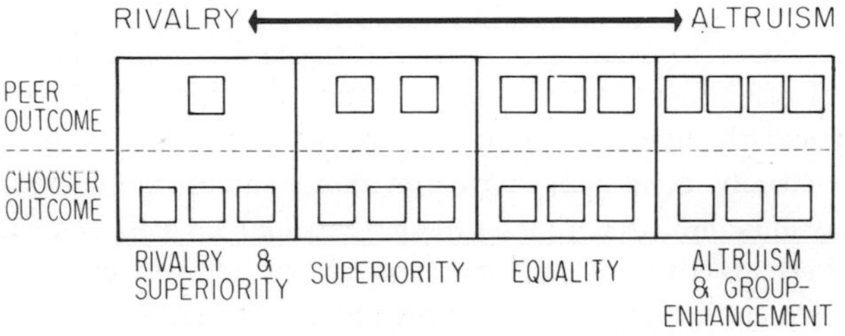

FIGURE 9. The social behavior scale.

In the first study to use the social behavior scale, Anglo-American and Mexican-American children were presented with the card for 10 choices in three different conditions. In one condition, the peer was active and took turns making choices; in the second, the peer was present but passive; in the third, the peer was not present but imagined. The results indicated that children's performance is highly correlated between the imaginary and passive peer conditions, so the card may be used with some confidence as an individual measure of social behavior preferences. The results of the first experiment, shown in Figure 10, also indicated that with increasing age Anglo-American children increasingly chose the rivalry and relative gains alternatives and decreasingly chose the cooperative alternatives. In contrast, Mexican-American children, as they got older, tended to choose the cooperative alternatives increasingly and the competitive alternatives decreasingly. Among Anglo-American children, upper middle SES children developed competitive behaviors more intensely than lower SES children.

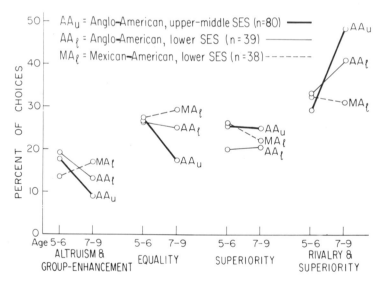

FIGURE 10. Percentage of altruism, equality, superiority, and rivalry choices on the social behavior scale (Culture x Age, sex collapsed). [From Knight & Kagan, in preparation.]

The social behavior scale also indicated marked sex differences in all groups at all ages, reflecting a more prosocial orientation among girls than among boys; girls were particularly likely to choose equality. The results with the four-choice card are not entirely consistent with previous findings, which indicated smaller sex differences and indicated that as they get older all children are increasingly competitive. Perhaps the four-choice card allows more accurate expression of motives than two-choice or game measures permit. It may be that the four-choice card allows a greater correspondence between social motives and social behaviors than do measures that force choices from among fewer alternatives.

Projective Material

In a quite different approach to understanding the social motives of Mexican-American children, several experiments have been conducted using projective techniques. These studies used traditional methodology for assessing needs through projective stories. Generally children were asked to write short stories in response to minimal verbal or pictorial cues, and the stories were then analyzed. The results of projective studies were remarkably consistent with those from experimental game studies.

The studies as a group have been primarily concerned with *n* affiliation and *n* achievement, but in some a number of other needs have been assessed. Generally, the studies sampled progressively younger subjects. The first study was concerned with college males, the next with adolescents, and the remaining three with children. The last three studies, because they focus on children, are most relevant to the present review.

Logan (1966), comparing Mexican and Anglo-American cultural values, predicted that Mexican-American college males would score below Anglo-Americans and above Mexicans on *n* achievement but that they would score above Anglo-Americans and below Mexicans on *n* affiliation and *n* power. The results indicated that Mexican-Americans were lower than Anglo-Americans and higher than Mexicans on some measures of *n* achievement but not others. Mexicans were highest on *n* affiliation. The remaining preductions were not confirmed. It is difficult to generalize from Logan's results because Mexican-American college males may be unrepresentative of Mexican-Americans in general.

Ramirez, Taylor, and Petersen (1971) predicted Mexican-American junior and senior high school students from Sacramento would differ from Anglo-American students on a number of needs. They predicted Mexican-American children in general would be lower on *n* achievement because the Mexican-American culture deemphasizes competition and individual achievement in favor of cooperation and achievement for the family group; because Mexican-American culture has authoritarian childrearing practices emphasizing dependency, passivity, and collectivism; because Mexican-Americans might fear the envy associated with achievement; and because the Mexican-American culture discourages motivation to excel in school. The authors also predicted that Mexican-American children would score lower on *n* affiliation and higher on *n* rejection because of "the culture's emphasis on close ties to the family group and its suspiciousness of strangers"; and that Mexican-Americans would score higher on *n* power "because interpersonal relationships in the Mexican-American culture are based on roles of dominance and submission."

More specific predictions were made, based on the unique sex roles thought to be characteristic of Mexican-American culture. Mexican-American males were expected to express more *n* succorance toward females because of the special support male children get in the Mexican-American family, and they were expected to show more *n* aggression toward domineering females because the Mexican-American male adolescent's masculinity is easily threatened by authoritarian females. Mexican-American females were expected to be higher on *n* autonomy because of their rebellion against traditional roles, and *n* infavoidance because of their need to compete for authority.

The results confirmed a lower *n* achievement and a higher *n* power and *n* rejection among Mexican-Americans. The prediction of a lower *n* affiliation was not confirmed. It is remarkable that the largest cultural differences occurred with the sex-role variables. Mexican-American males were far higher than Anglo-American on *n* succorance toward females and *n* aggression toward domineering females, and Mexican-American girls expressed higher *n* autonomy than Anglo-Americans. The predictions with regard to *n* infavoidance and competition for authority among Mexican-American females were not confirmed.

The findings and conclusions of the Ramirez *et al.* (1971) study relate in several interesting ways to the social motive matrix. The authors interpret the lower *n* achievement among Mexican-American children as the result of cultural orientation among Mexican-Americans that "emphasizes achievement for the family and ethnic group rather than for the self." If this interpretation is true in terms of the social motive matrix, Mexican-Americans are less individualistic and more group enhancement oriented. The authors, however, explain the greater *n* power among Mexican-Americans as the result of interpersonal relations in Mexican-American culture based on roles of dominance and submission. Thus the group enhancement orientation among Mexican-Americans is probably not associated with an intense motive for equality, a conclusion also supported by the results of the experimental game studies. In both the Avellar and Kagan (1976) and Knight and Kagan (in press) studies, the only ones in which the equality motive could be separated from the other cooperative motives, equality motivation proved not to distinguish Mexican-American children from Anglo-American. Apparently Mexican-Americans do have a high group enhancement motive, but they do not manifest all elements of a cooperative social orientation. This conclusion is supported by the findings of higher *n* rejection and the absence of a higher *n* affiliation among the Mexican-American adolescents sampled.

To determine specifically the strength of individualistic achievement in contrast to family achievement, Ramirez and Price-Williams (1976) asked 180 fourth-grade children to tell stories about seven line drawings depicting persons in settings related to education. The children were equally divided among Mexican-Americans, blacks, and Anglo-Americans from Catholic parochial schools in Houston. The stories were scored for individualistic achievement motives and family achievement motives. The results indicated that on individualistic achievement Anglo-American children scored highest as a group, followed by Mexican-Americans. Black children scored lowest. The difference between Mexican and Anglo-American children was relatively small and was accounted for entirely by the females; Mexican-American males scored slightly higher than Anglo-American males. The results of the family achievement scoring indicated that Mexican-American children scored highest, followed closely by black children. Anglo-American children showed extremely little achievement need for the family.

In terms of the social motive matrix, it appears that Mexican-American children are considerably higher on the group enhancement motive than Anglo-American, but as a group, they are not consistently lower on the individualism motive. This general conclusion is consistent with those of the experimental game studies.

In a second study, Ramirez and Price-Williams (Note 2) rescored the same stories for two additional needs: *n* affiliation and *n* guidance. The results indicated that Mexican-American and black children scored higher than Anglo-American children on *n* affiliation and *n* guidance, but the differences in *n* guidance were not significant. Mexican-American males and females both showed higher *n* affiliation than Anglo-American children, but the difference was most marked among the females; Mexican-American females demonstrated considerably more *n* affiliation than any other group.

The tendency of Mexican-American children to show higher *n* affiliation is generally consistent with the experimental game results, which indicate greater group enhancement and/or altruism motivation among Mexican-American children.

In the fourth study to use projective techniques to study the social motives of Mexican-American children, Sanders, Scholz, and Kagan (1976) analyzed the *n* achievement, *n* affiliation, and *n* power of 184 Anglo-American and Mexican-American fifth- and sixth-grade children using sentence cues that had been developed to test social motives among children of that age.

The results indicated that Anglo-American children had higher *n* achievement and *n* power than Mexican-American children, who tended to have higher *n* affiliation. The magnitude of all these differences, however, was not great. Nevertheless, the differences were generally consistent with the previous two studies and with results of the experimental game studies. The only discrepancy among all of the studies was the finding of greater *n* power among Mexican-American adolescents in the Ramirez *et al.* (1971) study and less *n* power among Mexican-American children in the Sanders *et al.* (1976) study. This difference could represent sampling differences or perhaps a developmental difference indicating greater development of *n* power among Mexican-Americans increasing with age. Logan (1966) however, did not find *n* power differences among his college samples.

Role Plays

To determine if Mexican-American and Anglo-American children differ in interactions with their mothers, Hoppe, Kagan, and Zahn (in press) had Anglo-American and Mexican-American mother-child dyads perform in three role-play situations designed to provoke conflicts over issues of maternal authority and children's independence. For example, children and mothers were asked to pretend they were in a shoe store and each preferred a different pair of shoes for the child. They were asked to speak only to each other and make a decision. The role plays were tape recorded, transcribed, and analyzed.

The results indicated that although Anglo-American and Mexican-American mothers differed only slightly in the three role plays, children of the two cultural groups were quite different. Anglo-American children more often made statements of what they wanted, more often justified those statements, more often disagreed with their mothers, more often directly spoke back to their mothers, and more often contradicted their mothers. These differences could not be attributed to amount of verbal interaction, for the two groups did not differ in that respect.

The results of the mother-child interaction role plays indicated that Mexican-American children less often enter into overt conflict with their mothers, and in this regard their behavior was analogous to the less frequent occurrence of conflict moves observed among Mexican and Mexican-American children on the circle matrix board. The behavior in both situations was quite complex and is not readily interpreted in terms of the social motive matrix. Nevertheless, the behavior observed was certainly consistent with what one might expect if Mexican-American children have a relatively more developed group enhancement orientation.

Conflict Questions

In an initial attempt to determine whether verbal responses to imagined potential conflict situations might parallel actual behavioral responses in game situations, Kagan (Note 3) asked 259 Anglo-American, Mexican-American, and rural Mexican children two simple conflict questions: "What would you do if someone your age hit you?" and "What would you do if someone your age took away your toy?" The open-ended responses were classified into three types: direct conflict (hit, take the toy back), mediated conflict (go to teacher or parent), and nonconflict (do nothing, run, hide, feel bad). The results indicated that rural Mexican children far more often chose nonconflict responses than Mexican-American and Anglo-American children, who did not differ markedly. When they did differ, however, Mexican-American children were more like rural Mexican children than were Anglo-American children. In response to the question about having a toy taken away, 7% of the Anglo-American children said that they would give the toy to the other child or share it, as did 15% of the Mexican-American children and 24% of the rural Mexican children. In contrast, more Anglo-American children (14%) responded that they would hit the other child, whereas only 8% of the Mexican-American children, and 3% of the rural Mexican children did so.

Although not too much can be concluded from a study based on two simple questions, and transcultural equivalence of the meaning of being hit or having a toy taken away cannot be assumed, the results of the experiment were consistent with the interpretations that can be drawn from the other studies. Mexican and Mexican-American children answered in ways consistent with a more cooperative and less competitive social orientation more often than Anglo-American children. The responses of giving the toy to the other or sharing it were consistent with motives toward altruism, group enhancement, and even equality; taking the toy back or hitting back were more consistent with motives of rivalry and superiority. In general, the greater tendency toward conflict among Anglo-American children was consistent with a competitive social orientation; the tendency of Mexican-American children to prefer alternatives to direct interpersonal conflict was consistent with their more cooperative social orientation.

CORRELATES OF SOCIAL MOTIVE DIFFERENCES

Several studies have been conducted to document possible causes, correlates, and consequences of the differences in social development between Anglo-American and Mexican-American children. This research, however, is quite recent and is mostly still in preparation.

Social Behavior and Maternal Reinforcement Styles. Using the social behavior scale in conjunction with an experimental game measure of maternal reinforcement patterns developed by Kagan and Ender (1975), Knight and Kagan are attempting to determine if more prosocial behaviors of Mexican-American children are associated with differential maternal reinforcement styles. The maternal reinforcement game allows mothers to reward or punish the successes or failures of their children so that maternal reinforcement may be evaluated with regard to frequency and patterns of reward and punishment. It will therefore be possible to determine if these maternal reinforcement styles measured by the Kagan and Ender game are systematically related to children's social motives.

Role-Taking Ability. Because numerous studies suggested that Mexican-American children develop prosocial motivation more intensely than Anglo-American children, Knudson and Kagan (in press) speculated that the prosocial orientation of Mexican-American children might be caused by or result in superior ability to take the role of another. In the initial test of this hypothesis, seven visual perspective role-taking tasks were administered to Anglo-American and Mexican-American children aged 5 to 6 and 7 to 9. The results indicated that children of both cultures were able to take the roles of others at an earlier age than indicated by previous research, but that Anglo-American and Mexican-American children did not differ significantly in this ability.

Social Motives and School Achievement. McClintock (1974) speculated that the differences in the rate of development of competitive responding between Anglo-American and Mexican-American children may lead the latter to be "ontogenetically out of phase with the educational system of the majority culture." In an attempt to bring empirical data to bear on that question, Kagan *et al.* (in press) analyzed the relation between competitiveness and individualism in their choice-card task (see above) to performance on standardized tests of school achievement. The results indicated that the more cooperative orientation of Mexican-American children is not consistently associated with poorer school achievement.

SUMMARY OF THE MOTIVATIONAL ANALYSIS

The empirical literature to date supports a broad conclusion about the development of social motives and behaviors among Mexican-American children.

Mexican-American children develop stronger group enhancement and/or altruism motives than Anglo-American children, who develop stronger competitive motives. The greater cooperativeness of Mexican-American children manifests itself as they more often choose the cooperative alternative on the cooperation board (Madsen & Shapira, 1970), tend more often to behave spontaneously as though they have a group or "we" set, in contrast to Anglo-American children who, faced with the same situation, behave as though under an individualistic or "I" set on the circle matrix board (Kagan & Madsen, 1972a), less frequently contradict their mothers in potential conflict situations (Hoppe *et al.* in press), and tend to be higher on need for achievement for the family group (Ramirez & Price-Williams, 1976).

The more cooperative orientation of Mexican-American children in comparison with Anglo-American children cannot be attributed to cultural differences in individualism. Although satisfaction of individualism was possible only by cooperation in the early experimental game studies, it was controlled or directly measured in the later studies. Greater cooperation of Mexican-American children was found in studies that controlled individualism (Avellar & Kagan, 1976; Kagan *et al.*, 1977; Knight & Kagan, in press), and no cultural differences in strength of individualistic motives was observed when that variable was directly measured (Kagan *et al.*, 1977). There is clear evidence that Mexican-American children prefer achievement for the family group more than other children do; a general tendency for Mexican-Americans to be lower on individualistic achievement, however, has not been established.

Motivationally, the most interpretable cultural differences occurred in situations that control individualism. In those situations, Mexican-American children preferred alternatives that satisfy the group enhancement and/or altruism motives more than Anglo-American children. In cards 2 and 3 of the Avellar and Kagan (1976) study, in the B games of the Kagan *et al.* (1977) study, and in the Knight and Kagan (in press) study, absolute gains were controlled so the individualistic motive was not better satisfied by the altruism-group enhancement alternatives than by the rivalry-superiority alternatives. In those situations, Mexican-Americans more often chose the alternatives that satisfied motives for altruism and group enhancement.

The developmental trends indicated tendencies for the cultural differences in cooperativeness between Anglo-American and Mexican-Americans to increase between the ages of 5 and 9, after which they remained relatively constant. Of the four studies which sample children of 5 to 6 and 7 to 9 years, there was a significant culture-by-age interaction in three studies (Avellar & Kagan, 1976; Kagan & Madsen, 1971; Knight & Kagan, in press) and a trend in that direction in the fourth (Kagan *et al.* 1977). In the studies that sampled children beyond the second grade, Anglo-American — Mexican-American differences remained relatively constant with age (McClintock, 1974; Kagan *et al.*, 1977). Most studies indicated a tendency for all children to become more competitive with age. On the social behavior scale of Knight and Kagan, however, as they get older, Mexican-American children increasingly choose the cooperative alternatives, unlike Anglo-Americans, who increasingly chose the alternatives that would satisfy competitive motives.

Antecedents of the Observed Differences

A motivational analysis of the empirical literature supports the conclusion with some confidence that Mexican-American children are more cooperatively motivated than Anglo-American children and display a concern for group enhancement and/or altruism rather than a more competitive orientation that includes concern for superiority and/or rivalry. The question arises of how Mexican-American children develop their more cooperative social orientation. Speculation and research on this question are relatively recent, and definitive answers are not yet possible. Nevertheless, a number of explanations can be ruled out with a fair degree of confidence, and several explanations appear plausible and merit further research.

Economic Class. Although higher economic class is clearly related to higher levels of competition (Knight & Kagan, in press; Madsen, 1967), economic class per se cannot explain the greater cooperativeness of Mexican-American children. In all studies except McClintock (1974), Mexican-American children sampled were from the same economic class as the children to whom they were compared.

Urbanization Level. Children from rural settings are more cooperative than children from more urban settings (Madsen, 1967; Madsen & Yi, 1975; Marin, Mejia, & Oberle, 1975; Miller & Thomas, 1972; Shapira & Lomaranz, 1972; Shapira & Madsen, 1969; Sommerland & Bellingham, 1972; Thomas, 1975; Uribe, 1973). Nevertheless, in all studies reviewed, including comparisons within major cities and within semirural settings, Mexican-American children were compared with Anglo-American children of the same level of urbanization. This factor thus cannot explain the observed differences.

School and Community Characteristics. In most of the cooperation studies reviewed, Mexican-American and Anglo-American children came from different schools and different communities within the same cities. Thus school and community characteristics could contribute to the observed Anglo-American-Mexican-American differences. Nevertheless, in a number of the more recent studies, Mexican-American children were compared with other children in the same schools and from the same communities; and cooperation and affiliation differences still appeared (Hoppe *et al.*, in press; Kagan *et al.*, 1977; Knight & Kagan, in press; Sanders *et al.*, 1976). It is important to note, however, that of the experimental game studies, the largest cooperation differences were observed in studies by Kagan and Madsen (1972a), McClintock (1974), and Avellar and Kagan (1976), all of which sampled Mexican-Americans from different schools and communities from those of the children with whom they were compared. In the more recent experimental game studies of Knight and Kagan (in press) and Kagan *et al.* (1977), Mexican-American children were sampled from the same school as their Anglo-American counterparts, and although Mexican-American children were significantly more cooperative, the differences were not so great as those found in previous studies. Thus, while school and community characteristics do not fully explain the observed differences, they may contribute to the differences observed in some studies.

Minority Status. Minority status within the United States conceivably may contribute to the observed differences, but this interpretation is highly speculative. Some studies indicate that blacks, like Mexican-Americans, tend to be more cooperative than Anglo-Americans (Richmond & Weiner, 1973; Sampson & Kardush, 1965). Nevertheless, in the only study that included blacks and Mexican-Americans (Madsen & Shapira, 1970), Mexican-Americans were more cooperative than blacks, who did not differ from Anglo-Americans. Although it is not possible to make definitive conclusions about the effects of minority status, the little evidence available is not consistent with the conclusion that minority status per se explains the observed differences.

Cognitive Styles. In their provocative book, *Cultural Democracy, Bicognitive Development, and Education*, Ramirez and Castañeda (1974) reviewed early research on cooperativeness among Mexican-Americans and suggested that the greater cooperativeness of Mexican-American children is related to their more field-dependent or field-sensitive cognitive style. Numerous studies have indicated that Mexican-American children are not as field independent as Anglo-American children (Buriel, 1975; Canavan, Note 4; Kagan & Zahn, 1975; Ramirez & Price-Williams, 1974; Sanders *et al.*, 1976).

Several recent studies evaluated the relation of field dependence to the cooperativeness of Mexican-Americans. The results confirmed that Mexican-Americans are less field independent than Anglo-Americans, and that they are less competitive and more cooperative, but that these differences tend not to be related empirically. Kagan *et al.* (1977), found that the greater field dependence of Mexican-American children was not correlated with their tendency to choose the more cooperative alternatives from choice cards. Hoppe *et al.* (in press) found that the less intense competitiveness of Mexican-American children in comparison to Anglo-American children in their mother-child conflict role plays was not related to field dependence-independence. Sanders *et al.* (1976) found field independence to be related to the greater *n* achievement of Anglo-American children, but that field dependence was unrelated to the greater *n* affiliation of Mexican-American children.

In general, these results suggest that Mexican-American children may differ consistently from other children on numerous dimensions and that no single construct like field dependence-independence can explain the various cultural differences. It may be that field dependence-independence differences relate primarily to the cognitive domain, in contrast to cooperation and affiliation differences, which relate primarily to the social domain. Consistent with this interpretation are the findings that field dependence-independence relates to school achievement and other cognitive variables (Kagan & Buriel 1977) but not to *n* affiliation and cooperativeness.

Socialization Practices. Considerable literature exists about the Mexican-American family, and a complete review of how socialization might relate to the greater cooperativeness of Mexican-American children is beyond the scope of this chapter. Unfortunately, a great deal of what has been written about Mexican-American families is tied only weakly to quantitative and empirical studies (see, for example, Montiel, 1973; Murillo, 1976; Peñalosa, 1968; Staples, 1971; Stanton, 1972). Nevertheless, two related trends in Mexican-American families have been repeatedly described and have received some empirical documentation: the closeness of family ties and the fostering of obedience and respect in children (Jones, 1948; Kearns, 1970; Ramirez, 1967; Ramirez & Castañeda, 1974; Steward & Steward, 1973, 1974; Tharp, Meadow, Lennhoff, & Satterfield, 1968).

Two studies are noteworthy because they have used large samples and empirical methods. Both indicate the importance among Mexican-Americans of both close family ties and emphasis on respect and obedience.

Ramirez (1967) summarized his work with the family attitudes scale and the *F*-scale, which involved large numbers of college students in various settings. His results indicated that Mexican-Americans place more emphasis on family solidarity and conformity to adult and family expectations than on individualism. Some of the items which most strongly discriminated Mexican-Americans from Anglo-Americans were (*a*) For a child, the mother should be the dearest person in existence; (*b*) More parents should teach their children to have unquestioning loyalty to them; (*c*) There is hardly anything lower than a person who does not feel a great love, gratitude, and respect for his parents; and (*d*) Obedience and respect for authority are the most important virtues children should learn. Although the Ramirez questionnaire does not counterbalance either acquiescence or extremity response biases, Ramirez has sampled large numbers of Anglo-Americans and Mexican-Americans in a number of settings, always with similar results.

Using more sophisticated sampling techniques designed to increase the representativeness of their sample, and using multivariate analyses to control socioeconomic status, Rusmore and Kirmeyer (Note 5) also recently found that Mexican-American parents believe more strongly in the importance of close family relations and respect for adult authority. It is important that many of their questions centered around behaviors rather than beliefs; and their questions were varied in response types, including true-false, multiple choice, short answer, and free-response questions, so their results are not easily interpreted as a function of response biases. Rusmore and Kirmeyer found that, compared to Anglo-American parents, Mexican-American parents indicated (*a*) the importance of close ties with their own parents; (*b*) warm and friendly feelings toward relatives; (*c*) that a child's best friend should be a brother or sister; and (*d*) that loyalty to family members is important, right or wrong. Further, Mexican-Americans reported that they behave in ways likely to create strong family ties and respect for and obedience to authority more often than Anglo-Americans. Mexican-Americans more often report (*a*) requiring their children to play closer to home; (*b*) worrying more when their children were not home; (*c*) less often allowing their children to bring friends home to play; (*d*) less often allowing their children to make independent decisions, such as what to wear and when to go to bed; and (*e*) expressing more disapproval when their children talked back to or interrupted adults. Rusmore and Kirmeyer indicated that "Mexican-American parents in contrast to their Anglo-American neighbors, held more family-centered attitudes, reflecting a greater concern for maintaining close, warm relationships within the family, and appear to encourage similar family-centered attitudes and behaviors in their children by requiring them to play close to home with siblings and to respect the authority of their elders."

These socialization practices may be related to the greater cooperativeness of Mexican-American children in a number of ways. It is possible that the greater emphasis on family unity creates a "we" set or group enhancement orientation that is generalized to other settings. This group orientation may occur at both the affective and cognitive levels and may result from many processes, including modeling, prescription, reinforcement, and attachment. Further, emphasis on respect and obedience toward authorities may increase the tendency of children to act in conformity to adult norms, which may include cooperativeness and inhibition of competition and/or individualism. It may be that Mexican-American children first learn to be cooperative in their relations with their parents and that the cooperativeness is then generalized to other relationships. Prescriptive parental value systems are associated with greater altruism among children (Olejnik & McKinney, 1973). Socialization practices that create family unity and place clear authority in parents provide clear norms and expectations that also may produce a sense of identity and security in children and in turn may diminish the need for competition. Abraham Maslow and Rogelio Diaz-Guerrero collaborated on a seldom cited article in which they attempted to explain the lower levels of sibling rivalry and higher levels of respect, helpfulness, and affection among Mexican children in contrast to United States children. Maslow and Diaz-Guerrero (1960) interpreted this cooperativeness and lack of competitiveness among Mexican children as a result of the sense of structure and security children felt because of the clear norms their parents provided, norms rooted in traditional Mexican cultural values.

At this point, the relation of socialization practices to the development of cooperativeness among Mexican-American children is not established; the suggested relations remain speculative, awaiting confirmation or disconfirmation by empirical studies.

Cultural Background. Causal analyses can usually be carried back one step further. Even if it were established that the socialization practices common in Mexican-American families produced the greater cooperativeness of Mexican-American children, the question would arise of how Mexican Americans came to have the socialization practices they favor. Economic class, urbanization level, and cultural background probably influence socialization practices among Mexican-Americans.

Although the vast majority of Mexican-American families now live in urban centers, many of these families historically came to the United States from the most rural, traditional, and low-income areas of Mexico (Gamio, 1930; Grebler, 1965; Samora, 1971), and Mexico itself is enormously more rural and low income than the United States (Grebler, 1965). Children from rural and poor areas of Mexico are far more cooperative than children in more urban and middle-class areas of Mexico and the United States (Madsen, 1967; Madsen & Shapira, 1970; Kagan & Madsen, 1971, 1972a, b). These findings are consistent with the general tendency for children from rural and traditional settings in various parts of the world to be less competitive and individualistic than children in modern urban settings (Bethlehem, 1975; Feather & Hutton, 1974; Madsen & Yi, 1975; Marin, Mejia, & Oberle, 1975; Miller & Thomas, 1972; Shapira & Lomaranz, 1972; Shapira & Madsen, 1969; Sommerland & Bellingham, 1972; Sumotirto, 1962; Thomas, 1975; Uribe, 1973; Whiting & Whiting, 1973). Thus, the urbanization and class backgrounds of some Mexican-Americans may be related to their greater cooperativeness.

Historically, core aspects of the Mexican culture are rooted in Mexico's predominantly rural and agricultural history. Many studies have indicated an emphasis among Mexicans on affiliation, conformity, and cooperativeness and a deemphasis or avoidance of aggressiveness, competitiveness, and individual assertiveness (Fromm & Maccoby, 1970; Kagan, 1974, 1975, 1976; Kagan & Carlson, 1975; Kagan & Madsen, 1972a; Lewis, 1951; Minturn & Lambert, 1964; Romanucci-Ross, 1973; Whiting & Whiting, 1973). These values are suited to life in traditional agricultural settings where land is all allotted. In such settings, an individual can often increase his own gains or superiority only at the direct expense of another, leading to an "image of limited good" (Foster, 1965). In such settings, unchecked individualism and competition lead to direct interpersonal conflict and are not tolerated, a situation that perhaps explains the generally greater cooperativeness and avoidance of conflict among people from rural settings.

To some extent, the cooperativeness observed by Redfield (1930) and the fear, envy, and distrust observed by Lewis (1951) may have resulted from a common cause, for cooperativeness may be a strategy to avoid conflict in situations of potential direct interpersonal conflict, situations that also inspire fear and distrust. The attempt to avoid direct interpersonal conflict that underlies some forms of cooperativeness is eloquently described by Murillo (1976), who noted:

> There is one area in which the Anglo and the Mexican-American are likely to be markedly disparate. This is the area of manners, courtesy, interpersonal relations — call it what you will. The Anglo is taught to value openness, frankness, and directness. He is much more likely to express himself simply, briefly, and frequently bluntly. The traditional Latin approach requires the use of much diplomacy and tactfulness when communicating with another individual. The Mexican-American often finds himself in difficulty if he disagrees with an Anglo's point of view. To him,

direct argument or contradiction appears rude and disrespectful. On the surface
he may seem agreeable, manners dictating that he not reveal his genuine opinion
openly unless he can take time to tactfully differ [p. 18-19].

Certainly, however, not all cooperativeness behavior is historically rooted in
avoidance of conflict. As Whiting and Whiting (1973) noted:

In the simpler, kin-oriented societies, with economies based upon subsistence
gardening, altruistic behavior is highly valued and individual egoistic achievement
frowned upon. Women must work in the fields, and the children must help in
order for the family to subsist. To offer help, to support others, and to be responsible are taught both by precept and practice [p. 64].

Although the cooperativeness of Mexican-Americans may to some extent
be historically related to their cultural background and values, which are rooted
in the Mexican experience, the cooperation of Mexican-Americans today cannot
be reduced to avoidance of conflict or mere maintenance of historical cultural
forms. As noted, in a number of the experimental situations, the cooperativeness
of Mexican-Americans is adaptive. Similarly, in a number of life situations the
cooperativeness of Mexican-American children is adaptive, not only because it con-
forms to the values, expectations, and models provided by Mexican-American
parents but also because cooperative behaviors lead to rewarding interpersonal
relations.

A treatment of the historical roots of the intense competitiveness that is
found among Anglo-American children is beyond the scope of this chapter. It is
interesting to speculate, however, that the value placed on competition among
United States children is related to the breakdown of fixed status roles and also
to the expanding United States frontiers and markets, all environmental factors
that would reinforce competitiveness. Furthermore, as Whiting and Whiting (1973)
note, "in more complex societies, where no child knows what he is going to be
when he grows up, individual achievement and success must be positively valued.
To help a friend sitting next to you in an examination is defined as cheating [p.
64]."

Conclusion

The evidence to date is consistent with the conclusion that Mexican-American
children are more concerned than other children with cooperative motives, especially group enhancement and altruism. When they are presented with behavioral
alternatives across a variety of situations, Mexican-American children choose
alternatives that might satisfy cooperative motives rather than competitive motives
more often than other children. Although motives can never be inferred from behavior with certainty, several lines of evidence converge to support the conclusion
that observed ethnic differences reflect differences in general cross-situational
motivational orientations, not just situation-specific behavioral tendencies, First,

a similar pattern of motives may be inferred from a rather wide range of behaviors, including six experimental games, verbal role plays, projective techniques, and verbal questions. Second, the observed differences, as noted, are consistent with cultural differences noted by nonempirically oriented studies such as that of Murillo (1976). Third, the observed differences are consistent with the verbal comments of children. For example, when faced with the social behavior scale and the cooperation-competition individualism choice cards, children choosing the relative gain alternatives often spoke of getting more than their peer; children choosing the equality alternatives spoke of being fair or making it even; children who chose the altruism alternatives commented about being nice.

The observed cooperativeness of Mexican-American children is relatively robust in a number of respects. Not only does it occur across a variety of measurement situations, but also across a variety of populations. The studies reviewed sample subjects from Texas and California, from the middle class as well as lower classes, and from urban as well as semirural settings. The cooperativeness of Mexican-American children is also robust in its resistance to melting-pot pressures of acculturation that have shaped diverse groups into people now described as "Anglo-Americans." Mexican-Americans appear to resist acculturation pressures over time. In most of the studies reviewed, Mexican-American children were second and third generation residents of the United States. Further, in a number of the studies, Mexican-American children were sampled from settings where they interact daily with non-Mexican-American children, in the school room, playground, and to some extent, in their neighborhoods. In spite of this contact, the difference between Mexican-American and other children in cooperativeness tends to increase as they develop, at least from ages 5 to 9.

The causes of the observed differences are not yet established, but the evidence suggests that economic class, urbanization level, minority status, and cognitive styles cannot account for them. Community characteristics, socialization practices, and cultural background appear more likely causal determinants, but research along those lines is just beginning.

The present review indicates a number of possible research avenues that might lead to increased understanding of both the nature of social motive differences, and the causes, correlates, and consequences of such differences.

The introduction of the social motive matrix and the motivational analysis of the empirical literature suggested that research to date leaves the motivational bases for the observed differences somewhat ambiguous. For example, the motives for group enhancement and altruism have not been independently assessed. The motives for rivalry and superiority have also been confounded. These motives could be independently assessed through the use of measurement situations where own gains are not salient, situations where there is no outcome interdependence. The introduction of the social motive matrix also suggested the need for new social motive choice cards that include negative and zero outcomes, so the minor motives might all be assessed and the usefulness of that construct evaluated. Further research is also needed to determine the extent to which the tendency toward group enhancement among Mexican-American children represents an affective rather than a cognitive difference. That is, further research might be determine if Mexican-American children are more cooperative because they feel more positive toward others, because they more often see themselves and others as a group, or both. Research that determines how Mexican-American and other children conceptualize social interaction situations could clarify the nature of the observed differences.

As indicated, a great deal of research is needed to explain how the cooperative orientation of Mexican-American children is developed and maintained. Several recent studies included generation level and family histories that should allow some test of the hypothesis that the cooperativeness of Mexican-American children is related to traditional rural Mexican traditions. Research is also being conducted to determine the relation of maternal reinforcement patterns to social motives and behaviors, but, as indicated, the differences may occur to some extent as a function of modeling, prescription, reinforcement, and attachment processes. A great deal of research is needed if the causes of the cooperativeness among Mexican-Americans are to be understood in terms of socialization practices.

Although initial research suggested that the cooperativeness of Mexican-American children is probably not strongly related to their academic performance, other possible consequences of cooperativeness merit investigation. Important areas for future research include the development of empathy and interpersonal liking. Although the research to date indicated that Mexican-American children are not superior to other children in visual perspective role taking, they might be superior in affective role taking or empathy. Children who have positive experiences for themselves paired with the positive experiences of others become more empathic and altruistic (Aronfreed & Paskal, Note 6; Midlarsky & Bryan, 1967). A joint-gain or group enhancement orientation should produce more frequent pairings of positive experiences, and there is some basis for predicting that Mexican-American children should develop higher levels of empathy. Because cooperative activities also produce liking and good will among children (Gottheil, 1955; Sherif, Harvey, White, Hood, & Sherif, 1961), there is also a basis for prediciting higher levels of interpersonal attraction among Mexican-American children.

Defining the nature and causes of social motivation and behavior development among Mexican-Americans should prove to have some important practical implications beyond understanding how a cultural group maintains social values. For example, if Mexican-American children are more group and family oriented, they may be discriminated against by educational and psychotherapeutic practices predicated upon strong individualistic motivation. Understanding the social motive development of Mexican-Americans may provide a basis for more responsive public institutions.

REFERENCE NOTES

1. McClintock, C.G. Social motivation in settings of outcome interdependence. In D. Druckman (Ed.), *Negotiations: A social psychological perspective*. In preparation.

2. Ramirez, M., & Price-Williams, D.R. Need affiliation and need guidance in the ethnic groups in the United States. In preparation.
3. Kagan, S. Resolution of simple conflicts among Anglo-American, Mexican-American, and Mexican children of three ages. Paper represented at the Western Pscyhological Association Meeting, Los Angeles, April 1976.
4. Canavan, D. Field dependence in children as a function of grade, sex, and ethnic group membership. Paper read at American Psychological Association, Washington, D.C., 1969.
5. Rusmore, J., & Kirmeryer, S. Family attitudes among Mexican-American and Anglo-American parents in San Jose, California. Paper presented at the 56th annual meeting of the Western Psychological Association, Los Angeles, California, April 1976.
6. Aronfreed, J., & Paskal, V. Altruism, empathy and the conditioning of positive affect. Unpublished manuscript, University of Pennsylvania, 1965.

REFERENCES

Atkinson, J.E. (Ed.), *Motives in fantasy, action, and society*. Princeton, N.J.: Van Nostrand, 1958.

Avellar, J., & Kagan, S. Development of competitive behaviors in Anglo-American and Mexican-American children. *Psychological Reports*, 1976, *39*, 191-198.

Bethlehem, D. The effect of westernization on cooperative behavior in Central Africa. *International Journal of Psychology*, 1975, *10*, 219-224.

Buriel, R. Cognitive styles among three generations of Mexican-American children. *Journal of Cross-Cultural Psychology*, 1975, *6*, 417-429.

Diaz-Guerrero, R. The passive-active transcultural dichotomy. *International Mental Health Research Newsletter*, 1965, *7*, 8-10.

Diaz-Guerrero, R. The active and the passive syndromes. *Revista Interamericana de Psicologia*, 1967, *1*, 263-272.

Feather, N.T., & Hutton, M.A. Value systems of students in Papua, New Guinea and Australia. *International Journal of Psychology*, 1974, *9*, 91-104.

Foster, G.M. Peasant society and the image of limited good. *American Anthropologist*, 1965, *67*, 293-315.

Fromm, E., & Maccoby, M. *Social character in a Mexican village*. Englewood Cliffs, N.J.: Prentice-Hall, 1970.

Gamio, M. *Mexican immigration to the United States*. Chicago, Ill: University of Chicago Press, 1930.

Gottheil, E. Changes in social perceptions contingent upon competing or cooperating. *Sociometry*, 1955, *18*, 132-137.

Grebler, L. *Mexican immigration to the United States: The record and its implications. Mexican-American Study Project-Advance Report 2*. Los Angeles: Division of Research, Graduate School of Business Administration, University of California, 1965.

Griesinger, D., & Livingston, O. Towards a model of interpersonal motivation in experimental games. *Behavioral Science*, 1973, *18*, 173-188.

Hoppe, C.M., Kagan, S.M., & Zahn, G.L. Conflict resolution among field-independent and field-dependent Anglo-American and Mexican-American children and their mothers. *Developmental Psychology*, in press.

Jones, R.C. Ethnic family patterns: The Mexican family in the United States. *American Journal of Sociology*, 1948, *53*, 450-452.

Kagan, S. Field dependence and conformity of rural Mexican and urban Anglo-American children. *Child Development*, 1974, *45*, 765-771.

Kagan, S. Preferred levels of achievement and aspiration in rural Mexican and urban Anglo-American children. *The Journal of Comparative Cultures*, 1975, *2*, 113-126.

Kagan, S. Preference for contol in rural Mexican and urban Anglo-American children. *Interamerican Journal of Psychology*, 1976, *10*, 51-59.

Kagan, S., & Buriel, R. Field-dependence-independence and Mexican-American culture and education. In J.L. Martinez, Jr. (Ed.), *Chicano Psychology*. 1977. New York: Academic Press, 279-328.

Kagan, S., & Carlson, H. Development of adaptive assertiveness in Mexican and United States children. *Developmental Psychology*, 1975, *11*, 71-78.

Kagan, S., & Ender, P. Maternal response to success and failure of Anglo-American, Mexican-American, and Mexican children. *Child Development*, 1975, *46*, 452-458.

Kagan, S., & Madsen, M. Cooperation and competition of Mexican, Mexican-American, and Anglo-American children of two ages under four instructional sets. *Developmental Psychology*, 1971, *5*(1), 32-39.

Kagan, S., & Madsen, M. Experimental analysis of cooperation and competition of Anglo-American and Mexican children. *Developmental Psychology*, 1972, *6*, 49-59. (a)

Kagan, S., & Madsen, M. Rivalry in Anglo-American and Mexican children of two ages. *Journal of Personality and Social Psychology*, 1972, *24*, 214-220. (b)

Kagan, S., & Zahn, G.L. Field dependence and the school achievement gap between Anglo-American and Mexican-American children. *Journal of Educational Psychology*, 1975, *67*, 643-650.

Kagan, S., Zahn, G.L., & Gealy, J. Competition and school achievement among Anglo-American and Mexican-American children. *Journal of Educational Psychology*, 1977, *69*, 432-441.

Kearns, B.J.R. Childbearing practices among selected culturally deprived minorities. *Journal of Genetic Psychology*, 1970, *116*, 149-155.

Kluckhohn, F.R. Dominant and variant value orientations. In C. Kluckhohn & H.A. Murray (Eds.), *Personality in nature, society, and culture*. New York: Alfred A. Knopf, 1954.

Kluckhohn, F.R. Dominant and variant value orientations. In C. Cluckhohn and H.A. Murray (Eds.), *Personality in nature, society, and culture*. New York: Alfred A. Knopf, 1954.

Kluckhohn, F.R., & Strodtbeck, R. *Variations in value orientations*. New York: Row Peterson, 1961.

Knight, G., & Kagan, S. Development of prosocial and competitive behaviors in Anglo American and Mexican American children. *Child Development*, in press.

Knudson, K.H.M., & Kagan, S. Visual perspective role taking and field-independence among Anglo-American and Mexican-American children of two ages. *Journal of Genetic Psychology*, in press.

Kuhlman, D.M., & Marshello, A.F.J. Individual differences in game motivation as moderators in preprogrammed strategy effects in prisoner's dilemma. *Journal of Personality and Social Psychology*, 1975, *32*, 922-931.

Kuhlman, D.M., & Wimberly, D.L. Expectations of choice behavior held by cooperators, competitors, and individualists across four classes of experimental game. *Journal of Personality and Social Psychology*, 1976, *34*, 69-81.

Lewis, O. *Life in a Mexican village: Tepoztlan restudied*. Urbana, Ill: University of Illinois Press, 1951.

Logan, D.L. An empirical investigation of the cultural determinants of basic motivational patterns. (Doctoral dissertation, University of Arizona, Tuscon, 1966). University Microfilms Order No. 67-1077.

Madsen, M. Cooperative and competitive motivation of children in three Mexican sub-cultures. *Psychological Reports*, 1967, *20*, 1307-1320.

Madsen, M., & Shapira, A. Cooperative and competitive behavior of urban Afro-American, Anglo-American, Mexican-American, and Mexican village children. *Developmental Psychology*, 1970, *3*, 16-20.

Madsen, M., & Yi, S. Cooperation and competition of urban and rural children in the Republic of South Korea. *International Journal of Psychology*, 1975, *10*, 269-274.

Marin, G., Mejia, B., & Oberle, C. Cooperation as a function of place of residence in Colombian children. *The Journal of Social Psychology*, 1975, *95*, 127-128.

Maslow, A.H., & Diaz-Guerrero, R. Juvenile delinquency as a value disturbance. In J. Peatman and E. Hartley (Eds.), *Festschrift for Gardner Murphy*. New York: Harper, 1960. Reprinted as Adolescence and juvenile delinquency in two different cultures. In A.H. Maslow, *The farther reaches of human nature*. New York: Viking Press, 1971.

McClintock, C. Development of social motives in Anglo-American and Mexican children. *Journal of Personality and Social Psychology*, 1974, *29*, 348-354.

McClintock, C.G., Messick, D.M., Kuhlman, D.M., & Campos, F.T. Motivational bases of choice in three-choice decomposed games. *Journal of Experimental Social Psychology*, 1973, *9*, 572-590.

Menninger, K. *Man against himself*. New York: Harcourt, 1938.

Messick, D.M., & McClintock, C.G. Motivational bases of choice in experimental games. *Journal of Experimental Social Psychology*, 1968, *4*, 1-25.

Messick, D.M., & Thorngate, W.B. Relative gain maximization in experimental games. *Journal of Experimental Social Psychology*, 1967, *3*, 85-101.

Midlarsky, E., & Bryan, J.H. Training charity in children. *Journal of Personality and Social Psychology*, 1967, *5*, 408-415.

Miller, A., & Thomas, R. Cooperation and competition among Blackfoot Indian and urban Canadian children. *Child Development*, 1972, *43*, 1104-1110.

Minturn, L., & Lambert, W.W. *Mothers of six cultures: Antecedents of childbearing*. New York: Wiley, 1964.

Montiel, M. The Chicano family: A review of research. *Social Work*, 1973, *18*, 22-31.

Murillo, N. The Mexican-American family. In C.A. Hernandez, M.J. Haug, & N.N. Wagner (Eds.), *Chicanos: Social and psychological perspectives*. St. Louis: C.V. Mosby, 1976.

Nelson, L., & Madsen, M. Cooperation and competition in four-year-olds as a function of reward contingency and subculture. *Developmental Psychology*, 1969, *1*, 340-344.

Olejnik, A.G., & McKinney, J.P. Parental value orientation and generousity in children. *Developmental Psychology*, 1973, *8*, 311.

Peñalosa, F. Mexican family roles. *Journal of Marriage and the Family*, 1968, *30*, 680-688.

Ramirez, M. Identification with Mexican family values and authoritarianism in Mexican-Americans. *The Journal of Social Psychology*, 1967, *73*, 3-11.

Ramirez, M., & Castañeda, A. *Cultural democracy, bicognitive development and education*. New York: Academic Press, 1974.

Ramirez, M., & Price-Williams, D.R. Cognitive styles of children in three ethnic groups in the United States. *Journal of Cross-Cultural Psychology*, 1974, *5*, 212-219.

Ramirez, M., & Price-Williams, D.R. Achievement motivation in children of three ethnic groups in the United States. *Journal of Cross-Cultural Psychology*, 1976, *7*, 49-60.

Ramirez, M., Taylro, C., & Petersen, B. Mexican-American cultural membership and adjustment to school. *Developmental Psychology*, 1967, *73*, 3-11.

Redfield, R. *Tepoztlan – A Mexican village*. Chicago: University of Chicago Press, 1930.

Richmond, B.O., & Weiner, G.P. Cooperation and competition among young children as a function of ethnic grouping, grade, sex, and reward condition. *Journal of Educational Psychology*, 1973, *64*, 329-334.

Romanucci-Ross, L. *Conflict, violence, and morality in a Mexican village*. Palo Alto, Calif.: National Press Books, 1973.

Samora, J. *Los mojados: The wetback story*, Notre Dame, Ind.: University of Notre Dame Press, 1971.

Sampson, E., & Kardush, M. Age, sex, class, and race differences in response to a two-person non-zero-sum game. *Conflict Resolution*, 1965, *9*, 212-220.

Sanders, M., Scholz, J., & Kagan, S. Three social motives and field independence-dependence in Anglo-American and Mexican-American children. *Journal of Cross-Cultural Psychology*, 1976, *7*(4), 451-462.

Shapira, A., & Lomaranz, J. Cooperative and competitive behavior of rural Arab children in Israel. *Journal of Cross-Cultural Psychology*, 1972, *3*, 353-359.

Shapira, A., & Madsen, M. Cooperative and competitive behavior of Kibbutz and urban children in Israel. *Child Development*, 1969, *40*, 609-617.

Sherif, M., Harvey, O.J., White, B.J., Hood, W.R., & Sherif, C.W. *Intergroup conflict and cooperation: The robbers cave experiment*. Norman: Institute of Group Relations, University of Oklahoma, 1961.

Sommerland, E.A., & Bellingham, W.P. Cooperation-competition: A comparison of Australian, European and Aboriginal school children. *Journal of Cross-Cultural Psychology*, 1972, *3*, 149-157.

Staples, R. The Mexican-American family: Its modification over time and space. *Phylon*, 1971, *32*, 179-192.

Stanton, R.D. A comparison of Mexican and Mexican-American families. *The Family Coordinator*, 1972, *21*, 325-330.

Steward, M., & Steward, D. The observation of Anglo-, Mexican-, and Chinese-American mothers teaching their young sons. *Child Development*, 1973, *44*, 329-337.

Steward, M.S., & Steward, D.S. Effect of social distance on teaching strategies of Anglo-American and Mexican-American mothers. *Developmental Psychology*, 1974, *10*, 797-807.

Sumotirto, B.W. Social attitudes among high school students in Indonesia. *British Journal of Educational Psychology*, 1962, *32*, 3-11.

Tharp, R.G., Meadow, A., Lennhoff, S.G., & Satterfield, D. Changes in marriage roles accompanying the acculturation of the Mexican-American wife. *Journal of Marriage and the Family*, 1968, *30*, 404-412.

Thomas, R. Cooperation and competition among Polynesian and European children. *Child Development*, 1975, *46*, 948-953.

Uribe, B.M. *Estudio comparative del motivo a cooperar en niños de poblacion urbana y rural de primer año elemental*. Bogota: Pontificia Universidad Javeriana, 1973.

Veroff, J. Social comparison and the development of achievement motivation. In C.P. Smith (Ed.), *Achievement-related motives in children*. New York: Russell Sage Foundation, 1969.

Vinacke, W.E. Variables in experimental games: Toward a field theory. *Psychological Bulletin*, 1969, *71*, 293-318.

Whiting, J.W.M., & Whiting, B.B. Altruistic and egoistic behavior in six cultures. In D.H. Maybury Lewis (Ed.), *Anthropological studies*. L. Nader & T.W. Maretzki (Eds.), *Cultural illness and health, essays in human adaptation* (No. 9), Washington, D.C.: American Anthropological Association, 1973.

CHAPTER 6

CHICANO POWER AND INTERRACIAL GROUP RELATIONS

ALBERT RAMIREZ

University of Colorado

Introduction

Interracial relations is one of the most extensively researched areas in social psychology. One need only glance at contemporary social psychology textbooks to find entire chapters or sections devoted to such topics as interracial conflict and hostility, as well as strategies for increasing intergroup harmony and positive relations (Ashmore, 1970; Secord & Backman, 1974; Wrightsman, 1972). The focus of interracial group processes in American social psychology has been on black-white relations, and apparently no body of literature within traditional social psychology has attempted to study those factors that lead to either Chicano-Anglo group conflict and hostility or positive contact and relations when members of these two groups come into contact.

Any discussion of ethnic group relations is incomplete if it excludes the concept of social power. Several years ago, Cartwright (1959) referred to power as a neglected variable in social psychology, accusing social psychologists of converting the problem of power into "one of attitudes, expectations, and perceptions." Cartwright stated that "there is more interest in authoritarianism than authority; expectations are made the critical element in the notion of role rather than behavioral restrictions or compulsions; prestige is studied because it can be investigated apart from any specific situation of interpersonal interaction and influence." Again, one searches the literature of social psychology in vain to find studies focusing on the social power of Chicanos, although much has been written on Chicano power outside the mainstream of traditional psychology (Acuña, 1972; Rendon, 1971). It is obvious that the two topics — power and intergroup relations — are interrelated. In discussing this relationship, Cartwright emphasized the

importance of knowledge about power structures in understanding intergroup relations. This chapter is an attempt to look at the interdependency between these two
areas, particularly as they relate to Chicano-Anglo group relations.

The Equal-Status Contact Hypothesis in Interracial Group Relations

It is clear from the extensive research conducted that interracial contact
per se does not necessarily lead to reduction in prejudice or hostility (Allport,
1954; Amir, 1969; Cook, 1962; Sherif, 1966) and that what is important is the
attributes of the contact situation as well as the attributes or characteristics of
the participating group members. From his review of the research findings on ethnic intergroup contact, Amir (1969) concluded that some of the favorable conditions that tend to reduce prejudice occur

1. When there is equal-status contact between the members of the various
ethnic groups.
2. When the contact is between members of a majority group and *higher*
status members of a minority group.
3. When an "authority" and/or the social climate are in favor of and promote
the intergroup contact.
4. When the contact is of an intimate rather than a casual nature.
5. When the ethnic intergroup contact is pleasant or rewarding.
6. When the members of *both* groups in the particular contact situation
interact in functionally important activities or develop common goals or super-
ordinate goals that are higher rankings in importance than the individual goals of
each of the groups.

All of these conditions, in varying degrees, involve power relations. Although
all are important in their implications for Chicano-Anglo relations, the focus of
this paper is primarily on one of them — the principle of equal status, which states
that if contact is to result in positive relations, the groups involved must meet on
equal terms. Many studies conducted in a variety of different settings have demonstrated the importance of equal-status contact between groups. These settings
include the military (Star, Williams, & Stouffer, 1965), integrated housing projects
(Wilner, Walkley, & Cook, 1955), and work settings (Harding & Hogrefe, 1952;
MacKenzie, 1948). Cook and his colleagues (Cook, 1970; Blanchard, Weigel, &
Cook, 1975) have attempted to set up experimental conditions favorable to prejudice reduction. Because of the extensive research demonstrating the importance
of this type of contact, the equal-status hypothesis has received wide acceptance
by researchers in intergroup relations.

Several theoretical models suggest why equal-status contact is important.
Most of them are based on the ideas of stereotype destruction (Ashmore, 1970),
role congruency (Secord & Backman, 1974), and perceived similarity (Pettigrew,
1971; Rokeach, Smith, & Evans, 1960). Thus, equal-status situations can be con-

ceptualized as giving a member of the dominant group the opportunity to discover that

  1. The minority person holds similar attitudes, beliefs, and values.
  2. The minority person is not *really* that different from him or her.
  3. The minority person can function as well as he or she does in the same roles.

The following passage from a popular and current social psychology textbook (Wrightsman, 1972) describes one of the optimal aspects of the contact situation that results in favorable attitude change, and it also illustrates the possible inequality of the equal-status concept:

> Particularly beneficial to favorable attitude change are contacts in which the participating minority-group members differ from commonly held, unflattering stereotypes of their group. Interacting and working with a black who is hardworking, bright, restrained, and not particularly musical or religious may be the stimulus for attitude change. It is also helpful if the member of the minority group resembles the majority-group member in regard to background, interests, and personality. The prejudiced white who realizes that his black co-worker is similar to him may be able to overcome his stereotyped beliefs about blacks [p. 324].

A major concern is that some of the current theoretical models and methodological approaches concerning the equal-status hypothesis may in fact limit its potential as a principle for promoting intergroup relations. This is particularly apparent when equal-status contact is defined for and superimposed upon the minority person in the contact situation by others, and when being "equal" means being like the white, Anglo subjects with whom the minority person is in contact. To the extent that equal status is conceptualized in this way, the status of the minority person in such an equal-status situation is obviously anything but equal.

There are other problems with some of the current approaches to equal-status contact. For example, although equal status is often assumed to exist, few (if any) measures are obtained to ascertain whether the participants involved do in fact ascribe equal status to each other. In addition, what is meant by the effects of equal status are most often measures of liking, attraction, and acceptance; but if status is defined as "the amount of respect, prestige, and privilege that is accorded to the person who occupies a particular position" (Raven & Rubin, 1976), measures of these dimensions are also necessary. From this definition of status it becomes obvious that status is linked to legitimate authority and that we cannot adequately understand the concept of equal status without the concept of social power.

Social Power and Social Influence

For purposes of this paper, social power is defined as potential social influence, or the ability of one person or group to influence another (French & Raven,

1959, Raven, 1965). Social influence is viewed as change in a person's cognitions, attitudes, or behaviors which has its origin in another person or group. In the area of persuasive communications, the person or group that is attempting to influence others is called the communicator or source. Studies have shown that among those factors that affect the source's potential influence are status variables derived from the source's role position. In general, the influence of a high status source is greater than that of a low status source. It is evident that in contemporary American society ethnicity and race are inextricably bound to status, role, authority, and power relations. Several years ago the writer became interested in studying the potential influence of ethnically different communicators. A series of studies was conducted that involved a black or white communicator presenting different levels of fear-arousing dental health messages to black students. We were interested in finding out what effect, if any, the race of the communicator would have on dental health attitudes and on toothbrushing behavior. The studies utilized a pretest-treatment-multiple posttest design. During the pretest, students responded to paper-and-pencil measures of dental attitudes and were also scored with respect to cleanliness of teeth. Cleanliness of teeth was measured by an index of oral debris developed by Podshadley and Haley (1968) that was found to be a fairly good predictor of toothbrushing behavior in an earlier study (Ramirez, Lasater, Bethart, & McNeal, 1971). During the two or three week interim periods between the pretest and treatment, students were randomly assigned to two communication conditions (high fear, low fear) and two communicator conditions (black, white). On the day of the presentations, students were exposed to slide-tape presentations. Slides of the person giving the talk were interspersed throughout the message although actually the same voice was used in all the communicator-communication conditions. After the presentations, the students were given a dental health kit consisting of disclosing tablets (a tablet which, when chewed, reddens the places on the teeth where debris has accumulated), a toothbrush, toothpaste, and dental floss. They then answered another questionnaire similar to the one used in the pretest but also including reactions to the talk, the communicator, and retention of information presented in the message. On the subsequent posttests, the paper-and-pencil measures, as well as the behavioral measure of toothbrushing, were again administered.

The results of two studies, one conducted in St. Petersburg, Florida and the other in Birmingham, Alabama were essentially the same. In comparison with the white communicator and independent of level of fear communication, the black communicator (*a*) produced significantly more immediate behavior change, (*b*) produced significantly more information retention for the affective part of the message, (*c*) generated rather positive evaluations and similar amounts of anxiety regardless of the fear level. With the white communicator, reported anxiety and attitudinal evaluations were positively associated with level of fear communication (Dembroski, Lasater, & Ramirez, Note 1).

The results of these studies not only indicated the importance of the race of the communicator but also raised a number of questions. Is ethnicity of communicator a significant factor in an ethnically heterogenous audience? Does the minority communicator have the same influence on the minority and nonminority members of his audience? Can the results obtained with respect to black-white communicator comparisons be generalized to Chicano-Anglo comparisons?

In order to investigate some of these questions, a Chicano or an Anglo communicator, named for purposes of the study Dr. Martinez or Dr. Martin, presented high- or low-fear appeals to 45 Chicano and 159 Anglo elementary and junior high school students (Ramirez & Lasater, 1977). The study was conducted in a small town about 15 miles from Denver. The students were fifth and sixth graders at an elementary school and seventh and eighth graders at a junior high school. Their age range was ten to fifteen years. The design of the study was similar to that described earlier and combined four factors at two levels each: (*a*) ethnicity of communicator (Anglo versus Chicano), (*b*) level of fear (high versus low), (*c*) ethnicity of student (Anglo versus Chicano), and (*d*) self-esteem (high versus low). No significant differences were found with respect to ethnicity of student. As in the studies performed with black and white communicators, a significant interaction was found between levels of fear and race of communicator on the evaluations of the communicator and presentation. The evaluation of the Chicano communicator and the Chicano presentation were equally positive in both the low-fear and high-fear conditions, while the Anglo communicator and presentation were evaluated more positively in the high-fear condition than in the low-fear condition. Reactions to the ethnicity of the communicator were influenced by the self-esteem levels of the students. Self-esteem was measured by having the student evaluate the concept "Myself As I Really Am" on eighteen bipolar adjectives in a semantic differential format. High self-esteem students reacted more favorably to the Chicano communicator while low self-esteem subjects reacted more favorably to the Anglo communicator. In addition, the students exposed to the Anglo communicator indicated greater anxiety arousal. Anxiety arousal was measured by a series of items asking the subjects how worried or upset they felt while they were watching the presentation. The most significant result, from the perspective of social power and influence, was the effect on toothbrushing behavior. The results described so far are similar to those of the earlier study. In the previous study, however, the black communicator had a greater short-term influence on toothbrushing behavior. In the present study, the students exposed to the Anglo communicator developed significantly cleaner teeth than the students exposed to the Chicano communicator. The social influence of the Anglo communicator on both Chicano and Anglo students was greater than that of the Chicano communicator. These results probably reflect the fact that both Chicano and Anglo students have little exposure to a Chicano occupying a power position, particularly within the school system where the study took place. Such an interpretation would account for the difference in results between the earlier study and this one, since in the earlier study the school administration and faculty — the power structure within the school — were black.

These two studies had the following characteristics: (*a*) They occurred in a school setting, (*b*) they involved an adult and therefore older communicator attempting to influence younger students; and (*c*) the influence attempt was directed toward a group.

In the next study (Ramirez, in press), the generalizability of these results was tested by having a young Chicano or Anglo communicator present a brief dental health message to an older Chicano person in the latter's home. The Chicano and Anglo communicators, who were both students at the University of Colorado, presented five-minute talks, with slides, to Chicano adults living in a predominantly Chicano housing project in Denver. A total of 116 Chicano adults were individually exposed to the presentations. After each talk, the communicator gave the person a dental kit and asked him or her to answer a brief questionnaire evaluating the presentation. Before leaving, the communicator requested the person to fill out another questionnaire at his leisure and mail it in the stamped envelope provided by the communicator, addressed to the "Dental Health Education Project." Reactions to both communicators were equally positive. The Anglo communicator, however, was significantly more effective than the Chicano communicator in obtaining compliance to the request for the completed questionnaires. Thus, 30% (n = 18) of the adults exposed to the Anglo communicator mailed the questionnaire, while only 12.5% (n = 7) complied with the request of the Chicano communicator ($p < .05$).

If social power is defined as potential influence and influence is viewed as the change in another person's behavior that can be attributed to the communicator, the results of these studies clearly indicate that the Anglo has higher social power and influence. On measures of attraction, both communicators were equally liked and both received positive evaluations. However, on the behavioral measures, the measures of social influence and power, the Anglo was the more effective.

Results similar to those reported above were obtained with respect to the effect of the ethnicity of test administrator on the self-esteem scores of junior high school students. Little and Ramirez (1976) found that the self-esteem scores of Anglo and Chicano junior high students were higher when the test was administered by an Anglo tester. The self-esteem measure was an 18 bipolar adjective Semantic Differential in which the student responded to the concept "Myself As I Really Am." The ethnicity of the test administrator had no effect on elementary school children. These results can also be interpreted within a social power framework. Older students taking a self-evaluation test like the one of self-esteem may attempt to describe themselves more positively when the test is administered by an Anglo because it is usually an Anglo who evaluates them. In the school system where this study took place there were no Chicanos occupying positions of authority. Older students were probably influenced by tester ethnicity because they were aware of power and authority differences between Anglos and Chicanos in their area. Studies performed in other areas have obtained similar results. For example, Acosta (1975), in his study of Chicanos' and Anglos' reactions to Chicano and Anglo therapists, found that the Anglo professional therapist received more favorable responses from both Anglos and Chicanos than the Chicano professional therapist. Acosta interprets this to indicate that the Chicano was not seen "as credible, as truly qualified." Another way of stating this is that the Chicano was viewed as the possessor of less legitimacy of authority and social power.

Social Power and Equal Status

Further research is needed to test the generalizability of the results described above in the preceding section. It may be that if the content area of the message were not dental hygiene, different results would be obtained. Nor can one rule out unique characteristics of the particular Chicano and Anglo communicators used in these studies. Perhaps if the same studies were conducted on other samples of Chicanos, the results would be different. If these results can be generalized to other situations, however, they point to some important implications with respect to Chicano-Anglo relations in this country. If equal-status contact is an important characteristic resulting in positive interethnic group relations and if one component of equal status is equal social power, then one implication of our research is that an important and requisite condition for positive intergroup contact between Anglos and Chicanos is not being met. Some may feel that activist cries of "Chicano Power" are dangerous and need to be tempered. However, if we take the role of equal status in producing positive interethnic group relations seriously, it is essential to increase the social power of Chicanos. It is therefore necessary to focus on what provides the basis of power. An understanding of these bases is important if one is to affect power relations between groups. Understanding will be facilitated by examining the five bases of power described by French and Raven (1959). These are (*a*) reward power, (*b*) coercive power, (*c*) legitimate power, (*d*) referent power, and (*e*) expert power. These bases of power are not independent and are often concurrent. From the brief presentation below, it will be apparent that these bases of social power have not been accessible to the Chicano.

Reward power is based upon the ability to reward and depends upon the perception by the person being rewarded that the influencing agent has the ability as well as the resources to provide the reward. In order to increase the reward power of Chicanos so that others recognize this as a power base, Chicanos would have to be in positions usually associated with the distribution of resources and rewards; employers, supervisors, and managers. Just as these positions utilize the promise of reward, they also provide the threat of punishment. Coercive power is based on a person's perception that the influencing agent has the ability to punish. Legitimate power is based on the person's acceptance of the agent's right to influence him on the basis of perceived obligation to comply. This acceptance of the agent's legitimacy to influence is based on the internalization of norms and values that individuals, groups, and institutions represent legitimate sources of authority. Since Anglos have traditionally held positions of authority, their legitimate power has been higher than that of Chicanos. The fourth type of power, referent power, has its basis in the identification of the person with the influencing agent. Modeling is an important component, as is perceived similarity. The referent power of the Chicano individual in a position of leadership should increase if he can serve as a role model for other Chicanos. Expert power is exerted by an individual when another person attributes special knowledge or ability to him. The effectiveness of expert power increases as the attribution of expertise increases and also generalizes to other areas. If the expert power of the Anglo is higher than that of the Chicano, a person will be more influenced by the Anglo professional than by the Chicano professional. In our society, we are more likely to see Anglos in expert roles than we are to see Chicanos. The results of our studies with Dr. Martin and Dr. Martinez described above were probably most affected by the attribution of the subjects to Dr. Martin of higher expert and legitimate power, although the other bases of power no doubt were also operating.

Although it is obvious that political and economic change can effect the social power of Chicanos, psychology can also play a significant role. Psychologists can focus on the five bases of power and develop research programs that systematically attempt to delineate variables that influence the power base of Chicanos. They can contribute to defining the conditions necessary to effect real, equal-status contacts between groups rather than the same-as-me status contacts that have occurred all too frequently in the past in the research paradigms comparing minorities and nonminorities. Same-as-me status contacts between groups are a product of traditional Anglo psychology. The standard of comparison and point of reference, not surprisingly, have been the Anglos' values, beliefs, and lifestyles. If the full potential of bona fide equal-status relationships between Chicanos and Anglos is to be achieved, then a psychology is needed that concerns itself with Chicanos' values, beliefs, and lifestyles and considers them to be equally valid. Although the term *ethnopsychology* has been used to describe a psychological approach that goes beyond using one particular sociocultural value system as the standard of behavior (Thomas, Note 2), the present author prefers the term *ethnic psychology*. The foundation of an ethnic psychology would be cultural pluralism, rather than cultural assimilation, that would accept the Chicano as his own referent.

As mentioned above, an important factor in the development of equal-status relationships is social power. Ethnic psychology can develop programs to study socialization processes that lead to *increased social power and influence*. Such processes could be called ESPI processes or systems. Such systems could be tested and developed in many settings. For example, a number of psychologists are involved in developing learning systems that foster a culturally pluralistic approach to education and devising measures to assess the effectiveness of such programs. One measure vital for assessing such programs would be the degree to which participation in them leads to a greater acceptance of the social power of individuals from diverse ethnic backgrounds. To the extent that such an education program accomplished this objective, it would be characteristic of an ESPI system. One goal of bilingual-bicultural programs, therefore, would be creating socialization processes that lead to equal social power and influence among groups. Equal power and influence among groups is, after all, an important measure of cultural diversity and cultural pluralism.

In terms of future directions for research, psychologists need to (*a*) delineate those socialization processes that lead to equal social power and influence among groups, called ESPI processes, (*b*) study how these ESPI processes interact with these factors that promote positive intergroup relations, and (*c*) develop programs, based on the empirical findings, that have as one of their goals maximizing positive interracial group relations. This paper has focused on only one factor that research has shown to affect positive contact. A general research program would include the other variables, as indicated in Figure 1.

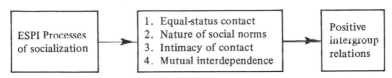

FIGURE 1. The ESPI model of intergroup relations.

This model is only a modification of earlier ones focusing on intergroup relations (Ashmore, 1970; Amir, 1969). The present model, however, is guided by the premise that in the promotion of positive interracial group relations, it may be less important that the two groups be similar to each other than that they be aware of and learn to respect their unique differences.

REFERENCE NOTES

1. Dembroski, T.M., Lasater, T.M., & Ramirez, A. Evaluative and behavioral reactions of Black adolescents to fear arousing persuasion and race of communicator. Unpublished manuscript. Available from senior author, Eckerd College, St. Petersburg, Florida 33733.
2. Thomas, C.W. II.*The science and social power of ethnopsychology*. Invited address presented at the meeting of the Rocky Mountain Psychological Association, Phoenix, May, 1976.

REFERENCES

Acosta, F.X. Mexican-American and Anglo-American reactions to ethnically similar and dissimilar psychotherapists. In R. Alvarez (Ed.), *Delivery of services for latino community mental health*. Monograph No. 2. Los Angeles: Spanish Speaking Mental Health Research and Development Program, 1975.

Acuña, R. *Occupied America: The Chicano's struggle toward liberation*. New York: Canfield Press, 1972.

Allport, G.W. *The nature of prejudice*. Cambridge, Mass.: Addison-Wesley, 1954.

Amir, Y. Contact hypothesis in ethnic relations. *Psychological Bulletin*, 1969, *71*, 319-342.

Ashmore, R.D. Solving the problem of prejudice. In B.E. Collins, *Social Psychology*, Reading, Mass.: Addison-Wesley, 1970.

Blanchard, F.A., Weigel, R.H., & Cook, S.W. The effect of relative competence of group members upon interpersonal attraction in cooperating interracial groups. *Journal of Personality and Social Psychology*, 1975, *32*, 519-530.

Cartwright, D. Power: A neglected variable in social psychology. In D. Cartwright (Ed.), *Studies in social power*. Ann Arbor: University of Michigan Press, 1959.

Cook, S.W. The systematic analysis of socially significant events: A strategy for social research. *Journal of Social Issues*, 1962, *18*, 66-84.

Cook, S.W. A preliminary study of attitude change. In M. Wertheimer (Ed.), *Confrontation: Psychology and the problems of today*. Glenview, Ill.: Scott, Foresman, 1970.

French, J.R., & Raven, B.H. The bases of social power. In D. Cartwright (Ed.), *Studies in social power*. Ann Arbor: University of Michigan Press, 1959.

Harding, J., & Hogrefe, R. Attitudes towards Negro co-workers in an eastern urban department store. *Journal of Social Issues*, 1952, *8*, 18-28.

Little, J., & Ramirez, A. Ethnicity of subject and test administrator: Their effect on self-esteem. *Journal of Social Psychology*, 1976, *99*, 149-150.

MacKenzie, B.K. The importance of contact in determining attitudes towards Negroes. *Journal of Abnormal and Social Psychology*, 1948, *43*, 417-441.

Pettigrew, T.F. *Racially separate or together?* New York: McGraw-Hill, 1971.

Podshadley, A.G., & Haley, J.V. A method for evaluating oral hygiene performance. *Public Health Reports*, 1968, *83*, 259-263.

Ramirez, A. Social influence and ethnicity of the communicator. *Journal of Social Psychology*, in press.

Ramirez, A., & Lasater, T.M. Ethnicity of communicator, self-esteem, and reactions to fear-arousing communications. *Journal of Social Psychology*, 1977, *102*, 79-91.

Ramirez, A., Lasater, T.M., Bethart, H., & McNeal, D.R. The patient hygiene performance method as an indication of behavioral change following persuasive communications: A study of validity. *Journal of Public Health Dentistry*, 1971, *31*, 188-190.

Raven, B.H. Social influence and power. In I.D. Steiner & M. Fishbein (Eds.), *Current studies in social psychology*. New York: Holt, Rinehart, and Winston, 1965.

Raven, B.H., & Rubin, J.Z. *Social psychology: People in groups*. New York: Wiley, 1976.

Rendon, A.B. *Chicano manifesto*. New York: Macmillan, 1971.

Rokeach, M., Smith, P.W., & Evans, R.I. Two kinds of prejudice or one? In M. Rokeach, *The open and closed mind*. New York: Basic Books, 1960.

Secord, P.F., & Backman, C.W. *Social Psychology*. New York: McGraw-Hill, 1974.

Sherif, M. *In common predicament: Social psychology of intergroup conflict and cooperation*. Boston: Houghton Mifflin, 1966.

Star, S.A., Williams, R.M., Jr., & Stouffer, S.A. Negro infantry platoons in white companies. In H. Prohansky & B. Seidenberg (Eds.), *Basic studies in social psychology*. New York: Holt, Rinehart, and Winston, 1965.

Wilner, D.M., Walkley, R.P., & Cook, S.W. Residential proximity and intergroup relations in public housing projects. *Journal of Social Issues*, 1952, *8*, 45-69.

Wrightsman, L.S. *Social psychology in the seventies*. Belmont, Calif.: Wadsworth, 1972.

CHAPTER 7

PERSONAL CONTROL AND FATALISM IN CHICANOS AND ANGLOS: CONCEPTUAL AND METHODOLOGICAL ISSUES

RAYMOND T. GARZA

University of California, Riverside

Introduction

The controversy over personal causation reaches back to the origins of philosophical concern about human behavior. Some have taken a teleological image of man, insisting that self-determination and personal choice play a central role in explaining the dynamics of human behavior. Others have proffered a highly mechanistic image, arguing that we are products and, to a great extent, victims of the environmental influences we encounter. Within the realm of psychology, this controversy is clearly exemplified in the perennial bifurcation between the schools of behaviorism and humanism. Taking sides with one of these lines of thought against the other can result in unnecessary polemics of little or no heuristic importance. The lines of theoretical research that seem to be most fruitful are those adopting some form of an interactional perspective, taking into account the effects of environmental rewards and punishments, but not ignoring the role of personal control or self-produced consequences. These interactional perspectives can explain variations among individuals socialized into the same environment in terms of the relative contributions of personal choice and environmental determinism in the development of the individual's personality structure.

Rotter's (1966) locus of control construct seems to provide an extraordinarily fruitful approach for studying individual differences in the generalized notion that individuals can control their own destinies. The concept of internal versus external control of reinforcement was developed from the work of social learning theory (Rotter, 1954; Rotter, Chance, & Phares, 1972). Rotter's internal-external scale (I-E) provides a reasonably adequate means of measuring the extent to which people believe they exercise control over their lives (internally controlled) or the degree to which they feel their destinies are beyond their personal control and are determined by external forces (externally controlled).

Whether individuals perceive internal or external control of their behaviors could very well be influenced by the values, perspectives, and socialization practices of the cultures in which they live. In one of his recent articles, Rotter (1975) suggested that members of cultures with fatalistic orientation could be expected to manifest a great deal of externality in their locus of control orientation. It is therefore conceivable that some cultures foster the development of externality, while others promote greater internality. Several empirical investigations have indeed shown cross-cultural differences in locus of control orientation (Parsons, Schneider, & Hansen, 1970; Reitz & Groff, 1972; Tin-Yee Hsieh, Skyhut, & Lotsof, 1969).

Fatalism and many other forms of passivity are cultural characteristics commonly attributed to Chicanos (Cabrera, 1964; Justin, 1970). Most ethnographic and anthropological accounts depict Chicanos as passive — controlled by the external forces of luck, fate, and chance. This stereotypic characterization is practically identical to that attributed to Mexican nationals. Mexicans have been consistently characterized by the traits of passivity and subjugation (Lewis, 1959; Diaz-Guerrero, 1967, 1975).

If fatalism and passivity are indeed salient charcteristics of the Chicano culture, it would be expected that Chicanos manifest a greater external locus of control orientation than members of cultures like Anglo-American, which lack fatalistic, passive orientations. Although it seems tenable on the basis of most ethnographic and observational accounts, this contention has not received consistent support from empirical investigations comparing Chicanos and Anglos on locus of control. Some researchers report greater externality in Chicanos, while others report either no difference or greater internality. Graves (Note 1) found that Anglo adolescents and adults feel greater personal control than their Chicano counterparts. Scott and Phelon (1969), using a sample of subjects who had spent years on the welfare rolls and were virtually unemployable, reported that Blacks and Chicanos were less internal on the I-E scale than Anglos. On the other hand, Jessor, Graves, Hanson, and Jessor (1968) were not able to replicate the findings reported by Graves. Scott and Phelon found no differences between the Chicano and Anglo adolescents in their sample. Using college students as subjects and controlling for socioeconomic factors, Garza and Ames (1976) showed that Chicanos are actually more internal than Anglos on the I-E scale. By breaking down Rotter's (1966) I-E scale into various dimensional categories, Garza and Ames were able to show that Chicanos are less external than Anglos in the luck-fate and interpersonal respect dimensions of locus of control.

What caused this inconsistency in the locus of control findings? One explanation seems to be a blatant lack of theoretical and conceptual objectivity. Socioeconomic status generally seems to be confounded with cultural background

(Casavantes, 1970). With one exception (Garza & Ames, 1976), socioeconomic background was never taken into account in any of these studies. A careful examination of the characteristics of the samples used suggests that most findings showing greater externality in Chicanos may be attributed to socioeconomic background and not to cultural differences. The Scott and Phelon (1969) study was actually based on a sample of unemployable subjects. In the other studies (Graves, Note 1; Jessor *et al.*, 1968), the socioeconomic status of the Anglo samples was higher than that of the Chicano samples. Even though there is ample evidence showing a consistent relationship between socioeconomic standing and locus of control (Guren & Ottenger, 1969), conclusions like those reported here are still generalized to the entire Chicano population. Externality in Chicanos seems quite consistent with anthropological descriptions, which psychologists have accepted without proper empirical demonstration (Padilla, 1976); most researchers have felt little or no need to qualify the generalizations that can be derived from their findings.

A careful examination of the literature on the antecedents of locus of control revealed that certain aspects of Mexican-American culture could easily foster the development of internality. In his chapter reviewing the antecedents of locus of control, Phares (1976) concluded that family environments characterized by warmth, protection, and nurturance tend to foster the development of internal perceptions of locus of control. If those aspects of family life that may be caused by a devastated socioeconomic background are set aside, then the family environments described by Phares are prototypical of those found in the Chicano community (Ramirez & Castañeda, 1974). If this is true, why do researchers appear unconcerned about such a blatant conceptual fallacy? The unfortunate, but nonetheless highly probable, answer is ethnocentrism and lack of cultural insight. Most researchers have virtually no understanding of the cultural dynamics of the Chicano community. Furthermore, most psychological research involving Chicanos seems predominantly to view Chicano culture only in terms of the damage it causes to the individual's affective and cognitive processes. It appears that the notion that certain characteristics of Chicano culture may result in positive attributes rarely crosses the minds of most researchers.

Since a lack of theoretical and conceptual objectivity can be readily inferred from much of the research into locus of control concerning Chicanos, it is tempting to dismiss it as an ethnocentric aberration and call for a moratorium on this kind of research. However, such polemical attitudes are likely to be seen as both unprofessional and devoid of heuristic value. Since it is virtually impossible to change ethnocentric attitudes and other forms of prejudice, a more constructive course would be to approach the matter from a methodological perspective. As Padilla (1976) noted, most of the existing psychological knowledge of the Chicano was obtained through poorly formulated and inadequately controlled cross-cultural investigations.

It is conceivable that the contradictory findings on locus of control reported earlier may be caused by methodological inadequacies. Although some studies did employ instruments that were subjected to appropriate validation and standardization procedures, they attempted to test neither the cultural equivalence of the locus of control construct nor the validity of the instrument for Chicano populations. Triandis (1972, p. 36) noted that it is methodologically indefensible to compare two cultural groups on variables that may not be culturally equivalent. Triandis (1972, p. 36) further noted that instruments validated in one culture are inappropriate for cross-cultural research unless substantial invariance in the factorial structure can be demonstrated across cultures. The cross-cultural comparibility of a personality instrument can be assessed by examining the factorial structure of the test items in each population sample. This can be done by using the congruence procedure developed by Cliff (1966). The coefficient of congruence (r_c) gives an indication of the extent to which factors a and b are similar (Cattell, 1966, p. 196). Thus, it is quite feasible to examine the factorial validity of a personality instrument across groups. The primary purpose of this study was to determine the appropriateness of Rotter's (1966) locus of control scale for Chicano populations. If substantial invariance in the patterns of scores for the Chicano and Anglo groups could be demonstrated, then the Rotter would be an appropriate instrument for comparing these two groups on locus of control.

Several studies have attempted to identify the number of dimensional categories that make up Rotter's 23-item locus of control instrument (Collins, 1974; Levenson, Note 2; Mirels, 1970). Although not all researchers reported the same number of factorial dimensions, the consensus seems to suggest that the I-E scale may be classified into five subcategories: beliefs concerning (*a*) luck, fate and chance, (*b*) respect and world justice, (*c*) political matters, (*d*) academic fairness, and (*e*) power, leadership, and success. These dimensions seem quite similar to those rationally derived by Schneider and Parsons (1970) who found the five subscales useful in cross-cultural comparisons and predicting national stereotypes. For example, Reitz and Groff (1972) used the five subscales to compare American, Mexican, and Thai workers; and Garza and Ames (1976) used the Schneider and Parsons categories to compare Chicano and Anglo college students.

Since these five dimensional categories have been useful in cross-cultural comparisons and appear to have reasonable construct validity, the basic strategy of the present study was to determine empirically the appropriateness of the five categories for comparing Anglo and Chicano populations. This was done by factor analyzing the Chicano and Anglo responses to Rotter's scale separately and then comparing the corresponding factor pairs by using Cliff's (1966) congruence procedure.

Method

Rotter's (1966) I-E scale was administered to 203 Anglo and 244 Chicano college undergradutes enrolled in psychology and sociology classes at Texas A & I University. The Chicano subjects used in this study constituted a predominately bilingual and bicultural group from South Texas communities with large proportions of Chicano residents (above 50% in many instances). In terms of the typology proposed by Ramirez and Castañeda (1974), the Chicano subjects would probably fall into the Dualistic category.

The data from the Anglo and Chicano subjects were factor anlayzed separately. In each case, the responses to the 23 scored I-E scale items were intercorrelated and, entering squared multiple correlations in the main diagonal, the principal factor method was used to extract the factors from the resulting matrix. Kaiser's (1958) varimax technique was used to rotate the components to an orthogonal simple structure. To test the similarity of the factorial structure, Cliff's (1966) congruence procedure was used to compare the factor patterns of the Chicano and Anglo groups. This procedure yields an index (coefficient of congruence) of the similarity of the corresponding factor pairs. The coefficient of congruence (r_c) gives an indication of the extent to which two independently generated factors are similar (Cattell, 1966, p. 196). The coefficients thus obtained are generally evaluated subjectively, since no statistical test of significance is yet available. However, Evans (Note 3) suggested a reasonable set of criteria for evaluating the congruence coefficients. Coefficients in the .90s indicate "good" correspondence, coefficients in the .80s demonstrate "fair" correspondence, coefficients in the .70s show "poor" correspondence, and coefficients lower than .70 indicate virtually no correspondence between a pair of factors. The Evans criteria were used to evaluate the congruence coefficients obtained in the present study.

Results and Discussion

The factor analysis results implied strong construct validity for the five conceptually based factors. The anticipated factors emerged in almost the same order for the Chicano and Anglo samples. In the case of the Chicano sample, factor I (luck-fate) accounted for 12.5% of the variance, factor II (leadership-success) for 7.2%, factor III (academics) for 6.7%, factor IV (politics) for 6.0%, and factor V (respect) for 5.4%. In the case of the Anglo sample, factor I (luck-fate) accounted for 17.6% of the variance, factor II (academics) for 7.1%, factor III (politics) for 6.6%, factor IV (leadership-success) for 6.0%, and factor V (respect) for 5.5%. Table 1 presents the item loadings for the Chicano and Anglo samples on the five factors. The numbering of the items is after Rotter (1966), and the filler items are omitted. Note that the alphabetical factor sequence does *not* represent the same order of factor emergence for both samples. The corresponding factors are paired for clearer comparisons between the groups. The coefficients of congruence for each factor pair are shown in the bottom row of Table 1.

Items loading high on factor A deal with the subject's tendency to attribute greater or lesser importance to personal effort and ability than to luck, fate, or chance influences that have a bearing on personality related behavioral outcomes. Each item in this factor poses a statement affirming the subjects' control over their

TABLE 1

Locus of Control Rotated Factor Loadings for Chicanos[a] and Anglos[b]

	Locus of Control Factors									
	A		B		C		D		E	
	Luck-Fate		Leadership Success		Academics		Politics		Respect	
	Chicano	Anglo	Chicano	Anglo	Chicano	Anglo	Chicano	Anglo	Chicano	Anglo
2. Many of the unhappy things in people's lives are partly due to bad *luck*.	.19	.13	.22	.38	-.01	.19	.12	-.11	-.17	.00
3. One of the major reasons why we have wars is because people don't take enough interest in politics.	.19	.45	-.17	-.38	-.10	-.06	.23	.32	.11	.06
4. Unfortunately, an individual's worth often passes unrecognized no matter how hard he tries.	.10	.36	.23	.06	.06	.12	.01	-.02	.10	.03
5. Most students don't realize the extent to which their grades are influenced by accidental happenings.	.04	.04	.07	.28	.50	.26	-.09	.09	.03	-.05
6. Without the right breaks one cannot be an effective leader.	.03	.12	.30	.25	.03	.17	.04	.18	-.06	.24
7. No matter how hard you try some people just don't like you.	.01	.05	.02	.24	.22	.01	.05	.14	.22	.37
9. I have often found that what is going to happen will happen.	.29	.41	.03	-.02	-.02	.31	.00	.05	.05	-.06
10. Many times exam questions tend to be so unrelated to course work that studying is really useless.	.36	.14	.01	.11	.32	.51	.06	-.01	.12	.14
11. Getting a good job depends mainly on being in the right place at the right time.	-.06	.17	.61	.25	.25	.43	.00	.18	.06	.21

Item										
12. This world is run by a few people in power, and there is not much the little guy can do about it.	.10	.08	.13	.13	.21	.39	.27	.56	.03	.07
13. It is not always wise to plan too far ahead because many things turn out to be a matter of good or bad fortune anyhow.	.49	.43	.13	.14	.02	.11	.12	.12	.10	.09
15. Many times we might just as well decide what to do by flipping a coin.	.33	.41	.41	.22	-.01	.15	-.06	.06	.04	.15
16. Who gets to be the boss often depends on who was lucky enough to be in the right place first.	.22	.07	.49	.30	.07	.24	-.02	.11	.08	.14
17. As far as world affairs are concerned, most of us are the victims of forces we can neither understand nor control.	.06	.29	-.02	.05	-.01	.14	.61	.42	.07	.01
18. Most people don't realize the extent to which their lives are controlled by accidental happenings.	.34	.28	.10	.45	.05	.01	.13	.14	.09	.02
20. It is hard to know whether or not a person really likes you.	.16	.17	.00	.02	.09	-.08	.02	.09	.47	.54
21. In the long run the bad things that happen to us are balanced by the good ones.	-.02	.16	.16	.28	.42	.02	.00	.02	.00	.10
22. It is difficult for people to have much control over the things politicians do in office.	.04	-.02	.03	.04	.06	-.08	.44	.42	.04	.06
23. Sometimes I can't understand how teachers arrive at the grades they give.	.04	.21	.03	.00	.40	.53	.17	-.04	.00	-.05
25. Many times I feel that I have little influence over the things that happen to me.	.50	.55	.26	.35	.10	.12	.14	.03	-.26	.21

(Continued)

103

TABLE 1 (Continued)

	Locus of Control Factors									
	A		B Leadership Success		C Academics		D Politics		E Respect	
	Luck-Fate									
	Chicano	Anglo	Chicano	Anglo	Chicano	Anglo	Chicano	Anglo	Chicano	Anglo
26. There's not much use in trying hard to please people, if they like you, they like you.	.04	.03	.06	.01	.00	.15	.09	-.06	.40	.52
28. Sometimes I feel that I don't have enough control over the direction my life is taking.	.39	.44	.08	.14	.18	.06	-.07	.01	.11	.11
29. Most of the time I can't understand why politicians behave the way they do.	.26	.03	.24	.40	-.05	-.02	.05	.30	.16	.10
	.85		.77		.68		.74		.70	

NOTE: Each item is represented by the alternative scored for external control. Omitted items 1, 8, 14, 19, 24, and 27 are unscored fillers.

[a]n = 244
[b]n = 203

104

own destinies against one that assigns control to external forces ("It is impossible for me to believe that chance or luck plays an important role in my life" versus "Many times I feel that I have little influence over the things that happen to me ." Items 13, 25, and 28 load ±.30 or greater for both Chicanos and Anglos. Adhering to the customary ±.30 criteria (Mirels, 1970), items 10 and 18 load on the luck-fate factor for the Chicano but not for the Anglo sample. Conversely, items 3, 4, 9, and 15 appear to be Anglo specific. The coefficient of congruence for this factor pair is quite high (0.85), and hence, a good indication of factor invariance.

High item loadings for factor B are related to the internal-external controversy on matters dealing with leadership and success ("Who gets to be boss often depends on who was lucky enough to be in the right place first" versus "Getting people to do the right thing depends upon ability; luck has little to do with it"). Only item 16 loads ±.30 or greater for both Chicanos and Anglos. Items 6, 11, and 15 are Chicano specific, whereas items 2, 18, and 29 are Anglo specific. In spite of the lack of common items, the coefficient of congruence (0.77) indicates an acceptable degree of factor correspondence.

The item loadings of the third factor are related to academic fairness and the extent of control a respondent perceives over such matters ("Sometimes I can't understand how teachers arrive at the grades they give" versus "There is a direct connection between how hard I study and the grades I get"). Under the ±.30 cut-off criterion, items 10 and 23 load for both samples, items 5 and 21 load for Chicanos only, and items 11 and 12 load for Anglos only. However, a factor similarity coefficient of 0.68 is considered quite low, suggesting little correspondence between this factor pair.

The internal-external controversy addressed in factor D falls within the realm of world affairs and political justice ("With enough effort we can wipe out political corruption" versus "It is difficult for people to have control over the things politicians do in office"). The common items are 17 and 22. Item 12 emerged only in the Anglo sample, and there were no Chicano-specific items in this factor. The congruence coefficient (0.74) for this factor pair indicates only a moderate degree of factor similarity.

High item loadings on factor E are related to the extent of control a respondent feels over issues dealing with personal dignity and interpersonal respect ("People are lonely because they don't try to be friendly" versus "There's not much use in trying too hard to please people, if they like you, they like you"). The loading of items 20 and 26 are high in both samples. As in the case of factor D, no Chicano-specific items appeared on this locus of control dimension. However, item 7 did load on this factor in the Anglo sample. The factor similarity coefficient (0.70) is indicative of a somewhat weak factor stability in this pair.

It should be noted that items did not always reach the ±.30 factor loading criterion for both samples. Seven of the items loaded to an acceptable degree only in the case of the analysis performed on the Anglo sample, whereas three items loaded only on the factors extracted from the Chicano sample. This could be a strong indication of the lack of semantic equivalence of some of the items employed to measure the locus of control construct. In other words, the seven items that do not load on any of the Chicano-based locus of control dimensions might not be appropriate for eliciting I-E responses in Chicano populations. Of course, this could also be seen as evidence for the unidimensional nature of the I-E personality construct. However, only three items failed to load on the Anglo-based factors. That some of the items take on different meanings for Chicanos seems to be a more likely explanation. These items might not even be perceived as relating to internal-external locus of control.

The fact that most factors contain a number of sample-specific items also reflects the differences in the meanings conveyed by the various items. This can readily be seen from an examination of the factor loadings of item 11 in the Chicano and Anglo samples. The respondent is asked to choose (agree with) one of these two statements: "Becoming a success is a matter of hard work, luck has little or nothing to do with it" or "Getting a good job depends mainly on being in the right place at the right time." As can be seen in Table 1, Chicano responses load on the leadership-success factor, whereas Anglo responses tend to load on the academics dimension. In other words, while item 11 conveys "leadership" qualities for Chicanos, it conveys "academic" qualities for Anglos.

What can be concluded regarding the validity of the I-E dimensions for Chicano populations? The luck-fate factor shows a great deal of invariance across the two samples and can hence be regarded as an indication of adequate standards for cultural equivalence. The stability of the leadership-success factor also seems reasonable. However, the cultural equivalence of the remaining three dimensions is somewhat questionable. As indicated by congruence coefficients in the low 70s, the correspondence of the politics and respect factors across the two samples is modest. The academics dimension shows virtually no cultural equivalence. Hence, although an internal-external factor dealing with "academic" matters does emerge in both samples, the concept itself does not appear to convey the same meaning for Chicanos and Anglos. It would, therefore, be methodologically indefensible to use this dimension to compare the two groups on their internal-external beliefs in academic situations.

Conclusions

The conceptual and methodological issues addressed in this paper underscore the intricate problems involved in assessing and comparing Chicanos and Anglos on a seemingly straightforward psychological dimension such as locus of control. The potential problems are much more complicated than most researchers are willing to admit. Using Anglo personality tests or Anglo-derived experimental manipulations without determining their appropriateness for Chicano populations is irresponsible and lacks both scientific validity and sociocultural objectivity. The problem of cultural equivalence is extremely complex and entails more than merely controlling for such obvious factors as readability and language usage.

As clearly indicated by the data presented in the present paper, even simple statements regarding beliefs in internal as opposed to external control may evoke totally different meanings for Chicanos in comparison with Anglos. It is conceivable that a great deal of the research literature comparing Chicanos and Anglos may be based on equivocal measurements of a given psychological construct, casting serious doubt on the validity of the findings.

It is hoped that the issues raised in this article will discourage the indiscriminate usage of Anglo personality tests with Chicanos populations. In accord with established cross-cultural research procedures (Triandis, 1972), the following criteria should be met in comparing Chicanos and Anglos on a given psychological construct: (*a*) The perception of the demand characteristics and other socioenvironmental aspects of the testing conditions, including the experimental manipulation, should not differ across populations; (*b*) differences in response styles and levels of anxiety produced by the testing situation should be assessed and minimized; (*c*) familiarity with the test instrument and experimental format should also be reasonably equivalent across populations. Moreover, researchers should familiarize themselves with the intricate sociocultural dynamics of the Chicano population. In addition to the essential differentiation between the effects of cultural aspects and those of socioeconomic status, intragroup variations with regard to numerous other intervening variables, such as regionality and levels of acculturation, must be carefully considered and the findings appropriately qualified. Accordingly, the findings reported in the present study may only hold for dualistic (bicultural) Chicano communities and hence should not be generalized to the entire Chicano population. In conclusion, investigations based on inappropriate methodologies and ethnocentric interpretations should no longer be tolerated within the scientific community, *ya basta!*

REFERENCE NOTES

1. Graves, T.D. *Time perspective and the deferred gratification pattern in a tri-ethnic community*. University of Colorado, Tri-Ethnic Research Project, Research Report No. 5, 1961.
2. Levenson, H. *Reliability and validity of the I, P, and C scales — A multidimensional view of locus of control*. Paper read at the annual meeting of the American Psychological Association, Montreal, August 1973.
3. Evans, G.T. *Congruence transformations: Procedures for comparing the results of factor analyses involving the same set of variables*. The Ontario Institute for Studies in Education, 1970.

REFERENCES

Cabrera, Y.A. A study of American and Mexican-American culture values and their significance in education. *Dissertation Abstracts International*, 1964, *25*, 309.

Casavantes, E. Pride and prejudice: A Mexican-American dilemma. *Civil Rights Digest*, Winter, 1970, *3*, 22-27.

Cattell, R.B. (Ed.). *Handbook of multivariate experimental psychology*. Chicago: Rand-Mc-Nally, 1966.

Cliff, N. Orthogonal rotation to congruence. *Psychometrika*, 1966, *31*, 33-42.

Collins, B.E. Four separate components of the Rotter I-E scale: Belief in a difficult world, a just world, a predictable world and a politically responsive world. *Journal of Personality and Social Psychology*, 1974, *29*, 381-391.

Diaz-Guerrero. R. The active and passive syndromes. *Revista Interamericana de Psicologia*, 1967, *1*, 263-272.

Diaz-Guerrero, R. *Psychology of the Mexican: Culture and personality*. Austin, Tex.: University of Texas Press, 1975.

Garza, R.T., & Ames, R.E. A comparison of Chicanos and Anglos on locus of control. In C.A. Hernandez, M.J. Haug, & N.N. Wagner (Eds.), *Chicanos: Social and psychological perspectives* (2nd Ed.). C.V. Mosby, 1976.

Gruen, G.E., & Ottinger, D.R. Skill and chance orientations as determiners of problem-solving behavior in lower- and middle-class children. *Psychological Reports*, 1969, *24*, 204-214.

Jessor, R., Graves, D.T., Hanson, R.C., & Jessor, S.L. *Society, personality, and deviant behavior*. New York: Holt, Rinehart, & Winston, 1968.

Justin, N. Culture, conflict, and Mexican-American achievement. *School and Society*, 1970, *98*, 27-28.

Kaiser, H.F. The varimax criterion for analytic rotation in factor analysis. *Psychometrika*, 1958, *23*, 187-200.

Lewis, O. *Five families: Mexican case studies in the culture of poverty*. New York: Basic Books, Inc., 1959.

Mirels, H.L. Dimensions of internal versus external control. *Journal of Consulting and Clinical Psychology*, 1970, *34*, 226-228.

Padilla, A.M. Psychological research and the Mexican-American. In C.A. Hernandez, M.J. Haug, & N.N. Wagner (Eds.), *Chicanos: Social and psychological perspectives* (2nd Edition). C.V. Mosby, 1976.

Parsons, O.A., Schneider, J.M., & Hansen, A.S. Internal-external locus of control and national stereotypes in Denmark and the United States. *Journal of Consulting and Clinical Psychology*, 1970, *35*, 30-37.

Phares, E.J. *Locus of control in personality*. Morristown, N.J.: General Learning Press, 1976.

Ramirez, M., & Castañeda, A. *Cultural democracy, bicognitive development, and education*. New York: Academic Press, 1974.

Reitz, H.J., & Groff, G.K. Comparisons of locus of control categories among American, Mexican, and Thai workers. *Proceedings of the Annual Convention of the American Psychological Association*, 1972, *7*, 263-264.

Rotter, J.B. *Social learning and clinical psychology*. Englewood Cliffs, NJ: Prentice-Hall, 1954.

Rotter, J.B. Generalized expectation for internal vs. external control of reinforcement. *Psychological Monographs*, 1966, *80* (1, Whole No. 609).

Rotter, J.B. Some problems and misconceptions related to the construct of internal versus external control of reinforcement. *Journal of Consulting and Clinical Psychology*, 1975, *43*, 56-67.

Rotter, J.B., Chance, J., & Phares, E.J. (Eds.). *Applications of a social learning theory of personality*. New York: Holt, Rinehart, & Winston. 1972.

Schneider, J.M., & Parsons, O.A. Categories on the locus of control scale and cross-cultural comparisons in Denmark and the United States. *Journal of Cross-Cultural Psychology*, 1970, *1*, 131-138.

Scott, J.D., & Phelon, J.G. Expectancies of unemployable males regarding source of control of reinforcement. *Psychological Reports*, 1969, *25*, 911-913.

Tin-Yee Hsieh, T., Skyhut, J., & Lotsof, E.J. Internal vs. external control and ethnic group membership: A cross-cultural comparison. *Journal of Consulting and Clinical Psychology*, 1969, *33*, 122-124.

Triandis, H.C. *The analysis of subjective culture*. New York: Wiley, 1972.

PART II
Bilingualism

CHAPTER 8

CHILD BILINGUALISM: INSIGHTS TO ISSUES

AMADO M. PADILLA

University of California, Los Angeles

In the past few years the study of language acquisition in children who simultaneously learn two languages has become an intriguing research problem to some investigators of child language development[1]. The reasons for this are many. First, the acquisition of a single language by a child almost constitutes a miracle in itself when the acquisition process is examined closely. Many earlier theoretical interpretations of language acquisition (Skinner, 1957) have been found inadequate in attempts to write a grammar for child language (Brown, 1973). Consider that a large number of children learn not one, but two languages. The first major study of child bilingualism was conducted by Leopold (1939), yet today relatively little is known about the intricacies of learning two languages. Second, the relationship between language and cognition in young children is a topic often discussed in developmental psychology, but relatively little is known about how bilingual children keep two linguistic systems separated and even less is known about how "concepts" are learned, stored, and retrieved in two languages. Third, what is the best way to teach children two languages? A number of strategies have been proposed, but little systematic information exists to support any of them. A number of statements have appeared in the literature about the pros and cons of child bilingualism and strategies for teaching children more than one language.

The purpose of this chapter is to analyze some of the arguments, pro and con, that surround the question of child bilingualism. This analysis draws upon

[1]Work on this paper was supported by Research Grant MH 24854-02 from the National Institute of Mental Health to the Spanish Speaking Mental Health Research Center at the University of California, Los Angeles.

some of the writer's own research, as well as upon information that exists in the literature. Before proceeding to these arguments, however, a definition of bilingualism is needed, since the question of what constitutes bilingualism is itself a problem.

What Is Bilingualism?

Bilingualism is a commonly misunderstood phenomena. So misunderstood, in fact, that at least one international seminar has been convened to discuss the definition and measurement of bilingualism (Kelley, 1969). In its simplest sense, bilingualism refers to the ability to communicate in two languages. Although this definition of bilingualism is accurate, it is not sufficient to convey all of the complexities involved. For instance, even the word "communicate" does not reveal all that is needed; that is, do we mean that bilingualism is the ability to speak, write, read, or merely understand a second language? For a person to claim mastery of a language implies the ability to both encode and decode in the language. For instance, mastery of English implies the ability to speak and write (encoding skills) in English, as well as the ability to listen and read with understanding (decoding skills). Drawing upon the work of Macnamara (1967), a finer analysis can also be made within each of these encoding or decoding skills. To be able to encode or decode further implies mastery of the basic sound and alphabetic system of the language (phonemes or graphemes), of the vocabulary of the language (lexicon), of the grammatical rules of the language (syntax), and of the signification of words (semantics).

To carry this discussion further, the speaker of a language, to claim complete mastery of the language, must demonstrate mastery of the 16 skills shown in Table 1. The bilingual, to claim complete fluency in two languages, must demonstrate mastery in 32 skills — 16 for each language.

TABLE 1
Major Encoding and Decoding Language Skills and the Four Subcomponents of Each

Encoding Skills		Decoding Skills	
Speak	Write	Listen	Read
Phonemes	Graphemes	Phonemes	Graphemes
Lexicon	Lexicon	Lexicon	Lexicon
Syntax	Syntax	Syntax	Syntax
Semantics	Semantics	Semantics	Semantics

The scheme allows a better definition of bilingualism with which it is possible to distinguish among balanced bilinguals, bilinguals dominant in one language (Spanish or English), receptive but not expressive bilinguals, and so on. Each of these types of bilingualism is different as applied to language competency in the bilingual. The term *balanced* bilingual is used to describe someone equally skilled in two languages. Technically, this implies skill in all aspects of encoding and decoding in both languages. However, the term is generally used in a more limited sense and applied to someone who appears to be able at least to comprehend and speak two languages. A receptive bilingual, on the other hand, can understand (comprehend) two languages, but cannot speak (produce) one of them. This phenomenon usually occurs among individuals whose parents were immigrants from a country where a different language is spoken. There are other types of bilingualism (another form is found among individuals who can read and write in a second language but have great difficulty speaking it), but these will be of less concern here. It is of importance, however, that bilingualism can be regarded as a skill existing along a continuum ranging from monolingualism to complete and balanced bilingualism.

The complete elaboration of this continuum is presented in Table 1. Mastery of a language demands linguistic competence in 16 skills of the language; and bilinguals, to claim mastery of two languages, must be competent in all 16 skills of both languages. This latter situation would be the balanced bilingual. To simplify the discussion of bilingualism in children, reading or writing will not be considered here; and this discussion will deal only with specifying a continuum of bilingualism that relies on speaking and listening. The purpose of confining the discussion to speaking and listening in the child bilingual is twofold: first, attention to the matrix of Table 1 demonstrates that the question of language competency in the bilingual is complex and, for the sake of simplicity, best to limited speaking and listening skills; second, the reading and writing skills of children between the ages of 6 and 12 are not so advanced that their inclusion in this conceptualization is essential.

One way of representing the possible types of bilingualism is shown in Figure 1. The numbers in the cells of the cube represent the linguistic skills involved in

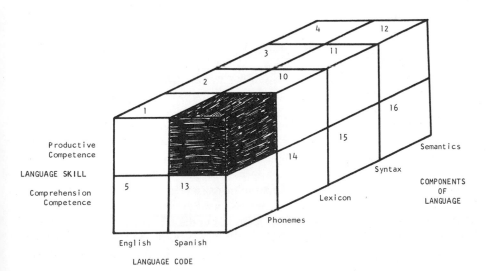

FIGURE 1. Three-dimensional space depicting the relationship among language skill, language code, and components of language. The cell numbers are referenced in Table 2.

speaking or listening in either Spanish or English. To be perfectly fluent, the monolingual speaker of English possesses skills 1 through 8; the fluent monolingual speaker of Spanish possesses skills 9 through 16. In Figure 1, the shaded cell of the cube (cell 9) represents a Spanish speaker's fluency with the phonetic system of the Spanish language. This representation permits a discussion of the large degree of variability that exists among children learning two languages — in the home, school, or on the playground. Table 2 presents, in summary form, the continuum of bilingual competency that results from combining the various linguistic skills in English and Spanish depicted in Figure 1.

TABLE 2

A Proposed Continuum of Bilingualism from Monolingualism in English or Spanish to Balanced Bilingualism, Based on the Skills Shown in Figure 1

Type of Spanish-English Speaker	Linguistic Skills Possessed by the Speaker
(1) Monolingual English speaker	1 - 8 (only)
(2) Dominant English speaker, and	1 - 8 (plus)
(a) Receptive Spanish-minimal expression	9, 10, (12), 13, (14), (16)
(b) Receptive Spanish-moderate expression	9, 10, 11, 12, 13, 14, (15), 16
(3) Balanced bilingual	1 - 16
(4) Dominant Spanish speaker, and	9 - 16 (plus)
(a) Receptive English-moderate expression	1, 2, 3, 4, 5, 6, (7), 8
(b) Receptive English-minimal expression	1, 2, (4), 5, (6), (7)
(5) Monolingual Spanish speaker	9 - 16 (only)

As can be seen from Table 2, many degrees of ability are possible to describe a child as bilingual. Any child's specific degree of bilingualism depends on a number of factors; one of the most obvious being the amount of language exposure the child receives in each of the two languages. Presumably, if a child hears two languages equally often and is encouraged to speak both, then the child, in all probability, will develop into a balanced bilingual. The importance of language input was noted in a previous study (Padilla & Liebman, 1975) when one of the children observed spoke more Spanish if his mother was instructed to speak only Spanish to him for at least 1 hour prior to an observation session. From Table 2, it becomes obvious, according to the model presented, that an individual's degree of bilingualism is defined as the sum of that individual's linguistic skills.

Defining bilingualism as a multidimensional skill that can be conceptualized along a continuum such as that depicted in Table 2 provides the necessary framework for proceeding to the first issue to be discussed in this chapter. Observers of bilingual children have often stated that bilingualism results in children who cannot adequately speak either language. Chicanos, for example, have often heard their language referred to as "Spanglish," a reference to the fact that Chicanos, who vary in their degrees of bilingualism, frequently mix Spanish and English. The best example of this phenomenon is seen in the work of the Chicano poet, Alurista.[2]

[2]Alurista's work is characterized by the rhythmic mixing of Spanish and English in such a way that a consonant flow emerges.

It is important to examine the question of language mixing in the context of the child bilingual.

Linguistic Interaction

The term *linguistic interaction* refers to the mutual influence of the two language systems of a bilingual. From Figure 1 it can be seen that the young child exposed to two languages must ultimately learn to differentiate between two linguistic systems. Previous work on simultaneous language acquisition indicates that children acquiring two languages from birth to early infancy pass from a stage in which the two languages are undifferentiated to a gradual separation of the two systems (Imedadze, 1967; Leopold, 1939, 1945, 1949a, b; Swain, Note 1). Elsewhere, Padilla and Liebman (1975) have shown that, at least for Chicano children who demonstrate productive capability in Spanish and English early in life, the phase of undifferentiation is relatively short. Differentiation of linguistic systems, however, was particularly evident at the phonological level, but could also be seen at the lexical and syntactic levels. Table 3 presents language utterances from three children described in more detail in an earlier report (Padilla & Liebman, 1975). Inspection of utterances similar to these led us to the conclusion that the appropriate use of both languages, even in mixed utterances, was evident; that is, correct word order was preserved. For example, there were no occurrences of "raining *está*" or "a *es* baby," but there were such utterances as "*está* raining" and "*es* a baby horsie." There was also an absence of redundance in mixed utterances as well as an absence of unnecessary words that might confuse the meaning. That is, "*dámelo* that" or "*es un* a baby horsie" did not appear, whereas "*dame* that" and "*es un* baby horsie" did occur.

The clearest evidence for separate systems was found at the phonological level. Even in mixed utterances, where evidence for some assimilation of sounds, particularly in young language learners, might have appeared, none was found. English morphemes were pronounced with an English accent and Spanish morphemes with a Spanish accent. Within a word boundary, there was no switching from one language to the other (Padilla & Liebman, 1975).

TABLE 3
Examples of Mixed Language Utterance Observed in the Speech of Selected Spanish-English Bilingual Children

Michelle 21 months	Bobby 25 months	Joaquin 26 months
baila mommy	a man *tu casa*	*es* a baby horsie
hello *papá*	daddy *está*	*está* raining
that *papel*		*dame* that

Although language mixing does occur, it is also apparent that mixes cannot be used as evidence that bilingualism is detrimental to the mastery of either language or both. The causes of linguistic interaction in children are complex and thus far largely unexplored. It is clear, however, that children in becoming bilingual bear a linguistic "load" caused by their bilingual environment heavier than that borne by children growing up in a monolingual environment. In spite of this, they are capable of learning the linguistic rules of both languages and applying them more or less appropriately.

Swain and Wesche (1975), in one of the only two studies of linguistic interaction to date, studied the speech of a French-English bilingual child and found that language mixing can often be attributed to the fact that the child knows the word in only one language. In cases where the child knows the word in both languages, the immediate verbal context appears at times to make a word or phrase more available than its counterpart in the other language. Swain and Wesche also claimed that the insertion of isolated words from one language into the other indicated a lack of differentiation of the languages by the child. The importance of Swain and Wesche's (1975) observations of linguistic interactions in a bilingual child lies in their demonstration of the usefulness of studying "natural speech" in investigating the processes underlying speech production. This is especially true with respect to linguistic interactions, which form the basis for many of the arguments against child bilingualism (Padilla & Ruiz, 1973).

In a second study designed to investigate linguistic interactions in bilingual children, Lindholm and Padilla (in press) examined language samples of five Spanish-English bilingual children, ranging in age from 2 years 10 months to 6 years 2 months. Of a total of 5177 separate language utterances examined, only 110, or 2%, contained a language switch. These language switches were divided into two categories: lexical (the introduction of a single word from the second language into the utterance); and phrasal (the use of a phrase from the second language). Table 4 provides a breakdown of the two types of interactions. It is evident that switching occurred predominately at the lexical level. Moreover, the insertion of English nouns into Spanish utterances accounted for most of the linguistic interactions. Several examples of these switches are 1. *Una vez estaba una* bird.[3] (Once

TABLE 4
Breakdown of Linguistic Interactions by Type[a]

Type	Spanish Utterance with English Insertion	English Utterance with Spanish Insertion
Lexical		
Noun	71	12
Verb	3	3
Conjunction	5	2
Adjective	2	-
Phrasal	4	8
Total	85	25

[a]Based on a total of 5177 utterances in both Spanish and English.

[3]It should be noted that a few words can take either gender depending on the translation used. Bird can be translated as *"pajaro"* or as *"ave"*. In the first instance it is masculine, and in the second it is feminine. Thus, the use of the feminine *una* is correct if the child was thinking of *ave*, but incorrect if *pajaro* was intended.

there was a bird.) 2. *Dónde está la* clock?[4] (Where is the clock?) 3. *Por qué voy a limpiar esa* window? (Why am I going to clean this window?)

Of major importance was the fact that switching did not occur randomly. In those few instances where switching did occur, the switch involved an English noun inserted into a Spanish utterance. Moreover, when the switch was made, the grammatical consistency of the utterance was maintained. Both of these points support the notion that bilingual children are able to differentiate their two linguistic systems (Padilla & Liebman, 1975) and manipulate their two languages for social impact at an early age.

The notion that child bilingualism creates a situation where the child cannot speak either language adequately and, as a consequence, speaks a hybrid mixture of the two languages must be rejected. Language mixing is a phenomenon observed in all bilingual communities and among bilingual speakers of all ages (Weinreich, 1953). Moreover, mixing languages is not indicative of lack of fluency in a language. It may occur, as suggested above, because of psychological (cognitive) factors and because of social conditions that may play an important role in bilingualism but have not been explored with child bilinguals.

Sociolinguists (Fishman, 1970; Gumperz, 1970 ; Hymes, 1967) pointed out that language choice and use are often affected by social milieu. People within a community behave according to the rules and actions of other members of the community. Thus children acquire not only language(s) in a social setting, but also the habits, attitudes, and values governing the use of language(s). Gumperz (1970) suggested that a child will acquire language(s) most suited to the community, its values, its actions, and its social pressures. Thus, in a bilingual community, the appropriate language system to learn is one that includes relatively frequent use of language mixes. The work of Gumperz and Hernandez (1972) suggests the social impact of language switching in the speech of bilingual children. In other words, Spanglish may be considered the norm in some Spanish-English communities, and its use does not denote lack of fluency in either language.

In sum, many children reared in a bilingual environment learn to differentiate the two linguistic systems relatively early. When linguistic interactions (mixes) do occur, there may be several possible explanations, ranging from the child's lack of familiarity with the word in one language to the child's acquisition of discourse strategies that demand a switch in language. Each of these explanations has a linguistic basis, and each, in one way or another, acknowledges the complexity — linguistic, psychological, social — of early child bilingualism. None of the explanations necessitates the assumption of a language deficit on the part of the child bilingual.

In a discussion of the issue of linguistic interaction, the role played by cognition in bilingualism must be considered. It is possible that some interactions could

---

[4]The use of the feminine article *la* is incorrect. Clock or *el reloj* is a masculine noun. When switching occurred, the child was as likely as not to be incorrect in the gender of the article that preceded the English noun, as this example illustrates.

be explained if more were known how the bilingual processed information in two languages. Although relatively little is known about this process (Kolers, 1966), it is within reason to argue that however it occurs, it may be related to overall enhanced cognitive ability on the part of the bilingual. It is possible that bilinguals, in carrying out their daily functions in two languages, must have more cognitive capacity than their monolingual counterparts. Otherwise, how can the bilingual's ability to encode and decode information in two linguistic systems without confusion or chaos be explained? This hypothesis is not unique and has been advanced by others. Nonetheless, it has received relatively little attention, especially within the context of child bilingualism.

Child Bilingualism and Cognition

Many studies in the early psychological literature conclude that child bilingualism has deleterious effects on intellectual development as measured by standard tests of intelligence. For reviews, see Darcy (1953, 1963) and Peal and Lambert (1962). Careful examination of this early literature, however, leads to questions concerning the validity of this conclusion. Almost without exception, the monolingual groups in these studies who gave significantly higher performances on standardized intelligence tests were speakers of a sociolinguistically dominant language — dominant in the sense that it enjoyed greater prestige and greater communicative utility in the larger society from which the groups were selected. Moreover, in the majority of these studies, the bilinguals, regardless of their proficiency in the dominant language, suffered from socioeconomic and environmental factors specific to the lower status bicultural communities in which they were socialized. Because of these and other shortcomings, the studies that concluded that bilingualism of itself produces an intellectual deficit should be dismissed for their lack of responsible scientific inquiry.

There is more recent literature bearing on the relationship between bilingualism and cognitive development — the processing of environmental events that depend upon the translation of experience into symbolic form. Specifically, cognitive development refers to those cognitive activities such as thinking and insight learning that depend upon language and to the extraordinary and distinctively human capacity for symbolically mediated learning and the cultural transmission associated with it.

Leopold (1939) was the first investigator of child bilingualism to note the type of relationship between language and cognition that will be emphasized here. Leopold, in the study of Hildegard, his German-English speaking child, noted that a child raised to be bilingual appeared to possess a noticeable looseness in the link between the phonetic word and its meaning. What Leopold meant is that not only is there an absence of confusion between two languages at the level of personal meaning, but the bilingual child at an early age is less bound to one specific kind of word-object or word-event link than is the monolingual child. The monolingual child is more predisposed to notice objects and events in one particular way. The bilingual child, on the other hand, is more predisposed to treat them in a variety of ways because of the greater flexibility of linguistic experience. Having alternative ways of looking at the same thing, the child is able to see the arbitrary nature of any one way of perceiving and learns to attend to the object or event itself.

Leopold's early observation was also made by Peal and Lambert (1962) in what is perhaps the best controlled study comparing monolingual and bilingual children on a series of intellectual tasks. Peal and Lambert observed that exposure to two cultures seemed to give French-English bilinguals advantages monolinguals did not enjoy. Intellectually their experiences with two languages seemed to result in mental flexibility, superiority in concept formation, and a more diversified set of mental abilities, in the sense that the patterns of abilities developed by bilinguals were more heterogeneous. In contrast, the monolinguals appeared to Peal and Lambert to have more unitary structures of intelligence that they had to use for all types of intellectual tasks.

Peal and Lambert's attempts to explain their interesting results centered on hypotheses first suggested by Leopold (1939) and independently collaborated by Imedadze (1967). These hypotheses suggest that the child bilingual is reinforced ". . .to conceptualize environmental events in terms of their general properties without reliance on their [being encoded into] linguistic symbols. . . [Peal & Lambert, 1962, p. 14]." The early "detaching" of words from the objects they represent appears to be associated with a number of advantages for cognitive development. Imedadze (1967), studying bilingual children, concludes that at the very first encounter the fact that an object can have two names, a separation of object and name begins. Thus, a word, freed from its referent, can easily become an object of special attention.

Although the observations of Imedadze (1967), Leopold (1939), and Peal and Lambert (1962) are no longer novel, little experimental work has been conducted comparing monolinguals to bilinguals on standard cognitive developmental tasks. Only one such study has used Mexican-American bilingual children. In it, Feldman and Shen (1971) compared the performance of monolingual and bilingual children on several Piagetian cognitive ability tasks. One task involved *object constancy*, the ability to recognize an object after its shape had been partially altered. The second included a variety of *naming* tasks, using common names for objects such as "cup," then using nonsense labels such as "wug" in place of "cup," and finally, substituting associated names like "plate" for the word cup. The third task required children to demonstrate the ability to *construct sentences* using three names. The results indicated that bilingual children were superior to monolingual children on all three tasks. These results supported Feldman and Shen's (1971) hypothesis that the mere presence of two language codes, possessed by bilingual children, may facilitate a shift from the notion of meaning as word reference to the notion of meaning as a function of use, a shift that may be the precursor of an adult meaning system. The Feldman and Shen study does not resolve all the problems bearing on the relationship between bilingualism and cognition, since the study suffered from a number of methodological flaws. Nonetheless, the results of the study are generally supportive of the thesis that bilingualism can have potentially beneficial effects on the overall cognitive development of children.

Using Leopold's (1939) classic work on child bilingualism Ianco-Worrall (1972, Note 2) also advanced the notion that bilingualism is a source of enriched early experience. This led her to two hypotheses: (a) Child bilingualism results in accelerated development in specific areas of cognitive functioning; and (b) child bilingualism equips individuals with greater reasoning strategies and cognitive flexibility. To test these hypotheses, Ianco-Worrall compared the performance of Afrikaans and English-speaking bilingual children to monolingual children in a number of tasks involving semantic or phonetic preference, name-object relationship, coding, classification, and discrimination problems. Although not all of the tasks yielded findings that supported this hypothesis, enough empirical evidence was obtained to suggest that the hypotheses were at least tenable. Ianco-Worrall concluded that, given the present state of knowledge of psychological variables inherent in bilingualism, it was almost inevitable that not all of her empirical findings supported her assumptions. This fact, however, does not detract from the inherent value of exploring and developing new techniques for investigating the relationship between bilingualism and cognition.

An investigator who has explored new avenues in this area is Bain (1974). Bain compared the performance of bilinguals and monolinguals on tests of mathematical ability, ability to make verbal analogies, and sensitivity to emotional expression. In his studies, Bain found that groups of French-English and German-English bilinguals from age 5 to adulthood tend to perform all these tests more readily and consistently than do matched groups of monolinguals. His work led Bain (1974) to conclude that, in general, the bilingual child tends to have a greater cognitive plasticity than the unilingual. Bain cautioned his readers, acknowledging a myriad of unresolved problems and contentious issues in this area of inquiry. But Bain concurs that being raised and schooled bilingually represents a unique form of child development.

From the literature it is becoming clear that potential beneficial effects on cognitive development are associated with bilingualism. The challenge is to design well-controlled studies better to specify the parameters of bilingualism that facilitate cognition. Such studies present many problems to be sure, but until they are conducted, there will be an incomplete picture of child bilingualism. Moreover, studies of the type suggested need to be conducted most especially by Chicano psychologists because so many Chicano children are raised in bilingual environments.

An issue discussed in this section and to be raised in the following section is an observation made several centuries ago by the famous German author, Goethe, who said ". . .that someone who does not know a second language does but poorly know his first." In other words, the acquisition of a second language not only introduces another store of knowledge, it also serves to raise the level of understanding of the first language. In an analogous situation, the learning of algebra raises the level of understanding of simple arithmetic. In mathematics, better performance on simple arithmetic tasks occurs because the possession of algebraic knowledge frees mathematical thinking from the constraints of understanding at a simple arithmetic level. Algebraic knowledge permits simple arithmetic to be seen as a particular case of mathematical knowledge and, in turn, permits a richer appreciation of mathematics in general. This situation also applies to language. Knowledge of a second language permits the first language to be seen as a particular pattern of meanings. The bilingual does not simply learn ways of labeling the same event in both languages but comes to see more clearly the particular meaning of the event, in both languages and from the perspective of each linguistic-cultural group. This kind of insight into meaning is not available to the monolingual. This argument can be summarized in the observation that those who want to know their first language, not superficially and reflexively but profoundly and reflectively, *must* learn a second language; similarly, if they wish truly to know the second, they must also study the first. A form of this argument was accepted at one time by educators as the basis of what constituted a truly educated individual. Not too many years ago Latin or Greek was an integral part of the school curriculum, the belief being that learning these languages was good training for the "mind." Latin or Greek, of course, do not have any properties as languages that make them better than other languages for training thinking and reasoning (Taylor, 1976), but this observation does not detract from the notion that instruction in a second language and bilingualism may serve to free the individual from the limited confines of thinking and speaking about events in a single language. The result is an individual with a unique form of cognitive flexibility not observed in the monolingual.

This point raises the last issue to be examined: How should bilingual instruction be carried out? This question implies strategies for maintaining a bilingual environment.

Strategies for Implementing Bilingual Instruction

The most pervasive strategy about the teaching of a second language in education circles is that instruction in a second language should begin only after complete mastery of the primary language has been achieved. When complete mastery is supposed to have occurred is not clear, but presumably it implies not only fluency in speaking but also good reading ability. This may explain why second-language instruction is traditionally not begun before high school. Ironically, as noted earlier, for many years this strategy of instruction was tied to an educational philosophy that learning a foreign language, such as Greek or Latin, had positive and beneficial effects. In essence, this educational philosophy parallels Goethe's comment about bilingualism. The decline in second-language instruction in secondary schools and colleges in this country is sad testimony to a misplaced educational philosophy about second language instruction.

Little research has actually been done on ways of implementing bilingualism in children. Clearly instruction in two languages can proceed simultaneously before the child has mastered the primary language. Ronjat (1913) was perhaps the first investigator to explore the consequences of child bilingualism systematically. Ronjat observed a child being raised according to the principle of *one person-one language*. In Ronjat's study, this principle meant that the father spoke to his child only in French and the mother spoke to the same child only in German. Other persons in the child's milieu spoke to him alternately in French or German, but the child's most important educators − his mother and father − tried, as much as possible, to adhere to the *one person-one language* principle. Ronjat's main findings were that by age 5 this child had learned both languages simultaneously; he could alternate between the two with minimal lexical and grammatical confusion; and his level of fluency in both was greater than that of the average child raised in a monolingual family. Ronjat's findings have been supported subsequently in other studies with children learning other language combinations (Leopold, 1939; Padilla & Lindholm, 1976, in press; Swain, Note 1; Fantini, Note 3). In all cases, the researchers reported an initial period of apparent confusion of languages for very young children. Very young children tend to use an amalgam of both languages that can be very confusing to those unfamiliar with their speech. But it is more confusing for adults (particularly monolingual adults) than for the children, whose confusion is more apparent than real. They know what they mean. Moreover, their apparent confusion is, in reality, an early example of mutual compensation. These children use what they know best, which may be words from one language interspersed with words, grammar, or parts of grammar from the other language, and describe their perceptions in the manner that makes the most sense to them. Bilingual and monolinugal children *both* make speech errors (Brown, 1973); but during the initial period, very young bilingual children make mistakes in two languages rather than one. Moreover, as Ronjat's (1913) and others' research showed, the two languages tend to become more or less functionally independent by age 4 if the parents adhere to the one person-one language principle. If they do not, this process can take longer.

Two points need to be emphasized. First, it appears from the limited research available that a strategy that emphasizes a separation of the two languages, such as the one person-one language principle, will maximize the simultaneous acquisition of two languages. But the research is limited, and other strategies such as one language for the first part of the day and a second language for the second half of the day, or one language for one part of the house and a second language for the other part of the house, have not been studied. To be totally systematic, this kind of research should also include monolingual control groups of children learning the target languages in unilingual settings. No one has ever attempted this type of longitudinal study, and the number of controls necessary to do it well may result in this research never being conducted. Thus, the studies of Ronjat (1913) and others are only suggestive. The second point that needs emphasis, and may reduce the hesitancy a cautious scientist would have about drawing conclusions from the writings of Ronjat and others, refers to the importance of speech errors in the language of children. The discussion of Spanglish is an example of the overemphasis placed on speech errors made by Spanish-English bilinguals. An observer of the speech of monolingual children will note more than a few passing errors. All children make frequent speaking errors that adults usually either do not notice or ignore as the "cute" mumblings of innocent children (Brown, 1973). Why the speech errors of bilingual children should appear to be more salient is an interesting question beyond the scope of this discussion. It is possible that observers of speech errors may be particularly attentive to such errors when observing bilingual speakers.

The scanty literature on the simultaneous acquisition of two languages favors the view that children can learn two languages well before the age of school entry and that when a child is to be exposed to two languages, instruction should be carried out systematically. The best strategy appears to be instruction that keeps the two languages separated as much as possible — the principle of *one person-one language*. In practice, this strategy is probably unrealistic in the case of Chicanos, who are more accustomed than other bilinguals to mix their two languages readily. Nonetheless, separation of the two linguistic systems occurs and the use of mixed utterances as proof of the lack of differentiation between linguistic systems may not be useful with Spanish-English bilingual children in the Southwestern and Western United States (Padilla & Liebman, 1975). This is most likely true because Chicano Spanish-English bilingual children may be far more accustomed to hearing mixed utterance from their adult language models than children studied elsewhere.

Before concluding this section, two points about child bilingualism, regardless of how instruction is carried out, must be raised. For two reasons, the learning of two (or more) languages is best done during the early years of the learner; one based on neurological evidence and the other on social modeling. Penfield, a noted neuroscientist, has advocated bilingualism for many years as a way in which the cortex of the young child can be given additional stimulation (Penfield & Roberts, 1959). Of equal importance is the fact that the brain seems to possess a greater plasticity and capacity for acquiring languages at an early age. The secret lies in the action of a switch mechanism, a conditioned reflex, that works automatically in the brain. This mechanism enables the child to switch easily from the vocabulary of one language to that of another, so that both are learned directly and without confusion. This cortical plasticity, discussed by Penfield and Roberts (1959), disappears once there is functional localization of the speech area in the left hemisphere of the brain. Since functional localization of speech occurs early, the advantage of early instruction in two languages may be lost if parents delay too long.

As for the second reason, children are highly dependent on *social models* and this dependence results in *identification* with the people who satisfy their needs. The readiness of children to learn the language of their environment is greater than that of older persons and is associated with strong need for membership in the cultural-linguistic group of their peers. Puberty, with its passage into adolescence, leads to a consolidation of personality that in large measure inhibits the kind of submission necessary to learn a second language. When a second language is learned during adolescence, the learner must be willing to submit to new language rules and norms and be able to tolerate the ridicule of peers for second language errors. Often the consolidation of personality during adolescence makes bilingualism an impossibility, whereas there is an openness in children that allows them to tolerate language learning in themselves and others.

It is important to note that these issues are interrelated; and other issues involved in child bilingualism are not discussed in this paper. It is felt that a review of the most salient issues rather than a comprehensive discussion of child bilingualism would provide some insight and coherence to the current state of knowledge. Accordingly, information from a wide variety of disciplines and a diverse number of language combinations was drawn together.

To summarize, child language acquisition has begun to receive widespread attention from investigators in a variety of disciplines. Child bilingualism, however, a more complex form of language acquisition, has not received the same kind of attention. This may be because researchers have found themselves confronted with both general questions about what constitutes bilingualism and many specific misconceptions surrounding child bilingualism. In this paper, an attempt is made to provide a definition of bilingualism and summarize some of the major issues in child bilingualism. Thus bilingualism was defined as encoding and decoding skills in two languages. Further, a continuum of ability to encode or decode in two languages was presented. This conceptual scheme led to a discussion of the linguistic complexity involved in the acquisition of two languages by children.

In addition, three issues in child bilingualism were addressed: (*a*) linguistic interactions: (*b*) the relationship between child bilingualism and cognitive development; and (*c*) strategies for implementing bilingualism. With respect to the first issue, it was argued that linguistic interaction or mixing two languages is not reflective of lack of fluency. The importance of early separation of linguistic systems was also discussed. As for the second issue, literature was summarized that suggested a positive and facilitory effect of child bilingualism on cognitive development. Finally, a *one person-one language* strategy was proposed as the best possible way to instruct children in two languages. It was also argued that instruction in two languages should begin early for both neurological and social modeling reasons.

REFERENCE NOTES

1. Swain, M.K. *Bilingualism as a first language* . Unpublished doctoral dissertation. University of California, Irvine, 1972.
2. Ianco-Worrall, A. *Bilingualism and cognitive development*. Unpublished doctoral dissertation. Cornell University, 1970.
3. Fantini, A. *Language acquisition of a bilingual child: A sociolinguistic perspective*. Unpublished doctoral dissertation. University of Texas at Austin, 1974.

REFERENCES

Bain, B. Bilingualism and cognition: Toward a general theory. In S. Cary (Ed.), *Bilingualism, biculturalism, and education.* Edmonton, Alberta: University of Alberta Press, 1974.

Brown, R. *A first language: The early stages.* Cambridge, Mass.: Harvard University Press, 1973.

Darcy, N.T. A review of the literature on the effect of bilingualism upon the measurement of intelligence. *Journal of Genetic Psychology,* 1953, *82,* 21-57.

Darcy, N.T. Bilingualism and the measurement of intelligence: Review of a decade of research. *Journal of Genetic Psychology,* 1963, *103,* 259-282.

Feldman, C., & Shen, M. Some language-related cognitive advantages of bilingual five year olds. *Journal of Genetic Psychology,* 1971, *118,* 235-244.

Fishman, J.A. *Sociolinguistics: A brief introduction.* Rowley, Mass: Newbury House, 1970.

Gumperz, J.J. Verbal strategies in multilingual communication. *Report on the twenty-first annual round table meeting on linguistics and language studies.* Washington, D.C.: Georgetown University, 1970.

Gumperz, J.J., & Hernandez, E. Bilingualism, bidialectalism, and classroom interaction. In C. Cazden, V.P. John, & D. Hymes (Eds.), *The function of language in the classroom.* New York: Teachers College Press, 1972.

Hymes, D. Models of interaction of language and social setting. *Journal of Social Issues,* 1967, *23,* 8-28.

Ianco-Worrall, A. Bilingualism and cognitive development. *Child Development,* 1972, *43,* 1390-1400.

Imedadze, N.V. On the psychological nature of child speech formation under condition of exposure to two languages. *International Journal of Psychology,* 1967, *2,* 129-132.

Kelley, L.G. *Description and measurement of bilingualism: An international seminar.* Toronto: University of Toronto Press, 1969.

Kolers, P.A. Reading and talking bilingually. *American Journal of Psychology,* 1966, *79,* 357-376.

Leopold, W. *Speech development of a bilingual child: A linguists' record.* Vol. 1: *Vocabulary growth in the first two years,* 1939. Vol. 2: *Sound learning in the first two years,* 1945. Vol. 3: *Grammars and general problems in the first two years,* 1949(a). Vol. 4: *Diary from age two,* 1949(b). Evanston, Illinois: Northwestern University Press.

Lindholm, K.J., & Padilla, A.M. Linguistic interaction in bilingual children. *Journal of Child Language,* in press.

Macnamara, J. The bilingual's linguistic performance – A psychological overview. *Journal of Social Issues,* 1967, *23,* 58-77.

Padilla, A.M., & Liebman, E. Language acquisition in the bilingual child. *The Bilingual Review/La Revista Bilingüe,* 1975, *2,* 34-55.

Padilla, A.M., & Lindholm, K.J. Acquisition of bilingualism: An analysis of the linguistic structures of Spanish-English speaking children. In G.D. Keller, R.V. Techner, & S. Viera (Eds.), *Bilingualism in the bicentennial and beyond.* New York: Bilingual Press, 1976.

Padilla, A.M., & Lindholm, K.J. Development of interrogative, negative and possessive forms in the speech of young Spanish/English bilinguals. *The Bilingual Review/La Revista Bilingüe,* in press.

Padilla, A.M., & Ruiz, R.A. *Latino mental health: A review of literature.* Washington, D.C.: U.S. Government Printing Office, 1973.

Peal, E., & Lambert, W. The relation of bilingualism to intelligence. *Psychological Monographs,* 1962, *76,* 1-23.

Penfield, W., & Roberts, L. *Speech and brain mechanisms.* Princeton, N.J.: Princeton University Press, 1959.

Ronjat, L. *Le développement du language observé chez un enfant bilingue.* Paris: Champion, 1913.

Skinner, B.F. *Verbal behavior*. New York: Appleton-Century-Crofts, 1957.

Swain, M., & Wesche, M. Linguistic interaction: Case study of a bilingual child. *Language Sciences*, 1975, *37*, 17-22.

Taylor, I. *Introduction to psycholinguistics*. New York: Holt, Rinehart, and Winston, 1976.

Weinreich, U. *Languages in contact*. New York: Linguistic Circle of New York, 1953.

CHAPTER 9

BILINGUAL MEMORY RESEARCH: IMPLICATIONS FOR BILINGUAL EDUCATION

MIKE LÓPEZ

University of Minnesota

The widespread initiation of bilingual education programs in public schools is probably the most significant development toward improving the education of Chicanos in the past century. As programs have proliferated, the demand for teachers trained in bilingual education has increased, and this has led to the initiation of bilingual teacher education programs in many colleges and universities.

One unfortunate consequence of the rapidly growing popularity of bilingual education has been the increased classroom and consultation workload of specialists in the field, resulting in concentration on practical problems and pragmatic solutions and consequent neglect of the development of theoretical aspects of bilingual education. Research into psychological foundations of bilingualism and bilingual education has largely been ignored by workers in the area. Except for the work of Ramirez and Castañeda (1974), no truly significant theoretical advance in the foundations of bilingual education has been made in the past decade.

Research into the theoretical aspects of bilingualism has been carried on in recent years by linguists and psychologists. Rather than making any real contribution to bilingual education, however, developments in linguistics and psychology at best have largely been ignored by bilingual educators and misunderstood or misapplied at worst. The purpose of this paper is to examine some of the popular misconceptions about bilingualism, to demonstrate how linguists, psychologists, and bilingual educators may have contributed to the development of these misconceptions, and finally to propose a modern conceptualization of bilingual semantic memory that should help to resolve some current theoretical problems in the area of bilingual memory.

Central to most of the misunderstandings of the working of the bilingual mind are the concepts of compound and coordinate bilingualism. These concepts have been at the center of discussions of bilingualism for the past 20 years, but, as Diller (1970) pointed out, they have never been well defined. The following is a composite, consensus definition of compound and coordinate bilingualism gleaned from several different sources (Ervin & Osgood, 1954; Haugen, 1956; Macnamara, 1967; Weinreich, 1953): Compound bilinguals acquire both languages in the same environmental context; for example, both may have been spoken in the home by the same people. A corresponding pair of words in the two languages (translation equivalents) thereby come to acquire the same meaning. That is, since both words have been used to refer to the same object, both words acquire the meaning represented by that referent. Coordinate bilinguals, on the other hand, have acquired two languages in different contexts, for example, one language at home and the second in school; and because of this, the corresponding terms in the two languages have different referents. The relationship between words and their referents in compound and coordinate bilingualism is illustrated in Figure 1.

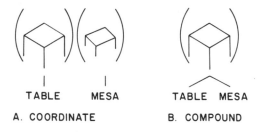

TABLE   MESA   TABLE   MESA

A. COORDINATE   B. COMPOUND

FIGURE 1. Coordinate and compound bilingual representation.

The concepts of compound and coordinate bilingualism had an impact on the structure of many bilingual education programs (Michel, 1967; Gaarder, 1967, 1970). Much of this impact, however, was based not on what compound and coordinate bilingualism have to say about the representations of individual words in a bilingual's memory, but on speculative conclusions about other aspects of a compound or coordinate bilingual's cognitive abilities, and even about aspects of personality in compound versus coordinate bilinguals. Most of these conclusions were based on a misunderstanding of the concepts as they were originally proposed by Weinreich (1953); they will be explored later in this chapter.

The best way to illustrate the extent to which the concepts of compound and coordinate bilingualism have been extended is to quote what various authorities have said about the two types of bilingual individuals. Saville and Troike (1971) in the *Handbook of Bilingual Education* maintain that "The compound bilingual. . . formulates his thoughts first in one language (usually his native one) and then goes through a high-speed translation process into the second language. Similarly, messages received in the second language are translated back into the first language before their meaning can be apprehended [p. 18] ." This opinion is echoed by another author who states "The compound bilingual (if we can call him a bilingual) first encodes his message in his mother tongue, then restates it . . . in the second language . . . . The compound bilingual never experiences the intellectual freedom and satisfaction of expressing his thought directly in the second language [Brooks, 1969, p. 308] ." The Clearinghouse on Early Childhood Education (1971) of the ERIC system states that "The compound bilingual has a single language system. He mixes both languages unknowingly . . . . Psycholinguists generally agree that the coordinate bilingual is probably less confused using two languages than is the compound bilingual [pp. 12, 13] ." Another author states "It is presumed that there is less mental interference in the coordinate system than in the compound system [Cardenas, 1971, p. 168] ."

Such statements led to the notion, formulated by various authorities (Dugas, 1967; John & Horner, 1971; Michel, 1967; UNESCO, 1963), that the coordinate bilingual is the ideal product of bilingual education. These statements are probably responsible for the feeling among many teachers of Chicano children that bilingualism is a liability and a source of mental confusion. Teachers of Chicano children, who were interviewed by Carter (1970) in his study of Mexican Americans in school and were quoted as saying that bilingualism "is confusing because one has to translate one language into another. . ." and "You have to think in two languages and translate from one to the other... [Carter, 1970, p. 51] ." Perhaps these statements illustrate this type of sentiment best.

There seems to be a general feeling that a bilingual automatically translates from one language to the other, or as stated in the psychological literature (Goggin & Wickens, 1971), from the nondominant to the dominant language. A corollary to this belief is the idea that bilingualism causes some sort of mental confusion and interference with normal cognitive processes. Let us see what available evidence exists about these notions.

The literature on the intelligence of bilingual children has been surveyed elsewhere (Jensen, 1962; Padilla & Ruiz, 1973), and this paper will have nothing to add to this topic other than to reiterate the general conclusion: Other things being equal, bilingual children are not at an intellectual disadvantage relative to monolinguals.

The notion that speaking two languages might interfere with a Chicano bilingual's ability to perform in a school situation was tested in a study reported recently (López, Note 1). This study compared the grade point averages and ACT scores of Mexican-American college students with varying degrees of fluency in English and Spanish, ranging from English monolinguals to bilinguals fluent in both languages. Contrary to the interference expectations, absolutely no differences in obtained grade point averages or ACT scores were found between any of the groups. However, it should be pointed out that negative results do not conclusively demonstrate that interference does not play a role in academic success.

The notion of bilingual interference probably arose from a misunderstanding of the concept of linguistic interference first proposed by Weinreich (1953). He defined it as being "those instances of deviation from the norms of either language which occur in the speech of bilinguals as a result of their familiarity with more than one language. . . . The term interference implies the rearrangement of patterns that result from the introduction of foreign elements into the more highly structured domains of language, such as the bulk of the phonemic system, a large part of the morphology and syntax, and some areas of the vocabulary [p. 1]." Certainly, this is a very clinical, innocuous description of the speech of many Chicano bilinguals. Fishman (1968), however, attacked the orientation of many linguists and educators who saw interference as something deleterious and harmful, to be avoided at all costs (cf. Haugen, 1970).

In point of fact, linguistic interference is not interference at all. There is no interference with the primary purpose of language — communication. A heavy foreign accent does not interfere with the ability to understand a nonnative speaker, even though the speaker may manifest a great deal of phonological interference. In many cases, lexical or vocabulary interference may even facilitate communication. Gumperz and Hernandez (1969) provided excellent examples of linguistically motivated code switches that might be considered instances of lexical interference where one or two words of English are inserted into ongoing Spanish. As a result, this behavior smooths the flow of communication, which is certainly not interference with communication.

Another phenomenon often found in the Spanish of many Chicano bilinguals is the use of words such as *lonche*, *taipiar*, and *brekas*, which is often cited as one of the worst examples of linguistic interference caused by languages in contact. Other linguists, however, point out that it is difficult, if not impossible, to specify which instances of lexical transfer from one language to the other are interference and which are actually some form of integration of these lexical items into the other code (Mackey, 1970). There is evidence of a growing tendency among sociolinguists to accept words that might once have been called instances of phonological and lexical interference in the speech of Chicano bilinguals as instances of integration into the Chicano Spanish dialect (Hernandez-Chavez, Cohen, & Beltramo, 1975; Saville-Troike, 1976). For these reasons, some linguists have suggested that the term *interference* be exchanged for another, possibly *transfer* or *enrichment* (Haugen, 1970).

A second notion, based partly on the compound-coordinate distinction, is that bilinguals develop some mechanism to perform high speed translation from their first language to their second. This idea has been proposed and supported by several psychologists (Tulving & Colotla, 1970; Goggin & Wickens, 1971) and used to explain some aspects of bilingual memory, notably the bilingual equivalence effect. A well-known phenomenon in the area of verbal learning is that the repetition of a word in a list presented for free recall will result in an increase in the probability that that word will be recalled. The presentation of the translation of a word in a mixed-language free recall list will result in an increase in the probability of recall equal to that obtained when the word is repeated in the same language (Kolers, 1966a). This bilingual equivalence effect has been explained in terms of a model of bilingual memory in which the presentation of a word and its translation activate the same representation in memory. In essence, this is a compound system. In other studies, Kolers (1963, 1966b) demonstrated that it is quite unlikely that bilinguals automatically translate each language into the other as it is presented. In one study, Kolers (1963) found that the associations given to a stimulus word were not the same in both languages, as would be expected if subjects were automatically translating all linguistic input. In another experiment Kolers (1966b) had subjects read either unilingual passages in English or French or mixed-language passages in which the word order was English or French. A comprehension test was given following the reading of the passage. It was expected that the necessary translating of the mixed-language passages into one language (or the constant code switching if translation was not required) would be reflected in a lower comprehension score for subjects in the mixed-language condition. In fact, there was no difference in comprehension scores following silent reading of unilingual or mixed-language passages, a finding that makes it difficult to believe that subjects waste any information-processing capacity in a bilingual situation on switching back and forth or translating between languages.

Despite the previous findings, the idea that the translation habit involves translation from the weaker language to the dominant language has persisted in the psychological literature. For most Chicano high school students, such a situation would mean that they automatically translate Spanish into English, but not English into Spanish. A study conducted by López and Young (1974) directly attacked the notion of unidirectional translation. Figure 2 presents part of the design of the experiment. Bilinguals were first asked to read a list of English or

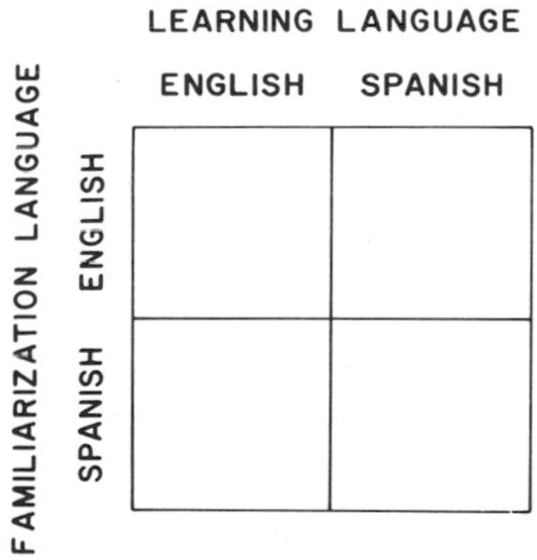

FIGURE 2. Design of the López and Young (1974) bilingual familiarization experiment.

Spanish words. Then, without knowing about it beforehand, they were asked to learn by free recall a list composed of either the same words as those in the first list or the same words translated. If bilinguals actually did translate from Spanish to English, having them read a list of Spanish words and later asking them to learn those words translated into English should be equivalent to having them read a list of English words and later asking them to learn those words in a free recall list. On the other hand, reading a list of English words and then learning the Spanish translations should not be the same as reading Spanish words and then learning those words, because the unidirectional translation hypothesis holds that there should be no translation from English to Spanish. In fact, the effect of familiarization in this study was uniform; both within and between languages there was no differential facilitation. The results (Koler, 1966a ,1968) indicated that the same unitary memory representation was activated by a word or by its translation.

The two misconceptions discussed thus far, mental interference caused by bilingualism and automatic translation from one language to the other, have their roots in the concepts of compound and coordinate bilingualism and the way these concepts have been misunderstood and misapplied. We turn now to an examination of these concepts.

Weinreich (1953) is usually given credit for originating the classifications of compound and coordinate bilingualism, although he was preceded by others (de Saussure, 1915). Weinreich proposed that the relationship between a pair of translation equivalents and their meaning could be characterized in one of three ways. Coordinate pairs would have separate *signifiers* and *signifieds* (a signifier can be thought of as a word and a signified as the meaning of that word). Compound pairs would have two signifiers but only one compounded signified. A third type of bilingual sign would be the subordinate. Subordinate pairs are the result of learning a new word in a second language by the so-called "indirect method" of translation. A subordinate pair might be produced, for example, in a foreign language class when a student learns that the word *Pferd* means *horse*, but the new word is never applied to any real-life referents. The meaning of a subordinate word acquired in this manner can then be accessed only through the original word. Figure 3 illustrates all three types of signs.

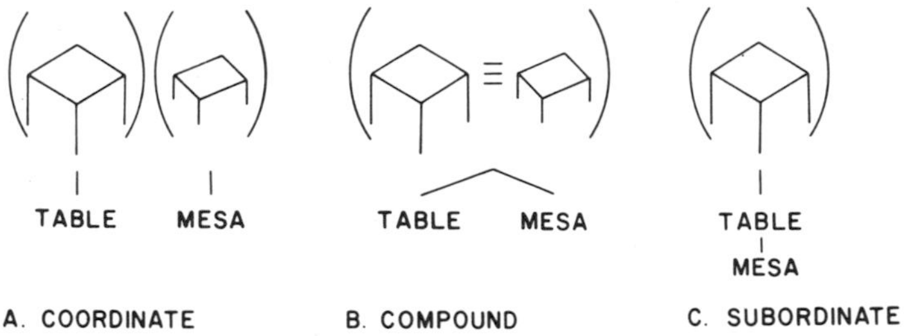

TABLE MESA	TABLE MESA	TABLE
		MESA
A. COORDINATE	B. COMPOUND	C. SUBORDINATE

FIGURE 3. Weinreich's (1953) bilingual classifications. From *Languages in Contact*, by U. Weinreich. [Copyright 1974 by Mouton and Co. Adapted by permission.]

Weinreich made it explicit that some signs of the same speaker may be compound while others are not. Moreover, he speculated that an originally coordinate sign may become compound through experience with the word in different surroundings. This speculation is a marked contrast to later authors who write in terms of coordinate or compound language systems, permanently fixed and determined by the language acquisition experience of each bilingual.

In 1954, Ervin and Osgood modified the Weinreich scheme in a way that has become almost universally accepted by later writers. They reasoned that, in both the compound and subordinate systems, words in a translation-equivalent pair are associated with the same set of representational mediation processes, or meaning, and that they are subsumed by the subordinate classification into the compound. That is, in both the subordinate and compound signs, the meaning of the word *table* is exactly the same as the meaning of the corresponding word *mesa* (as opposed to the coordinate sign where the corresponding words do not have the same meaning). Ervin and Osgood thus concluded that the compound and subordinate signs were isomorphic. Scientific parsimony would require that the two classifications, compound and subordinate, be merged into one classification. But merging required an accompanying change in the supposed language acquisition experiences hypothesized to produce compound bilinguals, so that Ervin and Osgood were forced to say that compound bilingualism was the result of growing up in a home where two languages were spoken interchangeably by the same speakers *or* the result of learning a foreign language in school by the traditional, "indirect" method. The "true bilingual" they go on to say, is the coordinate who has learned to speak one language at home and the other at school or work.

The compound-coordinate distinction went through additional attempts at reformulation. Lambert (1969) and Lambert and Rawlings (1969), for example, maintained that compound bilinguals acquire both languages in their homes before they begin school, and coordinates begin second-language learning after they enter school. This definition is almost impossible to reconcile with Ervin and Osgood's (1954) because Lambert makes no apparent distinction between second-language acquisition by traditional methods in a classroom and in a totally second-language environment.

This constant reformulation of the original Weinreich (1953) classification probably caused the unfortunate explanation of the two concepts to appear in the bilingual education literature, as found in *A Handbook of Bilingual Education*, by Saville and Troike (1971). This book is a required text in many bilingual education courses throughout the nation. On page 17 is an illustration of compound and coordinate bilingualism, reproduced as Figure 4. Notice that the figure labeled *coordinate* is *compound*, by Weinreich's (1953) definition, and the figure labeled *compound* is *subordinate*. In retrospect, it is easy to understand how this type of misunderstanding could occur. Certainly the figure labeled *compound* would be accurate if it were pointed out that this figure represented only part of the compound classification established by Ervin and Osgood (1954) and that this was defined as *subordinate* by Weinreich (1953). Given the Saville and Troike (1971) explanation of compound bilingualism, it is easy to see how the idea arose that compound bilinguals have to translate from the first to the second language and can never access meaning directly in the second language (Brooks, 1969; Cardenas, 1970; Carter, 1970). Given this misunderstanding of compound bilingualism, it is not surprising that many authorities in the field of bilingual education have characterized the coordinate bilingual as the only "true" bilingual (Clearinghouse on Early

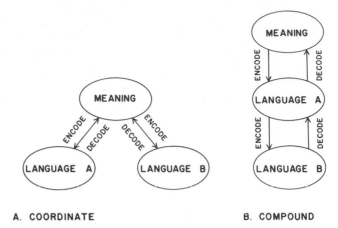

A. COORDINATE   B. COMPOUND

FIGURE 4. Saville and Troike's (1971) compound and coordinate bilingual representations. [From *A Handbook of Bilingual Education*, by M.R. Saville and R.C. Troike. Copyright 1971 by TESOL. Adapted by permission.]

Childhood Education, 1971; Dugas, 1967; John & Horner, 1971 ; Michel, 1967; UNESCO, 1963).

In light of this uncertainty about the definition of compound and coordinate bilingualism, we must ask, "Just how valid is this distinction?" A careful review of the psychological literature bearing on the subject suggests that it is not very valid at all.

The theoretical distinction between compound and coordinate bilingualism rested on a fragile empirical foundation (Lambert, 1969). After reviewing the relevant research, Macnamara (1967) concluded that the distinction was weak. He later (Macnamara, 1970) joined Diller (1970) in agreeing that the distinction was at best a conceptual artifact and expressed concern about the inferences concerning cognitive structures and personality differences among bilinguals based on the compound-coordinate distinction (Diebold, 1968). More recent research by investigators using short-term memory techniques has also failed to support the distinction (Dillon, McCormack, Patrusic, Cook, & Lafleur, 1973).

The basic problem with the compound-coordinate distinction is that it proposes that the language and semantic memory *systems* of a bilingual must be one or the other. Weinreich (1953), on the other hand, stated that the same person could have both types of representations for different words. Although the distinction could actually be a continuum from extreme compound to extreme coordinate, and a bilingual could lie anywhere on the continuum, most theory and research has emphasized compound or coordinate language systems, with their attendant cognitive consequences.

The supposed consequences of being either compound or coordinate lie behind educators' proposals that a coordinate bilingual system should be the ideal product of a bilingual education program. This goal has been present, either explicitly or implicity, in the structure of many bilingual education programs (Gaarder, 1967, 1970; Michel, 1967) in which certain subjects are taught in one language and other subjects are taught in the second language. However, rather than achieving the goal of producing true, balanced bilinguals, these programs may in fact be creating a type of diglossia (Ferguson, 1964) in which one language is appropriate for certain situations but not for others.

Recent developments in psychological theories of semantic memory (Anderson & Bower, 1973; Quillian, 1968, 1969; Rumelhart, Lindsay, & Norman, 1972; Smith, Shoben, & Rips, 1975) have provided a possible resolution of the compound-coordinate problem. In many of these models, the meaning of a word or concept is expressed in terms of a set of features or associations that may converge upon a single locus or node in memory. The actual word (a lexical entry) is stored in a separate lexicon with a pointer leading to the semantic locus. In the Rumelhart *et al.* (1972) model, for example, most of the meaning of a concept is captured in the form of three types of functional relations, ". . .the classes to which a concept belongs (i.e., its supersets), the characteristics which define it as a member of that class, and the examples or subsets of that concept [p. 203]." Rumelhart *et al.* (1972) use the notation *is a* to define set membership and the notation *has* or *is* to represent characteristics.

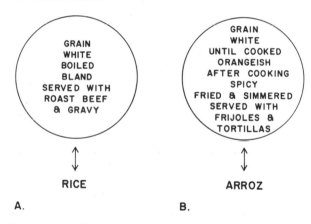

FIGURE 5. Possible features of the words *rice* and *arroz*.

The meaning that an individual might associate with the word *rice* might be represented as in Figure 5A. Rice is a grain, is white, is boiled, is bland, and is served with roast beef and gravy. *Arroz*, Figure 5B, is also a grain, but is white only until cooked, when it becomes orangeish, is spicy, is fried, then simmered, and is served with frijoles and tortillas. These are not, of course, exhaustive definitions of the terms. Notice that there is a certain degree of overlap in the attributes of the two words, *arroz* and *rice*. That is, there is some commonality of meaning that might be represented as in Figure 6A. In a similar fashion, all translation equivalents in two languages have some overlap of meaning ranging from almost total overlap

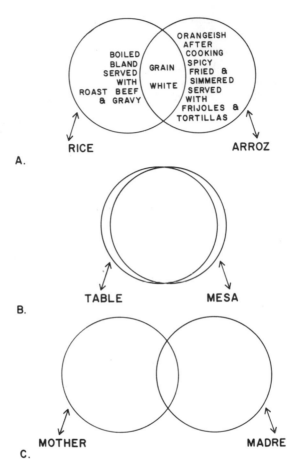

FIGURE 6. An overlapping features conceptualization of the representation of a word and its translation in bilingual memory.

to practically no overlap at all. (There must be some overlap, otherwise the words would not be translation equivalents.) This conceptualization, of course, is not a totally new idea, but rather a reformulation of Weinreich's original idea in the light of new theoretical developments.

The present conceptualization of the relationship between a word in one language and its translation in the other language explains results in bilingual memory research that are otherwise difficult to integrate into a theoretical model. The bilingual equivalence effect, for example (Kolers, 1966a; Lopez & Young, 1974) should be produced only when there is such an overlap of attributes that the presentation of the translation of a word activates a critical number of the attributes of that word. It should not be produced when there is not sufficient overlap, although there should be some increase in probability of recall similar to that which occurs when synonyms are presented in a free-recall list. The same line of reasoning would explain why some pairs of words would produce translation equivalents as high frequency associates and other pairs would not (Kolers, 1963; Lambert, 1969). Finally, the present conceptualization would explain why there is often confusion between translation-equivalent pairs when one word is presented in one list and its translation is presented in a subsequent list. All the common attributes have been activated, and it is difficult to pick one or the other word as the correct response solely on the basis of a "language tag" (López, Hicks, & Young, 1974).

With this conceptualization, the compound-coordinate distinction no longer makes any theoretical sense. It is interesting that the subordinate type of representation becomes a viable possibility. This type of representation is illustrated in Figure 7A, where a word and its translation activate exactly the same meaning, but the mode of access is different. That is, the subordinate word does not access the semantic network directly but only through another word in the lexicon. Words acquired through direct association with their translations in the other language should be only a small subset of the vocabulary of any bilingual.

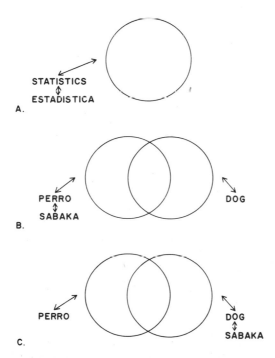

FIGURE 7. Subordinate bilingualism in terms of the overlapping features conceptualization.

The conceptualization of subordinate representations in memory is testable. Consider Figures 7B and 7C. If the words *dog* and *perro* constitute a compound pair, and *sabaka* is learned as the translation equivalent of *perro*, then it should take a measurably longer time to produce the English translation of *sabaka* than the Spanish translation. The opposite would be predicted if *sabaka* is learned as the translation of *dog*.

The importance of this new conceptualization of bilingual memory and the debunking of the compound-coordinate distinction for the education of Chicano bilinguals should be obvious. With the invalidation of the compound-coordinate distinction, the stigmatization of the so-called compound bilingual child who grows up speaking both languages in the home as being less than a "true" bilingual would no longer have a legitimate basis in psychological, linguistic, or educational theory. The insistence of so-called authorities that language switching in the middle of a conversation is to be avoided as a symptom of some underlying mental interference would also lose whatever theoretical support it may have had. The energies expended in trying to produce coordinate bilinguals as the ideal product of bilingual education could then be directed to more important endeavors.

REFERENCE NOTE

1. López, M. Linguistic interference and the academic achievement of Mexican-Americans. Paper presented at the meeting of the Rocky Mountain Psychological Association, Salt Lake City, May, 1975.

REFERENCES

Anderson, J.R., & Bower, G.H. *Human associative memory*. Washington, D.C.: V.H. Winston, 1973.

Brooks, N. The meaning of bilingualism today. *Foreign Language Annals*, 1969, *2*, 304-409.

Cardenas, D.N. Compound and coordinate bilingualism/biculturalism in the Southwest. In R.W. Ewton, Jr. & J. Ornstein (Eds.), *Studies in language and linguistics 1973*. El Paso, Tex.: Texas Western Press, 1972.

Carter, T.P. *Mexican-Americans in school: A history of educational neglect*. New York: CEEB, 1970.

Clearinghouse on early childhood education. *Early childhood programs for non-English speaking children*. Urbana, Ill.: ERIC, 1971.

de Saussure, F. Course in general linguistics. (W. Baskin, Trans.). New York: Philosophical Library, 1959. (French original, 1915.)

Diebold, R.A. The consequences of early bilingualism in cognitive development and personality formation. In E. Norbeck, D. Price-Williams & W.M. McCord (Eds.), *The Study of personality: An interdisciplinary appraisal*. New York: Holt, Rinehart, and Winston, 1968.

Diller, K.C. "Compound" and "coordinate" bilingualism: A conceptual artifact. *Word*, 1970, *26*, 254-261.

Dillon, R.F., McCormack, P.D., Patrusic, W.M., Cook, G.M., & Lafleur, L. Release from proactive interferences in compound and coordinate bilinguals. *Bulletin of the Psychonomic Society*, 1973, *2*, 293-294.

Dugas, D. *Research relevant to the development of bilingual curricula*. Report presented at the Annual Conference of Foreign Language Teachers, El Paso, Texas, November, 1967. ERIC Document Reproduction Service No. ED 018 298.

Ervin, S.M., & Osgood, C.E. Second-language learning and bilingualism. *Journal of Abnormal and Social Psychology* (Supplement), 1954, *49*, 139-146.

Ferguson, C.A. Diglossia. In D. Hymes (Ed.), *Language in culture and society*. New York: Harper and Row, 1964.

Fishman, J.A. Sociolinguistic perspective on the study of bilingualism. *Linguistics*, 1968, *39*, 21-49.

Gaarder, A.B. Organization of the bilingual school. *Journal of Social Issues*, 1967, *23*, 110-120.

Gaarder, A.B. The first seventy-six bilingual education projects. In J.E. Alatis (Ed.), Bilingualism and language contact. *Georgetown University Monograph Series on Languages and Linguistics*, No. 23, 1970.

Goggin, J., & Wickens, D.D. Proactive interference and language change in short-term memory. *Journal of Verbal Learning and Verbal Behavior*, 1971, *10*, 453-458.

Gumperz, J.J., & Hernandez, E. Cognitive aspects of bilingual communication. *Working Paper No. 28*, Berkeley: University of California. Language Behavior Research Laboratory, 1969.

Haugen, E. *Bilingualism in the Americas*. University, Alabama: American Dialect Society, 1956.

Haugen, E. Linguistics and dialinguistics. In J.E. Alatis (Ed.), *Bilingualism and language contact. Georgetown University Monograph Series on Languages and Linguistics*, No. *23*, 1970.

Hernandez-Chavez, E., Cohen, A.D., & Beltramo, A.F. (Eds.), *El lenguaje de los Chicanos: Regional and social characteristics of language used by Mexican-Americans*. Arlington, Va.: Center for Applied Linguistics, 1975.

Jensen, J.V. Effects of childhood bilingualism. *Elementary English*, 1962, *34*, 132-143; 358-366.

John, V.P., & Horner, V.M. *Early childhood bilingual education*. New York: Modern Language Association of America, 1971.

Kolers, P.A. Interlingual word associations. *Journal of Verbal Learning and Verbal Behavior*, 1963, *2*, 291-300.

Kolers, P.A. Interlingual facilitation of short-term memory. *Journal of Verbal Learning and Verbal Behavior*, 1966, *5*, 314-319. (a)

Kolers, P.A. Reading and talking bilingually. *American Journal of Psychology*, 1966, *79*, 357-376. (b)

Kolers, P.A. Bilingualism and information processing. *Scientific American*, 1968, *218*, 78-89.

Lambert, W.E. Psychological studies of the interdependencies of the bilingual's two languages. In J. Puhvel (Ed.), *Substance and structure of language*. Los Angeles: University of California Press, 1969.

Lambert, W.E., & Rawlings, C. Bilingual processing of mixed-language associative networks. *Journal of Verbal Learning and Verbal Behavior*, 1969, *8*, 604-609.

López, M., Hicks, R.E., & Young, R.K. The linguistic interdependence of bilinguals. *Journal of Experimental Psychology*, 1974, *102*, 981-983.

Mackey, W.F. Interference, integration and the synchronic fallacy. In J.E. Alatis (Ed.), Bilingualism and language contact. *Georgetown University Monograph Series on Language and Linguistics*, No. 23, 1970.

Macnamara, J. The bilingual's linguistic performance: A psychological overview. *Journal of Social Issues*, 1967, *23*, 58-77.

Macnamara, J. Bilingualism and thought. In J.E. Alatis (Ed.), *Bilingualism and language contact. Georgetown University Monograph Series on Languages and Linguistics*, No. 23, 1970.

Michel, J. Tentative guidelines for a bilingual curriculum. *Florida F L Reporter*, 1967, 5, 13-16.

Padilla, A.M., & Ruiz, R.A. *Latino mental health, a review of literature*. Washington, D.C.: U.S. Government Printing Office, 1973.

Quillian, M.R. Semantic memory. In M. Minsky (Ed.), *Semantic information processing*. Cambridge, Mass.: Massachusettes Institute of Technology Press, 1968.

Quillian, M.R. The teachable language comprehender. *Communications of the Association for Computing Machinery*, 1969, *12*, 459-476.

Ramirez, M. III, & Castañeda, A. *Cultural democracy, bicognitive development and education*. New York: Academic Press, 1974.

140 Mike López

Rumelhart, D.E., Lindsay, P.H., & Norman, D.A. A process of model for long-term memory. In E. Tulving & W. Donaldson (Eds.), *Organization of memory*. New York: Academic Press, 1972.

Saville, M.R., & Troike, R.C. *A handbook of bilingual education*. Washington, D.C.: TESOL. 1971.

Saville-Troike, M.R. *Foundations for teaching English as a second language*. Englewood Cliffs, N.J.: Prentice-Hall, 1976.

Smith, K.E., Shoben, E.J., & Rips, L.J. Structure and process in semantic memory: A feature model for semantic decisions. *Psychological Review*, 1974, *81*, 214-241.

Tulving, E., & Colotla, V.A. Free recall of trilingual lists. *Cognitive Psychology*, 1970, *1*, 86-98.

UNESCO. *Foreign languages in primary education: The teaching of foreign or second languages to younger children*. Hamburg: UNESCO Institute for Education, 1963.

Weinreich, U. Languages in Contact. *Publications of the Linguistic Circle of New York*, No. 1, 1953.

CHAPTER 10

THE STUDY OF EARLY CHILDHOOD BILINGUALISM: STRATEGIES FOR LINGUISTIC TRANSFER RESEARCH

EUGENE E. GARCIA

University of California, Santa Barbara

Prior to a discussion of investigatory strategies in early childhood bilingualism, it seems appropriate to comment on the scientific and social motivations for such research that will add to our undestanding of empirical phenomean. Language acquisition and bilingual acquisition (especially transfer effects) are but one of many of these. Yet it is impossible to separate scientific interest from social practice. Many people throughout the world are practicing bilingualism (Sorensen, 1967; U.S. Commission on Civil Rights, 1974); and there is no doubt that bilingualism will continue to exist. For example, Skarbanek (1970) reported the continued use of both Spanish and English along the southwestern border of the United States. He concluded that variables which might account for the continued maintenance of two languages seem to be stable. Since bilingualism is so predominant and seems to be here to stay, why is so little known of the phenomenon in this country? Haugen (1972) best characterized the answer in his discussion of social acceptance or nonacceptance of bilingualism: "In some countries bilingualism is considered a high attribute, in other countries (our own), bilingualism is a social stigma." For young children, bilingualism is too often considered an educational, intellectual, and linguistic liability.

With respect to linguistic research, it seems legitimate to counter pervasive negative attitudes with strong empirical work to delineate the exact relationship between bilingualism and the variables associated with language acquisition. Recent research in early bilingual development has taken on the methods of other psycholinguistic studies of early language acquisition: (*a*) Language samples are gathered over a reasonable period of time from the same children; (*b*) these samples are analyzed phonologically, morphologically, syntactically, and semantically for developmental changes correlated with age; and (*c*) most important, an analysis of language transfer is performed to indicate if, when, and how errors in either language might indicate transfer of forms between the two languages. This work is best exemplified by Ervin-Tripp (1973), Dulay and Burt (1972), and Padilla and Liebman (1975). In each of these reports, several bilingual children were observed to ascertain the linguistic acquisition modes for each language. Error patterns in language productions were identified to provide some analysis of interlanguage transfer. A contrastive analysis of Spanish and English in conjunction with this type of analysis has allowed Padilla and Liebman (1975), in particular, to make the conclusion that during early acquisition, languages tend to develop simultaneously but independently, with little or no phonological, morphological, syntactic, or semantic transfer. This form of research produces tentative conclusions because of the basic correlational nature of the method.

Two additional and experimental strategies are also available: (*a*) "No-Difference" research; and (*b*) "Language Manipulation" research. The first is a blend of naturalistic and experimental strategies, and it may be considered somewhat defensive. It typically provides evidence of "no-difference" (no difference between monolinguals and bilinguals) across a series of language tasks. This approach specifically asks: "Does learning two languages place the child at a language disadvantage or advantage?" The second strategy is more manipulative or experimental in nature. It manipulates one language while concomitantly assessing the effects of this manipulation (and change) on another language. This approach addresses the question: "If the child is learning a second language, what effect will this learning have on the first?" Each of these strategies is empirically sound, one directly attacks the notion of bilingual liability; the other may also do so, but it is primarily concerned with interactions that occur during language acquisition (positive or negative).

"No-Difference" Research

Carrow (1971, 1972) concentrated on the receptive language capabilities of bilingual Spanish-English children. Using a standardized set of stimulus cards portraying differential morphological and syntactic forms in each language, she investigated the acquisition of Spanish and English. In addition, she compared English receptive competence for bilingual and monolingual subjects from ages 3 to 7. Although the results of these studies are difficult to generalize, they seem to indicate that both languages showed developmental increases across the dependent measures assessed, but children were heterogenous with respect to this development. That is, some children scored higher in English than Spanish while others scored higher in Spanish than English. A comparison of monolinguals with bilinguals on English measures also indicated a superior competence for monolinguals up to the age of 7; at this age no significant difference in English receptive competence between these groups was observed.

Evans (1974) reported the comparison of word-pair discriminations and word imitations in Spanish and English between monolingual, English, and bilingual Spanish-English children. On these tasks, bilinguals did not differ from monolinguals on English tasks. Harris and Hassemer (1972) reported similar results from investigating the effects of modeling on sentence complexity in English monolinguals and Spanish-English bilinguals. Complex sentences (in terms of word length) were modeled in both languages for bilingual subjects. These models similarly enhanced both Spanish and English syntax in bilingual subjects. In addition, no differences were found between monolingual and bilingual subjects on enhanced English sentence competencies.

More recently, a study performed in our own preschool laboratory made use of a similar strategy. The study examined the differences in imitative productions for phonetic sound with high error predictions in Spanish and English. For monolingual Spanish speakers, a number of errors have been consistently found in the pronunciation of particular English phonemes (/ch/ for /dg/, /ch/ for /sh/, /s/ for /z/, /n/ for /ng/, /b/ for /v/, /t/ for /th/, /d/ for /th/, and /y/ for /j/). In addition, errors by monolingual English speakers for Spanish phonemes also exist (/r/ for /rr/, /n/ for /ñ/). This study assessed the differential production of these errors within bilingual and monolingual children. Three separate syntactic imitation tasks were likewise examined for error production. Thus a comparison of Spanish-English productive imitative competence was measured for the two languages within each group.

Two linguistically different groups of children were selected to participate in the study. The experimental group was composed of children defined as English-Spanish bilinguals. The control group was composed of children defined as English monolinguals. Bilinguals were defined as Spanish-surnamed children participating in a bilingual educational program and identified by their teacher as Spanish-English speakers. Monolinguals were defined as children participating in a monolingual English educational program and identified by their teacher as speakers of English only. A total of 60 subjects were selected randomly, 30 were bilingual and 30 were monolingual. Five age levels, 3, 4, 5, 6, and 7 years, were employed. Six subjects (three boys and three girls) were assigned to each age level.

Two experimental tasks were used:

1. *The phoneme imitation task* (see Table 1) was directed at examining specific types of verbal imitation errors predicted across specific phonemes.

2. *The syntax imitation task* (see Table 2) evaluated imitation across different syntactic emphasis in English and Spanish. This task contained three different emphases: (*a*) plurals, (*b*) possessives, and (*c*) adjectives. Each was presented in English and Spanish. Prior to the presentation of this task, each subject was randomly assigned to one of the six possible orders of presentation of the three types of syntactic units.

TABLE 1
Phoneme Imitation Task

	Words Modeled		Predicted errors	
Phonemes	English	Spanish	English	Spanish
/ch/for/dg/	ma*dg*e		ma*tch*	
	ri*dg*e		ri*ch*	
/ch/for/sh/	wit*ch*		wi*sh*	
/s/for/z/	ra*z*or		ra*c*er	
	bu*zz*		bu*s*	
/n/for/ng/	si*ng*		si*n*	
	ra*ng*		ra*n*	
/b/for/v/	ro*v*e		ro*b*e	
	*v*ail		*b*ail	
/t/for/th/	ba*th*		ba*t*	
	bo*th*		boa*t*	
/d/for/th/	*th*en		*d*en	
	*th*ey		*d*ay	
/y/for/j/	*j*ello		*y*ellow	
	ma*j*or		ma*y*or	
/n/for/ñ/		ni~n~o		ni*n*o
		ma~n~ana		ma*n*ana
/r/for/rr/		pe*rr*o		pe*r*o
		a*rr*oyo		a*r*oyo

TABLE 2
Syntax Imitation Task

English	Plural forms	Spanish
These are ducks.		Estos son patos.
These are cups.		Estas son copas.
These are rocks.		Estas son piedras.
These are blocks.		Estos son bloques.

English	Possessive forms	Spanish
This is my duck.		Este es mi pato.
This is my cup.		Esta es mi copa.
This is my rock.		Esta es mi piedra.
This is my block.		Este es mi bloque.

English	Adjective forms	Spanish
This is a big, red duck.		Este es un pato grande y rojo.
This a big, red cup.		Esta es una copa grande y roja.
This is a big, red rock.		Esta es una piedra grande y roja.
This is a big, red block.		Este es un bloque grande y rojo.

Tables 3 and 4 present the mean percentage of correct imitation of phoneme presentations for monolingual and bilingual children, respectively. These data indicate *no difference* between these two groups of subjects and no differences across age levels. Table 5 presents the results of the Spanish phoneme imitation task for both monolingual and bilingual subjects. Bilinguals scored higher than monolinguals on this task. Table 6 summarizes the results of the data for the sentence imitation tasks. On these tasks, bilinguals scored higher on all Spanish imitation tasks than monolinguals. There was no significant difference across these two groups on English tasks. In addition, no significant age differences were indicated. A significant decrease in correct imitation was found for bilingual subjects on the adjective sentence imitations in comparison with either the plural or possessive sentence imitations.

TABLE 3

Mean Percentage of Correct Imitation for English Items by Age Group and Phoneme Pairs for Monolingual Children

Age	CH-DG	CH-SH	S-Z	N-NG	B-V	T-TH	D-TH	Y-J	Means
3	85.00	100.00	50.00	75.00	85.00	100.00	100.00	100.00	86.88
4	70.17	100.00	91.67	50.00	83.33	95.83	100.00	95.83	86.98
5	70.83	100.00	95.83	83.33	100.00	95.83	100.00	87.50	91.67
6	75.00	100.00	79.19	70.83	95.83	100.00	100.00	75.00	86.98
7	83.33	93.67	91.67	87.50	100.00	95.83	95.83	95.83	92.71
Means	78.67	98.33	81.67	73.33	92.83	97.50	99.17	90.83	

TABLE 4

Mean Percentage of Correct Imitation for English Items by Age Groups and Phoneme Pairs for Bilingual Children

Age	CH-DG	CH-SH	S-Z	N-NG	B-V	T-TH	D-TH	Y-J	Means
3	95.00	90.00	85.00	60.00	85.00	75.00	80.00	80.00	81.25
4	58.33	91.67	95.83	79.17	87.50	66.67	95.83	75.00	81.25
5	83.33	100.00	100.00	66.67	100.00	91.67	100.00	100.00	82.71
6	66.67	91.67	100.00	79.17	100.00	95.83	100.00	79.17	89.06
7	83.33	100.00	100.00	75.00	100.00	95.83	100.00	100.00	94.27
Means	77.33	94.67	96.17	72.00	94.50	85.00	95.27	86.83	

TABLE 5

Mean Percentage of Correct Imitation of Spanish Phonemes for Monolingual and Bilingual Subjects by Age Group

Age	Monolinguals		Bilinguals	
	n	rr	n	rr
3	33.33	40.00	86.67	83.33
4	69.44	11.11	72.22	52.78
5	66.67	77.78	83.33	91.67
6	58.33	52.78	88.89	86.11
7	58.33	58.33	80.56	75.00
$\bar{x}$	57.22	48.00	82.33	77.79

In summary, bilingual children did not significantly differ from monolingual children in their production of English, but bilinguals were able to produce Spanish at a much higher level than monolinguals. Thus, although bilingual children indicated competence in Spanish, this did not seem to affect their English competence on these imitative tasks.

TABLE 6

Mean Percentage of Correct Imitation of English and Spanish Syntactic Categories for Bilingual and Monolingual Children by Age Group

Age	English				Spanish			
	Pls	Pos	Adj	Total	Pls	Pos	Adj	Total
				Bilingual children				
3	98.61	100	88.89	95.83	56.95	66.67	26.79	50.14
4	91.67	95.84	93.14	93.55	68.06	72.40	44.32	61.59
5	89.58	98.96	83.72	90.75	82.83	90.63	43.07	72.18
6	99.31	100	95.85	98.39	77.78	93.75	68.37	79.95
7	99.31	100	98.62	99.31	92.36	82.30	47.14	73.94
Total	95.70	98.96	92.04	95.57	75.6	81.15	45.94	67.56
				Monolingual children				
3	90.29	85.42	84.03	86.58	12.50	10.42	0	7.64
4	100	100	96.54	98.85	21.52	21.36	2.88	15.25
5	99.30	100	99.65	99.65	59.29	67.70	19.58	48.86
6	84.03	86.46	91.01	87.17	41.67	33.86	8.22	27.91
7	98.22	100	98.62	98.62	8.34	7.30	0	5.22
Total	94.37	94.38	93.97	94.14	28.66	28.13	6.14	20.98

These studies represent a correlational strategy that compares monolingual and bilingual subjects across specific linguistic categories. They were partially motivated by the present pervasive negative connotations of bilingualism. They are meant to demonstrate that bilinguals are not under some sort of linguistic handicap, and each of these studies suggests they are not. Further research will delineate the relationship between bilingualism and negative language transfer. One important methodological consideration needs to be raised here: namely, that studies of this type may necessarily have to prove the null hypothesis. It is also possible that bilingualism has *advantageous* effects on the acquisition of either language. These studies have addressed only the negative side of the issue.

"Language Manipulation" Research

One methodological criticism of the research strategy previously discussed has to do with types of internal and external validity issues related to experimental outcomes. From these data it is difficult to extrapolate a direct cause and effect relationship between bilingualism and the dependent measure of interest. This problem can be overcome by actually manipulating language in children so that any changes produced can be measured and related to "other" language change. The following experiment attempted to follow this strategy. Especially, the acquisition of prepositional concepts at the expressive level in one language (Spanish) was manipulated. Subjects were children, receptively competent on these prepositions in both Spanish and English but only expressively competent on them in English.

In this way, the transfer effect across receptive and productive domains was provided during the acquisition phase.

Three Mexican-American children, 4 years of age, all from bilingual Spanish-English home environments, served as subjects. These children were members of low socioeconomic families. The experimental stimuli consisted of nine black and white plastic drawings (4" x 5½") representing three prepositional concepts (*on [arriba de]*, *behind [detras de]*, and *under [debajo de]*) taken from the Northwestern Syntax Screening Test. (A description of each card is presented in Table 7.)

TABLE 7
Description of the Twelve Experimental Stimuli

English	Spanish
The cat on the table	El gato arriba de la mesa
The cat behind the table	El gato detras de la mesa
The cat under the table	El gato debajo de la mesa
The cat on the bed	El gato arriba de la cama
The cat behind the bed	El gato detras de la cama
The cat under the bed	El gato debajo de la cama
The cat on the chair *	El gato arriba de la silla*
The cat behind the chair *	El gato detras de la silla*
The cat under the chair *	El gato debajo de la silla*

*Probe items

Pretests were given to each subject to determine linguistic ability prior to any experimental manipulations. These pretests used the probe items identified in Table 7. Prior to any pretest all subjects were asked to point to items portrayed in the pictures to insure their linguistic labeling skills with respect to these items. Responding on these trials necessitated a 100% correct response prior to inclusion in the study. A receptive pretest was given to monitor the subjects' comprehension abilities. In this pretest, the experimenter instructed the subjects in either Spanish or English to point to the specific card that described specific concepts. An expressive pretest was also administered. It consisted of displaying the stimulus card and asking, "Where is the cat? Is he behind, under, or on the chair?" or "¿Donde esta el gato? ¿Esta detras de, debajo de, o arriba de la silla?" The order of the presentation of the three concepts was changed with each successive trial.

Following these pretests, training was introduced sequentially on one English preposition at a time. After each training session, subjects were exposed to an additional 30 trials consisting of 24 expressive probe trials. The probe items (Table 7) were used during these trials. Each concept was presented four times during this session, in random sequence. Six training trials were randomly interspersed among probe trials, and those items used in training trials represented the preposition trained during the last training session. The procedure during probe trials was the same as that used in the expressive pretest.

Following the completion of a training phase for each preposition (six training sessions), a receptive probe identical to the receptive pretest was given to each subject. This procedure was included in order to monitor any changes in the subject's receptive abilities as a result of expressive training in Spanish.

Results indicated that during training each subject reached near 100% correct responding for each separate Spanish preposition undergoing training. Probe results are presented in Figures 1, 2, and 3. These figures present percentage of correct responding for both receptive and expressive trials during pretesting and for successive probe sessions of the study for S_1, S_2, and S_3, respectively. During pretesting, all subjects responded at 100% in English and at 0% in Spanish on expressive trials. When Spanish training was introduced on any specific preposition for S_1 and S_2 correct responding in Spanish, expressive probes increased (from near 0% to near 100%) and correct English responding decreased (from 100% to 0%). This phenomenon was replicated with each prepositional concept in a sequential manner. For S_3, training on the first Spanish prepositional concept (*debajo*) resulted in an increase (to near 100% correct responding) during trials for all Spanish prepositions and a corresponding decrease (to 0%) in expressive responding for all English prepositions. When the English preposition (*under*) was trained, an increase in expressive responding for all English prepositions resulted in conjunction with a concomitant decrease in correct expressive Spanish responding. This effect was replicated by reintroducing the training of *debajo*.

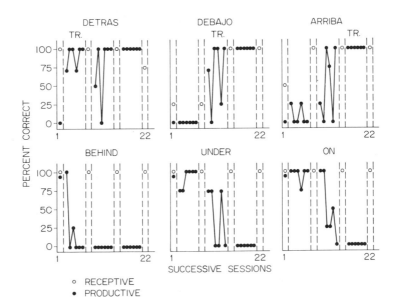

FIGURE 1. Percentage correct responding for receptive (o) and expressive (•) probe trials during pretesting (session 1) and successive sessions of the study for S_1. Specific prepositions which were undergoing training are indicated (TR.).

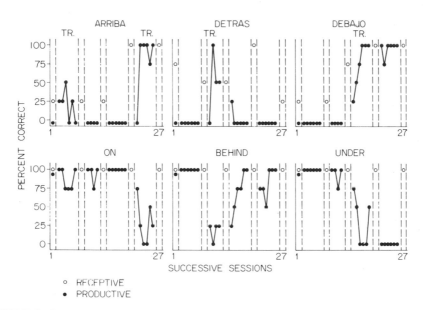

FIGURE 2. Percentage correct responding for receptive (o) and expressive (●) probe trials during pretesting (session 1) and successive sessions of the study for S_2. Specific prepositions which were undergoing training are indicated (TR.).

During receptive pretesting, English responding was at 100% for all subjects while Spanish responding ranged between 25% and 100%. English receptive responding remained at 100% throughout the successive components of the study for each subject. Spanish receptive responding fluctuated between 25% and 100% but tended to remain near 100% for each subject.

A qualitative analysis of subject expressive responding was performed by assessing the form of subject errors on expressive probes. Almost all response errors (85% to 100% of errors in each session) were of a language substitution type. For example, during the training of the preposition *debajo*, an error on an English probe trial almost always took the form of the conceptually correct but linguistically incorrect production, "*debajo*." That is, if the experimenter asked, "Where is the cat," the child would answer, "debajo de la silla." For S_3, who was trained in both English and Spanish, this effect was also observed. During Spanish training, English errors took the form of conceptually correct English productions.

The present study has suggested an experimental analysis of bilingual development during acquisition. Manipulating the linguistic competence in one language and monitoring the effects of this manipulation on both languages permitted a cause and effect analysis of interaction between languages. The results of this study indicate that expressive acquisition of specific prepositional concepts in Spanish

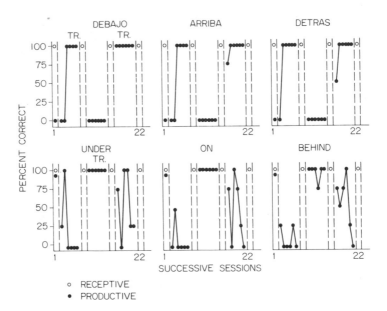

FIGURE 3. Percentage correct responding for receptive (o) and expressive (●) probe trials during pretesting (session 1) and successive sessions of the study for S3. Specific prepositions which were undergoing training are indicated (TR.).

led to a distinct change in the expressive use of these same prepositions in English. Although this change took place, there was never any indication of English receptive linguistic change. This receptive competence might be considered as a constant conceptual (or cognitive) measure. Therefore, acquisition of linguistic competence in one language did not disrupt the conceptual framework of these children. The error analysis further indicates that linguistic disruption only occurred in the form of one language usage. Similar studies using this methodology across other linguistic parameters will add significant understanding to the transfer effects that occur during bilingual acquisition. Although the present study indicates expressive linguistic disruption of one language during the acquisition of a second, there is no reason to believe that linguistic enhancement might not also occur. Present research in our laboratory is addressing this question.

In summary, strategies for research in the area of bilingual transfer have been discussed. These seem to fall into three separate categories:

1. Longitudinal language acquisition research combined with a linguistic error analysis.

2. "No-Difference" research, calling for the comparison of monolinguals to bilinguals within a series of linguistic tasks.

3. "Language Manipulation" research calling for specific linguistic manipulation of one language and the concomitant assessment of this manipulation on a second language.

Each of these approaches should be valuable in obtaining much needed information dealing with bilingual acquisition during early childhood.

REFERENCES

Carrow, E. Comprehension of English and Spanish by preschool Mexican-American children. *Modern Language Journal*, 1971, *55*, 229-306.

Carrow, E. Auditory comprehension of English by monolingual and bilingual preschool children. *Journal of Speech and Hearing Research*, 1972, *15*, 407-412.

Dulay, H.C., & Burt, M.K. Goofing: An indication of children's second language learning strategies. *Language Learning*, 1972, *22*, 235-252.

Ervin-Tripp, S. *Language acquisition and communicative choice*. Stanford, Calif.: Stanford University Press, 1973.

Evans, J.S. Word-pair discrimination and imitation abilities of preschool Spanish-speaking children. *Journal of Learning Disabilities*, 1974, *7*, 573-580.

Harris, M.B., & Hassemer, W.G, Some factors affecting the complexity of children's sentences: The effect of modeling, age, sex, and bilingualism. *Journal of Experimental Child Psychology*, 1972, *13*, 447-455.

Haugen, E. *The ecology of language*. Stanford, Calif.: Stanford University Press, 1972, 307-324.

Padilla, A.M., & Liebman, E. Language acquisition in the bilingual child. *The bilingual review/ La revista bilingüe*, 1975, *2*, 34-55.

Skarbanek, R.L. Language maintenance among Mexican-Americans. *International Journal of Comparative Sociology*, 1970, *11*, 272-282.

Sorensen, A.P. Multilingualism in the northwest Amazon. *American Anthropologist*, 1967, *69*, 670-684.

U.S. Commission on Civil Rights. *Toward quality education of Mexican-Americans: Report IV: Mexican-American education study*. U.S. Commission on Civil Rights, Washington, D.C.: U.S. Government Printing Office, 1974.

PART III

Psychological Testing

CHAPTER 11

IDENTIFYING THE GIFTED CHICANO CHILD

JANE R. MERCER

University of California, Riverside

Relatively few Chicano children are identified as gifted by the public schools, and disproportionately large numbers are labeled as mentally retarded (Mercer, 1973, 1975a, b).[1] This situation is common throughout the Southwest. Most of the litigation relating to testing and assessment in public education has focused on the Chicano children labeled as mental retardates. This paper, however, will focus on a related phenomenon, the disproportionately small number of Chicano children labeled as gifted. Both situations limit the access of Chicano children to equal educational opportunities.

Following a brief review of the philosophical and historical background of present assessment practices, the paper presents an alternative system of pluralistic assessment that may be useful in identifying the gifted Chicano child.

Present Assessment Procedures

THE ANGLO CONFORMITY MODEL AND ANGLICAZATION

Historically, the majority group in American society has been the English-speaking Caucasians, carriers of the English cultural tradition. During the eighteenth century, the English conquered the eastern seaboard of the United States by de-

[1]Research findings reported in this paper were supported by Public Health Service Research Grant No. R01 MH25044 from the National Institute of Mental Health, Department of Health, Education, and Welfare. The opinions and conclusions stated in the paper are not to be construed as officially reflecting the policy of the granting agency.

feating the French, Dutch, and Spanish and by subjugating or driving out the native American inhabitants. Subsequently, the English established the English language as the dominant tongue and English social and political institutions as the dominant agencies. As later migrants arrived, the dominant Anglo-Saxon group adopted a policy of Anglicazation with the intention of building a society based on conformity to the Anglo linguistic and cultural tradition.

In the nineteenth century, the established Anglo elites of Boston and New York set up common schools as private philanthropies to educate the children of immigrant families to the Anglo-Saxon tradition and teach them the English language. Those who established the common schools had only contempt for the parents of immigrant children and excluded them from any participation in the educational process (Karier, 1973; Katz, 1972).

When the public schools were established, they perpetuated the Anglo-Saxon model. The goal of public education was to "Americanize" the children of immigrants and to wean them from the language and culture of their parents. All instruction was in English, and only the Anglo-Saxon traditions, institutions, values, and history were taught. Thus, the implicit goal of public education was to produce monolingual, monocultural, Anglicized children and to allow non-Anglo cultural traditions to die.

THE IMPACT OF ANGLO CONFORMITY ON STANDARDIZED TESTING

All current standardized tests are designed to predict which children are likely to succeed in the public schools. Thus, the values of Anglicazation are implicit in standardized tests geared to the public schools. Tests serve as a bulwark to Anglo conformity and as a method for legitimating the Anglicazation process. As a consequence of the assumption that cultural homogeneity is the societal model in America, current testing procedures have the following characteristics: All standardized tests regularly used in the public schools are written in English, and test content is culture specific to the Anglo culture. A single normative framework is used to judge the quality of performance. Consequently, all children are compared with the children of the Anglo majority, and tests are interpreted against the assumption that all children are or ought to be Anglicized. The "validity" of tests is determined by the extent to which they predict success in a single social role, that of student in the public schools. Anglo conformist scholars argue that any test which predicts accurately who will fail in the public schools is, by their definition, "fair" and "unbiased" because it does precisely what it was designed to do. The value framework of Anglo conformity is taken for granted (Cleary, Humphreys, Kendrick, & Wesman, 1975). The monocultural framework led to the belief that "achievement" tests and so-called "intelligence" tests tap psychologically distinct dimensions (Jensen, 1971; Eysenck, 1971). This particular fallacy has now been abandoned by representatives of the American Psychological Association (Cleary *et al.*, 1975) but will probably continue to confuse discussion of testing issues for many years. Finally, Anglo conformity assumptions resulted in the confusion of prognosis in psychological assessment with diagnosis. Prognosis is the process of predicting outcomes; diagnosis is the process of identifying causes. Tests designed as prognostic measures to predict future performance in the role of student have been interpreted as if they yielded diagnostic information on the cause of the predicted outcome. Mental retardation, for example, is a diagnosis frequently made on the basis of performance on a single test that was designed as a prognostic measure.

THE IMPACT OF ANGLO CONFORMITY AND ANGLICAZATION ON CHICANO CHILDREN

Because tests are used to determine which children will be regarded as a "success" in the monocultural institutions of the public school, they have served as a powerful mechanism for implementing and legitimating the Anglicazation process (Katz, 1972; Kariar *et al.*, 1973). Anglo conformity and Anglicazation have restricted the educational opportunities of Chicano children by assigning disproportionately large numbers of them to classes for the mentally retarded and disproportionately few to classes for the gifted (Mercer, 1973). They have placed too many Chicano children in "slow" tracks and reduced the number with access to accelerated programs and college preparatory programs. Placing them in programs for subnormal children has stigmatized Chicano children and produced unidimensional assessment that does not give children credit for their ability to cope with complex social situations in the family, the community, the economy, and the peer group. Children have been viewed in relation to one role in one social system, the role of student in the public school. This effectively devalued the cultural background of Chicano children (Mercer, 1975a). Finally, the monolingual, monocultural, and monocognitive development of children has deprived Chicano children of the opportunity to become literate in Spanish and be educated in the cultural heritage of their birth. Diagram A in Figure 1 depicts the Anglo conformity model of American society.

STRUCTURAL AND CULTURAL PLURALISM

Pluralistic assessment is based on the view that American society is characterized by cultural and structural pluralism. Although Anglicazation has been practiced by the dominant Anglo group through the policy called Americanization, the pluralistic perspective suggests that non-Anglo ethnic groups have never acquiesced completely to the Anglicazation process and that the Anglo conformity model, which assumes that all peoples are acculturated, is not an accurate picture of American society (Gordon, 1964). Diagram B in Figure 1 presents some of the complexities of cultural and structural pluralism in America today. The large circle represents the Anglo core culture whose domination has existed since colonial times and has been maintained through public education. Descendents of some non-Anglo immigrants have been culturally and structurally absorbed into the Anglo sector of society, notably the German Protestants, the Scots-Irish, the Swedes, and the Norwegians. Other culturally integrated groups, such as the Irish

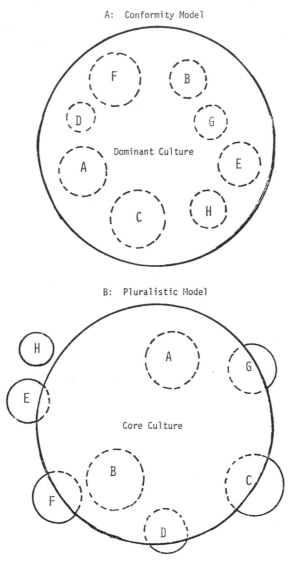

FIGURE 1. Two models of a culturally diverse society.

Catholics and the Jews, have maintained sufficient structural separatism through religious and communal ties to be ethnically identifiable. They are represented by circles A and B, located within the larger cicle of the Anglo core culture. Still other groups appear to span the boundaries of the core culture, as indicated by circles C, D, E, F, and G. Some members of these groups are culturally integrated with the core culture, while other members lie at varying sociocultural distances from the Anglo core culture. Some members may be recent immigrants, who do not speak English and share none of the values and behaviors of the core culture, while others may be indistinguishable from the core groups except for their surnames. Within each ethnic group, there are also socioeconomic differences. The Chicano community is one of these groups, structurally, culturally, and socioeconomically heterogeneous.

THE VALUE PREMISES OF CULTURAL DEMOCRACY

The ideology of cultural democracy, so eloquently described by Ramirez and Castañeda (1974) supports the maintenance of cultural pluralism. Unlike the ideology of Anglicazation, cultural democracy regards all languages and cultures as equally valuable. It supports the perpetuation of non-Anglo languages and cultures as a matter of public policy, as well as the perpetuation of the Anglo core culture. It would provide educational alternatives within the public schools so children would have the option of participating in bilingual and multicultural educational programs. From the value premises of cultural democracy, the goal of public education would be the development of the bilingual, bicultural, bicognitive child who can operate effectively not only in the Anglo core culture but also in one or more other linguistic and cultural systems.

THE IMPACT OF STRUCTURAL AND CULTURAL PLURALISM ON TESTING

The consequences of a theory of structural and cultural pluralism for assessment are somewhat speculative because pluralism is a new framework, not yet seriously explored by more than a few scholars. Among these consequences, first, test language and content should become increasingly multilingual and multicultural. Greater effort should be expended in developing culture-specific tests for non-Anglo groups. Second, there should be increasing use of multiple normative frameworks rather than the single Anglo conformity model. In this fashion, children could be compared with others from the same sociocultural background who had similar opportunities to learn the test material and acquire the skills covered in the test. Third, the definitions of test "validity" should be broadened to include predictions to performance in roles other than that of student in the public schools. All tests should be treated as measures of learned behavior, that is, as achievement tests. There should be a clear separation of prognostic information from diagnostic interpretation.

THE IMPACT OF STRUCTURAL AND CULTURAL PLURALISM
ON CHILDREN

A pluralistic approach to assessment will, it is hoped, open up educational opportunities for Chicano children and redress the problem of overlabeling them as mentally retarded and underlabeling them as gifted. Such a multidimensional approach would reduce the stigmatization to which Chicano children have been subjected. It would permit their performance in social roles, in the family, community and peer groups to become part of the evaluation process and the viewpoint of their parents to be systematically included as part of the assessment data. It would stop penalizing Chicano children for their cultural heritage and provide a means to credit them for being bilingual, bicultural, and bicognitive. Surely, a child who can speak two languages and participate in two cultural traditions is enriched by this experience and demonstrates a more complex level of development than a monocultural, monolingual child (Peal & Lambert, 1962).

A System of Multicultural Pluralistic Assessment

The System of Multicultural Pluralistic Assessment (SOMPA) is designed to assess the current level of functioning and the potential of children from Anglo, Chicano, and black cultural backgrounds. The measures were standardized on 700 English-speaking Caucasian, 700 Chicano, and 700 black children, 5 through 11 years of age. Each ethnic sample was representative of the population of children attending the public schools of California from that ethnic group. There were 100 children, 50 boys and 50 girls, at each age level for each ethnic group.

SOMPA is based on three conceptual models: the medical model, the social system model, and the pluralistic model. Each model is based on a different definition of the nature of abnormality and a different set of assumptions. Thus each model provides a different conceptual vantage point from which the child's performance can be viewed.

THE MEDICAL MODEL

The Medical Model was developed in medicine to understand biological malfunctioning and disease, such as measles, tuberculosis, or rheumatic fever. It is one of the most powerful conceptual tools ever invented to explain and control biological illnesses. Consequently, other disciplines, such as psychology and education, attempted to adopt this model as a tool for conceptualizing their problems. The attempt to use a medical model to explain nonmedical phenomena has been a source of much confusion in assessment.

The medical model identifies biological pathology by specifying symptoms. Since pathologies are defined by their symptoms, this model has also been called a deficit model. "Normal" remains a residual, undefined category consisting of those persons who *do not* display symptoms. The model assumes that pathological symptoms are caused by a biological condition. Because the human organism is similar for all members of the species, sociocultural factors are not relevant to diagnosis with the medical model. Tuberculosis can be diagnosed without knowing what language the patient speaks or the nature of his cultural heritage. Pathology is viewed as a characteristic of the organism being diagnosed. Using a medical model, one says that a patient "is" tubercular or "has" the measles. Cause and effect reasoning are appropriate in this model because the tendency is to seek biological causes for observed symptoms. Finally, within a medical model a pathology can exist unrecognized and undiagnosed. For example, one can have tuberculosis and not be aware that he is ill. Thus within a medical model it makes sense to do epidemiologies, in which the investigator seeks out hidden or undiagnosed illnesses by screening a sample population for tuberculosis, high blood pressure, cancer, or other biological conditions.

Since the medical model focuses on pathologies, measures operating from a medical model will focus on deficits. Measures operating from this model will tend to count or enumerate pathological signs and differentiate cases in the negative tail of the population distribution. There will be little differentiation among those diagnosed as normal, however, because the normals comprise the large mass of persons who have no symptoms. The validity of measures operating from a medical model is determined by their correlation with other information about the biological organism. Although high correlations with sociocultural characteristics would not be expected, there might be greater pathology in those populations exposed to greater risk of disease because of socioeconomic conditions or limited access to adequate health care facilities. Scores on measures of biological characteristics within a medical model can be interpreted without reference to the individual's cultural background. The measures are not culture bound.

There are six sets of measures within the SOMPA that met the assumptions of the medical model when tested on the standardization sample of 2100 children: (*a*) the physical dexterity tasks, (*b*) the Bender-Gestalt test, (*c*) the health history inventory, (*d*) visual acuity, (*e*) auditory acuity, and (*f*) the weight-by-height ratio. There is no listing of "intelligence," "aptitude," or "acheivement" tests among measures that can be appropriately interpreted within a medical model. None of these measures meet the basic assumptions of a medical model. They *cannot* be interpreted from a strictly medical framework.

THE SOCIAL SYSTEM MODEL

The social system model is derived from sociology rather than medicine. Sometimes called the social deviance model, it defines abnormality as behavior that violates social system norms, while normal behavior meets the expectations of others in the system for persons occupying particular roles in that system. Thus, there are multiple definitions of normal. Each role in each social system has its own set of expectations. For example, the behavior expected of a child playing first base on the softball team differs from that expected of the same child when playing clarinet in the band, which in turn differs from the behavior expected when playing the role of student in the sixth grade social studies class. To judge whether a particular set of behaviors is "normal" or "abnormal" requires four kinds of information: (*a*) the system in which the child is functioning, (*b*) the role the child is playing at the time the judgment is made about his or her behavior, (*c*) the expectations others in the system have for behavior of persons playing that role, and (*d*) the actual behavior of the child. Thus there are many definitions of normal. Norms are both role specific and system specific.

Another significant aspect of the social system model is the fact that the norms for any social system are determined not by the biological organism of the species but by political processes within the social system. Whichever group is dominant in the system and has the authority to establish the rules that govern behavior within the group will determine the norms for various social roles. As we discussed earlier in this paper, the norm that a successful student in the public schools speaks standard English and has a knowledge of the Anglo core culture was established by the politically dominant group in American society. These expectations immediately make "deviants" of all those who do not match the Anglo conformity model. Present assessment tools are focused on a single role in a single social system: the role of the student in the public school. The norms for that role were determined in a historical-political process through which carriers of the Anglo cultural tradition emerged as the dominant group.

The social system model has seven characteristics that follow from these assumptions. It is a multidimensional model with norms for each role in each social system. It is an evaluative model; the values of the most powerful groups are enforced. Definitions of behavior are both role bound and system bound. To make an assessment it is necessary to specify both the role and the system within which the assessment is being made. It is both a deficit and an asset model because both the poor performers and the outstanding performers in various social roles can be identified. Consequently, measurements made within a social deviance model should form a normal distribution rather than truncated distributions such as are expected in the medical model. The social system model makes judgments about specific behavior and, hence, it is not appropriate to think in terms of attributes or traits as somehow residing "in" the child. Since the political process defines what behaviors will be regarded as deviant, cause and effect reasoning appropriate to the medical model is inappropriate from a social system perspective. Finally, social deviance, by definition, is behavior judged to violate social norms. Hence, deviance cannot exist apart from the process of being defined. The notion of unrecognized or "undiagnosed" deviance is not logical within the assumptions of the social system model.

Assessment devices operating within a social system model will have several identifying characteristics. Scores will tend to form a normal distribution because there should be a full range of differentiation. Measures should assess competencies as well as deficits. Scores on measures should reflect social system norms as revealed in the judgments about the behavior made by members of the system. The validity of a measure within a social system model will be determined by the extent to which scores on the measurement correlate with independent judgments of the person's behavior made by members of the system.

It is clear from this discussion that the Wechsler Intelligence Scale for Children-Revised (WISC-R) is a social system measure and should be interpreted within a social system model. It focuses on identifying persons likely to meet the expectations for the role of student in the public schools. Hence it is a measure of scholastic functioning level in the public schools as they are now constituted. The validity of the WISC-R and similar measures has always been established by correlating scores on the test with teacher judgments, teacher grades, or some other measure of the extent to which children are meeting the expectations of powerful groups in the social system of the school. It is important to remember that the scores on measures operating from a social system model relate to a specific role in a specific social system and should not be generalized beyond that role.

Within the SOMPA, two sets of measures meet the assumptions of the social system model: the WISC-R using the standard norms and the Adaptive Behavior Inventory for Children (ABIC). The WISC-R is treated as a social system measure because it is designed to correlate with successful performance in the student role in the social system of the school. The ABIC is a social system measure because it measures the child's role behavior in the family, community, peer group, nonacademic school situations, self-maintenance, and earner-consumer roles from the viewpoint of the family.

THE PLURALISTIC MODEL

The pluralistic model is a third model that can be used in assessing the child. Its definition of *normal* and set of assumptions are different from those used in either the medical or social system models. The initial idea for this model developed during earlier studies of the labeling of mentally retarded in the community (Mercer, 1973). It was clear that school psychologists and clinicians believed that the scores they obtained on so-called measures of intelligence indicated something about children's ability or aptitude in general. They did not limit their interpretations of such scores entirely to predictions about scholastic performance. At that time, it was theorized that it would be possible to make inferences about a child's learning potential if the following assumptions from which such inferences are made were rigorously observed: that the children whose performances were being compared (*a*) had similar opportunities to learn the materials and acquire the skills needed to respond to test items; (*b*) had been similarly motivated by the significant other persons in their lives to learn these materials and acquire these skills; (*c*) had similar experience with taking tests and responding in a one-on-one test situation with a strange adult; (*d*) had no emotional disturbances or anxieties that might interfere with test performance; and (*e*) had no sensory or motor disabilities that might have interfered with prior learning or might influence their ability to respond in the test situation. If all these factors could be held constant, it would be possible to make inferences about children's learning potential from their performance in a test of learned behavior. When everything else is held constant, the pluralistic model assumes that the child who has learned the most probably has the most "learning potential."

From this line of reasoning, it follows that "normal" performance can be defined as performance near the average for a group of children from similar sociocultural backgrounds. The SOMPA uses multiple regression equations as a mechanism for estimating the average performance for children from similar ethnic, sociocultural, and socioeconomic backgrounds. The score for each child is compared with the average for others from precisely the same sociocultural and socioeconomic backgrounds.

In SOMPA four sociocultural scales; (*a*) urban acculturation, (*b*) socioeconomic status, (*c*) family structure, and (*d*) family size, measure background characteristics. Twenty-two questions covering family background were factor analyzed and yielded the nine original factors listed on Table 1. These factors were then factor analyzed to yield the four sociocultural factors that make up the four sociocultural scales and the weight given to each factor in calculating a child's raw score on each scale. The weights were based on the factor loadings of each of the original factors in the analysis. These scales were used to place the child in the sociocultural space of American society, as depicted in Figure 1. To determine the appropriate normative group with which to compare a child's performance, the scores for the child's background on the four sociocultural scales were substituted into the appropriate multiple regression equation to estimate the average score for his or her sociocultural group.

TABLE 1
Nine Sociocultural Factors Combined to Form Four Sociocultural Scales: SOMPA

Sociocultural Scales	Original Factor	Weight	Raw Score Range
Urban acculturation	Anglicazation	6	0-88
	Sense of efficacy	2	
	Community participation	2	
	Urbanization	1	
Socioeconomic status	Occupation of head of household	1	0-12
	Source of income	1	
Family structure	Marital status	4	0-18
	Relationship of child to parents	3	
Family size	Family size	1	0-30[a]

[a]A high score on Urban Acculturation, Socioeconomic Status, and Family Structure characterizes families which are more like the dominant Anglo culture, while a high score on Family Size characterizes families which are less like the dominant Anglo culture.

TABLE 2
Multiple Regression Equations for Estimating Learning Potential from Sociocultural Scale Scores for WISC-R Full Scale, Verbal, and Performance Scores, Chicano Children

SES (.42) Family size (.29) + urban acculturation (.20) + family structure (0) + 84.86 = Est. full scale $R = .39$ $R^2 = .149$ Standard error = 12.84

SES (.27) Family size (.38) + urban acculturation (.30) + family structure (0) + 78.58 = Est. verbal $R = .47$ $R^2 = .218$ Standard error = 13.39

SES (.47) Family size (.16) + urban acculturation (.08) + family structure (0) + 93.67 = Est. performance $R = .19$ $R^2 = .036$ Standard error = 13.02

Table 2 presents the three regression equations used to calculate average scores for Chicano children of various sociocultural backgrounds. For example, to determine the average full scale score expected for a child with a particular set of sociocultural scores (*a*) substitute the score for socioeconomic status in the proper place and multiply by the weight of .42; (*b*) subtract the family size score times its weight of .29; (*c*) add the urban acculturation score times its weight of .20; and (*d*) add the constant term of 84.86. This calculation yields the average full scale score on the WISC-R expected for a child from a background with that particular combination of sociocultural characteristics. The child's actual score on the test is compared with the average score for the child's sociocultural group. Such scores are interpreted as a measure of "estimated learning potential." They can be expressed either as a standard score with a mean of 100 and a standard deviation of 15 or as a percentile. It should be noted that the weight for family structure is zero. This scale does not have to be calculated in the equation for Chicano children but does have a weight for both black and Anglo children, whose equations are not presented in the table. Sociocultural factors account for 21.8% of the variance in verbal scores (r = .47) but only 3.6% of the variance in performance scores (r = .19). This difference indicates a greater cultural loading in the verbal than in the performance subtests.

Under the assumptions made by the pluralistic model, *subnormal* is defined as a test score that is low when compared to a child's own sociocultural group. The model assumes that all tests measure learned behavior, that inferences can be made about learning potential if the opportunity to learn, the motivation to learn, and test experience are held constant, and that children from similar sociocultural settings are roughly similar with respect to these factors. The model further assumes that emotionally disturbed or physically disabled children have been identified by other measures, such as those in the medical model and those in the social system model.

The characteristics of the model fall between the medical and the social system models. The pluralistic model has multiple "normal" distributions, as many distributions as there are possible combinations of scores on the four sociocultural scales. It is an evaluative model that assumes it is better to have high potential than low. The model is completely culture bound. Test scores reveal a child's relative rank among children from similar sociocultural backgrounds. It is primarily an "asset" model, and in actual practice, scores significantly changed as a result of using the pluralistic model are modified primarily in a positive direction. This is particularly characteristic of scores for Chicano children on the verbal and full scale scores. Table 3 presents the frequency distribution of the difference between estimated learning potential (ELP) and standard full scale IQ or scholastic functioning level (SFL) for the Chicano children in our study. The average difference in the two scores for the verbal tests is 11.28. It is only 2.17 for the performance tests, however, and 7.39 for the full scale. Sociocultural factors do not greatly influence performance scores for Chicano children.

TABLE 3

Difference between Scholastic Functioning Level and Estimated Learning Potential for Chicano Children[a]

Difference ELP Minus SFL		Verbal		Performance		Full Scale	
		f	%	f	%	f	%
- 7	- 8			1	0.2	1	0.2
- 5	- 6			7	1.3	1	0.2
- 3	- 4			25	4.7	14	2.7
- 1	- 2	1	0.2	78	14.5	17	3.3
No Difference (0)		2	0.4	54	10.0	21	4.0
+ 1	+ 2	9	1.9	140	25.8	49	9.4
+ 3	+ 4	22	4.8	106	19.6	76	14.6
+ 5	+ 6	48	10.4	70	12.9	69	13.2
+ 7	+ 8	68	14.8	45	8.3	66	12.7
+ 9	+10	70	15.3	12	2.3	60	11.6
+11	+12	67	14.6	2	0.4	40	7.7
+13	+14	63	13.7			32	6.2
+15	+16	48	10.4			40	7.6
+17	+18	25	5.5			21	4.0
+19	+2 -	17	3.7			9	1.8
+21	+22	13	2.8			3	0.6
+23	+24	5	1.1			1	0.2
+25	+26	2	0.4				
$\overline{X}$		11.28		2.17		7.39	
SD		7.29		3.24		5.68	
n		524		540		520	
F-Ratio		820.21		1337.11		826.40	
Sig Level p		$< .001$		$< .001$		$< .001$	

[a]Scholastic functioning level (SFL) is the standard IQ score in the WISC-R while estimated learning potential (ELP) is the child's score compared to the predicted score for persons from his or her sociocultural background.

The pluralistic model assumes that *learning potential* is an attribute of the child. It assumes that scholastic potential can exist unrecognized because the child's potential may be masked by the cultural difference between the child and the culture of the school.

Table 4 presents the distribution of estimated learning potential for the Chicano children in our sample. The ELP is completely normalized. The mean for verbal is 98.99, for performance, 99.65, and for full scale 99.21.

The question of defining validity within a pluralistic model is a matter for future exploration. It seems reasonable to hypothesize that ELP should be a better predictor of future academic performance, within ethnic group, than the IQ test

TABLE 4

Percentage Distribution of Estimated Learning Potential (ELP) for WISC-R Verbal, Performance, and Full Scale Scores for Chicano Children, 6 through 11 years

ELP	Verbal %	Performance %	Full Scale %
50 - 54		.37	.19
55 - 59	.19	.55	
60 - 64	.76		.77
65 - 69	1.14	1.47	2.88
70 - 74	3.43	3.33	1.73
75 - 79	4.00	2.95	3.84
80 - 84	6.86	5.73	5.37
85 - 89	9.52	9.61	9.98
90 - 94	11.62	13.12	13.44
95 - 99	14.48	12.01	14.01
100 - 104	10.67	11.28	9.98
105 - 109	12.57	13.31	11.71
110 - 114	9.52	10.54	10.75
115 - 119	7.43	7.02	7.87
120 - 124	4.76	4.44	3.26
125 - 129	2.10	2.40	2.11
130 - 134	.38	1.29	1.34
135 - 139	.38	.55	.58
140 - 144	.19		
145 - 149			.19
n	525	541	521
Mean	98.99	99.65	99.21
SD	14.62	14.94	15.02

score (SFL), if indeed it is tapping unrecognized potential.[2] Pairs of children are being followed — matched in their IQ test scores (SFL) but with significantly different estimated learning potential — to determine if the children with higher ELP do perform better in school after three years than children with lower ELP.

A combination of the child's performance on the adaptive behavior inventory for children (ABIC) and the child's ELP provides a basis of detecting the gifted Chicano child using the SOMPA. There were 22 Chicano children in the California sample with an estimated learning potential of 125 or higher. There is no space in this paper to describe each child, but two case descriptions provide a picture of what is implied by the measure of ELP.

[2]We are in the process of developing a research design to follow up those children in our California sample whom we found to have an ELP which was 15 or more points higher than their SFL, i.e., a "latent potential group." We will match them with other children of the same ethnic group who had the same SFL as the "latent potential group" but did not have an ELP higher than the SFL. On the basis of an identical SFL (IQ test score), we would predict that children in the two groups should have equivalent performance in the public school. Thus, the null hypothesis is no difference between groups. However, if our measure of estimated learning potential is identifying children who have greater potential than is manifested by their standard score (SFL), we would hypothesize that the "latent potential group" will be doing significantly better in school than the group in which SFL and ELP were approximately the same. In this fashion, we will approach the question of the "validity" of the ELP as a measure of potential.

Anthony Piedros is 5 years old and lives with his mother, father, and six brothers and sisters in East Los Angeles. His father was born and reared in a rural Mexican town, had two years of formal education in Mexico, and supports his family as a boilermaker. His mother was reared in the same rural area and had three years of formal schooling. The family lives in a rented three-room dwelling. The mother speaks only Spanish, and the interview was conducted entirely in Spanish. She reported that the family speaks only Spanish in the home, the neighborhood, and other places in the community. The mother never goes to meetings of church groups or to school for conferences or other activities and does not belong to any social groups, but occasionally she attends meetings of groups working for the welfare of the Chicano community. She feels somewhat fatalistic about the future, thinking that much is determined by luck and that planning is likely to make people unhappy because plans usually do not work out. Given the family circumstances, such feelings may be a realistic appraisal of her situation.

Anthony, who has just entered kindergarten, made a score of 105 on the full scale WISC-R. The average score for a child from sociocultural background so culturally distant from the Anglo core culture is 83.5. Thus his score is more than 21 points highers than average. Interpreted within pluralistic norms, his score would be 125, approximately the ninety-fifth percentile.

Anthony's mother expects him to complete college. On the ABIC, she rates him at about the ninety-fifth percentile in peer group roles and about the sixty-sixth percentile in nonacademic school roles. She reports average role performance in family, community, earner-consumer, and self-maintenance activities. His total ABIC was a scaled score of 56, slightly above the average, which is set at 50 for the adaptive behavior inventory for children.

Maria Gonzales is 7 years old and lives with her mother, father, and five brothers and sisters in a four-room house that the family is buying in Santa Ana, California. Her mother and father were both reared in the same small town in rural Mexico where her father finished second grade and her mother fourth grade in the village school. Her mother, like Anthony's, is fatalistic about the future and believes planning makes for unhappiness. Although she can speak some English, the interview was conducted in Spanish. Maria's mother is somewhat more involved in community affairs than Anthony's. She goes to meetings of church groups about once a month, attends meetings at the school once or twice a month, and participates in community improvement groups about once a year. Although they speak English occasionally at home, they speak only Spanish in the neighborhood and in the community near their home.

Maria's school functioning level, using the standard norms for the WISC-R, was 114. However, when her sociocultural background was taken into account using the pluralistic norms, her estimated learning potential on the full scale was 133. Considering her age and background, her performance on the WISC-R was truly outstanding.

Her mother also reported that Maria was outstanding in her role performance, especially family roles and peer group roles, which she reported as above the ninety-eighth percentile on the ABIC. Her performance was at approximately the sixtieth percentile on the other ABIC scales, and her overall adaptive behavior inventory score was at the sixty-sixth percentile.

Anthony and Maria are probably gifted Chicano children. They were selected for presentation because they are young and because appropriate educational planning could greatly enhance their growth. However, the type of program planned for gifted Anglo children would not be appropriate. Anthony and Maria are developing bilingually, biculturally, and bicognitively, and the Anglo programs are geared only for the monolingual, monocultural child. Children like Anthony and Maria are probably among those who will become the next generation of leaders in the Chicano Community and represent a relatively uncultivated human resource. Programs need to be developed to nurture their potential and that of children like them.

Conclusion

Other approaches to the development of assessment procedures that are not racially or culturally discriminatory have been proposed. There have been (a) attempts to develop "culture-free" tests, (b) attempts to develop "culture-fair" tests, (c) adaptations of present tests for cross-cultural applications, and (d) the development of culture-specific tests for non-Anglo cultures.

CULTURE-FREE TESTS

Attempts to develop "culture-free" tests rest on the assumption that it is possible to develop a test consisting of items free of all cultural influence. We agree with Wesman (1968) and Williams (1975) that the search for a culture-free test is "sheer nonsense." All learning takes place in a sociocultural setting; all tests measure learned behavior.

CULTURE-FAIR TESTS

Four approaches have been used in developing culture-fair tests. The common-culture approach assumes that there are tasks or problems common to all cultures and that a test can be developed using only common-culture items. "To be equally fair to all persons, an intelligence test should present problems that are equally familiar or equally unfamiliar to all [Eells *et al.*, 1951, p. 16]." Davis's and Eells' early attempts to develop tests using the common-culture approach were unsuccessful in achieving culture fairness (Cronbach, 1975). Research on the culture fairness of Cattell's culture-fair tests for measuring intelligence (Institute for Personality and Ability Testing, 1973) is limited and inconclusive. Some investigators have used Raven's progressive matrices (Raven, 1960) and the Goodenough draw-a-man test (Harris, 1963) for cross-cultural assessment on the assumption that the tasks required in these measures are common to all cultures. However, differences in average group performance persist (Dennis, 1966; Irvine, 1966). Paper-and-pencil tests present special difficulties in cross-cultural testing (Swartz, 1963). The psychosituational context of the testing situation presents numerous complexities in communication that make it difficult to interpret performance cross culturally (Bersoff, 1973; MacKay, 1974; Mehan, 1971; and Roth, 1974). Other investigators attempted to develop culture-fair measures by including an equal number of items from each of the cultural traditions of persons taking the test. Breland *et al.* (1974) questioned the cross-cultural stability of test items and tests based on balancing items because they suffer from the additional problem of not being adequate predictors of performance in any particular cultural milieu.

Two promising approaches have recently been reported. Budoff (Note 1) has experimented with a test-train-retest paradigm using nonverbal reasoning tasks such as those in Raven's progressive matrices. He interprets the gain score resulting from teaching as a measure of the child's "learning potential." Other investigators (Bernal, 1975; De Avila, 1975) have hypothesized that the developmental stages described by Piaget can provide a cross-cultural framework for assessment. De Avila has developed test instruments for this purpose.

MODIFICATIONS OF EXISTING TESTS

Any attempt to make existing tests culture fair is fraught with difficulties. Smith (1974) studied 14 different versions of the Binet, revised for nine countries from 1908 to 1960, and concluded that each Binet item had a different cultural loading bound to a particular time and locale. Studies of Spanish translations of the Wechsler scales report similar difficulties (Moran, 1962; Coyle, 1965). Direct translation of vocabulary items is frequently impossible. Translation also changes the difficulty level of items, because words used frequently in one language system may be less frequent in another. In any case, the content remains culture specific. Another common adaptation of existing tests is to weight the nonverbal portion of the test more heavily than the verbal, on the assumption that performance tests are more culture fair than verbal tests. This procedure has varying degrees of utility, depending on the culture of the child being evaluated (Darcy, 1952, 1963; Johnson, 1953; Jones, 1952). Some investigators have varied the speed and power components of the test on the assumption that, given adequate time, persons from differing cultural backgrounds will perform in similar fashion. Swartz (1963) contends that there are unpredictable complexities when the speed-power factor in test administration is varied and that adequate power tests are, in general, the most difficult to devise and use cross culturally. Probably the most cogent objection to modifying the language, procedures, scoring, or speed-power characteristics of a standardized test is that such modifications make the scores earned on a modified test impossible to interpret within any existing normative framework. A new norming of the test based on the modified procedures is required before scores can be interpreted.

CULTURE-SPECIFIC TESTS

It may be possible to develop culture-specific tests for each sociocultural group. For example, the BITCH-100 (Black Intelligence Test of Cultural Homogeneity), developed by Williams (1975), is a vocabulary test of 100 words selected from the *Dictionary of Afro-American Slang*. Using the BITCH-100, Williams studied 100 black and 100 white high school students in St. Louis and found that the black group averaged 36 points higher than the white group. The distribution of scores for blacks was negatively skewed, indicating that the items were "easy" for them. The distribution of white student scores was positively skewed, indicating that the items were "difficult". Williams concluded: "(1) A culture-specific test clearly shows the ability of the population for which the test was intended and (2) a culture-specific test does not accurately reflect the abilities of a nonrepresentative group [p. 110] ."

While culture-specific tests for each ethnic minority are a distinct possibility, such tests would face the same problem, in reverse, as the Anglocentric culture-specific tests now being used, the problem of deciding which child can appropriately be evaluated by which test. Non-Anglo culture-specific tests would provide information on a child's level of functioning in relation to the expectations of family and class but would not provide information on level of functioning in relation to American core culture.

The SOMPA system of assessment uses multiple measures to triangulate the assessment process and uses multiple normative frameworks to interpret the meaning of scores on standardized measures. It involves modifying neither the content nor the procedures used in administering existing measures, nor does it involve the development of common-culture or culture-specific test items. The school psychologist looks at the child through a *medical model* and screens him for possible biological anomalies that may interfere with optimal performance. In cases where the child presents a health history, performance on the physical dexterity battery, or tests of vision or hearing that suggest that there may be organic problems, a thorough medical examination with possible medical intervention is indicated. Using a *social system model*, the psychologist looks at the child's social role performances in those primary social systems where the child is functioning: family roles, peer group roles, community roles, earner-consumer roles, self-maintenance roles, nonacademic school roles, and academic school roles. Using a *pluralistic model*, the psychologist evaluates the child's performance relative to others from the same sociocultural background on the WISC-R measure of school functioning and makes inferences about the child's estimated learning potential. Through this process, we hope that it will be possible to identify the gifted Chicano child whose potential may be masked by the inability of present assessment procedures to take into account the cultural specificity of the test and the distance between the child's location in sociocultural space and the culture of the school.

REFERENCE NOTE

Budoff, M. Measuring learning potential: An alternative to the traditional psychological examination. Paper presented at the First Annual Study Conference in School Psychology, Temple University, Philadelphia, June, 1972.

REFERENCES

Bernal, E.M., Jr. A response to "Educational uses of tests with disadvantaged subjects." *American Psychologist*, 1975, *30*, 93-95.

Bersoff, D.N. Silk purses into sow's ears: The decline of psychological testing and a suggestion for its redemption. *American Psychologist*, 1973, *28*, 892-899.

Breland, H.M., Stocking, M., Pinchack, B., & Abrams, N. *The cross-cultural stability of mental test item: An investigation of response patterns for ten sociocultural groups*. Princeton, N.J.: Educational Testing Service.

Cleary, T.A., Humphreys, L.G., Kendrick, S.A., & Wesman, A. Educational uses of tests with disadvantaged students. *American Psychologist*, 1975, *30*, 15-41.

Coyle, F.A. Another alternate wording on the WISC. *Psychological Reports*, 1965, *16*, 1276.

Cronbach, L.J. Five decades of public controversy over mental testing. *American Psychologist*, 1975, *30*, 1-14.

Darcy, N.P. Performance of bilingual Puerto Rican children on verbal and on non-language tests of intelligence. *Journal of Education Research*, 1952, *45*, 499-506.

Darcy, N.P. Bilingualism and the measurement of intelligence: Review of a decade of research. *Journal of Genetic Psychology*, 1963, *103*, 259-282.

De Avila, E.A., & Havassy, B.E. Piagetian alternative to IQ: Mexican-American study. In N. Hobbs (Ed.), *Issues in the classification of children* (Vol. 2). San Francisco: Jossey-Bass Publishers, 1975.

Dennis, W. Goodenough scores, art experience, and modernization. *Journal of Social Psychology, 68*, 211-228, 1966.

Eells, K., Davis, A., Hairghurst, R., Herrick, V., & Tyler, R. *Intelligence and cultural differences*. Chicago: University of Chicago Press, 1951.

Eysenck, H.J. *The IQ argument: Race, intelligence and education*. New York: The Library Press, 1971.

Gordon, M. *Assimilation in American Life: The role of race, religion, and national origins*. New York: Oxford University Press, 1964.

Harris, D.B. *Children's drawings as measures of intellectual maturity*. New York: Harcourt, Brace, Jovanovich, 1963.

Institute for Personality and Ability Testing. *Measuring intelligence with the culture fair tests: Manual for scales 2 and 3*. Los Angeles: Western Psychological Services, 1973.

Irvine, S.H. Toward a rationale for testing attainments and abilities in Africa. *British Journal of Educational Psychology*, 1966, *36*, 24-32.

Jensen, A.R. Do schools cheat minority children? *Education Research*, 1971, *14*, 3-28.

Johnson, G.B., Jr. Bilingualism as measured by a reaction-time technique and the relationship between a language and a non-language intelligence quotient. *Journal of Genetic Psychology*, 1953, *82*, 3-9.

Jones, W.R. The language handicap of Welsh-speaking children: A study of their performance in English verbal intelligence tests in relation to their non-verbal ability and their reading ability in English. *British Journal of Educational Psychology*, 1952, *22*, 114-123.

Karier, C.J., Violas, P.C., & Spring, J. *Roots of crisis: American education in the twentieth century*. Chicago: Rand McNally, 1973.

Katz, M.B. *Class, bureaucracy, and schools*. New York: Praeger Publishers, 1972.

MacKay, R. Standardized tests: Objective/objectified measures of competence. In A.V. Cicourel, K. Hennings, S. Hennings, K. Leiter, R. MacKay, H. Mehan, & D. Roth, (Eds.), *Language and school performance*. New York: Academic Press, 1974.

Mehan, H. Assessing children's language using abilities: Methodological and cross cultural implications. In M. Armer & A.D. Grimshaw (Eds.) *Comparative social research: Methodological problems and strategies*. New York: Wiley, 1971.

Mercer, Jane R. *Labeling the mentally retarded*. Berkeley: University of California Press, 1973.

Mercer, Jane R. Psychological assessment and the rights of children. In N. Hobbs (Ed.), *The classification of children*, Vol. 1. San Francisco: Jossey-Bass, 1975. (a)

Mercer, Jane R. Sociocultural factors in educational labeling. In M.J. Begab & S.A. Richardson (Eds.), *The mentally retarded and society: A social science perspective*. Baltimore: University Park Press, 1975. (b)

Moran, R.E. Observations and recommendations on the Puerto Rican version of the Wechsler intelligence scale for children. *Pedagogia, Rio Piedras*, 1962, *10*, 89-98.

Peal, E., & Lambert, W.E. The relation of bilingualism to intelligence. *Psychological Monographs*, 1962, *76*, 1-23.

Ramirez, M., III, & Castañeda, A. *Cultural democracy, bicognitive development, and education*. New York: Academic Press, 1974.

Raven, J.C. *Guide to the standard progressive matrices*. London: H.K. Lewis, 1960.

Roth, D.R. Intelligence testing as social activity. In A.V. Cicourel, K. Jennings, S. Hennings, K. Leiter, R. MacKay, H. Mehan, & D. Roth, (Eds.), *Language use and school performance*. New York: Academic Press, 1974.

Smith, M.W. Alfred Binet's remarkable questions: A cross-national and cross-temporal analysis of the cultural biases built into the Stanford-Binet intelligence scale and other Binet tests. *Genetic Psychology Monographs*, 1974, *89*, 307-334.

Swartz, P.A. Adapting tests to the cultural setting. *Educational and Psychological Measurement*, 1963, *23*, 673-686.

Wesman, G. Intelligence testing. *American Psychologist*, 1968, *23*, 267-274.

Williams, R.L. The Bitch-100: A culture-specific test. *Journal of Afro-American issues*, 1975, *3*, 103-116.

CHAPTER 12

PSYCHOLOGICAL TESTING AND THE CHICANO: A REASSESSMENT

ESTEBAN L. OLMEDO

University of California, Los Angeles

Psychological testing of Chicanos and other ethnic minorities has been a source of controversy for over four decades.[1] As early as 1934, George I. Sánchez warned that the uncritical use of assessment instruments had resulted in numerous abuses in the testing of school children, primarily on the part of practitioners who failed to consider the importance of individual differences and environmental factors. Nevertheless, the testing community, ignoring its critics, has failed to take decisive action to alleviate this most critical problem. For example, at their January 1976, meeting the American Psychological Association Council of Representatives postponed indefinitely a resolution introduced by Division 12 (Clinical) urging that all test manuals include a warning concerning the potentially harmful consequences of using the test on populations differing from those for which the test was standardized. Instead, the council overwhelmingly passed a self-serving resolution introduced by Division 5 (Evaluation and Measurement) that praised the value of standardized testing by "competent and well trained psychologists" and recommended that "abuses in testing are to be avoided" ("Warning Labels for Tests?" 1976, p. 8).

Actions of this type by our professional organizations raise the question of whether *any* positive change has taken place over the past 40 years. This paper will first review evidence indicating that although limited progress has been a-

[1]Preparation of this paper was supported in part by the Spanish Speaking Mental Health Research Center at the University of California, Los Angeles. The center is funded by Research Grant MH24854 from the National Institute of Mental Health, Center for the Study of Minority Mental Health Programs. An earlier version was presented at the First Symposium on Chicano Psychology at the University of California, Irvine, May 15-16, 1976.

chieved, the continued occurrence of abuses in testing necessitates a reassessment of the issues involved and the strategies utilized in the pursuit of an ameliorative policy. Within this context, the nature of psychological tests and the assumptions underlying their application will be reviewed, followed by a critical examination of methodological issues pertaining to test bias. Throughout the paper, areas in need of further research will be delineated, and promising approaches toward the solution of critical problems will be described.

Certainly some change has taken place. As Oakland (1973) pointed out, some school districts with a significant number of minority children, such as New York, Chicago, Los Angeles, and Houston "have drastically curtailed or eliminated the use of norm-referenced tests in assessing academic aptitude and achievement and are evaluating the suitability of developing criterion-referenced measures to replace them [p. 296]." Following the 1970 publication of guidelines by the Equal Employment Opportunity Commission (EEOC), which has required the demonstration of the validity of selection tests for minority groups, a number of investigations were conducted in industry with the intended goal of establishing culture-fair selection procedures. Studies have also been conducted to investigate the validity of standardized tests in predicting the success of minority students in institutions of higher education. Finally, psychology departments in some universities (including the universities of Colorado, Utah, Washington, and Wyoming) have waived the Graduate Record Examination (GRE) requirements for Chicano students (Ramirez, Note 1).

However, abuses in the use of psychological tests with Chicanos and other minorities continue to take place. The work of Mercer (1972, 1973, 1976) dramatically illustrates how Anglocentric IQ tests are being misused to label many Chicano and black children as mentally retarded by not taking into account their sociocultural characteristics. Garcia (1972, 1975) pointed out that IQ tests are being misused when the data they provide are utilized in comparing the relative intelligence of biosocial groups, as in the work of Jensen (1969). A study of the evolution of IQ tests indicates that the assumptions, biases, and limitations built into their design render them inappropriate for use in such comparisons. "The use of I.Q. data for group comparisons changes the social contract [between educators and mental testers] into a social conspiracy to label particular groups inferior and to propagate the status quo [Garcia, 1972, p. 40]." Finally, tests are being abused when minority applicants are refused admission to educational and industrial institutions on the basis of scores whose applicability to minority populations has not been properly established. A majority of the studies that claim to find no evidence of cultural bias in test-based selection procedures in educational and industrial settings (see, for example, Cleary, 1968; Cleary, Humphreys, Kendrick, & Wesman, 1975; Gael & Grant, 1972; Gael, Grant, & Ritchie, 1975a, b; Temp, 1971) are based on a definition of culture-fair selection that has been seriously questioned in the recent psychometric literature (Cole, 1973; Darlington, 1971, 1976; Thorndike, 1971).

The issues pertaining to the psychological testing of Chicanos have been brought into a sharper focus, but they remain unsettled. The concepts of unbiased assessment and culture-fair selection are the object of public concern and scholarly debate, but their implementation remains, in the view of many, largely in the realm of wishful thinking. This paper will attempt to reassess the problem objectively in the light of current literature. It is hoped that this process will lead to the discovery of more effective approaches to a solution.

Substantive versus Methodological Issues

It is impossible, within the scope of this paper, to provide even a cursory survey of the substantive literature. There are recent reviews, such as *Latino Mental Health* by Padilla and Ruiz (1973) and Samuda's (1975) *Psychological Testing of American Minorities*. A more technical discussion, incorporating genetic, psychological, and anthropological perspectives is provided by Loehlin, Lindzey, and Spuhler (1975) in *Race Differences in Intelligence*. Examination of these sources and other relevant literature leaves no doubt about the ambiguous and often contradictory nature of current findings. For example, in summarizing their review on intelligence testing of the Spanish surnamed, Padilla and Ruiz (1973) pointed out a variety of deficiencies such as inadequate norms and culturally biased test items that led them to conclude, "the tests available lack validity, and that validity is lowered even further by the manner in which they are used [pp. 89-90]." Jensen (1974), on the other hand, compared the performance of Anglo, black, and Chicano children on the Peabody picture vocabulary test (PPVT) with performance on the Raven's progressive matrices test. He concluded that the Raven (considered to be a "culture-reduced" test) was not biased against Chicanos. However, the results concerning the PPVT (considered to be one of the most "culture-loaded" IQ tests) were ambiguous since some of the analyses were "consistent with the predictions from a culture bias hypothesis [p. 243]." Finally, on the basis of an extensive review of empirical findings and theoretical arguments, Loehlin *et al.* (1975) concluded that differences in IQ between ethnic groups "probably reflect in part inadequacies and biases in the tests themselves [p. 238]," in addition to environmental and genetic differences. The authors indicated that although their conclusions were limited, the present state of scientific evidence did not justify stronger ones.

The empirical evidence now available often leads to ambiguous and contradictory conclusions. It is suggested that this state of affairs will continue until fundamental methodological issues are resolved. More research on ethnic-group differences in intelligence will not provide any further clarification until there is agreement about what is being measured. Further research on test bias will not help unless a commonly accepted definition of test bias is reached. More validation studies will not satisfy the critics no matter how "valid" tests are shown to be, unless consensus is developed about how validity is to be determined. Finally, debate as to whether test-based selection procedures and classification decisions are or are not culture fair will not subside until opponents arrive at a mutually acceptable methodology for determining what constitutes a culture-fair procedure.

In view of the foregoing discussion, it is important to concentrate on the clarification of these methodological issues. Critics of psychological testing have often been ineffective because they have substituted passionate rhetoric for a clear understanding of the complex problems involved. Let us not succumb to that temptation.

The Nature of Psychological Tests

"A psychological test is essentially an objective and standardized measure of a sample of behavior [Anastasi, 1976, p. 23]." In order for a test to conform to this definition it must meet certain well specified criteria of *standardization, validity,* and *reliability*.[2]

Standardization involves two important aspects: (*a*) establishing standard procedures to be followed in administering and scoring the test that should be the same for all individuals whose scores are to be compared; and (*b*) establishing the norm or average performance on the test for a large group of subjects representative of the individuals for whom the test was designed. Individual scores are evaluated by comparing them to this norm. It is important to note that in standardized testing an individual score value has meaning only within the context of the norm against which it is compared. Thus, the degree to which the standardization sample is representative of individuals being tested is crucial to the interpretation of their scores.

The concept of validity applies to drawing inferences from a test score with respect to (*a*) what is being measured, and (*b*) performance on some other variables presumably related to scores on the test. Thus, the validity of a test refers in general to how well the scores represent that characteristic the test is intended to measure and the extent to which the scores are related to other pertinent variables. Although there are various types of validity, the issues discussed in this paper are concerned primarily with criterion-related validity. This concept is applicable in cases where individuals' most probable standings on a variable called the *criterion* are inferred from their scores on a test. If the test scores are obtained prior to the criterion measure, then the term *predictive validity* applies, which is a special case of criterion-related validity. Within this context, the *validity coefficient* is the correlation between test and criterion scores. For example, the correlation coefficient between Scholastic Aptitude Test scores (SAT) and grade point average (GPA)

---

[2]A comprehensive treatment of these topics is beyond the scope of this paper. The following discussion is based on the *Standards for educational and psychological tests* (American Psychological Association, 1966) and Anastasi (1976). The interested reader should consult these sources for a more thorough exposition of the subject.

in college would indicate the validity of the SAT (the test) as a predictor of GPA (the criterion).

There are also various types of reliability, but in general the concept refers to the *consistency* of the scores obtained by the same individual in the same or equivalent tests. The estimation of reliability coefficients involves correlating at least two sets of measurements. For example, *test-retest* reliability is estimated by correlating test scores obtained at one point in time with scores obtained by the same individuals on the same test at a later time. Alternatively, *equivalent forms* reliability is estimated by administering two alternate forms of the same test to a group of subjects and then correlating the two sets of scores. A third method involves establishing the *internal consistency* of a test through various procedures designed to assess the extent to which the items are correlated with each other.

Current uses of psychological tests may be classified into four broad categories (Anastasi, 1976).

1. Clinical: tests used in the detection of intellectual deficiency and diagnosis of the emotionally disturbed

2. Counseling: tests used to enhance self-understanding, personal development, and as an aid in vocational guidance

3. Educational: tests used in the classification of children for differential instruction, the diagnosis of academic failures, and the selection of applicants for professional schools

4. Industrial: tests used in personnel selection and classification

Within each of these categories, tests have been classified according to a variety of typologies. Most textbooks on psychological testing (see, for example, Anastasi, 1976) list and describe tests of each type and discuss the specific assumptions involved in their development and use. This discusssion, however, will focus primarily on fundamental issues pertaining to educational and industrial applications. These areas have generated by far the greatest amount of controversy reflected in the literature. It should be pointed out that interest in issues of test bias concerning clinical and counseling applications is increasing. Padilla and Ruiz (1975), for example, indicated that although little research is available on personality assessment of Mexican-Americans, the evidence suggested that they might differ in response patterning on projective tests and that language problems may contaminate interpretation of findings with objective instruments. In addition, Turner and Horn (1975) found that Mexican-Americans showed distinctive patterns of responding to the Guilford-Zimmerman temperament survey and the Kuder occupational interest survey, suggesting that there may be a need to validate personality and interest tests for the Mexican-American population.

Assumptions in Psychological Testing

A number of assumptions underlie the use of psychological tests. Some pertain to particular instruments or types of instruments, and such assumptions are usually specified in a test manual. Other assumptions, more general in nature, are fundamental to the testing process. An excellent, nontechnical summary of the latter may be found in Newland (1973). Although they are recognized and emphasized by experts, these assumptions are not necessarily taken into consideration by field technicians or test consumers. This may result in the inadequate assessment of tested individuals and the misuse of their test scores.

Two fundamental assumptions mentioned by Newland (1973) are particularly relevant to testing Chicanos and other minorities. The first states that the *examiner is properly trained to administer the test*. There are actually two distinct issues implicit in this assumption: (*a*) competence in administering tests in general; and (*b*) competence in testing minority individuals. With respect to the first issue, many, often subtle, aspects of the examiner's behavior are crucial to accurate assessment. Some examples are (*a*) establishing rapport with the examinee, (*b*) reinforcing cooperation in the testing situation, (*c*) allocating sufficient time for responses, (*d*) handling failure frustration adequately, (*e*) properly recording all psychologically relevant aspects of the response, and (*f*) being sensitive to cognitive differences implied by different albeit "correct" responses (Newland, 1973).

With respect to the second issue, research reviewed by Zirkel (1972) on the "examiner variable" indicated that special training is required for testing linguistically different learners. A complex interaction among linguistic, cultural, and psychological factors deeply affects the results obtained from testing a Spanish-speaking individual. Some of these factors are (*a*) ethnic background, sex, and testing style of the examiner; (*b*) degree of acculturation of the examinee; (*c*) whether the test is administered in English, Spanish, or both (and if so, in what order); and (*d*) whether a bilingual interpreter is used in addition to a monolingual examiner.

The second assumption is that *subjects being tested should have had exposure to comparable acculturation* (Newland, 1973). If tests are used on atypical populations, they may have decreased reliability because of restrictions in the range of scores (Fishman, Deutsch, Kogan, North, & Whiteman, 1964). These authors also listed a variety of factors that may impair validity such as poor test-taking skills, anxiety, and misunderstanding test instructions, all of which usually seem to act to the detriment of minority individuals. Controversy is lively as to whether specially developed tests and norms should be used with members of culturally different groups. Garcia (1972) suggested including items that favor Chicanos or developing separate Chicano tests standardized for Chicano reference groups. Anastasi (1976), on the other hand, argued that this type of approach might drastically reduce the predictive validity of such tests. The technical problem is clear cut in this case; as long as criteria are culturally biased, then culturally biased tests will, in general, be better predictors than culture-fair tests. The issue then becomes one of priorities, or what Darlington (1971) called "a conflict between the two goals of low cultural discrimination and high validity [p. 78]." The solution requires a value judgment, but it is not an "all or nothing" proposition. Linn (1973) showed that for moderate values of criterion-culture correlations (r_{yc} = .40) it is theoretically possible to achieve reasonable predictor-criterion correlations (r_{xy} = .30 to .70) with tests that are essentially independent of culture (that is, r_{xc} approximates zero). Later in the paper, a methodology for formalizing the incorporation of value judgments into the decision-making process is discussed.

Careful consideration of the foregoing assumptions pertaining to the competence of the examiner and the acculturation of the examinee is essential to the accurate psychological assessment of Chicanos and other minorities. An individual's potential may be grossly underestimated when it is inferred from scores on tests standardized on culturally different populations or administered by improperly trained examiners. Under these conditions, using test scores as the basis for making a decision that will adversely affect an individual's educational or occupational future constitutes a clear abuse of the testing process. A concentrated effort must be undertaken to eradicate uncritical test administration and interpretation permanently. This effort should be first directed at re-educating those who conduct the testing and those who use the resulting information to make decisions about Chicanos, particularly in educational and industrial settings.

Bilingualism and Psychological Testing

Reviews of the literature in this area (Padilla & Ruiz, 1973; Peal & Lambert, 1962) indicated that no consensus exists as to whether bilingualism per se impairs intellectual functioning. Earlier studies showing that bilinguals performed below monolinguals on ability and achievement tests have been criticized because sociocultural variables were not adequately controlled. The finding that bilinguals often score lower on verbal than nonverbal tests was interpreted as an indication that bilingualism interferes with language development. Recently, some authors suggested that "structural and idiomatic differences between the English and Spanish languages [Hickey, 1972, p. 24]" and the "underdeveloped perception of English phonology [Matluck & Mace, 1973, p. 365]" have a detrimental effect on the test performance and learning ability of bilingual children. As these authors pointed out, the latter problem involves auditory discrimination and is not an indication of intellectual deficit.

A growing body of literature (Bryen, 1974; Killian, 1971; Padilla & Ruiz, 1973; Peal & Lambert, 1962) suggests that bilingualism per se does not interfere with intellectual functioning and that the "deficit" observed may be a function of inadequate assessment procedures. Thus, a "linguistic difference" model should be preferred over the traditional "linguistic deficit" model.

Contemporary Issues in Test Bias

DISTINCTION BETWEEN INTERNAL AND EXTERNAL CRITERIA OF TEST BIAS

It has been argued by psychometric experts that the mere presence of mean differences in test scores between majority and minority populations does not indicate that the test is biased, because the populations may indeed differ in the quality being measured. As a result, a great deal of recent research has focused on the search for psychometrically defensible criteria of test bias. As Jensen (1974) pointed out, these criteria may be classified into two categories: (*a*) *external criteria*, which pertain to the study of bias in test-based prediction of criterion measures (usually scholastic and job performance); and (*b*) *internal criteria*, which pertain to the study of bias intrinsic to the test, such as the presence of items that have characteristics that differ for various cultural groups. Of the two, external criteria have received by far the greatest attention and are considered in a later section of this paper.

The problem of internal criteria, although perhaps more directly relevant to the issue of cultural bias, has not often been the focus of sophisticated research. Critics of testing have usually pointed out the presence of culturally loaded items, but whether they are biased is a different question that may be answered empirically (Jensen, 1974). Mere inspection of items is not sufficient to determine whether bias is present. In an interesting study, Armstrong (1972) compared ratings indicative of perceived item bias by Anglos and those of various minority groups. He found that it is extremely difficult for subjects of one culture to judge bias against another culture.

Psychometrically acceptable internal criteria of test bias involve item analyses, usually performed using analysis of variance (ANOVA) (Angoff & Sharon, 1974; Cleary & Hilton, 1968; Jensen, 1974). The presence of interactions between items and groups indicates that some items vary in difficulty across cultural groups and could thus be considered biased. It should be noted, however, that a statistically significant interaction is not necessarily interpreted as an indication of bias, unless the interaction accounts for a substantial proportion of total variance (Cleary & Hilton, 1968) and no "counter hypothesis" can reasonably be advanced to explain the interaction in terms other than cultural bias. Conversely, the lack of significant interaction in the presence of a significant main effect for groups is no proof that bias does not exist, if it can be hypothesized that the biasing factor affects all items equally (Jensen, 1974).

The only study using the ANOVA approach (and other ANOVA-derived indices) that involves a Chicano sample seems to be the one by Jensen (1974) mentioned previously which investigated the performance of Anglo, black, and Chicano children on the PPVT and the Raven. It is of interest that by the traditional criteria of internal bias, neither test seemed biased against Chicanos. However, a more sensitive index was derived that showed the Raven to be considerably less biased than the PPVT for Chicanos. The procedure involved matching the PPVT and Raven item by item for difficulty in the Anglo sample. When the matched scales were administered to the Chicano group, it was found that their mean performance was significantly lower on the PPVT than on the Raven. As Jensen (1974) concluded, "this indicates that the [Chicano] group is somewhat handicapped on the culture-loaded PPVT relative to the culture-reduced Raven [p. 239]." The author then speculated that some verbal factor associated with bilingualism was probably operating to depress PPVT performance equally for all items.

It is then possible to demonstrate by means of certain psychometrically sound procedures that, for Chicanos, one test is intrinsically biased compared to another test. Further efforts to develop an adequate methodology would be a useful strategy in developing cogent arguments for the presence of bias in many tests. Smith (1974), for example, presented strong evidence that the Binet tests have built in cultural biases that can be demonstrated by using similar methods. Showing, by *psychometrically acceptable* procedures, that item bias does exist in currently used tests is an essential step in any effort to modify such tests or eliminate their use with Chicanos. If no defensible rationale, based on scientific criteria, can be formulated for rejecting or modifying current tests and developing new measures, the testing controversy will not transcend the realm of heated rhetoric.

"CULTURE-FREE" AND "CULTURE-FAIR" TESTS

Many attempts have been made over the past 30 years to develop culture-free and culture-fair tests. Cattell's "Culture-Free Intelligence Test," published in 1944, was perhaps the first (Samuda, 1975). The consensus today seems to be that there is no such test. Perhaps "culture reduced" may be a more appropriate term. Recent literature has raised serious doubts about the utility of such an approach (Arvey, 1972; Hart, 1973). The consensus of psychologists and psychometricians is that minority individuals have not benefited from the use of "culture-fair" tests because, in general, their level of performance on these tests is just as low or even lower than on conventional measures (Samuda, 1975).

A related issue for Chicanos is the translation of existing intelligence tests into Spanish. The current evidence indicates that this approach has not been successful because of translation problems (Padilla & Ruiz, 1973), differences between the Spanish spoken at home or the community and the Spanish used in tests, and the fact that the test content remains culture bound (Samuda, 1975).

NORM-REFERENCED VERSUS CRITERION-REFERENCED MEASURES

One result of the testing controversy has been the reevaluation of the assessment process involving, in particular, an increased interest in criterion-referenced measurement (Samuda, 1975). The distinction between this process and the more traditional norm-referenced procedures was stated by Popham and Husek (1969):

> A norm-referenced measure is used to identify an individual's performance in relation to the performance of others on the same measure. A criterion-referenced test is used to identify an individual's status with respect to an established standard of performance [p. 1].

As Simon (1969) pointed out, however, the distinction is in terms of *scores* from a test and does not necessarily apply to the format or content. Consequently, the term *criterion-referenced measure* is to be preferred.

The use of criterion-referenced evaluation has received strong support (Drew, 1973; McClelland, 1973; Samuda, 1975) because it serves educational purposes more effectively by presenting information in terms of actual skills to be mastered by the individual without any comparisons with the performance of other individuals that could lead to unwarranted bias and discrimination. As Drew (1973) warned, however, criterion-referenced measures are also vulnerable to bias, and issues such as who determines the criteria and what is to be included in them must be settled if criterion-referenced evaluation is to make a significant contribution to culture-fair assessment.

Some Models of Culture-Fair Selection

Assessing current issues involving external criteria of test bias, Humphreys (1973) noted, following the publication of EEOC guidelines in 1970, that a number of studies were conducted to establish the predictive validity of employment tests for minority groups. Frequently, the method used was that of testing the null hypothesis of zero predictor-criterion correlation for the minority group.[3] Humphreys (1973) criticized this approach on various empirical and theoretical grounds (such as the frequent small size of minority samples) and suggested that the proper null hypothesis to be tested was that of no difference between majority and minority validity coefficients. It should be noted that in the first approach the null hypothesis must be rejected for a test to be declared valid, while in the second case, retaining the null hypothesis leads to the conclusion that the test has the same validity for majority and minority groups. Thus in the first case, the chances of falsely declaring a test valid are associated with the probability of making a Type I error, which is easily specified at some level of significance. In the second case, however, the chances of falsely declaring a test equally valid are associated with the probability of making a Type II error, which is not specified in the studies reported.

Neither approach is really adequate from a psychometric point of view. On the other hand, a number of apparently defensible culture-fair selection procedures have recently been proposed and have generated a heated controversy among experts (Darlington, 1976; Cole, 1973; Novick & Petersen, 1976; Petersen & Novick, 1976; Sawyer, Cole, & Cole, 1976; Thorndike, 1971). Some of these models will now be examined in the context of the selection process.[4]

[3]The discussion in this section assumes knowledge of certain elementary statistical topics such as correlation, regression, probability theory, and hypothesis testing. Readers unfamiliar with these concepts should consult a textbook on statistics such as Hays (1973) for an explanation.
[4]The models to be examined have been discussed under various labels. The classification system and nomenclature used here are from Petersen, N.S. and Novick, M.R. An evaluation of some models of culture-fair selection. *Journal of Educational Measurement*, 1976, *13*, 3-29. Copyright 1976, National Council on Measurement in Education, Inc., East Lansing, Michigan. Used by special permission.

THE SELECTION PROCESS

Figure 1 is a hypothetical bivariate frequency distribution that illustrates the selection process based on the prediction of a criterion (Y), usually a measure of academic or job performance, from some aptitude or ability test (X). Y' represents the least-squares regression line of Y on X, and indicates the predicted criterion performance for any given value of X. y^* represents minimum acceptable

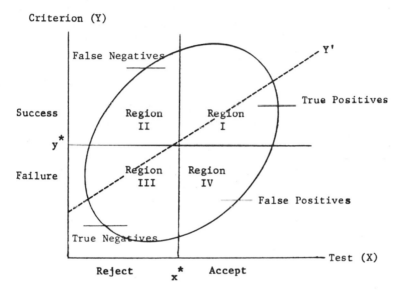

FIGURE 1. A hypothetical bivariate frequency distribution illustrating the selection process. From N.S. Petersen and M.R. Novick. An evaluation of some models of culture-fair selection. *Journal of Educational Measurement*, 1976, *13*, 3-29. P. 10. Copyright 1976, National Council on Measurement in Education, Inc., East Lansing, Michigan. Adapted by special permission.

criterion performance and x^* represents the test score corresponding to predicted minimum acceptable criterion performance. As such, x^* is the cutoff point for selection: applicants who score   above x^* are selected; those who score below x^* are rejected. Note that four outcomes are possible: the two correct outcomes (represented by regions I and III) are the acceptance of applicants that will be successful and the rejection of applicants that would fail; the two incorrect outcomes (represented by regions II and IV) are the rejection of applicants who would be successful and the acceptance of applicants who would fail (Petersen & Novick, 1976).

THE REGRESSION MODEL

This model was stated by Cleary (1968): "A test is biased for members of a subgroup of the population if, in the prediction of a criterion for which the test was designed, consistent nonzero errors of prediction are made for members of the subgroup [p. 115]." Basically, this model defines bias in terms of the discre-

pancy between predicted and actual (obtained) *criterion* scores for minority individuals. *Overprediction* occurs when actual scores are consistently *below* the predicted scores. *Underprediction* occurs when actual scores are consistently *above* the
predicted scores. In the latter case, the test may be considered unfair to those
individuals whose criterion scores are underpredicted.

The implementation of the regression model involves statistical procedures
proposed by Gulliksen and Wilks (1950) used to test sequentially for equality of
slopes and intercepts between separate regression lines for majority and minority
groups. If the statistical tests are not significant (that is, regression slopes and intercepts are equal across groups), then the test is considered fair and a common cutoff point in selection is recommended.

This procedure has received wide acceptance in the literature and has been
the basis for most studies of bias in the predictive context (Anastasi, 1976; Bartlett & O'Leary, 1969; Cleary *et al.*, 1975; Einhorn & Bass, 1971; Jones, 1973;
Linn, 1973; Temp, 1971). Most studies using this method have involved black
versus Anglo comparisons and have in general found no evidence of bias against
the minority group. If anything, criterion scores for minorities are some times
overpredicted if a common regression equation is used (Cleary *et al.*, 1975; Schmidt,
Berner, & Hunter, 1973; Stanley, 1971). Few studies involving Chicano samples
have been reported. Goldman and Richards (1974) found that the regression
equations for predicting freshman grade point average from Scholastic Aptitude
Test scores differed significantly for Anglo and Chicano students at the University
of California, Riverside. The Scholastic Aptitude Test was slightly more valid
for Anglos than for Chicanos when separate equations were calculated. However,
when an Anglo-derived equation was used with Chicanos, it resulted in an *overprediction* of their grade point average. It is interesting to note in this context
that Borup (1971) using an ANOVA technique demonstrated the presence of
ethnic bias in American college test prediction of grade point average. Although
American college test scores were significantly lower for Chicanos than for Anglos,
actual first-semester grade point averages were not significantly different for the
two groups.

With respect to industrial applications, Gael and associates at the American
Telephone and Telegraph Company conducted two recent studies (Gael *et al.*,
1975a, b) applying the regression model in the validation of various tests for
black, Spanish surnamed, and Anglo clerks and telephone operators. In both
studies they found that the use of a common regression equation did not under-
predict criterion performance for minority applicants, although both studies
showed separate ethnic regression lines to differ in intercepts, and one study
showed that they also differed in slope. Thus, a common cutoff point was recommended for both majority and minority applicants.

Findings of this nature led some experts to question the adequacy of the
regression model as a criterion of fairness for minority groups. Thorndike (1971),
for example, argued that when two groups show substantial differences in mean
test scores the regression model is unfair to the lower scoring *group* because the

proportion passing the test will be smaller (when compared with the higher scoring group) than the proportion that will perform successfully on the criterion.

This argument is demonstrated in Figure 2 where π_1 and π_2 represent minority and majority subpopulations, respectively, and π_c is the common regression line.[5] In this case, although the regression line is identical for both groups, the difference between means is greater for test scores than for criterion scores. The regression model would lead to the decision that x_2^* is a fair cutoff point for both subpopulations, although it would lead to rejection of virtually all minority (π_1) applicants. Note, however, that a substantial proportion of minority applicants would do well if selected. This proportion is represented by the area under π_1 that falls above y^* (Petersen & Novick, 1976).

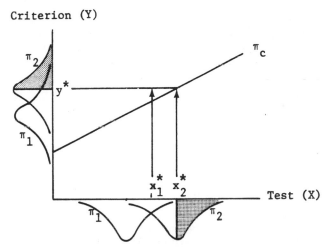

FIGURE 2. Subpopulations with common regression line but differing in mean test score more than in mean criterion score. From N.S. Petersen and M.R. Novick. An evaluation of some models of culture-fair selection. *Journal of Educational Measurement*, 1976, *13*, 3-29. P. 8. Copyright 1976, National Council on Measurement in Education, Inc., East Lansing, Michigan. Reprinted by special permission.

THE CONSTANT RATIO MODEL

Thorndike (1971) consequently suggested an alternate model which states that ". . .qualifying scores on a test should be set at levels that will qualify applicants in the two groups in proportion to the fraction of the two groups reaching a specified level of criterion performance [p. 63]." According to this model, x_1^* (see Figure 2) would be a fair cutoff point for the minority subpopulation.

[5]When subpopulation regression lines differ in slopes and/or intercepts, the situation changes. However, since this is not the point of contention, a discussion is omitted. The interested reader is referred to Anastasi (1976) and Petersen and Novick (1976).

As Petersen and Novick (1976) explain, "This definition assumes that the selection procedure is fair if applicants are selected so that the ratio of the proportion selected to the proportion successful is the same in all subpopulations [p. 7]." In terms of Figure 1, the model requires that the ratio of areas (I + IV)/(I + II) be constant for all subpopulations.

THE CONDITIONAL PROBABILITY MODEL

Cole (1973) proposed a model that emphasizes fairness to potentially successful applicants. This model states that ". . . for both minority and majority groups whose members can achieve satisfactory criterion scores . . . there should be the same probability of selection regardless of group membership [p. 240]." In essence, this means that the conditional probability of selection, given success, should be constant for all subpopulations. In terms of a practical selection situation, suppose, for example, that the cutoff point on a test is chosen so that, for the majority group, the potentially successful individuals have a .80 probability of being selected (that is, four out of five potentially successful applicants are selected); then, in order for the selection process to be fair according to the conditional probability model, a cutoff point must be chosen for the minority group so that potentially successful minority individuals *also* have a .80 probability of being selected (Cole, 1973). In terms of Figure 1, the ratio of areas I/(I + II) should remain constant for majority and minority subpopulations (Petersen & Novick, 1976).

A COMPARISON OF THE THREE MODELS

Schmidt and Hunter (1974) demonstrated that the regression and constant ratio models "can and do lead to very different conclusions about the fairness of tests used in every day life to make decisions about people [p. 6]."[6] Petersen and Novick (1976) contrasted the regression, constant ratio, and conditional probability models. In Figures 3, 4, and 5, one subpopulation (π_1) shows lower mean test and criterion scores but the regression is identical to that of the other subpopulation (π_2). According to the regression model, a fair strategy would be to select all applicants who score above x^* regardless of group membership (Figure 3). The constant ratio model (Figure 4) and the conditional probability model (Figure 5), however, require that different and lower cutoff points (x_1^*) be specified for members of subpopulation π_2 than the cutoff point x_2^* for members of subpopulation π_2.

Which model should be used? Unfortunately, experts are not in agreement. Petersen and Novick (1976) have criticized the constant ratio and conditional probability models because they take into account only the selection-success as-

---

[6]Other similar models have been proposed such as the Equal Risk Model (Einhorn & Bass, 1971) and the Equal Probability Model (Linn, 1973). However, these models do not raise any substantially different issues. As Linn (1976) pointed out, for example, the Regression Model and the Equal Risk Model involve the same strategy for evaluating test bias.

Criterion (Y)

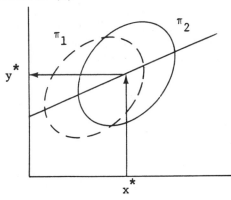

Test (X)

FIGURE 3. Subpopulations with common regression line. Selection strategy fair according to regression model. From N.S. Petersen and M.R. Novick. An evaluation of some models of culture-fair selection. *Journal of Educational Measurement*, 1976, *13*, 3-29. P. 11. Copyright 1976, National Council on Measurement in Education, Inc., East Lansing, Michigan. Reprinted by special permission.

FIGURE 4. Subpopulations with common regression line. Selection strategy fair according to constant ratio model. From N.S. Petersen and M.R. Novick. An evaluation of some models of culture-fair selection. *Journal of Educational Measurement*, 1976, *13*, 3-29. P. 12. Copyright 1976, National Council on Measurement in Education, Inc., East Lansing, Michigan. Reprinted by special permission.

Criterion (Y)

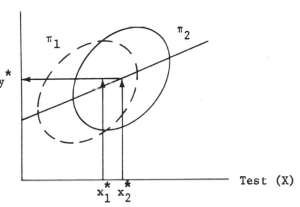

Test (X)

Criterion (Y)

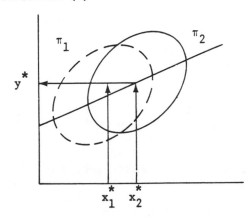

Test (X)

FIGURE 5. Subpopulations with common regression line. Selection strategy fair according to conditional probability model. From N.S. Petersen and M.R. Novick. An evaluation of some models of culture-fair selection. *Journal of Educational Measurement*, 1976, *13*, 3-29. P. 12. Copyright 1976, National Council on Measurement in Education, Inc., East Lansing, Michigan. Reprinted by special permission.

pects of fairness without considering the rejection-failure side of the issue. They point out that the *converse* models are of equal importance. For example, the converse constant ratio model would dictate that the ratio of the proportion rejected to the proportion failing be equal for all subpopulations. Similarly, the converse conditional probability model would dictate that the conditional probability of being rejected, given failure, should be the same for all subpopulations. These authors have developed ingenious mathematical proofs showing that the constant ratio and conditional probability models and their corresponding converse models are internally contradictory because fairness criteria specified in terms of selection-success and rejection-failure cannot both be satisfied in the typical selection situation.[7] They have also pointed out that these two models might "discriminate" against certain other minorities, such as Japanese-Americans, who may have mean criterion and predictor scores higher than those of the majority population.

THE CULTURE-MODIFIED CRITERION MODEL

Darlington (1971) rejected models based on the assumption that issues of cultural fairness in test-based selection can be reduced to "purely mechanical procedures." He proposed a "rational" approach to personnel selection that emphasizes value judgments on the part of the decision maker. The criterion to be predicted is then modified for various cultural subgroups by introducing a factor representing those value judgments on the part of the decision maker. Thus, the selection process is based on maximizing the correlation between the predictor and the culture-modified criterion.

DECISION THEORETIC APPROACHES BASED ON UTILITY THEORY

Darlington's (1971) approach explicitly acknowledged the issue of value judgments. Unfortunately, until recently this emphasis has been largely ignored by most psychometricians. As Petersen and Novick (1976) pointed out:

> There are many different definitions of what constitutes culture-fair selection, and each implicitly, though unfortunately not explicitly, involves a particular set of value judgments with different implications for how selection should be accomplished [p. 3].

The contemporary trend seems to be that of explicitly acknowledging the presence of different values. This is resulting in a welcome effort to formalize the incorporation of value judgments into the decision-making process (Cronbach, 1976; Darlington, 1976; Gross & Su, 1975; Petersen & Novick, 1976; Sawyer *et al.*, 1976). The paradigm required for rational decision making is well stated by Petersen and Novick (1976):

[7]The mathematically sophisticated reader is strongly encouraged to consult the Petersen and Novick (1976) paper. A study of this excellent work will provide valuable insights into the intricacies of the technical issues involved.

In that paradigm the desirability or *utility* of each possible outcome is stated quantitatively. Then, given all available information concerning the person in question, the *probability* of each possible outcome is stated for each decision under consideration. Next, for each possible decision, the utility of each outcome is multiplied by the probability of each outcome and the products are summed to provide an *expected utility*. Finally, the decision is then made for which the expected utility is highest [p. 25].

This approach has the advantage of providing a general model that requires the values or utilities in any given situation to be explicitly stated and entered into the decision-making process. If utilities are conflicting for the different parties involved, such as educational institutions and minority applicants, then this approach provides for explicit quantitative statements of the conflicting values. Thus, through bargaining, a compromise may be reached as to a set of utilities mutually acceptable to all. For example, in the typical selection situation illustrated in Figure 1, the outcomes represented by regions I and III are desirable (that is, have high "utility") because they involve correct decisions. On the other hand, the outcomes represented by regions II and IV are undesirable (that is, have no "utility") because they reflect incorrect decisions. Note, however, that the rejection of potentially successful applicants (region II) is likely to be more undesirable to the applicants than to the institution, while the reverse is true concerning the acceptance of applicants that fail (region IV). The utility theory approach provides (*a*) methods for quantifying the degree of desirability associated with each outcome for the various parties affected by the decision process; and (*b*) methods for determining the "expected utility" of each decision by taking into account the probability of occurrence of the various outcomes in addition to their utility (Petersen & Novick, 1976).

Some specific utility models have already been proposed (Darlington, 1976; Gross & Su, 1975; Novick & Petersen, 1976; Petersen & Novick, 1976; Sawyer *et al.*, 1976). It is too early, however, to predict whether they will pass the test of consensus among test experts and consumers. Nevertheless, this seems to be the most promising approach to the solution of a most complex issue.

THE CRITERION PROBLEM

Another largely ignored issue is that of the nature and extent of bias present in the various criteria of success. Practically all discussions of culture-fair selection have assumed the existence of perfectly valid criteria. This assumption has been seriously questioned recently by Goldman and Slaughter (1976), Levine (1976), and Linn (1976). The problem seems more critical in educational than in industrial settings. Perhaps experts would do well to devote more of their energies to investigating just what it is that we are trying to predict and to what extent these criteria are biased against Chicanos and other minority groups.

Summary

The following points have been made in this paper:

1. Although some positive changes have taken place over the past few years in the effort to reduce the misuse of psychological tests with Chicanos, abuses still occur. We need to press for greater sensitivity to the problem, particularly in professional organizations such as the American Psychological Association.

2. The substantive literature provides a bewildering array of ambiguous and contradictory conclusions as to the presence of bias in instruments and test-based selection procedures currently used.

3. The contention has been presented and substantiated that further progress will depend upon the resolution of basic methodological issues.

4. Adherence by those who administer and use tests to the fundamental assumptions involved in the assessment process would result in a reduction of the abuses that take place. Of crucial importance is the assumption that subjects being tested should have had exposure to comparable acculturation.

5. Contrary to earlier findings, bilingualism per se does not appear to impair cognitive functioning. The "deficits" observed may be an artifact of faulty assessment procedures and failure to control confounding variables.

6. An increasingly sophisticated methodology is being developed to examine issues of intrinsic and predictive bias. Chicano scholars pressing for fairness in test construction and use should become cognizant of these technical advances in order to be more effective in their quest for ameliorative policies.

7. Certain early proposed solutions such as "culture-fair" tests and Spanish translations of standard instruments have been found unproductive. Two promising approaches seem to be criterion-referenced evaluation and the use of a decision theoretic model based on utility theory.

8. The problem of cultural bias in criteria, particularly in educational settings, should be one of the primary focuses of future research.

The long path toward fairness in the psychological testing of Chicanos is arduous indeed. Many grow impatient at continuing abuses that strike deep emotional discords of frustration and resentment. Nevertheless, passionate rhetoric alone will be no substitute for a thorough understanding of complex technical issues and the balanced consideration of conflicting value systems. Future efforts should focus on the formulation of scientifically defensible rationales for determining the nature and extent of biases present in current tests and test-based selection procedures. This process will then provide the solid foundation required for the development of alternate and more satisfactory procedures.

REFERENCE NOTE

1. Ramirez, A. *Admission requirements and recruitment for Ph.D. programs in psychology: Implications for Mexican Americans*. Paper presented at the Conference on Increasing Educational Opportunities for Chicanos in Psychology. University of California, Riverside, May 17-18, 1973.

REFERENCES

American Psychological Association. *Standards for educational and psychological tests.* Washington, D.C.: American Psychological Association, 1966.

Anastasi, A. *Psychological testing* (4th ed.). New York: Macmillan, 1976.

Angoff, N.H., & Sharon, A.T. The evaluation of differences in test performance of two or more groups. *Educational and Psychological Measurement,* 1974, *34,* 807-816.

Armstrong, R.A. Test bias from the non-Anglo viewpoint: A critical evaluation of intelligence test items by members of three cultural minorities. (Doctoral dissertation, University of Arizona, 1971). *Dissertation Abstracts International,* 1972, *33,* 1502.

Arvey, R.D. Some comments on culture fair tests. *Personnel Psychology,* 1972, *25,* 433-448.

Bartlett, C.J., & O'Leary, B.S. A differential prediction model to moderate the effects of heterogeneous groups in personnel selection and classification. *Personnel Psychology,* 1969, *22,* 1-18.

Borup, J.H. The validity of American College Test for discerning potential academic achievement levels: Ethnic and sex groups. *Journal of Educational Research,* 1971, *65,* 3-6.

Bryan, D.N. Special education and the linguistically different child. *Exceptional Children,* 1974, *40,* 589-599.

Cleary, T.A. Test bias: Prediction of grades for Negro and white students in integrated colleges. *Journal of Educational Measurement,* 1968, *5,* 115-124.

Cleary, T.A., & Hilton, T.L. An investigation of item bias. *Educational and Psychological Measurement,* 1968, *28,* 61-75.

Cleary, T.A., Humphreys, L.G., Kendrick, S.A., & Wesman, A. Educational uses of tests with disadvantaged students. *American Psychologist,* 1975, *30,* 15-41.

Cole, N.S. Bias in selection. *Journal of Educational Measurement,* 1973, *10,* 237-255.

Cronbach, L.J. Equity in selection — Where psychometrics and political philosophy meet. *Journal of Educational Measurement,* 1976, *13,* 31-41.

Darlington, R.B. Another look at "cultural fairness." *Journal of Educational Measurement,* 1971, *8,* 71-82.

Darlington, R.B. A defense of "rational" personnel selection, and two new methods. *Journal of Educational Measurement,* 1976, *13,* 43-52.

Drew, C.J. Criterion-referenced and norm-referenced assessment of minority group children. *Journal of School Psychology,* 1973, *11,* 323-329.

Einhorn, H.J., & Bass, A.R. Methodological considerations relevant to discrimination in employment testing. *Psychological Bulletin,* 1971, *75,* 261-269.

Equal Employment Opportunity Commission. Guidelines on employee selection procedures, 1970. In A. Anastasi, *Psychological testing* (4th ed.), New York: Macmillan, 1976.

Fishman, J.A., Deutsch, M., Kogan, L., North, R., & Whiteman, M. Guidelines for testing minority group children. *Journal of Social Issues Supplement,* 1964, *20,* 129-145.

Gael, S., & Grant, D.L. Employment test validation for minority and nonminority telephone company service representatives. *Journal of Applied Psychology,* 1972, *56,* 135-139.

Gael, S., Grant, D.L., & Ritchie, R.J. Employment test validation for minority and nonminority telephone operators. *Journal of Applied Psychology,* 1975, *60,* 411-419. (a)

Gael, S., Grant, D.L., & Ritchie, R.J. Employment test validation for minority and nonminority clerks with work sample criteria. *Journal of Applied Psychology,* 1975, *60,* 420-426. (b)

Garcia, J.I.Q.: The conspiracy. *Psychology Today,* September 1972, pp. 40; 42-43; 92; 94.

Garcia, J. The futility of comparative I.Q. research. In N.A. Buchwald and M.A. B. Brazier (Eds.), *Brain mechanisms in mental retardation.* New York: Academic Press, 1975.

Goldman, R.D., & Richards, R. The SAT prediction of grades for Mexican-American versus Anglo-American students at the University of California, Riverside. *Journal of Educational Measurement,* 1974, *11,* 129-135.

Goldman, R.D., & Slaughter, R.E. Why college grade point average is difficult to predict. *Journal of Educational Psychology*, 1976, *68*, 9-14.

Gross, A.L., & Su, W. Defining a "fair" or "unbiased" selection model. *Journal of Applied Psychology*, 1975, *60*, 345-351.

Gulliksen, H., & Wilks, S.S. Regression tests for several samples. *Psychometrika*, 1950, *15*, 91-114.

Hart, S.N. The culture fair assessment of intelligence. (Doctoral dissertation, Indiana State University, 1972.) *Dissertation Abstracts International*, 1973, *33*, 3284-3285.

Hays, W.L. *Statistics for the social sciences* (2nd ed.). New York: Holt, Rinehart, and Winston, 1973.

Hickey, T. Bilingualism and the measurement of intelligence and verbal learning ability. *Exceptional Children*, 1972, *39*, 24-28.

Humphreys, L.G. Statistical definitions of test validity for minority groups. *Journal of Applied Psychology*, 1973, *58*, 1-4.

Jensen, A.R. How much can we boost I.Q. and scholastic achievement? *Harvard Educational Review*, 1969, *39*, 1-123.

Jensen, A.R. How biased are culture loaded tests? *Genetic Psychology Monographs*, 1974, *90*, 185-244.

Jones, M.B. Moderated regression and equal opportunity. *Educational and Psychological Measurement*, 1973, *33*, 591-602.

Killian, L.R. WISC, Illinois Test of Psycholinguistic Abilities, and Visual-Motor Gestalt Test performance of Spanish-American kindergarten and first grade school children. *Journal of Consulting and Clinical Psychology*, 1971, *37*, 38-43.

Levine, M. The academic achievement test: Its historical context and social functions. *American Psychologist*, 1976, *31*, 228-238.

Linn, R.L. Fair test use in selection. *Review of Educational Research*, 1973, *43*, 139-161.

Linn, R.L. In search of fair selection procedures. *Journal of Educational Measurement*, 1976, *13*, 53-58.

Loehlin, J.C., Lindzey, G., & Spuhler, J.N. *Race differences in intelligence*. San Francisco: W.H. Freeman and Co., 1975.

Matluck, J.H., & Mace, B.J. Language characteristics of Mexican-American children: Implications for assessment. *Journal of School Psychology*, 1973, *11*, 365-386.

McClelland, D.C. Testing for competence rather than for "intelligence." *American Psychologist*, 1973, *28*, 1-14.

Mercer, J.R. I.Q.: The lethal label. *Psychology Today*, September, 1972, pp. 44; 46-47; 95-97.

Mercer, J.R. *Labeling the mentally retarded*, Berkeley: University of California Press, 1973.

Mercer, J.R. Pluralistic diagnosis in the evaluation of Black and Chicano children: A procedure for taking sociocultural variables into account in clinical assessment. In C.A. Hernandez, M.J. Haug, and N.N. Wagner (Eds.), *Chicanos: Social and psychological perspectives* (2nd ed.). St. Louis: C.V. Mosby, 1976.

Newland, T.E. Assumptions underlying psychological testing. *Journal of School Psychology*, 1973, *11*, 316-322.

Novick, M.R., & Petersen, N.S. Towards equalizing educational and employment opportunity. *Journal of Educational Measurement*, 1976, *13*, 77-88.

Oakland, T. Assessing minority group children: Challenges for school psychologists. *Journal of School Psychology*, 1973, *11*, 294-303.

Padilla, A.M., & Ruiz, R.A. *Latino mental health: A review of literature*. (DHEW Publication No. (HSM) 73-9143), Washington, D.C.: U.S. Government Printing Office, 1973.

Padilla, A.M., & Ruiz, R.A. Personality assessment and test interpretation of Mexican-Americans: A critique. *Journal of Personality Assessment*, 1975, *39*, 103-109.

Peal, E., & Lambert, W.E. The relation of bilingualism to intelligence. *Psychological Monographs*, 1962, *76*, 1-23.

Petersen, N.S., & Novick, M.R. An evaluation of some models of culture-fair selection. *Journal of Educational Measurement*, 1976, *13*, 3-29.

Popham, W.J., & Husek, T.R. Implications of criterion-referenced measurement. *Journal of Educational Measurement*, 1969, *6*, 1-9.

Sawyer, R.L., Cole, N.S., & Cole, J.W.L. Utilities and the issue of fairness in a decision theoretic model of selection. *Journal of Educational Measurement*, 1976, *13*, 59-76.

Samuda, R.J. *Psychological testing of American minorities: Issues and consequences.* New York: Dodd, Mead, 1975.

Sánchez, G.I. Bilingualism and mental measures: A word of caution. *Journal of Applied Psychology*, 1934, *18*, 765-772.

Schmidt, F.L., Berner, J.C., & Hunter, J.E. Racial differences in validity of employment tests: Reality or illusion? *Journal of Applied Psychology*, 1973, *58*, 5-9.

Schmidt, F.L., & Hunter, J.E. Racial and ethnic bias in psychological tests: Divergent implications of two definitions of test bias. *American Psychologist*, 1974, *29*, 1-8.

Simon, G.B. Comment on "Implications of criterion-referenced measurement." *Journal of Educational Measurement*, 1969, *9*, 259-260.

Smith, M.W. Alfred Binet's remarkable questions: A cross-national and cross-temporal analysis of the cultural biases built into the Stanford-Binet Intelligence Scale and other Binet tests. *Genetic Psychology Monographs*, 1974, *89*, 307-334.

Stanley, J.C. Predicting college success of the educationally disadvantaged. *Science*, 1971, *171*, 640-647.

Temp. G. Validity of SAT for blacks and whites in thirteen integrated institutions. *Journal of Educational Measurement*, 1971, *8*, 245-251.

Thorndike, R.L. Concepts of cultural fairness. *Journal of Educational Measurement*, 1971, *8*, 63-70.

Turner, R.G., & Horn, J.M. Standard psychological test responses of a group of Mexican-Americans. *Catalog of Selected Documents in Psychology*, 1975, *5*, 210.

Warning label for tests? *American Psychological Association Monitor*, March 1976, p. 8.

Zirkel, P.A. Spanish-speaking students and standardized tests. *The Urban Review*, 1972, *5/6*, 32-40.

CHAPTER 13

INTELLIGENCE TESTING: QUOTIENTS, QUOTAS, AND QUACKERY

JOHN GARCIA

University of California, Los Angeles

So much has been said about race and intelligence that the author of any new study must first exhume the dead horse long ago buried under an avalanche of words and then attempt to beat some more life into its decayed remains. Jane Mercer's (1977) fascinating discussion of the prejudicial assumptions of acculturation made by Anglos in New England, who canonized themselves forever in the format of the American intelligence test, and Esteban Olmedo's (1977) crisp analysis of the further abuses occurring when modern intelligence testers violate their own biased test procedures are both prefatory to this discussion. How in the world can a Chicano ever cope with a monolingual educational establishment that considers bilingual children handicapped because they know two languages? But the problem with mental tests is not a dead horse; it is a source of grief to every minority child in public school and every minority applicant to a graduate or professional school. We need to review some *basic truths* about testing methods if we are not to be confused by the sophistries of psychometrics, population genetics, and heritability statistics.

Race and Intelligence as Polemics, Not Research Issues

Racial comparison of intelligence is a controversial issue because any data on the question are biased by arbitrary assumptions and value judgments of the persons studying the issue. Furthermore, anyone in the testing business knows that IQ differences between groups are fundamentally meaningless, as was previously pointed out (Garcia, 1975). Those attempting to find meaning in such data find their scholarship and motives becoming suspect no matter how erudite and academic their phrasing might be. Thus, any statement on race and intelligence necessarily becomes a polemic, advocating a specific method for dealing with the various biological and social distinctions in our diverse society.

Let me make my own advocacy clear. I am a student of biology and ethology as well as of psychology. I believe that research on the behavior of animals is critical to understanding man's behavior, particularly when that behavior reflects the functioning of homologous structures in animals and man. I also believe that the social behavior of animals is equally relevant to man. Furthermore, I believe behavioral genetics is a legitimate research area of paramount importance, and poses no threat to ethnic groups. It is specifically the misuse of psychometric tests that distresses me, for reasons I hope to make clear. I advocate drastic reforms in the application of tests to human groups differing in biology or culture and removal of racial, sexual, and cultural bias from criterion measures as well as tests.

The Impossibility of Ethnic IQ Differences

Intelligence tests are designed so that, when they are appropriately applied, all biological and social groups appear equal in measured intelligence. To repeat this *truth* in the jargon of the trade, IQ is a scale of within-group variance in test performance, where the trait measured is assumed to be normally distributed with a root mean square of approximately 15, around a mean of 100. The fundamental assumption that all groups are equal in intellectual capacity made IQ measurement possible by circumventing arbitrary value judgments on human differences.

Sex differences are an interesting example. Men in our common culture tend to do better on some mechanical, spatial, and quantitative tests and women on some perceptual, memory, and verbal tests. Lewis Terman (a man) and Maud Merrill (a woman), who designed the Stanford-Binet (Terman & Merrill, 1960), were fully aware that men and women are biologically different and that men and women play different social roles in virtually every human society. But they could not decide whether the male biological attributes are more adaptive than the female biological attributes, or whether the male social role is more intellectual than the female role, or whether male test items are ultimately more valid than female test items. Terman and Merrill solved their problem by simply selecting items that favored neither sex and balancing sex-biased items so that males and females appeared equal in IQ. In doing this, they deliberately attenuated the socioeconomic validity and the predictive power of their test. Since males are economically and professionally more successful than females in America, it should be obvious that an IQ test indicating male superiority would have yielded higher correlations with socioeconomic scales. But, by and large, other mental testers have followed suit, using one statistical device or another to remove between-sex differences from their intelligence scales.

Ethnic differences in test performance present us with the same dilemma as do sex differences. In the case of black-white differences, for example, whites do better on intelligence tests devised for whites, but blacks do better on tests designed for blacks, as R.L. Williams (1975) demonstrated when he devised the BITCH-100 test utilizing the vocabulary of the black American subculture. (Recall that the vocabulary subtest is usually the most efficient part of an intelligence test.) There is no method for deciding which items are ultimately more valid, for the acquisition of words, concepts, grammars, and abstract solutions is the same intrinsic developmental process in all languages and for all mankind (Lenneberg, 1974). Whenever a human group, like black Americans, is isolated, segregated, or socially restricted, it tends to develop its own vocabulary, concepts, ethics, responses, motives, and incentives as a function of the degree of segregation. This is the stuff of which intelligence tests are made. It follows inevitably that black-white differences can be enhanced, reduced, or reversed by the selection of items from either the white or black subcultures.

The decision to phrase intelligence tests in the "good English" of the white middle class urban school was not based on any biological grounds; it was based upon the sociopolitical clout of the Anglos who assumed that all other folks naturally wanted to become Anglos and that if they would not or could not they were naturally inferior. Therefore, we should not be surprised by sociological surveys which indicate that the mean IQ score achieved by ethnic subgroups is related to other measures of conformity or to the socioeconomic rewards accompanying conformity. Chicanos should be forewarned by the plight of women that equality on IQ scales and superiority in scholastic achievement do not necessarily mean they will be cordially invited to share money and power equally with members of the dominant subculture.

The Change of Intelligence Tests over Age and Time

In a sense, infants, children, adolescents, young, and old belong to different subcultures. This poses a problem, since the validity of the intelligence tests rests on the simple assumption that children become more proficient in answering questions as they grow older. Consider the trouble we get into when we attempt to compare two groups, differing only in age, with a simple vocabulary test. The words must be selected with some care, for if they are too difficult, all children will score zero and the individual differences within each group and the average difference between the two groups will be zero. If the words are too easy, all children will respond without error, and again the within-group and between-groups differences will be zero. At this point, the test maker steps off into a morass of assumptions, making inferences about the course of mental development ambiguous. Taking a firm grip on his boot straps, he selects words for the test that will yield both within-groups differences and between-groups differences.

Let us take the simplest sort of between-groups comparison — for example, two groups made up of 8 and 10-year-old brothers from English-speaking families of the same socioeconomic status. In this case, the mental tester can select a single vocabulary list on which the 10-year-old will respond more frequently with correct English usage than will the 8-year-old. The tester, however, cannot assume that the superiority of the 10-year-old is due to his advanced biological maturity, since the 10-year-old has also had two more years of English speaking experience and cultural conditioning. Of course, we could use experimental methods to gather evidence on this issue, but this would require us rigorously to control all exposure to source materials and cultural conditioning. Humane treatment of children prevents such experiments.

There are added complications when the groups differ markedly in age. If the mental tester wishes to compare 4-year-olds with their 16-year-old brothers, he may have to devise a completely different vocabulary list for each group, thus making any comparison of performance impossible because, while the two groups are different in age, the two tests are different in content. As any thoughtful person might expect, when the same group of children are tested at two points in time, the correlation of their IQ performance is high when the points in time are close together and the content of the two tests is similar. The correlation is low if the two points in time are far apart and the tests do not contain overlapping items. In fact, the correlation obtained for very young children retested as youths is virtually zero. Practically, this means that the measured intelligence of a developing child can routinely be expected to change 15 IQ points or more and that changes of 30 IQ points or more are commonplace(McCall, Appelbaum, & Hogarty, 1973).Theoretically, this complicates the notions of the heritability of intelligence enormously, for we logically can ask "Which intelligence do we inherit?" Most mental testers like to believe that this occurs because the child's test is worthless, but it may be the youth's test that is worthless. In fact, the youth's test is more suspect, because another decade of cultural conditioning has operated upon the original biological potential.

The content of intelligence tests for any given age group necessarily changes over time, making the comparison of one generation with another dubious, to say the least. Vocabularies, information, problems, solutions, morals, and laws change, making IQ tests obsolete, so that items must be deleted, added, changed, and re-standardized every few decades. The same is true of college entrance and achievement tests. The apparent paradox, often discussed in academic halls and the popular press, that *students are getting higher grades but doing worse on standardized tests*, is no mystery. Grades are rising because students have gained power to challenge their parents, to sit on advisory committees, and to evaluate their teachers. Teachers have become more sensitive to student aspirations and more reluctant to saddle them with bad grades for life. Standard test scores have fallen because curriculums are becoming more "relevant" to student interests. Television, computers, and space travel have changed our language, our knowledge, and our skills. Students do not respond with yesterday's answers. In fact, since standardized scores are normative data, they cannot fall unless we are using yesterday's inappropriate norms.

To summarize, each sex has its own attributes; so does each ethnic group, each age, and each generation. Each group shares many attributes with nearby groups and fewer with more distant groups along a number of biological, cultural, and temporal dimensions. Before any test can be applied to any group, mental test procedures require that each test item represent something to which all members of that group have had equal exposure on the average, and construction of these items so that they differentiate members within the group. This means that each group should have its own valid tests, which may be more or less distinct from those of other groups. All things are assumed to be similar, and all groups are assumed to be equal along a singular capacity to cope with their own things. This may sound like madness, but this is IQ.

The Prejudicial Assumptions of Racial IQ Research

I have just thumbed through *Race Differences in Intelligence* by J.C. Loehlin and Gardner Lindzey of the University of Texas and J.N. Spuhler of the University of New Mexico (1975). This book is devoted entirely to comparisons of different ethnic groups and different generations, and it has received laudatory reviews for its lucid and scholarly approach to this "research area." Frankly, I found the book confusing and irritating because the authors, while obviously knowledgeable on method and fact, shift their premises without warning and make the most incredible assumptions to render the topic viable. Let me review a few examples.

On pages 137-138 they discuss comparisons between test performance of enlisted men in World War I and that of enlisted men in World War II which suggest that IQ increased 12-14 points. In Appendix J, however, the authors point out that interpretation of studies of population change over time is difficult because the tests as well as the populations change over time. But at another point (pages 46-47) I encountered an astounding passage where the authors discuss the consequences of differential selection on two hypothetical populations and state that "Population A will show an increase in average IQ level of approximately 0.024 IQ points, and that of Population B an increase of 0.064 IQ points." I was referred to Appendix D for the details of these incredibly precise calculations, but I did not bother because Appendix J had already informed me that it was impossible to interpret a change of 12.000 to 14.000 IQ points between the two world wars. The authors speculate that although the differences between populations A and B would be undetectable in a single generation, ". . . in 100 generations, assuming the relative degree of selection remained the same, there would be the equivalent of 4 IQ points difference between the population averages, and in 1000 generations, 40 IQ points." They admit that it is unlikely that selective conditions remain the same over such a long period, but if they could assume such constancy, then a small degree of differential natural selection ". . . could plausibly result in large differences between the populations in the genes influencing intelligence." Can unlikely assumptions ever lead to plausible conclusions?

In Chapter 3 entitled "Intelligence And Its Measurement," the authors draw misleading "analogies between the trait of intelligence and the trait of stature," as if the IQ scale is a physical yardstick with an absolute zero which can be transported across cultures and handed down to succeeding generations. But the authors know that IQ is at best a relative scale based upon ranking and rating procedures where the assumption of equal intervals and zero points "smacks of a kind of magic — a rope trick" as S.S. Stevens (1951) so aptly phrased the problem.

I can empathize with the authors' desire for a physicalistic analogy to help them out of the relativistic morass. I should say that intelligence is analogous to speed in an automobile. Speed seems to be a trait of automobiles but no sane mechanic would attempt to find the actual physical locus of speed by taking the automobile apart. He would know that if driving conditions are held constant, then the speed of an auto can be influenced by the adjustment of the carburetor, or the air pressure in the tires, or the fuel in the tank. If the automotive factors are held constant, then the speed of the auto can be influenced by the velocity of the wind, by the surface of the road, by rain, sleet, and gloom of night. Only a fool would attempt to apportion 100% of the speed to either automotive or environmental factors, because speed is an interaction of both sets of factors. Analogously to speed with automobiles, intelligence is of necessity a product of genetic and environmental interaction.

Heritability Statistics

I found that Loehlin *et al.* (1975) used the assumptions of heritability research in an even more confusing manner. E.O. Wilson (1975) defines heritability as follows: "A heritability score of 1 means that all of the variation in a population is due to the differences between genotypes, and no variation is caused in the same genotype by the influence of the environment. A score of 0 means that all of the variation is caused by the environment; in other words, genetic differences among individuals have no influence on that particular trait." Then Wilson goes on to warn us as follows: "Notice also that heritability depends upon the environment in which the population lives. The same population, with an unchanged genetic constitution, can yield a different heritability score for a given characteristic if placed in a new environment." These apparently contradictory statements can be reconciled if we understand the origins of heritability statistics.

Jeff Peck (Note 1) pointed out that heritability statistics were developed by plant geneticists to estimate the feasibility of selective breeding programs under given sets of environmental conditions. For example, if you are interested in a phenotypic trait of corn, such as yield per acre, and you know the productivity of the related parental stocks, you can use heritability statistics to estimate the increases in yield resulting from a positive eugenics program. However, the heritability estimates obtained with a given variety of corn in a given region will differ from heritability estimates obtained with that same variety in another region of the country. Furthermore, heritability estimates for the same genetic stock in the same region will change if cultivation methods are changed.

Peck said that educators should be especially aware that cultivation can change heritability estimates, since they are in the business of cultivating human minds. Ironically, it is a professor of astronomy, David Layzer (1974), who instructed us in technical detail on the limitations of heritability analysis. He discussed the systematic cultural differences between races and socioeconomic classes and the significant genotype-environment correlations inherent in IQ measurement that render the method meaningless for human populations.

The best evidence that IQ heritability estimates are meaningless is provided by Loehlin *et al.* (1975). On pages 84-85, they present quantitative "estimates of the broad heritability of IQ in the range of .60 to .85," though they concede that "critics can be certainly found who offer arguments as to why these estimates might run a bit high." In Appendix I, they attribute a broad heritability estimate of .45 to Jencks and attempt to pull this into line with the higher figures. They argue that "two plausible changes" in Jenck's analysis would modify his "best guess" values from .45 to .60 and that "still other assumptions could modify them either up or down." Why not all the way down to the range of .00 to .50 attributed to Layzen (1974) or the .00 attributed to Kamin (1974)? Make your own assumptions to fit your own prejudicial values of human diversity and arrive at your own heritability estimate!

Intelligence and Race as a Numbers Game

On pages 53-54, Loehlin *et al.* (1975) ponder the question of whether intelligence is the single general ability to solve various items proposed by Spearman or the nine primary abilities proposed by Thurstone or the 20 factors proposed by French or the 120 factors proposed by Guilford. They omit the millions proposed by Tryon (1935). They feel more comfortable in operating "at a Thurstonian than at a Guilfordian level of differentiation." They "take this to be merely a matter of convenience, not of basic theoretical commitment."

Tryon, however, was committed to millions, arguing that IQ test methods are in accord with the notion that there is a nearly infinite number of mental elements. IQ tests are based on large numbers of items that show low intercorrelations within the test but a reasonable correlation with the total score on the test. This implies that there are many independent elements to sample. Any of this multitude of mental elements could effect behavior, resembling the action of genes, which exist in similar abundance. Two tests, viewed as samples of the same elements, can account for the high intercorrelations between similar IQ tests. Two tests, viewed as samples containing different elements, can account for the low correlations between dissimilar tests. Nevertheless, the authors seem to prefer the nine suggested by Thurstone as a matter of convenience for the game they play.

Nine is also their numerological choice for the races of man. On pages 32-33, they discuss racial classification, saying that it is rather arbitrary since the number of local breeding populations in the human species may be something on the order of one million. This means that we could arbitrarily take the number of races to be anything from one to one million, but they suggest that nine is reasonable. In Chapter 2, there is a lot of pretentious discussion of blood types, gene frequencies, and genetic drift for differentiating the racial groups. When the nine races are chosen, however, they turn out to be the same races arrived at by those who rely upon superficialities of skin, hair, and bone.

The Intelligence-Race Game

In his "classic" twin studies, Cyril Burt (1966) allegedly compared identical twins when one of each pair was raised in a different home and went to a different school in London. He allegedly tested them with English IQ tests and found that they performed about the same. They were more alike than mere brothers raised under the same conditions and more alike than completely unrelated children living in the same London house. These results are unsurprising, perhaps even trivial, but the British government knighted Burt, and the American Psychological Association honored him with its Thorndike Prize in 1971 — because Sir Cyril had the gall to imply that his results indicated that intelligence was mainly genetic (85%) and that the environment did not count for much. Obviously the results would have been different if one twin had been raised in London and the other in the Kalahari desert of South Africa by the !Kung Tribe or even if one twin had been systematically conditioned and rewarded for intellectual pursuits and the other for nonintellectual activities while living in similar English homes.

Sir Cyril was influential in setting up a three-track system, to which British children were irrevocably channelled at age 11 on the basis of tests that presumably measured their fixed genetic capacity to learn. When Sir Cyril died in 1971, after living the good life for 88 years, Arthur Jensen, of the University of California at Berkeley, eulogized him as "one of the world's great psychologists" and Richard Herrnstein of Harvard called him "a towering figure of 20th Century Psychology." These are rich tributes indeed for such thin research.

I use "allegedly" in referring to Sir Cyril's research because Leon J. Kamin of Princeton voiced some blunt criticisms in lectures and later detailed them in an illuminating book, *The Science and Politics of IQ* (Kamin, 1974). Nicholas Wade reported in *Science* (1976) that a geneticist going over Sir Cyril's papers raised suspicions that Burt may even have invented research associates and subjects, in addition to fudging his statistical data. Everyone agrees now that his research is useless, but they argue about whether he was fraudulent or merely eccentric. Does it really matter whether he invented plausible data or plausible assumptions to inflate his heritability estimates? Presumably not, for Wade reported Jensen's opinion that all of Burt's salient results have been duplicated and that Burt did not lead people into error! Presumably, Sir Cyril's prejudicial instinct that lower class children should be tracked into training for labor was correct after all! It is not surprising that the British Royal establishment knighted him for sharing their elitist presumptions; it is much more disturbing that the American Psychological Association also honored him for his "research."

In an article for *The Atlantic*, Richard Herrnstein (1971) of the Harvard Psychology Department, suddenly left the obscurity of the operant conditioning laboratory and burst into prominence with IQ genetics speculations. He theorized that socioeconomic classes in time become genetically distinct because people tend to marry within their class; that is, people of high status mate with others of high status, and soon the genes influencing high status become concentrated in the upper strata of society. Social mobility and equal opportunity accelerate this selection process. The problem with this theory is that socioeconomic status depends upon money, and money can be earned by a wide variety of people. Money is accumulated rapidly by investment bankers and cattle ranchers, by 5-foot jockeys and 7-foot basketball players, by sexy women and handsome fortune hunters. In one generation, money is accumulated by warriors and pirates, in another by prospectors and inventors, and in another by the talented offspring of workers and slaves. Under these conditions, it is difficult to see how money mating money would ever result in a purebred monied race. It seems a little like asking a dog breeder to produce a pure, blue-ribbon breed by inbreeding blue-ribbon winners regardless of whether they were poodles, terriers, Great Danes or any other canine stock that happened to catch the fancy of dog owners. Nevertheless, we can save Herrnstein's theory with a few plausible assumptions borrowed from Larry Niven (1970), a legitimate author of science fiction. Assume that, within the upper classes, the opportunity to mate is more or less random. Assume further that those who get the most opportunities to mate are lucky. After a number of generations, we could expect a "lucky trait" to be naturally selected into the upper classes, and of course these lucky people would acquire fortunes with ease.

Faulty Criteria and Faulty Tests

Sir Cyril's notions were echoed in the *Harvard Educational Review* by Arthur Jensen (1969), of the Education Department of the University of California at Berkeley. He declared, "Compensatory Education has been tried and it apparently has failed." The failure, he argues, was a result of the limited genetic potential of children from the lower socioeconomic classes who also tend to be brown and black. Presumably, these children were placed in compensatory educational programs when it was suspected that regular educational methods and intelligence tests were not valid for them. Now what criteria did Jensen use to "evaluate" compensatory education? He used intelligence tests similar to those used to track such children into compensatory programs. He found their IQ tests to be low indeed, so he deemed the compensatory education to be a waste. Obviously, lower class children can never rise to the top in this whirlpool of "scholarly" logic.

We should not be too harsh with Jensen, for he has not had the advantages of a Chicano education. I still recall the ridicule and shame I felt in elementary school when one of my Spanish words intruded into my English recitation. I certainly felt dumb. My genuinely sympathetic Anglo teacher seemed justified in holding me back a year when I failed oral reading and arithmetic recitation. At the time, I did not appreciate the irony in the same teacher's asking me to assist her with some of my friends who could speak only Spanish. One of my tasks was to bring them back, like a Judas goat leading lambs to slaughter, when they fled from the misery of the Anglo school to the protective warmth of their Chicano homes. How different our education would have been with a bilingual teacher to teach us in both English and Spanish. How different the criteria of pass-fail would have been. But of course, the sympathetic Anglo teacher, backed up by a sympathetic Anglo school board, was preparing us to deal with the "English-speaking reality" of life. There were no "unrealistic" requirements that teachers learn Spanish, if only to help us to move from unreal Spanish to real English.

Normalized Grade Point Averages (GPAs) within Groups

Jensen's circular nonreasoning illustrates that there is no inherent difference between predictive measures and criterion measures and that both must be viewed in their educational context. An intelligence test is fundamentally an admissions test for the academic track in primary and secondary schools. Admissions tests are fundamentally group intelligence tests.

If we remove all ethnic bias from such tests, more minority admissions to our universities might result. These minority candidates will inevitably earn lower GPAs because GPAs are based on ratings and tests that have the very bias we removed from our admissions measures. Few teachers, if any, make systematic efforts to weed out biased test items or rephrase them so that they deal with subject matter in a way fair to all ethnic groups. I have heard teachers protest, "My grading is fair; geometry is geometry, after all." But the way geometry is taught may be unfair. The way geometry tests are graded may be unfair. The Chicano student's response could justifiably be, "Then teach us in Spanish; geometry is geometry, after all!"

It is essential that we remove cultural bias from GPAs because they are a major variable in admission to higher institutions of learning. In high school GPA s there is another source of bias beyond those discussed above. Middle class parents exert much more pressure to raise their children's GPAs than do lower class parents, as any high school teacher knows all too well. We have no assurance that a Chicano student in an inner city school will receive the same grade, even if his performance is identical to that of an Anglo student in an affluent suburban school. Therefore, the grades, like intelligence scores, must be scaled within groups. GPAs of minority students must be converted to standard scores or percentile scores based on minority student norms. GPAs of majority students must be converted to standard scores based on majority norms. The "raw GPA" must be discarded and selection made, under conditions "blind" to the ethnic origin of the student, on the basis of a normalized GPA. This is the procedure used in the GRE (Graduate Record Examination), where, for example, the verbal score of any given woman is converted to a percentile score based on group scores of women. Men are given a percentile score based on male performance. Since men, as a group, score lower on the verbal GRE, each man is assigned a higher percentile score than any woman who does as well as he on the test, and he receives a higher percentile score than many women who do better than he does. (The converse is true on the quantitative component of the GRE). This procedure candidly admits that men, as a group, are "disadvantaged" compared to women, in the verbal component of the GRE and that normalized scores increase their chance to get into graduate school. This establishes a clear precedent for normalizing GPAs within relevant ethnic groups.

College, Graduate School, and Professional Quotas

Higher education is expensive, so an absolute quota is set for each segment of a university and consequently on every ethnic group applying to every segment. Someone is always disappointed, and this disappointment is exacerbated when the rewards to those selected are great. Medical schools are a prime example, but the observation applies to all segments of the university. There are always more qualified applicants than there are places; hence any method of selection is arbitrary to a great degree. Testing often makes things worse, because tests tend to become codified forms of prejudice concealing the fundamental issues of admissions.

Figure 1 illustrates a hypothetical correlation between scores on an admissions test and performance in school. The oval represents the scatter of the hypothetical population of applicants along the diagonal regression line. The correlation is approximately .70, which means that this hypothetical test is better than most real ones. We cannot improve the correlation much because the elements that make up the test are vastly different from those that make up performance. On the one hand, the test measures the student's responses to many brief queries; on the other, professors evaluate laboratory and clinical proficiency and other long, drawn-out coping behaviors of the student. The vertical cutoff line divides the population into accept or reject; its position is more or less fixed by the number of openings in the class for the given year. The horizontal cutoff line divides the expected performance into pass or fail and intersects the accept-reject line near the contour of the population, dividing the oval into unequal quadrants. The position of the pass-fail line is fixed because a number of forces operate to keep the number of students in the admit-fail quadrant low. Failures represent a financial loss, and professors are reluctant to fail such carefully selected students. Every reasonable effort is made to train and develop all the accepted students.

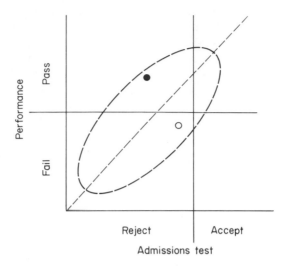

FIGURE 1. The correlation between an admissions test and school performance for a hypothetical population of applicants. The effect on the distributions of cutoff lines for accept-reject and pass-fail is depicted. The black dot represents an applicant who would have passed but was rejected. The white dot represents an applicant with a higher admission score who would have failed.

The upper left quadrant, however, contains a large segment of rejected students who would have passed if every effort had been made to train them. These students must swallow the bitter pill of rejection, made twice bitter because they are stigmatized as unqualified when, in fact, they were qualified.

Pseudoquantification, Discrimination, and "Reverse" Discrimination

The division of the population by the pass-fail line is obviously false and unjust. When a test contains systematic cultural bias such as testing experts have found in the Medical College Admissions Test (MCAT) and reported in Buros's *The Seventh Mental Measurements Yearbook* (1972), it follows that many minority candidates will be found in the upper left quadrant of the figure. Since large amounts of money hang in the balance on entry to medical schools, applicants bring suits in the courts for admission. Ironically, lawsuits are not always instigated to rectify discrimination against minorities but, in effect, to force that discrimination.

Consider two hypothetical students in our hypothetical population. The black dot in Figure 1 represents a worthy minority candidate who might be found by a committee using special admissions procedures to ameliorate the discrimination of the admissions test. As soon as such a candidate is admitted, every rejected candidate with a higher score on the admissions test can sue for admission in the courts on the grounds of "reverse discrimination." Moreover, even an unworthy candidate, represented by the white circle, can conceivably gain admission through the courts because he too has a higher score on the admissions tests. Presumably he can force admission without going through the special admissions procedures that established the worth of the minority candidate.

It is the minority candidates who should be suing for being subjected to such admission tests as the MCAT, for the courts have established that applicants cannot be subjected to tests which bear no relation to the occupation to which they apply. The expert reviews in Buros's *The Seventh Mental Measurement Yearbook* (1972) indicate that the MCAT has little, if any, validity for predicting a student's success in medical school. Nor has it any proven relationship to excellence in the practice of medicine, the job for which we are selecting medical students.

I am not criticizing medical school admissions procedures specifically. I use these procedures as an example of the limitations of testing because they represent the most thorough and conscientious selection process in university admissions. The problem is as bleak for all graduate departments that use GPA and the Graduate Record Examination (GRE). The accuracy of these tests in predicting student success was described as no better than modest (Willingham, 1974). One needs only to look at the effects that the cutoff lines have on the population oval in Figure 1. Validity data can be obtained only from those who were accepted, and the accept-reject line alters the scatter oval from one that resembles a validity correlation of .70 to one that resembles .00.

Figure 1 is a simplification illustrating the use of one test, but the correlational oval is generous; the actual scatter may be more circular. Admissions committees use interviews, vitas, and references, as well as tests and grades. These other sources are largely redundant and of dubious validity because they only tell us about the applicants' capacity to deal with the role of student or applicant as a youth. They tell us nothing about the applicant's ability to handle his occupation when he is older. Therefore validity correlations will always be low. Often this supplementary evidence is also scaled into numbers and statistically combined with grades and test scores into one number, a simplification that makes Figure 1 applicable.

Selecting Candidates by Lottery

The accept-reject division of the applicants above the pass line in Figure 1 is the pseudoquantification that causes legal problems. It is often suggested by harried admissions people that we should conduct a lottery to select applicants to fill the limited number of available openings. In effect, selection committees would simply attempt to determine whether applicants were reasonable candidates for training and then randomly select the members of the class for that year. Such a lottery would have many real advantages. The rejected but worthy applicant would be deemed unlucky, not unqualified, and be free to try again at another time or another place. The pressure from unlucky applicants would be directed toward increasing the number of openings in succeeding lotteries. The opportunities for minority applicants would be substantially increased, even with biased admissions procedures. Finally, the lottery would reduce the unreasonable pressure on applicants to achieve the highest possible grades and scores by whatever device possible.

The exaggerated importance of standardized testing has other pernicious effects on the educational process. If students know they must pass a standard test with grades higher than others, a premium is placed upon competitive tactics, perhaps even on cheating, rather than on cooperation. Competitive students must restrict themselves to classes that will raise their test scores and forego many enriching activities of university life. Moreover, tests like the national medical boards can direct students' attention away from areas of training vital to the healing arts that cannot be encapsuled in test items. Moreover, since the average performance of students on national tests reflects on their schools, there is pressure on faculties to train students to pass tests rather than master the arts and sciences. The selective pressure of testing may well present us with candidates we do not want as friends. As Michael Wallach said, "Tests tell us little about talent [1976]."

In the final analysis, tests and the spurious concept of "intelligence" exist because a testing industry offered universities the illusion of quantification to cope with the education of qualitatively diverse people. Racial differences in intelligence exist as a research area, and the genetic superiority of the privileged classes is proclaimed because historically the university has been a bastion of privilege. A great public univerity dedicated to unselfish inquiry and freely accessible to all sexual, racial, and social groups seems to be evolving. It needs all our strength to make it viable. But we must take warning from another lottery – the Selective Service. The quotas for Vietnam were too large among the black, the brown, and the poor. Equal opportunity became the cry, and random selection from a pool of eligible candidates loomed as the method. The draft vanished as pressure to make it fair increased; so might a fair university.

The Validity of Unfair Tests in an Unfair Society

Testing as a predictive device is limited by the social context in which it operates. Predict the chances for success of an attractive black male gynecologist in the white suburbs of Birmingham, Alabama in 1920, even if he were another Lister. Predict the chances of a Jewish politician in Germany in 1930, even if he were another Bismarck. Predict the chances of a female naval technician in the United States Navy in 1940, even if she were another Nelson. No matter how precisely we measured the talent and training of these three candidates, no matter how well these predictive measures were correlated with what was needed for success in their respective jobs, a few simple items revealing the race and sex of each candidate would be more predictive of their success in their chosen professions in their times. Criteria are ultimately provided by society. If society is unfair, then criterion measures are unfair, and unfair tests are more valid than fair tests. This simple truth quickly becomes lost in technical discussion of statistical and ethical implications of various definitions of test bias by psychometricians, who solemnly warn us that race, sex, and ethnicity may be valid predictors of performance above and beyond the effects of other variables (Hunter and Schmidt, 1976).

When the criteria are fair and objective, a condition that seems to be most closely approached in athletics, neither race nor quota concern us. We could probably learn much from the Wizard of Westwood, who assessed and developed basketball talent with cool detachment. With a keen eye on the basketball game, he freely shuffled black and white players with impunity. He steadfastly refused to compare one player with another, and he changed his strategy so as to win with the specific talents he had at hand. A remarkable diversity of individualistic personalities flourished under his firm discipline, as he neither imposed nor surrendered his own intense ethos. But not even the *Brujo* of the Bruins could have weaved his magic before basketball fans and alumni were ready for black players.

REFERENCE NOTE

1. Peck, J. Personal communication.

REFERENCES

Buros, O.K. *The seventh mental measurements yearbook, Volume 2*. Highland Park, N.J.: The Gryphon Press, 1972, 1509-1514.

Burt, C. The genetic determination of differences in intelligence: A study of monozygotic twins reared together and apart. *British Journal of Psychology*, 1966, *57*, 137-153.

Garcia, J. The futility of comparative IQ research. In N.A. Buchwald & Mary A.B. Brazier (Eds.), *Brain mechanisms in mental retardation*. New York: Academic Press, 1975, 421-442.

Hensen, A.R. How much can we boost IQ and scholastic achievement? *Harvard Educational Review*, 1969, *39*, 1-123.

Herrnstein, R. IQ. *The Atlantic*, 1971, *228*, 43-58.

Hunter, J.E., & Schmidt, F.L. Critical analysis of these statistical and ethical implications of various definitions of *test bias*. *Psychological Bulletin*, 1976, *83*, 1053-1071.

Kamin, L.J. *The science and politics of I.Q.* New York: Wiley, 1974.

Layzer, D. Heritability analyses of IQ scores: Science or numerology? *Science*, 1974, *183*, 1259-1266.

Lenneberg, E.H. On explaining language. *Science*, 1974, *164*, 635-643.

Loehlin, J.C., Lindzey, G., & Spuhler, J.N. *Race differences in intelligence*. San Francisco: W.H. Freeman and Company, 1975.

McCall, R.B., Appelbaum, M.I., & Hogarty, P.S. Developmental changes in mental performance. *Monogram of the Society for Research in Child Development*, 1973, *38*, 1-83.

Mercer, J. Identifying the gifted Chicano child. In J.L. Martinez, Jr. (Ed.), *Chicano Psychology*, New York: Academic Press, 1977, 155-173.

Niven, L. *Ringworld*. New York: Ballantine Books, 1970, 188-189.

Olmedo, F. Psychological testing and the Chicano: A reassessment. In J.L. Martinez, Jr. (Ed.), *Chicano Psychology*, 1977, 175-195.

Stevens, S.S. Mathematics, measurement, and psychophysics. In S.S. Stevens (Ed.), *Handbook of experimental psychology*, New York: Wiley, 1951.

Terman, L.M., & Merrill, M.A. *Stanford-Binet Intelligence Scale* (3rd ed.), Boston: Houghton, 1960.

Tryon, R.C. A theory of psychological components – an alternative to "mathematical" factors. *Psychological Review*, 1935, *42*, 425-454.

Wade, N. IQ and heredity: Suspicion of fraud beclouds classic experiment. *Science*, 1976, *194*, 916-919.

Wallach, M.A. Tests tell us little about talent. *American Scientist*, 1976, *64*, 57-63.

Williams, R.L. The BITCH-100: A culture-specific test. *Journal of Afro-American Issues*, 1975, *3*, 103-116.

Willingham, W.W. Predicting success in graduate education. *Science*, 1974, *183*, 273-278.

Wilson, E.O. *Sociobiology. The new synthesis*. Cambridge, Mass.: Belknap Press of Harvard University Press, 1975.

PART IV
Mental Health and Psychotherapy

CHAPTER 14

ETHNIC VARIABLES IN PSYCHOTHERAPY: THE MEXICAN AMERICAN

FRANK X. ACOSTA[1]

University of Southern California, School of Medicine

Although highly disadvantaged and subject to multiple stresses, the Mexican American has been substantially underrepresented among those who receive mental health services (Padilla & Ruiz, 1973; Padilla, Ruiz, & Alvarez, 1975). This has been true even in Los Angeles County, which has the nation's largest number of Mexican American residents and one of the nation's most comprehensive networks of mental health services.

A specific example of an underutilization profile is found in the rates of new admissions for outpatient mental health services for Mexican Americans in the Los Angeles County Mental Health Report (1973, 1975). While these rates have shown a slight increase, from 10.3% in 1970 to 12.5% in 1974, they are still strikingly low compared to the Mexican American population of about 21% in Los Angeles.

By contrast, overutilization is found in the use of the same kind of services by blacks. These rates show a greater increase, from 19.4% in 1970 to 26.10% in 1974, and are much greater in proportion to the black population, which is about 12%. Even in the Mexican American community of East Los Angeles, the rates of new admissions for outpatient mental health services from July 1973 to June 1974 were 22.9%, while in the black community of Southeast Los Angeles, the rates for the same period were 77.7% (Los Angeles County Mental Health Report, 1975). Although Mexican Americans are beginning to use mental health services in slightly increasing numbers, these figures underscore the fact that they are far below the expected proportion and present a sharply different utilization profile than the black minority group from the same geographic area.

A small body of research has recently begun to focus both on the paradoxical lack of participation of Mexican Americans in mental health programs and

[1]Preparation of this manuscript was assisted by a grant awarded to the author by the Social Science Research Council's Committee on Grants to Minority Scholars for Research on Racism and Other Social Factors in Mental Health. For his research contributions and work on this article, the author was awarded the First Annual Faculty Research Prize by the Department of Psychiatry, University of Southern California School of Medicine.

on the type of services they receive. This discussion examines how the Mexican American perceives and relates to psychotherapy, psychotherapists, and mental health services in general. How Mexican Americans' ethnic and cultural background may affect their participation in psychotherapy will also be explored. In addition, this discussion examines how such therapist factors as ethnicity, expertise, sociocultural background, and stereotypes may affect the initiation and process of therapy with an ethnic minority patient. Recommendations are made for future research that may promote better understanding of the needs of Mexican Americans and provide improved mental health services to them.

The Need for Psychotherapy and Mental Health Services

POVERTY AND DISCRIMINATION

Substantial evidence has recently affirmed that Mexican Americans are a disadvantaged group (U.S. Bureau of Census, 1974). They have experienced little social progress even though they have lived in the United States longer than most other ethnic groups. In fact, some families have lived in the United States since before the land annexations from Mexico. Mexican Americans' lack of social mobility and economic advancement has typically been explained by social scientists as a result of their approach to life and their distinct cultural values (Madsen, 1964; Saunders, 1954). These ascribed values, such as greater concern for the present than the future, being more dependent than individualistic, and being more nongoal oriented than goal oriented, are usually viewed as the opposites of Anglo American values and impediments to success in the United States (Vaca, 1970). Unfortunately, findings by investigators working with rural and isolated groups of Mexican Americans (Kluckhohn & Strodtbeck, 1961) have been generalized to the majority of Mexican American people, who reside primarily in large urban areas.

It has been established, however, that Mexican Americans have been the objects of discrimination by Anglo American society. Mexican Americans now find themselves markedly behind the larger society in total amount of education, occupations, income, housing, political representation, and professional identification (U.S. Census, 1974; Grebler, Moore, & Guzman, 1970). Discrimination against Mexican Americans has also been documented in the legal and judicial system (Morales, 1972).

These oppressive conditions should certainly make Mexican Americans particularly vulnerable to serious psychological distress and lowered levels of self-esteem. Several major urban studies have already demonstrated that lower socioeconomic status in itself is associated with a higher incidence of psychiatric problems (Hollingshead & Redlich, 1958; Srole, Langer, Michael, Opler, & Rennie, 1962). However, much research remains to be done to assess empirically the level of psychological distress experienced by Mexican Americans.

GENERATION LEVELS

In addition to being subject to poverty and to discrimination by the larger society, Mexican Americans must also deal with problems of acculturation and language. Census figures for 1970 estimate that, of the more than four and one-half million Mexican Americans living in the Southwest, more than two million were either born in Mexico or born to parents who had immigrated from Mexico (Hernandez, Estrada, & Alvirez, 1973). These figures, which probably underestimate the actual numbers of Mexican American people and do not reflect recent immigrants from Mexico, indicate that large numbers are either immigrants or first generation Mexican Americans. The 1970 census also indicates that a large majority of Mexican Americans specify Spanish as their native tongue or the language spoken in their home as children.

This profile suggests that a significant number of Mexican Americans are still relatively close to the Spanish language. It further suggests that, in years if not in practice, many Mexican Americans are close to the social, familial, religious, and cultural systems of Mexico.

FAMILY AND RELIGION

In the dominant family pattern among Mexicans, the husband and father tends to have a great deal of authority and receives respect and obedience. The wife and mother tends to be obedient and compliant to her husband and receives respect and emotional reward from her children. The younger children respect the older children (Peñalosa, 1968). While it is often claimed that Mexican American families, particularly extended families, are a strong source of personal communication and support for family members, the actual utility of the family for solving serious emotional problems has not been examined.

The Roman Catholic religion also seems to play a major role in the lives of most Mexicans (Peñalosa, 1968). Catholicism is also the predominant religion for Mexican Americans (Grebler *et al.*, 1970). Even if Catholicism is not practiced through regular church attendance, basic Christian beliefs and practices such as prayer may provide tremendous help to the Mexican American in time of need and emotional distress. This has not yet been specifically examined. Nor has the impact on an individual's mental health of such Catholic beliefs as the value of the confessional and the immortality of the human soul been examined.

ACCULTURATION AND SELF-IDENTITY

Little empirical research has been done on the psychological effects on Mexican Americans of acculturation to Anglo American lifestyles. Fabrega and Wallace (1968) found that among Mexican American patients hospitalized for psychiatric care, those more marginally acculturated had the highest number of hospitalizations, in comparison to those who were either traditional or highly acculturated.

The potential severity of the problem of ethnic self-identity for Mexican Americans as they move into the Anglo American lifestyle is not currently known. It is important to note that most Mexican Americans are several generations removed from immigrant status.

The magnitude of the problem of self-identity is hinted at in several studies. In a survey of 666 Mexican Americans in California, half of whom were born in Mexico and half born in the United States, respondents identified themselves as Mexican 54%, Mexican American 27%, American of Mexican descent 7%, and Chicano 6% (Padilla, Carlos, & Keefe, 1976). In a study with 94 native-born Mexican American junior college students in East Los Angeles, students identified themselves as Mexican American 48%, Chicano 30%, Mexican 10%, Caucasian 6%, white 4%, and other 2% (Acosta & Sheehan, in press). The differences between and within these two groups suggest that generation, age, and area of residence may be important factors in the ethnic self-identity of Mexican Americans. Identification with the label *Chicano* was seen in only a small minority of the Padilla *et al.* (1976) native-born and foreign-born respondents, and in less than one-third of Acosta and Sheehan's (in press) native-born group. Among the latter group about the same percentage identified themselves as Mexican or as Caucasian-white.

In summary, it strongly appears that the Mexican American is indeed subject to many conditions of psychological stress. It appears further that the Mexican American does have special needs for the intervention of mental health professionals.

Perceptions toward Psychotherapy

Does the Mexican American perceive psychological problems differently and thus not consider seeking psychiatric help? Karno and Edgarton (1969) interviewed large groups of Anglo Americans and Mexican Americans of similar socioeconomic status and concluded that the two groups did not differ significantly in their perceptions and definitions of mental illness. A further finding was that even though the majority of each group were unable to name or locate a single psychiatric clinic, the majority of both groups felt that a psychiatric clinic could help a person with a psychiatric disorder.

It is not clear, however, to what degree Mexican Americans perceive psychiatric clinics as useful in the presence of psychological problems that they would not categorize as mental illness. In the Karno and Edgarton (1969) study, the respondents were mainly presented with vignettes that described people manifesting psychotic conditions such as schizophrenia. The term mental illness thus referred primarily to psychosis. However, emotional or psychological problems may take the form of many conditions, such as anxiety neurosis or interpersonal conflicts, that do not include thought disorder or other signs of psychosis. Further research is needed to evaluate Mexican American definitions, attitudes, and perceived resources for such predominant nonpsychotic problems as situational reactions, depressive reactions, anxiety reactions, sexual dysfunctions, adjustment reactions, and marital problems.

In a recent study, Acosta and Sheehan (1976) investigated the reactions of large groups of Mexican American and Anglo American junior college students to psychotherapists and psychotherapy. One main finding revealed ethnic differences in the students' perceptions of the usefulness of therapy. Mexican Americans showed a significantly more favorable attitude toward the potential usefulness of therapy than Anglo Americans. No socioeconomic differences were found. Both the Karno and Edgarton (1969) and the Acosta and Sheehan (1976) findings that Mexican Americans see psychiatric clinics and psychotherapy as useful for some problems further underscores the contradictory and striking underrepresentation of Mexican Americans in psychiatric settings.

One explanation offered for this underrepresentation has been the Mexican American use of special folk healers or *curanderos* for the solution of many psychological and emotional difficulties. Several authors have reported that *curanderos* are both popular and often successful in both rural and urban areas of the Southwestern United States (Kiev, 1968; Madsen, 1964). These reports, however, have generally provided little data to support their claims. In sharp contrast to the reportedly widespread use of *curanderos*, Edgarton, Karno, and Fernandez (1970) found that only a few people out of a large sample of Mexican Americans residing in East Los Angeles would recommend a *curandero* for help with a psychological disturbance. However, these same subjects did specify physicians as the favored treatment resource for "mild, moderate, and severe mental illness."

In a recent study by Padilla *et al.* (1976), in which large groups of both native-born and foreign-born Mexican Americans were surveyed about mental health service utilization, it was again found that not one person would recommend a *curandero* to someone with an emotional problem. Padilla *et al.* also found that about half their respondents could name a mental health clinic, felt positive about it, and would be willing to use it. In actuality, however, very few claimed to use the clinic, and the majority would recommend a doctor for problems of anxiety and depression.

The inference of the Edgarton *et al.* (1970) and the Padilla *et al.* (1976) studies is that family physicians are perceived by Mexican Americans as a primary choice for treatment of psychological problems. In a survey of a random sample of private general physicians in a barrio of Los Angeles, Karno, Ross, and Caper (1969) found that the majority of these physicians reported that they were providing chemotherapy and brief supportive help to some of their Mexican American patients experiencing emotional disturbances. These investigators pointedly noted that no other institution in the community was as active and available a source of help for emotional problems.

It appears that Mexican Americans primarily receive chemotherapy from practitioners not psychiatrically trained. This agrees with Hollingshead and Redlich (1958) who found that lower class persons receive more chemotherapy and are more often labeled as psychotic than middle and upper class, who receive more psychotherapy and are seen as neurotic.

One explanation for the underrepresentation of Mexican Americans in psychotherapy and in psychiatric facilities may be the fact that there is a conspicuous lack of such facilities in Mexican American communities (Morales, 1971). In addition, where local facilities do exist, there is usually a marked absence of bilingual-bicultural staff.

From the studies reviewed here, it also appears probable that Mexican Americans are much more familiar with the functions of physicians than with the functions of psychotherapists. My own clinical impressions of psychiatric patients who apply for services suggest that Mexican Americans often seek help for somatic complaints, as well as many emotional, interpersonal, and environmental problems. The environmental problems often include oppressive living conditions, unemployment, and difficulties in dealing with government agencies. Psychosomatic complaints appear to be more pronounced among Mexican American patients, particularly if they are foreign-born, than among other low-income groups. It is not uncommon for people, particularly poor people (Hollingshead & Redlich, 1958), to experience physical symptoms caused by recent or sustained periods of psychological stress. For example, some common complaints among persons experiencing anxiety or situational reactions may include rapid heart palpitations; breathing difficulties; chest, neck, and shoulder tenseness and pain; sweating; headaches; and sleep disturbance. Empirical research is seriously needed to systematically evaluate the psychological states experienced by Mexican Americans. No direct within-culture or cross-cultural empirical data are yet available to test these clinical impressions about Mexican American patients.

Issues in Therapy for Spanish-Speaking and Bilingual Patients

Although the number of Mexican American mental health professionals has increased slightly since the miniscule numbers reported by Ruiz in 1971, the overwhelming majority continue to be Anglo American. It is primarily Anglo therapists who will see, evaluate, and treat Mexican Americans who decide to seek therapy.

In many cases, the language barrier makes it impossible for Spanish-speaking persons to communicate with monolingual Anglo therapists. Thus, services are virtually unobtainable among monolingual Spanish speakers. A few Anglo American therapists have probably learned enough Spanish at least to communicate with Spanish-speaking patients, but their numbers are likely to be small, and the depth of communication is probably not the same. Research and statistics are not available to determine how many patients have been refused services because of the absence of Spanish-speaking therapists or unreasonably long waiting lists or through being discharged prematurely by impatient therapists.

THE IMPACT OF INTERPRETERS AND COMMUNITY AIDES

In a recent effort to provide more Spanish-speaking patients with the opportunity to be seen — in response to a growing waiting list and in the light of professional hiring freezes — the author recently initiated a community aide and interpreter program at a busy psychiatric outpatient clinic in a Mexican American community. The program began in January 1975 with a training program for volunteer bilingual Mexican American college students who would interpret for psychiatric residents at the Psychiatric Outpatient Clinic of the Los Angeles County — University of Southern California Medical Center. In January 1976, it developed into a full-time community aide and interpreter program with the hiring of two full-time, bilingual staff members, Manuel Chavez and Mary Lou Alarid. Both community aides lived in the community they were serving.

Training the community aides to be interpreters involved close supervision including weekly meetings, feedback, and role-playing sessions in which tapes of their sessions with patients and therapists were reviewed. Accuracy of translation was stressed. Difficulties with nuances of expression, time delay in communication, depth of communication, and the problems inherent in triadic interactions are disadvantages to such a program.

In addition to translating, the community aides were able to help the therapists and patients identify community resources, help the Spanish-speaking patients in their contacts with various agencies, participate in Spanish-speaking and English-speaking group therapy with the professional staff, and serve as friends to a large number of patients.

Over a one and one-half year period, this program proved to be a major service for Spanish-speaking patients. For example, 125 new patients were seen with an interpreter from May 1975 through June 1976, and many of these patients either continued to work with the therapists and interpreters or were subsequently treated by Spanish-speaking professionals.

In order to evaluate the specific utility of interpreting for both the Spanish-speaking patient and the therapist, a comparative study was undertaken by Kline, Acosta, Austin, and Johnson (Note 1) in an early developmental phase of this program. This study evaluated the reactions to their first therapy sessions of 21 Spanish-speaking patients who had used an interpreter and 41 English-speaking Spanish-surnamed patients. The patients' responses were then compared with the questionnaire responses of 19 English-speaking psychiatric residents who had worked through interpreters. Some of the major results of the Kline *et al.* (Note 1) study indicated that Spanish-speaking patients interviewed with the help of an interpreter (*a*) felt better understood than bilingual patients spoken to only in English, (*b*) saw the interview as more helpful, and (*c*) were just as willing to return for a second visit. In contrast, the therapists overwhelmingly indicated that the patients interviewed with an interpreter felt less understood, less helped, and less willing to return for a second visit than patients interviewed directly in English. A key implication of this study is that therapists consistently underestimated the degree to which Spanish-speaking patients felt helped.

POTENTIAL THERAPIST PROBLEMS

Several potential therapy problems can occur for an Anglo American therapist treating a Mexican American patient. Such a relationship can easily evoke uncertainties and stereotypes for the Anglo therapist if he/she believes it is impossible to help someone who is socioculturally different. Several studies have reported, for example, that experienced therapists, trainees, and supervisors expressed discontent, frustration, and unwillingness to treat or offer therapy to low-income patients (Lorion, 1974).

Even the Anglo American therapist who is interested in helping a Mexican American patient may harbor myths, stereotypes, and misinformation about the Mexican American's cultural background that could distort the therapist's perception, diagnosis, and treatment. Thomas and Sillen (1972) argued cogently that this kind of distortion often occurs when white therapists treat blacks.

The fact that certain words may have different meanings for Chicanos may create problems for Anglo therapists. Martinez (1977) and his coinvestigators found that among high school and college students, the concept of father differed greatly for Chicano males compared to that perceived by Chicano females, Anglo males, and Anglo females.

Current mental health literature continues to reflect well-intentioned misperceptions and misconceptions of Anglo therapists that can only serve to maintain a belief that Mexican Americans are somehow extremely different and must therefore be treated in extremely different ways. Kreisman (1975), for example, recently published two cases in which he treated Mexican Americans with their "culturally bound concept of illness [p. 81]." In essence, he describes telling his two patients that he had special herbs from a *curandera* and thus could offer a "course of curanderismo [p. 81]." It was posited by Kreisman that Mexican Americans "often" seek the services of a *curandero* because of their cultural concept of illness. As indicated earlier, in the findings of Padilla *et al.* (1976) and Edgarton *et al.* (1970), *curanderos* are seldom, if at all, used by Mexican Americans.

It is important, then, for psychotherapists who treat Mexican Americans to be aware of cultural differences but not to stereotype the Mexican American.

Traditional Treatment Received

Since the Mexican American population is clearly subsumed within the poor classes of our nation, it is important to consider how social class factors may affect the client's participation in psychotherapy. Several studies in the past two decades have found that psychotherapy is traditionally available to clients in primarily middle and upper classes but not to clients in the working and poor classes (Brill, & Storrow, 1960; Garfield, 1971; Hollingshead & Redlich, 1958; Rosenthal & Frank, 1958).

In comprehensive reviews, both Cobb (1972) and Lorion (1973) cited numerous studies which indicate that people from the poor and working classes have the least opportunity to obtain professional help, even in public outpatient clinics and community mental health centers where services are virtually free to low-income groups. These reviews indicate that lower class patients are accepted less often for therapy, drop out more often, or are discharged sooner.

A few studies have found that patients from different social class levels who engage in individual therapy and stay with it exhibit no differences in treatment outcome or success. Albronda, Dean, and Starkweather (1964), for example, found that low-income patients even responded a little better to treatment than higher income patients after 11 interviews. The implication of this research is that therapists have been either highly discriminative about whom they treat or unwilling to adapt to the lifestyle and needs of lower class patients.

What kind of treatment do Mexican Americans encounter when they seek professional psychiatric assistance in public outpatient clinics? Both Yamamoto, James, Bloombaum, and Hattem (1967) and Karno (1966) have reported in separate studies that in spite of similar low social status, Anglo American patients received significantly more individual therapy than either Mexican American or black patients. The strong implication of both the Yamamoto *et al.* and the Karno studies is that it is not only the social class of ethnic patients that excludes them from psychiatric treatment but also their ethnic identification. For Mexican Americans the odds become even greater that they will not receive therapeutic help even if it is sought.

Preferences toward Psychotherapists

The effects of client perceptions of the psychotherapist in initial involvement and on the outcome of treatment seem to be particularly important for a study of client participation in psychotherapy, whether it be by Mexican Americans or any other group. A few investigators have recently begun to study systematically the different characteristics of therapists that lead to preferential selection by different clients (Boulware & Holmes, 1970; Wolkon, Moriwaki, & Williams, 1973).

Acosta and Sheehan (1976) recently examined the effects of therapist ethnicity and expertise on the preferences and attitudes toward therapists by Mexican Americans and Anglo Americans. In this study, 94 Mexican American and 93 Anglo American junior college students listened to one of two matched therapy audiotapes containing the same dialogue. The tapes presented a therapist working for the first time with an anxious, depressed, and at times angry young man. In one tape, the therapist spoke fluent English with a slight Spanish accent; in the other, he spoke fluent English without an accent. The therapist was identified as being in one of four categories: Anglo American professional, Anglo American nonprofessional, Mexican American professional, and Mexican American nonprofessional. The same therapist was introduced as either a professional (Dr.) or as a nonprofessional (Mr.), with corresponding high and low descriptions of his expertise. When he spoke English with a slight Spanish accent, he was also identified by a common Spanish name, Raul Sanchez, and it was stated that his parents came from Mexico. When he spoke unaccented English, he was identified by a common Anglo American name, William Jones, and it was stated that his ancestors came from Northern Europe before the Civil War. After hearing the tape, subjects indicated on rating scales their attitudes toward the therapist.

Acosta and Sheehan found that both Mexican Americans and Anglo Americans expressed significantly more positive attitudes toward the Anglo American professional and the Mexican American nonprofessional. More specifically, both ethnic groups attributed more skill, understanding, trustworthiness, and liking to the Anglo American professional and the Mexican American nonprofessional. It is important to note, however, that while the Anglo professional and the Mexican American nonprofessional were seen more positively than either the Anglo nonprofessional or the Mexican American professional, all therapists were seen with moderately positive attitudes.

Acosta and Sheehan concluded that while the Mexican Americans held generally favorable attitudes toward therapists and psychotherapy, they appeared to have less trust and credence in an expert therapist of their own ethnicity. The implication is that Mexican American professionals may not yet have achieved high public credibility among their own ethnic group.

Some social psychologists have argued that similarity to stimulus persons will lead to more credibility, trust, respect, and attraction (Berscheid, 1966; Brook, 1965; Minnick, 1957). Simons, Berkowitz, and Moyer (1970), however, argued that the bulk of research on the effects of similarity and dissimilarity remains equivocal. Many studies in the 1950s and 1960s with black and white children indicated that both groups tend to choose white stimuli or people as a preference (Brand, Ruiz, & Padilla, 1974). A few recent studies, however, have shown higher preference by blacks for black stimulus persons. Brand *et al.* (1974) suggested that these later findings may reflect black pride or may be the result of better experimental measures. Peñalosa (1970) argued that changes in self-identification will probably occur among many Mexican Americans as the result of the new Chicano movement. Ethnic similarity and dissimilarity between therapists and clients, therefore, warrant greater study for the Mexican American population.

Self-Disclosure Styles

How are the self-disclosure styles of Mexican Americans related to their use of psychotherapy? Self-disclosure tendencies could greatly affect participation in psychotherapy since it is primarily through self-disclosures that patients communicate their thoughts, feelings, and problems to the therapist.

The area of self-disclosure styles among Mexican Americans has been open to a great deal of speculation and little empirical evidence. For example, Heiman, Burruel, and Chavez (1975) noted that open discussion of feelings, particularly outside the family, is discouraged in Mexican American culture. Jaco (1959) has argued that, in fact, Mexican Americans rely a great deal on the family to discuss personal problems and receive emotional support in times of stress. Grebler *et al.* (1970) found that a slight majority of a large sample of Mexican American men and women responded that they turned to people other than their relatives for help in any kind of problem, be it personal, financial, political, or bureaucratic, in contrast to both Jaco (1959) and Heiman *et al.* (1975).

Acosta and Sheehan (in press) recently examined the self-disclosure styles of Mexican American and Anglo American junior college students in relation to therapists of different ethnic and professional identifications. Students listened to one of two matched therapy tapes of a therapist working with a disturbed young man. Therapists were described and identified as Anglo American professional, Anglo American nonprofessional, Mexican American professional, and Mexican American nonprofessional. Students then responded to a self-disclosure scale designed to measure degree of willingness to disclose information about themselves to the therapists. This scale contained five areas of self-disclosure: personal problems, sex, work, body concept, and general dissatisfaction. It was found that Mexican Americans showed significantly less willingness to self-disclose than Anglo Americans. Both groups, however, showed positive willingness to disclose to therapists.

Acosta and Sheehan's findings indicated that Mexican Americans are, in general, willing to make considerable disclosure to therapists, regardless of whether the therapist is professional or nonprofessional, Anglo American or Mexican American. This was true regardless of the area of self-disclosure or the student's sex and socioeconomic class. This finding is certainly in contrast to the generally held assumption that Mexican Americans, particularly males, are not likely to show much willingness to talk about personal matters. Nevertheless, the finding that Mexican Americans showed less willingness to disclose than Anglo Americans further suggests that Mexican Americans may be more reserved about disclosure to a stranger, in this case, a therapist. This implication needs to be investigated in future research.

Bilingual-Bicultural Treatment Approaches

Few reports deal with bilingual-bicultural treatment approaches with Mexican Americans, and virtually no empirical work has been reported. Padilla *et al.* (1975) reviewed several innovative approaches with the Spanish-speaking population grouping them into (*a*) professional adaptation, (*b*) family adaptation, and (*c*) barrio service centers. The professional adaptation model referred to clinics where greater numbers of professional and paraprofessional staff were Spanish-speaking and where treatment programs were more available to the Spanish-surnamed. The family adaptation model referred to group therapy programs in which therapists tried to approximate Puerto Rican family structure within the groups. The barrio service center model referred to mental health programs in which professional and paraprofessional staff provided help both for psychological problems and for a variety of other problems such as economic difficulties. Most of the programs reported were in preliminary stages of development; four dealt with Puerto Rican populations, three with Mexican American populations, and one with a Hispanic population. On the whole, Padilla *et al.* (1975) indicated that these programs, though few in number, had met with some success and deserved further exploration.

One of the first reported efforts to try to adapt services for Mexican Americans was described by Karno and Morales (1971). The major focus of this effort was the development of a bilingual-bicultural mental health center in the Mexican American community of East Los Angeles. The authors indicated that the program began with a predominantly bilingual Mexican American professional staff. In contrast to low utilization rates, 86% of the first 200 patients seen were Mexican American. The authors report some success in the early stages of their program but note the need for empirical investigation to assess the degree of the program's success.

Heiman *et al.* (1975) described the operation of a psychiatric outpatient clinic in Tucson. Again, the presence of a bilingual staff was emphasized; three of seven full-time staff members were bilingual. Half of the board of directors were Mexican American, and 61% of one month's patient load was Mexican American. The authors stressed the importance of advertising services on radio and in newspapers. The program provided both traditional psychotherapy and direct assistance in helping patients deal with such environmental problems as job hunting and applying for welfare assistance.

The efforts of a bilingual-bicultural staff to improve services available to Mexican Americans in Bexar County, Texas were reported by Serrano and Gibson (1973). Much of their work appears to be in building links with the community and in consulting with various community agencies and institutions. The authors report an increase of Mexican American patients in referrals from other agencies.

In treating Spanish-speaking Mexican American patients in a Mexican American community at the Psychiatric Outpatient Clinic of the Los Angeles County – University of Southern California Medical Center, I have seen a highly positive response from both men and women to the opportunity to participate in Spanish-speaking therapy. Rather than stereotypical poor time orientation and low self-disclosure styles, patients have typically shown high reliability in keeping appointments, once they are involved in treatment, and have self-disclosed a great deal in therapy. This pattern has been the norm in crisis intervention, time-limited or short-term therapy, long-term therapy, and group therapy.

I have noted relative differences in patients' responses to different treatment approaches, however. Patients have appeared to be more at ease and self-disclosing in individual therapy than in group therapy. Some explicitly state that they prefer to be seen by an individual therapist and not in a group therapy setting. Their reasons have included reluctance to make disclosures in public, fear of receiving less attention for their own problems, and reluctance to listen to other people's problems out of fear of increasing their own anxiety. Nonetheless, many patients who do join group therapy indicate that they are benefiting from the experience and are regular participants. It is important to note that, as with any group of people, some patients are more open and verbally active, while others are more reticent.

An eclectic approach with low-income Spanish-speaking patients has proved to be the most effective and has resulted in significant levels of improved functioning for many patients. Combined use has been made of the following approaches: (*a*) early determination of patient expectations — immediate or longer range needs; (*b*) evaluation of the patient's environmental constraints — degree of acculturation, problems of referral, or facilitation of contact with appropriate community agencies; (*c*) crisis intervention; (*d*) Gestalt therapy such as role playing and focus on experiencing present feelings; (*e*) client-centered listening; and (*f*) behavioral approaches such as setting outcome objectives together with the patient or teaching the patient specific techniques for relaxation or assertiveness.

Objective evaluation of approaches used in clinical practice or of the kind of services patients are receiving is often difficult to accomplish. Bergin (1971) has stressed the continuing need for the evaluation of therapeutic approaches with specific groups of people and specific types of problems. In the absence of any therapy studies done with Mexican Americans, empirical research is critically needed to evaluate the process and outcome of therapeutic interventions with bilingual or monolingual Spanish-speaking patients.

Conclusion

It appears, from recent empirical findings and clinical reports reviewed in this discussion, that Mexican Americans have a great need for psychotherapeutic intervention. It further appears that Mexican Americans express positive attitudes toward psychotherapists, psychotherapy, and mental health services (Padilla *et al.*, 1976; Acosta & Sheehan, 1976). Yet Mexican Americans remain consistently underrepresented in mental health services.

Some empirical information is now available about the interactive effects of at least young Mexican Americans' preferences and self-disclosures toward Anglo American and Mexican American psychotherapists (Acosta, 1975; Acosta & Sheehan, 1976). Much is still unknown, however, about the effects of generation, age, sex, language use, ethnic identity, status as a patient or client, patient treatment expectations and attitudes, treatment approaches, and therapist attitudes and characteristics on the success of psychotherapy with Mexican Americans. There are still no research studies concerning the ongoing therapy process between therapists and Mexican American patients.

The degree to which stereotypes and prejudice may exist among psychotherapists who see Mexican Americans as clients needs to be examined. From the large number of studies done with low-income patients (Lorion, 1973), it appears that discriminatory behavior toward treating the low-income patient has been the norm.

Promising approaches toward changing stereotypes and misinformation about Mexican Americans and their mental health needs probably will come from the following: (a) continued clinical research; (b) development of greater awareness and understanding of their cultural and ethnic characteristics and heterogeneity; (c) communication of more accurate information about them to Anglo American and even to Mexican American therapists, trainees, and supervisors; (d) greater supervised experience in working with Mexican American patients; and (e) increased bilingual-bicultural staffing of mental health clinics and departments of psychology, psychiatry, and social work.

Since Mexican Americans have been virtually ignored until recently by psychologists and other mental health professionals, many unproven generalizations and assumptions about them still exist. In this context, success or failure rates are not yet known in situations where different therapy approaches have been used with different subgroups of Mexican American patients. New therapeutic approaches more congruent with the sociocultural perspectives of different subgroups of Mexican Americans may need to be developed. Research is desperately needed to see which therapists and which therapeutic approaches or combinations of approaches are most effective with different subgroups of Mexican Americans.

As the field of clinical psychology continues to develop and assess various psychotherapeutic and behavioral approaches, these approaches should be available for use and comparative evaluation with Mexican Americans. Several clinical reports noted earlier in this discussion suggest that combinations of treatment approaches and resources can be effective in helping Mexican Americans to achieve not only relief from immediate pain but better levels of functioning in dealing with longer term problems within a stressful society. The final success of any therapeutic approach, however, will depend on the degree of sensitivity, interest, and open-mindedness which psychotherapists show toward Mexican Americans.

REFERENCE NOTE

1. Kline, F., Acosta, F.X., Austin, W., & Johnson, R. Subtle bias in the treatment of the Spanish-speaking patient. Paper presented at the meeting of the Section of Psychiatry, Neurology and Neurosurgery of the Puerto Rican Medical Association, the American Psychiatric Association, and the Caribbean Psychiatric Association, San Juan, Puerto Rico, May, 1976.

REFERENCES

Acosta, F.X. Effects of psychotherapists' ethnicity and expertise on self-disclosures by Mexican Americans and Anglo Americans. (Doctoral dissertation, University of California, Los Angeles, 1974.) *Dissertation Abstracts International*, 1975, *35*, 4157-B. (University Microfilms No. 75-2213, 119.)

Acosta, F.X., & Sheehan, J.G. Preferences toward Mexican American and Anglo American Psychotherapists. *Journal of Consulting and Clinical Psychology*, 1976, *44*, 272-279.

Acosta, F.X., & Sheehan, J.G. Self-disclosure in relation to psychotherapist expertise and ethnicity. *American Journal of Community Psychology*, in press.

Albronda, H.F., Dean, R.L., & Starkweather, J.A. Social class and psychotherapy. *Archives of General Psychiatry*, 1964, *10*, 276-283.

Bergin, A.E. The evaluation of therapeutic outcomes. In A.E. Bergin and S.L. Garfield (Eds.), *Handbook of psychotherapy and behavior change: An empirical analysis*. New York: Wiley, 1971.

Berscheid, E. Opinion change and communicator-communicatee similarity and dissimilarity. *Journal of Personality and Social Psychology*, 1966, *4*, 670-680.

Boulware, D.W., & Holmes, D.S. Preferences for therapists and related expectancies. *Journal of Consulting and Clinical Psychology*, 1970, *35*, 269-277.

Brand, E.S., Ruiz, R.A., & Padilla, A.M. Ethnic identification and preference: A review. *Psychological Bulletin*, 1974, *81*, 860-890.

Brill, N.Q., & Storrow, H.A. Social class and psychiatric treatment. *Archives of General Psychiatry*, 1960, *3*, 340-344.

Brook, T.E. Communicator-recipient similarity and decision change. *Journal of Personality and Social Psychology*, 1965, *1*, 650-654.

Cobb, C.W. Community mental health services and the lower socioeconomic class: A summary of research literature on outpatient treatment (1963-1969). *American Journal of Orthopsychiatry*, 1972, *42*, 404-414.

Edgarton, R.B., Karno, M., & Fernandez, I. Curanderismo in the metropolis. *American Journal of Psychotherapy*, 1970, *24*, 124-134.

Fabrega, H., & Wallace, C.A. Value identification and psychiatric disability: An analysis involving Americans of Mexican descent. *Behavioral Science*, 1968, *13*, 362-371.

Garfield, S.L. Research on client variables in psychotherapy. In A.E. Bergin and S.L. Garfield (Eds.), *Handbook of psychotherapy and behavior change: An empirical analysis*. New York: Wiley, 1971.

Grebler, L., Moore, J.W., & Guzman, R.C. *The Mexican-American People*. New York: The Free Press, 1970.

Heiman, E.M., Burruel, G., & Chavez, N. Factors determining effective psychiatric outpatient treatment for Mexican-Americans. *Hospital and Community Psychiatry*, 1975, *26*, 515-517.

Hernandez, J., Estrada, L., & Alvirez, D. Census data and the problem of conceptually defining the Mexican American population. *Social Science Quarterly*, 1973, *53*, 671-687.

Hollingshead, A.B., & Redlich, F.C. *Social class and mental illness: A community study*. New York: Wiley, 1958.

Jaco, E.G. Mental health of the Spanish-American in Texas. In M.E. Opler (Ed.), *Culture and mental health*. New York: Macmillan, 1959.

Karno, M. The enigma of ethnicity in a psychiatric clinic. *Archives of General Psychiatry*, 1966, *14*, 516-520.

Karno, M., & Edgarton, R.B. Perception of mental illness in a Mexican-American community. *Archives of General Psychiatry*, 1969, *20*, 233-238.

Karno, M., & Morales, A. A community mental health service for Mexican-Americans in a metropolis. *Comprehensive Psychiatry*, 1971, *12*, 116-121.

Karno, M., Ross, R.N., & Caper, R.A. Mental health roles of physicians in a Mexican-American community. *Community Mental Health Journal*, 1969, *5*, 62-69.

Kiev, A. *Curanderismo: Mexican-American folk psychiatry*. New York: The Free Press, 1968.

Kluckhohn, F.R., & Strodtbeck, F.L. *Variations in value orientations*. Evanston, Ill.: Row, Peterson & Co., 1961.

Kreisman, J.J. The *Curandero's* apprentice: A therapeutic integration of folk and medical healing. *American Journal of Psychiatry*, 1975, *132*, 81-83.

Lorion, R.P. Socioeconomic status and traditional treatment approaches reconsidered. *Psychological Bulletin*, 1973, *79*, 263-270.

Lorion, R.P. Patient and therapist variables in the treatment of low-income patients. *Psychological Bulletin*, 1974, *81*, 344-354.

Los Angeles County. *Patient and service statistics*. (Report No. 10.) Los Angeles: County of Los Angeles Department of Health Services, Mental Health Services, 1973.

Los Angeles County. *Patient and service statistics*. (Report No. 11.) Los Angeles: County of Los Angeles Department of Health Services, Mental Health Services, 1975.

Madsen, W. *The Mexican-Americans of South Texas*. New York: Holt, Rinehart, & Winston, 1964.

Martinez, J.L. Cross cultural comparison of Chicanos and Anglos on the Semantic Differential: Some implications for psychology. In J.L. Martinez (Ed.), *Chicano psychology*. New York: Academic Press, 1977, 29-43.

Minnick, W.C. *The art of persuasion*. Boston: Houghton Mifflin, 1957.

Morales, A The impact of class discrimination and white racism on the mental health of Mexican-Americans. In N.N. Wagner and M.J. Haug, (Eds.), *Chicanos: Social and psychological perspectives*. St. Louis: C.V. Mosby, 1971.

Morales, A. *Ando Sangrando (I Am Bleeding)*. La Puente, CA: Perspectiva Publications, 1972.

Padilla, A.M., Carlos, M.L., & Keefe, S.E. Mental health service utilization by Mexican Americans. In M.R. Miranda (Ed.), *Psychotherapy with the Spanish speaking: Issues in research and service delivery*. Monograph 3. Los Angeles: Spanish Speaking Mental Health Research Center, University of California, 1976.

Padilla, A.M., & Ruiz, R.A. *Latino mental health: A review of literature*. Washington, D.C.: U.S. Government Printing Office, 1973.

Padilla, A.M., Ruiz, R.A., & Alvarez, R.A. Community mental health services for the Spanish-speaking/surnamed population. *American Psychologist*, 1975, *30*, 892-905.

Peñalosa, F. Mexican family roles. *Journal of Marriage and the Family*, 1968, *30*, 680-689.

Peñalosa, F. Recent changes among the Chicanos. *Sociology and Social Research*, 1970, *55*, 47-52.

Rosenthal, D., & Frank, J.D. The fate of psychiatric clinic outpatients assigned to psychotherapy. *Journal of Nervous and Mental Disorders*, 1958, *127*, 330-343.

Ruiz, R.A. Relative frequency of Americans with Spanish surnames in associations of psychology, psychiatry, and sociology. *American Psychologist*, 1971, *26*, 1022-1024.

Saunders, L. *Cultural differences and medical care: The case of the Spanish-speaking people of the southwest*. New York: Russell Sage Foundation, 1954.

Serrano, A.C., & Gibson, G. Mental health services to the Mexican-American community in San Antonio, Texas. *American Journal of Public Health*, 1973, *63*, 1055-1057.

Simons, H.W., Berkowitz, N.N., & Moyer, R.J. Similarity, credibility, and attitude change: A review and a theory. *Psychological Bulletin*, 1970, *73*, 1-15.

Srole, L., Langer, T.S., Michael, S.T., Opler, M.K., & Rennie, T.A.C. *Mental health in the metropolis: The midtown Manhattan study*. New York: McGraw-Hill, 1962.

Thomas, A., & Sillen, S. *Racism and psychiatry*. New York: Brunner/Mazel, 1972.

U.S. Bureau of Census. *Statistical abstract of the United States: 1974* (95th ed.). Washington, D.C.: U.S. Government Printing Office, 1974.

Vaca, N.A. The Mexican-American in the social sciences. Part II: 1936-1970. *El Grito*, 1970, *4*, 17-51.

Wolkon, G.H., Moriwaki, S., & Williams, K.J. Race and social class as factors in the orientation toward psychotherapy. *Journal of Counseling Psychology*, 1973, *20*, 312-316.

Yamamoto, J., James, Q.C., Bloombaum, M., & Hattem, J. Racial factors in patient selection. *American Journal of Psychiatry*, 1967, *124*, 630-636.

CHAPTER 15

THE DELIVERY OF MENTAL HEALTH AND SOCIAL CHANGE SERVICES FOR CHICANOS: ANALYSIS AND RECOMMENDATIONS

RENE A. RUIZ

University of Missouri, Kansas City

Introduction

The focus of this chapter is on the effects of *stress* among Chicanos as a variable influencing the formation of problems of two different types: mental illness and social maladjustment. The first major division of the chapter presents the intrapsychic-extrapsychic dimension, a formulation designed to facilitate the identification of the *sources* of stress people experience. An earlier and less elaborate presentation of this formulation appears in Ruiz and Padilla (1977).

THE INTRAPSYCHIC-EXTRAPSYCHIC DIMENSION

Within the context of "mental health," certain cause-and-effect relationships have been identified between stress factors and problem development. Furthermore, and this is a significant point for the remainder of the chapter, some of these cause-and-effect relationships appear relatively independent of ethnicity or culture group membership. To illustrate this point, you are asked to imagine a typical undergraduate class in an American college. Assume further that students in this hypothetical classroom are both Chicano and non-Chicano. The unexpected announcement of a "pop" quiz would probably create consternation in all students, or at least the vast majority, independent of ethnic or culture group membership. More specifically, *test anxiety* would be elicited and would probably be distributed in approximately equal proportions among both the Chicano and non-Chicano students. Furthermore, among those students who performed poorly, regardless

233

of ethnicity, one would probably note the appearance of a more general form of subjective discomfort, probably depression. It should be noted here that all students are "alike" in this hypothetical situation, regardless of ethnicity, in the sense they are subjected to the same degree of stress stemming from their environment (that is, the same pop quiz). Individual responses to this same stress, however, will vary widely (again, independently of ethnicity). The personality style of the individual will determine the nature of the reaction. Henceforth, the term "intrapsychic" will be used to describe situations in which the response to stress is determined primarily by factors such as individual lifestyle or personal adjustment, and only minimally by social, sociocultural, or ethnic variables.

In addition to intrapsychic reactions to stress which both Chicanos and non-Chicanos experience, Chicanos also experience stress and develop problems that are relatively independent of personal lifestyle or adjustment. The term "extrapsychic" is used to define problems which originate in society rather than in the individual. A society can create extrapsychic problems for its members through such unfair practices as racial discrimination. The result of extrapsychic stress, as with intrapsychic stress, is the experience of *subjective discomfort*, including any possible combination of anxiety, depression, insecurity, inadequacy, loneliness, and so on. Internal factors such as individual "ego strength" or "coping ability" can facilitate a more adaptive response to extrapsychic stress but *cannot* influence the source of stress. In other words, a well-adjusted Chicano may be less distressed personally by racial discrimination than a less well-adjusted Chicano, but neither can "force" society to treat its members fairly.

It should be stated here that these two terms "intrapsychic" and "extrapsychic" represent extreme points on a hypothetical continuum rather than discrete, dichotomous variables. The labels are analogous to the concepts of "heredity" and "environment," in the sense neither occurs in isolation and both are always present and functional in the life of any organism.

A partial summary and restatement of key definitions may be helpful to lay the groundwork for the communication of several subtle, complex, and interrelated ideas. First, intrapsychic stresses are those experienced by all, regardless of ethnicity. Second, the kinds of symptoms which develop in response to intrapsychic stress depend upon the personality adjustment or "stress resistance" ability of the individual being stressed. Third, the symptoms which develop in response to intrapsychic stress are mental health problems that respond differentially to a variety of mental health treatment methods. Fourth, the success of a given treatment method depends primarily on the nature and severity of the target symptoms.

Fifth, with regard to extrapsychic stress, in addition to experiencing all the intrapsychic stresses that everyone experiences (both Chicanos and non-Chicanos), Chicanos are subjected to the stresses of second-class membership in the dominant social organization. Sixth, the same, or highly similar, patterns of symptoms may develop regardless of whether the source of stress is intrapsychic or extrapsychic. Thus, a Chicano may appear depressed because of intrapsychic stress associated with failure to achieve satisfactorily at some individually determined level of performance. A second Chicano may become depressed to an equivalent degree of severity because of stress which is extrapsychic in origin. To illustrate this difference, consider a Chicano student who is aware of satisfactory performance at one level of academic endeavor and believes such a performance warrants continued study at higher levels. Consider further that this student may be denied admission to higher levels of education because of relatively low scores on culturally biased tests designed to predict academic achievement (Mercer, 1972).

Several conclusions of maximum importance to this chapter can be derived from the intrapsychic-extrapsychic distinction as illustrated by the examples provided in the preceding paragraph. Note that in both examples the persons experiencing stress, whether intrapsychic or extrapsychic in origin, will almost certainly develop "depression" or some manifestation of a more general construct, "subjective discomfort." Note further that this depression will appear highly similar in terms of some decline in self-esteem, energy, confidence, and ambition. It should also be noted that the person with "good" coping mechanisms can resist intrapsychic stress more effectively; for example, can try harder to perform better. The quality of individual coping skills is much less important in reducing extrapsychic stress, however, since the source is societal rather than individual. No matter how much individual effort a Chicano exerts to reduce social pressure such as racial discrimination, his or her individual efforts will have little immediate impact. Finally, and most important, it should be noted that the depressive syndrome associated with intrapsychic stress may become a mental health problem and, as such, will respond to mental health treatment methods. To be as precise as possible, the dysphoria implied in the statement, "I feel bad because I'm not studying enough and subsequently am doing poorly in school," can be alleviated if the person studies more, or more efficiently. If the self-dissatisfaction stated above becomes depression, then some form of treatment intervention may become necessary, that is, any combination of counseling, psychotherapy, medication, hospitalization, and so forth.

The depression described in the statement, "I feel bad because I performed poorly on the admissions test," is extrapsychic whenever the "admissions test" in question is invalid because of cultural bias (Mercer, 1972) in predicting quality performance among Chicanos, as seems to be the case with many so-called tests of intelligence, achievement, or ability. Greater effort by a culturally different person (such as a Chicano) will probably not be reflected in higher test scores. Thus, factors such as "improved adjustment" or "enhanced coping" will be relatively ineffectual in reducing extrapsychic depression, since the source of the stress lies in society, not in the individual. Furthermore, mental health treatment methods that alleviate intrapsychic depressions are ineffective with extrapsychic depressions for the same reasons, that is, the stress emanates from societal "pathology," not individual maladjustment.

With the presentation of this background information, it is now possible to make a point of major significance concerning the intrapsychic-extrapsychic dimension. Mental health workers insensitive to or unaware of this dimension may tend to misperceive all distress as intrapsychic in origin and will subsequently misapply mental health treatment methods. The treatment approach that alleviates intrapsychic depressions (some combination of medication and supportive and insight psychotherapy) is of little help in minimizing extrapsychic depressions associated with discrimination from the larger society. Furthermore, the basic problem — a prejudicial society — remains untouched and unchanged by a mental health treatment approach aimed at individual "pathology." What seems to be needed instead is some approach that helps the patient fully grasp the societal source of the distress and helps him or her seek alternative means of achieving desired goals. Ultimately, of course, social action programs may be necessary to minimize influences that hinder psychological growth at the individual level. Be that as it may, it is incumbent upon those delivering *both* mental health and social change services to be sensitive to the intrapsychic-extrapsychic dimension because it helps clarify whether the distress experienced stems from some maladaptive aspect of a client's life style or emanates from some aspect of the greater society beyond the immediate control of the individual.

Chicanos involved in the delivery of mental health or social welfare services are probably already sensitive to the intrapsychic-extrapsychic dimension and thus can discriminate accurately between sources of stress for a specific client and select judiciously the appropriate treatment method or intervention strategy. This statement is not designed to imply that Chicanos are somehow "supersophisticated" compared to non-Chicanos, or that their "sensitivity" and service delivery skills cannot be improved. It merely means that the "Chicano experience," including familiarity with Chicano culture and personal contact with societal discrimination, enhances sensitivity to the intrapsychic-extrapsychic dimension. Unfortunately, however, the number of Chicanos in the core disciplines is infinitesimally small and unlikely to increase significantly within the near future (El-Khawas & Kimzer, 1974; Padilla, Boxley, & Wagner, 1973; Ruiz, Note 1). Thus, the overall goal of this chapter is to provide mental health and social welfare personnel with basic information about Chicanos that will help them identify sources of stress and formulate appropriate remedial or intervention strategies. This information is presented below as a series of "summary statements" as follows: (*a*) demographic characteristics, (*b*) ethnohistory and cultural diversity, (*c*) assimilation and acculturation, (*d*) sources of stress, and (*e*) factors reducing self-referral. Each summary statement consists of a brief synopsis of information presented in much greater detail in Padilla and Ruiz (1973); Padilla, Ruiz and Alvarez (1975); Ruiz and Padilla (1977); and Ruiz, Padilla and Alvarez (in press). The chapter closes with conclusions and recommendations. This closing section is further subdivided into two major portions. A subsection on research priorities identifies a variety of problem areas in which information about Chicanos is deficient. The dissemination of accurate, empirically based information on Chicanos will not only facilitate the discrimination between intrapsychic and extrapsychic sources of stress but also ultimately lead to a process whereby valid and appropriate solutions become available to Chicanos for their unique problems. The second subsection of the concluding portion deals with service delivery and consists basically of a series of recommendations for personnel and agencies involved in the delivery of mental health and social change services.

Summary Statements

DEMOGRAPHIC CHARACTERISTICS OF CHICANOS

Analyses of recent census data indicate that the number of Latinos, and of Chicanos in particular, is increasing. The 1974 census of the United States identified 6.45 million Chicanos and the 1975 census counted 6.9 million (U.S. Bureau of the Census, 1975, p. 23, Table 1; 1976, p. 20, Table 1). The net increase of 240,000 indicates an annual growth rate of 3.7%. Using this percentage for a short range projection, one predicts 7.19 million Chicanos by 1977 and 7.46 million by 1978. Considering that census enumerations of Latinos are almost certainly underestimated, for a variety of reasons (Padilla & Ruiz, 1973, pp. 2-3), it seems likely that current estimates and future projections are highly conservative. Other analyses of census data indicate that Chicanos tend largely to be urban dwellers, reside mostly in the Southwestern part of the United States, are vastly overrepresented in the lowest socioeconomic group, have extremely low levels of income, are undereducated (by multiple criteria: lower median years of education, more with less than five years of schooling, and fewer completing high school), have higher rates of unemployment, and are largely bilingual. These differences between Chicanos and non-Chicanos will be used later to make inferences concerning sources of stress and subsequent problems that develop among Chicanos at higher rates than among the general population.

ETHNOHISTORY AND CULTURAL DIVERSITY

At the recent First Symposium on Chicano Psychology (University of California, Irvine, May 15-16, 1976), a number of speakers agreed with the main point of this section by rebutting the myth that all Chicanos are "alike" or that they are members of a single, unified and homogeneous culture group. The individuals who spoke most directly to this point included the organizer of the symposium, Joe L. Martinez, Jr. ("Cross-Cultural Comparison of Chicanos and Anglos on the Semantic Differential: Some Implications for Psychology"), Rogelio Diaz-Guerrero ("A Sociocultural Psychology?"), and Maria Senour ("Psychology of the Chicana"). These papers may be found in this volume.

One distinguishing characteristic of Chicanos, primarily genetic in origin, is skin color. While exposure to the sun obviously affects skin color, Chicanos generally range from European "white" to Indian "brown." The variable of skin color is important because it relates to the amount of extrapsychic stress Chicanos experience and the kinds of problems that subsequently develop. This association between skin color and stress is particularly strong in the United States with its lengthy history of intense prejudice against people with dark skin.

Nongenetically based variables that differentiate among Chicanos (and to an extent, between Chicanos and non-Chicanos), include the date of arrival in, or incorporation into, the United States (from 1540 to the present); reasons for leaving the Mexican territory (exploration, colonization, economic opportunity, or political-military flight); origins in different areas of Mexico with different mixtures of an Indo-Hispanic culture; and differences in background (rural-agricultural versus urban-technological). While certain similarities among Chicanos can be inferred from demographic data (for example, Spanish fluency, nominal Catholicism, or certain Latino customs and traditions), the subculture group differences identified above seem larger than the similarities with respect to ease of adaptation to a new sociocultural, geopolitical environment. The significance of this highly summarized discussion is that, all things considered, and particularly with regard to the stresses people experience (for example, in adapting to a foreign environment), the heterogeneity of the Chicano group seems greater than its homogeneity.

ASSIMILATION AND ACCULTURATION

Differences among Chicanos with regard to degree of assimilation to the greater American society not only support the inference of cultural diversity but also provide insight into the kinds of problems that might develop in adjusting to a new culture. Some obvious differences include wide variations in degree of familiarity with critical aspects of the greater American society such as hiring practices, general decorum, etiquette, dress, and a tremendous number of other variables relevant to successful adaptation in the United States. The point is that among Chicanos who develop problems in living, the greater their similarity to the general population, the greater the probability that their problems will be intrapsychic. Furthermore, under these conditions, it seems probable that this intrapsychic problem will respond with more or less the same success rate found among non-Chicanos with similar problems receiving the same treatment. Conversely, the more Chicanos are "traditional" (that is, like Mexicans and other Chicanos), the greater the probability that their problems will be *extrapsychic*. The mental health treatment methods successful with intrapsychic problems may be applied, and often are; but they are typically ineffective because of their cultural irrelevance. Social intervention strategies need to be developed to deal effectively with the extrapsychic problems of Chicanos, and recommendations pertaining to this need appear in concluding sections of this chapter.

SOURCES OF INTRAPSYCHIC AND EXTRAPSYCHIC STRESS

Despite cultural diversity, examination of Chicanos as a group leads to the identification of a large number of "high stress predictors" known to be correlated with personality disintegration and the subsequent need for treatment within the general population. The most obvious of these for Chicanos include: (*a*) poor communication skills, (*b*) the poverty cycle − limited education, low income, depressed social status, deteriorated housing, and minimal political influence, (*c*) the survival of rural agricultural traits relatively ineffective in an urban, technological society, and (*d*) the necessity, for some, of seasonal migration to maintain employment. The major source of extrapsychic stress, of course, is the problem of adaptation to a prejudicial, hostile, and rejecting society. The example of extrapsychic stress used earlier is exclusion from educational or employment opportunities because of lower test scores on measures that are invalid because of low predictability among Chicanos. Extensive documentation of this point appears in Mercer (1972). More recent perspectives were presented by two speakers at the First Symposium on Chicano Psychology: Mercer ("Identifying the Gifted Chicano Child") and Olmedo ("Psychological Testing and the Chicano: A Reassessment"). These papers appear in this volume.

Further examination of intrapsychic and extrapsychic stress suggests that Chicanos should develop a greater number of mental health and social adaptation problems characterized by greater subjective discomfort. Thus, one would predict higher rates of self-referral to centers or agencies designed to deliver some form of amelioration. Analyses of available data, however, consistently indicate the reverse. Chicanos refer themselves significantly *less* often than non-Chicanos. For more current documentation of this point, see Bachrach (1975) and selected references from the works that represent the background for this section of the chapter (especially Padilla & Ruiz, 1973; Padilla *et al.*, 1975; Ruiz & Padilla, 1977; and Ruiz *et al.*, in press). The significant question concerning underutilization of ameliorative services despite the incidence of greater stress is, of course, "Why?"

FACTORS REDUCING SELF-REFERRAL

The most detailed presentation of a rationale to explain why Chicanos underutilize available mental health and counseling services for their intrapsychic problems appears in *Latino Mental Health* (Padilla & Ruiz, 1973). This rationale follows an outline suggested originally in a speech by Torrey (Note 2), and with supportive documentation by Bloombaum, Yamamoto, and James (1968), Edgerton and Karno (1971), Karno and Edgerton (1969), Kline (1969) and Phillipus (1971). The basic principle is that a set of five variables can be identified that actively operate to discourage self-referrals. These appear here in highly condensed form. First among them is discouraging institutional policies. This category is operationally defined to include long waiting lists, inflexible intake procedures, unreasonable delays in contacting patients after self-referral, and the delivery of irrelevant services. An example of the latter point would be offering medication (which might be effective with an intrapsychic depression) to deal with the sadness and frustrated rage associated with racial discrimination. A second discouraging factor involves geographic isolation − the placement of service delivery agencies at some distance from the target population. The absence of transportation or adequate child care facilities for potential Chicano clients further reduces self-referrals. Third, language barriers exist between service delivery personnel and the potential Chicano client group. The number of Spanish-speaking professionals and para-professionals, whether Chicano or non-Chicano, is far too small to meet the need. Fourth, class-bound values interfere with the delivery and success of appropriate services. With regard to psychotherapy, for example, personnel are largely middle class while the Chicano patient group is primarily lower class. Treatment conducted in a fifty minute hour once or twice a week can be expected to fail, and the available literature bears out this expectation (Bakelund & Lundwall, 1975; Lorion, 1974). By and large, therapists tend to project the blame upon the patient for his or her failure to respond to treatment of this type. Fifth, culture-bound values reduce communication between Chicano patients and non-Chicano therapists. For example, one study demonstrated that 90% of Anglo residents in psychiatry associate the phrase "hears voices" with the word "crazy"; whereas only 16% of a Mexican-American group of high school students made the same association (Phillipus, 1971).

Conclusions and Recommendations

In this concluding section the mass of information presented above as summary statements is integrated in the form of a series of observations and suggestions designed to implement constructive change. These recommendations are based on the assumption that the time for rhetoric is past (except, possibly, to communicate the nature and severity of Chicano problems to naive Americans) and that what is desperately needed from now on is a well-founded, empirically based fund of information to help us understand Chicano problems. Such information can also be used to better discriminate between intrapsychic and extrapsychic problems, to improve treatment methods for intrapsychic problems where possible, and develop new intervention strategies for extrapsychic problems. This philosophy of social change based on hard data is elaborated in what follows in two separate sections. In the section on research priorities, problem areas are identified that warrant new, more, or continued study (see also Padilla, Note 3). This is followed by a section on service delivery agencies which contains a series of suggestions on how mental health facilities can be modified to deliver more valid services for both intrapsychic and extrapsychic problems.

RESEARCH PRIORITIES

Intrapsychic-Extrapsychic Dimension

The intrapsychic-extrapsychic discrimination is important but seems to be consistently neglected, especially in traditional mental health centers and social service agencies. This neglect suggests strongly that the distinction requires greater publicity and the development of better measurement techniques to make this differentiation. With the best of intentions, too many mental health workers offer standard psychotherapeutic or medical intervention for the wrong kinds of problems — with little effect. Several times, the example has been used of a patient seeking help at some type of mental health center for some form of depression. Intrapsychic etiology is immediately assumed, that there is something wrong with the individual person in terms of low self-esteem, poor coping methods, maladaptive lifestyle, and so forth. In some cases, the intrapsychic assumption is warranted, and a lifting of the depression is to be anticipated following the application of whatever mental health treatment method seems appropriate, for example, psychotherapy, behavior modification, assertive training, or medication. With some problems, however, this assumption is totally inaccurate, and mental health intervention will be futile. Chicanos may seek help for extrapsychic depression due to social problems such as limited work skills and education in a declining economy. Once the problem is recognized as extrapsychic, the appropriate intervention strategies can be devised. In this instance, programs can be devised to train or educate people for new jobs. The major point, of course, is that mental health treatment methods such as insight psychotherapy or any other means of helping, improving, curing, or treating intrapsychic problems are not functional for extrapsychic problems.

Cultural Diversity, Assimilation, and Acculturation

The basic recommendations are first, for more refined means of discriminating between subgroups of Chicanos and second, for the development of measures of varying degrees of assimilation and acculturation. The rationale is that differences among Chicanos are probably related to differences in type and frequency of intrapsychic and extrapsychic problems. Furthermore, responses to different types of mental health treatment methods or intervention strategies may vary as a function of these differences. We need research to investigate the possibility that Chicanos from Northern New Mexico with intrapsychic problems may respond better to group psychotherapy than Chicanos from Southern California with the same problems but that this relationship might be reversed with extrapsychic problems. This simple example of one possible relationship could be complicated further by other interacting variables that influence response to treatment or to intervention, for example, degrees of assimilation and acculturation. Thus, the major question concerns the valid measurement of these variables. We cannot even begin such a program of research, however, until we know more about underlying variables such as ethnic identification and self-esteem (Brand, Ruiz, & Padilla, 1975; Rice, Ruiz, & Padilla, 1974; Stone & Ruiz, 1974).

Testing

This vague term has been selected deliberately to facilitate recommendations for a broad area of needed research. First, serious questions have been raised concerning the definition, conceptualization, and measurement of the psychological construct labeled *intelligence* in IQ tests that are culturally biased for Chicanos. At the First Symposium on Chicano Psychology, several people commented or presented papers on this exact point. This list includes John Garcia ("Intelligence Testing: Quotas, Quotients, and Quackery"), Jane Mercer ("Identifying the Gifted Chicano Child"), and Esteban Olmedo ("Psychological Testing and the Chicano: A Reassessment"). These three papers may be found in this volume. The second point concerns the use of tests to measure levels of scholastic function or to predict academic achievement. We are all aware that Chicano students obtain lower mean scores on a variety of tests designed to predict success at higher levels of learning. Despite lower mean scores, Chicanos graduate with doctoral degrees in the sciences and professions and function as well as non-Chicanos. Thus, the question of significance becomes how to measure academic potential validly at all levels of education. The third point concerns tests used to formulate treatment programs in mental health centers; for example, the Rorschach inkblot test, the Minnesota Multiphasic Personality Inventory, the Thematic Apperception Test, the Wechsler tests, and so on. Elsewhere, Padilla and Ruiz (1973, pp. 31-33) offer an extended discussion of how cultural differences influence diagnostic formulations and treatment decisions. A hypothetical anecdote reported there involves two very young children who relate to an Anglo adult a story which, to them, seems true. One child describes the appearance, costume, and benevolence of Santa Claus, but the second child relates a story about *La Llorona*. The reaction to the first story is one of amused tolerance, but the second story elicits suspicion of delusional or hallucinatory thinking from a listener unfamiliar with the folk mythology of Chicano culture. Thus once again, the strong recommendation is for additional research to demonstrate that Chicano response patterns that differ from those elicited from the general population do not necessarily denote psychopathology. This recommendation is justified further by Padilla and Ruiz (1975).

Effects of Bilingualism

Despite the absence of confirmatory evidence from linguists and psycholinguists, many social scientists assume that lower IQ and achievement test scores among Chicanos are due to some assumed inhibitory factor upon cognitive function associated with bilingualism. Two speakers at the First Symposium on Chicano Psychology (Mike López, "Bilingual Memory Research: Implications for Bilingual Education"; and Amado M. Padilla, "Child Bilingualism: Insights to Issues"), reported that some so-called experts have gone so far as to suggest that Chicanos unfamiliar with the grammatical and syntactical rules governing English and Spanish actually lack language. The untenable nature of this assumption is being demonstrated by the research programs of Professors López and Padilla. Thus, the basic recommendation here is for continued research on simultaneous dual language acquisition and subsequent bilingualism. In addition, we need further research on types or degrees of bilingualism (that is, passive, dominant, or balanced), and on the processes of language encoding and decoding. The ultimate goal is to learn how dual language comprehension influences thinking, regardless of how or when acquired, or degree of fluency.

Cognitive Style

It seems reasonable to assume that degree and type of bilingualism, and possibly other less obvious aspects of culture, influence how people solve problems. This is not meant as an implied value judgment in the sense that the conceptual approach is good while trial and error is bad. The intent is merely to acknowledge the fact that people differ in problem-solving styles. Ramirez and Castañeda (1974) demonstrated that culture group membership is related to differences in cognitive style. Obviously this relationship demands much additional and continued research, and new relationships must be sought.

Cultural Differences

Basically, this represents an elaboration and extension of the second and fifth points. Chicanos are known to be, or seem to be, different from non-Chicanos in a number of cultural variables that may bear upon the formation of both intrapsychic and extrapsychic problems. As a result, responses to different methods of treatment and intervention may also differ. These differences must be identified with greater precision. To provide an example, demographic data indicate that extended families are more common among Chicanos and that the number of children in each family is larger. If this type of family solidarity is stronger, then it may influence response to mental health treatment or social intervention programs. For example, family treatment approaches may be more successful than individual methods with Chicanos experiencing intrapsychic depression. Likewise, job retraining programs for Chicanos may be more effective when the entire family of the person experiencing the extrapsychic problem of undereducation is involved.

Sex Roles

One of the speakers at the First Symposium on Chicano Psychology (Senour, this volume) made a point consistent with the main thrust of this recommendation, namely, that the sex roles of Chicano men and women represent another important cultural difference warranting additional research. The well-circulated and accepted myth is that Chicano men are dominant and Chicano women are submissive. My personal and professional opinion is that measurable differences almost certainly exist between Chicano and non-Chicano sex roles but that they are not as caricatured or stereotyped as in the social science literature. It is exciting to report that some research is beginning to appear that refutes this myth (Cromwell, Note 4). Certainly, Chicano men are *macho* but this term does not denote compulsive promiscuity, explosive violence, or chronic drunkenness (Ruiz & Padilla, Note 5). When I think of the *machismo* of my father and uncles, the emotional responses elicited are in terms of a strong sense of personal honor, family loyalty, love for children, and respect for the aged. These impressions require documentation based on empirically generated data. Such research is not recommended to prove to others or ourselves how wonderful Chicano culture is, it is needed to provide a data base for treatment and intervention programs. To illustrate this point with a ludicrous example: If some aspect of Chicano culture such as *machismo* is the ultimate cause of undereducation, high unemployment, and significant drug abuse among Chicanos, then society, including both Chicanos and non-Chicanos, would benefit from some means of reducing *machismo*. One possibility might be the development of some type of antimacho medication to solve these social problems. If, on the other hand, these problems are due to societal discrimination that results in poor schools combined with limited educational and employment opportunities, then *machismo* is irrelevant as an explanatory or causal factor. Instead, what would be needed are educational programs designed to lessen prejudice within the majority group combined with the creation of more and better jobs for unemployed Chicanos.

Research Accountability

The term *accountability* was deliberately selected because of its broad connotations. In the scientific sense, the concept is synonymous with *validity*. If the preceding recommendations are followed — and new tests, treatment methods, or intervention strategies are developed — then we are obliged to test their efficiency. Whatever fails to meet the criterion of functional utility must be improved, modified, incorporated into some other kind of approach, or discarded. In the philosophical sense, accountability refers to *relevance*. Chicanos experience so many serious extrapsychic problems that basic, applied research with practical outcomes is necessary. This opinion should not be misconstrued to denote opposition to pure research (search for new knowledge merely for the sake of new information); it is, rather, a personal value judgment that some of the problems plaguing Chicanos are so serious that immediate attention is required.

More Intensive Dialogue: Practitioners and Scientists

It has been about 30 years since planning began for the Boulder, Colorado conference on the education and training of clinical psychologists (American Psychological Association, 1947). The model that emerged called for a scientist-practitioner who was to be a professional possessing both treatment and research skills who could simultaneously deliver and investigate methods of treatment. Unfortunately, this model works much better in concept than in life. In practice, some psychologists emphasize the delivery of services and conduct little research while the rest are committed primarily to the creation of new knowledge and seldom interact with patients or clients. While this is certainly a problem within psychology, I sense that such conceptual isolation may be even greater among Chicano psychologists, therapists, and practitioners. In terms of a positive recommendation, there is a strong need for closer collaboration between Chicano scientists and Chicano personnel involved in the delivery of mental health and social change services. To provide only one example of a general area of needed research, we need to know more about how bilingualism influences the kind of learning processes that underlie success in treatment methods such as psychotherapy or intervention strategies such as job retraining programs.

SERVICE DELIVERY AGENCIES

The reality of the Chicano experience includes underutilization of mental health services, as documented earlier. Furthermore, most Americans refer themselves to mental health professionals, centers, or agencies for help with what has been termed intrapsychic problems. Thus, it seems most likely that the help needed by Chicanos for both intrapsychic and extrapsychic problems will ultimately be provided in an agency setting. Service delivery centers are currently inappropriate for many of the problems of Chicanos, and Chicanos are not referring themselves. The following recommendations are designed to increase self-referral and expedite problem solving. Basically, they explain how agencies can change to help Chicanos.

Access to Services

Obviously, centers motivated to attract a Chicano clientele must be located close to the catchment area. If this is impossible, a number of modifications may help achieve the goal of attracting Chicano patients and clients; for example, outreach centers, transportation systems, telephone call-in services, child care or babysitting facilities, and so on. Clearly, bilingual personnel are crucial to the successful operation of services such as these.

Personalized Services

The earlier discussion on class and culture differences between Chicano patients and non-Chicano therapists leads to several recommendations which have the potential to increase self-referrals from Chicanos. First, since many Chicanos are working poor, it is necessary to keep agencies open at times other than Monday through Friday from eight to five. Chicano clients have been reported to be more comfortable when formal titles are avoided. Especially with the older generation, it seems important to emphasize physical nearness and body contact (for example, shaking hands). Current and detailed recommendations for the more personal treatment of Chicano clients in community centers appear in Padilla *et al.* (1975).

The Business Model

This recommendation involves the use of aggressive advertising techniques as a means of attracting a greater number of Chicano self-referrals. While this may appear unprofessional to some, well-established and successful precedents exist. For example, programs to achieve other positive social goals have been created, subsidized by tax funds, and well publicized. Obvious examples include programs designed to decrease alcohol abuse, drunken driving, venereal disease among teenagers, or illegal drug use. An article in *Newsweek* (Carter, Donev, & Keerdoju, 1975) describes how much social benefit derives from *inadvertent* publicity. This article reports a significant increase in the number of self-referrals for breast cancer examinations following the mastectomies of former First Lady Betty Ford and Happy Rockefeller. In a single hospital in Houston the number of breast cancers detected increased by 150%. Overall, the number of carcinomas which had spread to the lymph nodes decreased by 20%. In other words, inadvertent publicity motivated greater self-referral for examination. Earlier examinations resulted in the more frequent detection of premetastatic cancers and fewer American women died of cancer during that time period.

Community Involvement

It has been well established by now that one of the reasons Chicanos underutilize mental health services is that the delivery settings are perceived as alien, if not overtly hostile. This perception can be counteracted by including Chicanos at all levels of agency administration. The implementation of this recommendation requires that Chicano residents of the community assume authority for decisions concerning programs of treatment, service, and research.

Training Programs

It is unfortunate but accurate to state that the number of Chicano professionals available to provide services for intrapsychic and extrapsychic problems is extremely limited (Ruiz, 1971). Furthermore, non-Chicanos who are bilingual, adequately trained in service delivery, and familiar with Chicano culture are equally limited. Thus the solution for the immediate future is the development of educational endeavors to provide Chicanos with requisite skills or non-Chicanos with necessary fluency and cultural information.

Traditional Treatment for Intrapsychic Problems

Psychotherapy and counseling, as ordinarily delivered, have been remarkably unsuccessful with Chicanos. To oversimplify a complex problem, the major reasons seem to be that Chicanos have historically referred themselves to mental health agencies with a relatively low frequency; and when they do, the treatment methods are too often irrelevant to the problem presented (Padilla & Ruiz, 1973). Nevertheless, continued efforts to deliver these services seem worthwhile if, and only if, recommendations cited earlier for a strong research base combined with accountability are followed. Mental health agencies seem to have the potential to become settings for the development, refinement, validation, and delivery of new treatment methods for old problems.

Intervention Strategies for Extrapsychic Problems

Clearly implied throughout and made explicit in the preceding recommendation, is the assumption that mental health centers will ultimately become involved in the creation of new intervention strategies to deal with old problems. Ideally the development of a new program might begin with the assessment of local needs. To provide a hypothetical example, if the results identify a given extrapsychic problem such as undereducation and high unemployment, then the solution lies in some type of job retraining program. Treatment methods designed for intrapsychic problems (insight psychotherapy or medication for anxiety and depression) are not appropriate for the solution of vocational-academic problems.

REFERENCE NOTES

1. Ruiz, R.A. Mailing List: Analysis of Spanish surname ethnic minority group membership in associations of psychology, psychiatry and sociology. Unpublished manuscript, 1972. (Available from author at Department of Psychology, University of Missouri-Kansas City, 5319 Holmes, Kansas City, MO 64110).
2. Torrey, E.G. *The irrelevancy of traditional mental health services for urban Mexican-Americans.* Paper presented at the meeting of the American Orthopsychiatry Association, 1970.
3. Padilla, A.M. *Latinos in the United States: Some Research Priorities.* Paper presented at the Annual Meeting of the American Psychological Association, Chicago, 1975. (Available from author at Spanish Speaking Mental Health Research and Development Center, University of California-Los Angeles, 313 Kinsey Hall, Los Angeles, CA 90024).
4. Ruiz, R.A. and Padilla, A.M. *Chicano psychology: The family and the macho.* Manuscript submitted for publication, 1976. (Available from author at Spanish Speaking Mental Health Research and Development Center, University of California-Los Angeles, 313 Kinsey Hall, Los Angeles, CA 90024).
5. Cromwell, V.T. *A study of ethnic minority couples: An examination of decision making structures, patriarchy, and traditional sex role stereotypes with implications for counseling.* Unpublished doctoral dissertation, University of Missouri-Kansas City, 1976.

REFERENCES

American Psychological Association. Report of the Committee on Training in Psychology. *American Psychologist*, 1947, *2*. 539-558.

Bachrach, L.L. *Utilization of state and county mental hospitals by Spanish Americans in 1972*, Statistical Note 116, DHEW Publication No. (ADM). Washington, D.C.: U.S. Government Printing Office, 1975, 75-158.

Bakelund, F., & Lundwall, L. Dropping out of treatment: A critical review. *Psychological Bulletin*, 1975, *82*, 738-783.

Bloombaum, M., Yamamoto, J., & James, Q. Cultural stereotyping among psychotherapists. *Journal of Counseling and Clinical Psychology*, 1968, *32*, 99.

Brand, D.D., Ruiz, R.A., & Padilla, A.M. Ethnic identification and preference: A review, *Psychological Bulletin*, 1974, *81*, 860-890.

Carter, B., Donev, S., & Keerdoju, E. Women vs breast cancer. *Newsweek*, 1975, *86*, 13.

Edgerton, R.B., & Karno, M. Mexican-American bilingualism and the perception of mental illness. *Archives of General Psychiatry*, 1971, *24*, 286-238.

El-Khawas, E.H., & Kimzer, J.L. *Enrollment of Minority Graduate Students at Ph.D. Granting Institutions*, ACE, Washington, D.C.: 1974.

Karno, M., & Edgerton, R.B. Perception of mental illness in a Mexican-American community. *Archives of General Psychiatry*, 1969, *20*, 233-238.

Kline, L.Y. Some factors in the psychiatric treatment of Spanish-Americans, *American Journal of Psychiatry*, 1969, *125*, 1674-1671.

Lorion, R.P. Patient and therapist variables in the treatment of low-income patients. *Psychological Bulletin*, 1974, *81*, 344-354.

Mercer, J.R. I.Q.: The lethal label. *Psychology Today*, 1972, *6*, 44-47; 95-97.

Padilla, E.R., Boxley, R., & Wagner, N.N. The desegregation of clinical psychology training. *Professional Psychology*, 1973, *4*, 259-263.

Padilla, A.M., & Ruiz, R.A. *Latino mental health: A review of literature.* NIMH, Washington, D.C.: U.S. Government Printing Office, 1973.

Padilla, A.M., & Ruiz, R.A. Personality assessment and test interpretation of Mexican-Americans: A critique. *Journal of Personality Assessment*, 1975, *39*, 103-109.

Padilla, A.M., Ruiz, R.A., & Alvarez, R. Community mental health services for the Spanish-speaking/surnamed population. *American Psychologist*, 1975, *30*, 892-905.

Phillipus, M.J. Successful and unsuccessful approaches to mental health services for an urban Hispano-American population. *Journal of Public Health*, 1971, *61*, 820-830.

Ramirez, M., III, & Castañeda, A. (Eds.). *Cultural democracy, bicognitive development, and education*. New York: Academic Press, 1974.

Rice, A.S., Ruiz, R.A., & Padilla, A.M. Person perception, self-identity, and ethnic group preference in Anglo, Black and Chicano preschool and third-grade children. *Journal of Cross-Cultural Psychology*, 1974, *5*, 100-108.

Ruiz, R.A. Relative frequency of Americans with Spanish surnames in associations of psychology, psychiatry and sociology. *American Psychologist*, 1971, *26*, 1022-1024.

Ruiz, R.A. & Padilla, A.M. Counseling Latinos. *The Personnel and Guidance Journal*, 1977, *55*, 401-408.

Ruiz, R.A., Padilla, A.M., & Alvarez, R. Issues in the counseling of Spanish-speaking/surnamed clients: Recommendations for therapeutic services. In L. Benjamin (Ed.), *Counseling minority students*, in press.

Stone, P.C., & Ruiz, R.A. Race and class as differential determinants of underachievement and underaspiration among Mexican-Americans, *Journal of Educational Research*, 1974, *68*, 99-101.

U.S. Bureau of the Census. *Current Population Reports*, P-20, No. 280, "Persons of Spanish Origin in the United States: 1974," Washington, D.C.: U.S. Government Printing Office, 1975.

U.S. Bureau of the Census. *Current Population Reports*, P-20, No. 290, "Persons of Spanish Origin in the United States: March 1975," Washington, D.C.: U.S. Government Printing Office, 1976.

CHAPTER 16

CULTURE DISTANCE AND SUCCESS IN PSYCHOTHERAPY WITH SPANISH-SPEAKING CLIENTS

MANUEL R. MIRANDA
FELIPE G. CASTRO

University of Minnesota
University of Washington

A major problem in the successful delivery of mental health services to the Spanish-speaking has been the use of psychotherapeutic approaches incompatible or alien to the sociocultural needs of this minority population. The rigid adherence to traditional psychotherapeutic intervention techniques has left a large percentage of the Spanish-speaking population with no viable therapeutic alternatives to assist them in the complex process of adjusting to the dominant culture.

From their inception, traditional schools of psychotherapy were not oriented toward providing services to the general population. Only individuals with the qualities of "psychological mindedness," advanced education, and high level of acculturation were deemed successful candidates for the process (Goldstein, 1973). These criteria in effect served to exclude the uneducated, the marginally accultura-ted, and those (and their number is significant) afflicted by severe psychiatric disabilities from psychotherapeutic assistance. Contrary to the popular notion that one needs to be seriously disturbed to see a therapist, membership in the "association of former psychotherapy clients" appears restricted to the most highly developed individuals.

Acculturation and Mental Health

It is often pointed out by cross-cultural researchers that immigration to a new country reflects an inability to acquire a feeling of personal fulfillment in the old environment that motivates the search for an improved lifestyle (Spiro, 1955; Broom & Kitsuse, 1955). The Spanish-speaking peoples in this country, whether foreign or native born, are historical participants in this quest. Immigrants by necessity have worked their way up the American socioeconomic ladder by adopting or identifying with the values and lifestyles of the dominant culture. For the Spanish-speaking, this has frequently meant a negation or suppression of Latino cultural mores in order to learn the values inherent to the Anglo-American culture. Difficulties in adapting to or reconciling the conflicting values of two cultural systems result in an approach-avoidance conflict in which the individual is faced with a more provocative but also a more threatening alternative. A frequent result of this conflict is increasing psychological stress and eventual behavioral dysfunction (Graves, 1967a).

Ruesch, Jacobson, and Loeb (1948) have discussed the problems of American ethnic minority groups in terms of their "cultural distance" from the core values of the dominant society. The general perception of the situation is one in which the English-speaking, middle class population sets the preferred value standards and exerts pressure on newly arrived immigrants to conform to established cultural patterns. Quite simply, immigrant populations with cultural mores markedly different from the core value system of the dominant culture experience greater difficulty or greater "cultural distance" in adjusting relative to immigrant groups whose value bases are closer to the dominant culture. For the individual from a Spanish-speaking, lower class, agrarian, Catholic background, the cultural distance has historically been great. The process involved in adjusting to the dominant culture has been, and continues to be, stressful. For many individuals, the requirements for adjustment are so severe as to affect their ability to cope adversely.

With Spanish-speaking clients, cultural conflict must be considered in understanding the relative lack of success in providing effective mental health services. Because the Spanish-speaking are usually forced to interact with a mental health agency oriented to the middle class, a variety of interpersonal problems emerge. While disagreement exists about the best atmosphere for therapeutic gain, it is generally accepted that positive growth is enhanced in a setting utilizing cultural and societal variables consistent with a client's sense of self-worth. The absence of opportunities to meet culturally determined needs in a setting where ethnicity may be viewed as a barrier to personal growth creates a gap between individual aspiration and the perception of personal adequacy. This gap becomes the source of a great deal of mental anguish and can lead to the eventual termination of the therapeutic relationship (Sue, McKinney, Allen, & Hall, 1974). If the therapeutic relationship is seen from this broader perspective, as opposed to the myopic "illness model," it becomes apparent that Spanish-speaking clients, relative to their nonethnic counterparts, are generally hampered in achieving their therapeutic goals.

The failure to attract the Spanish-speaking to the existing mental health delivery system must be considered in terms of interacting social and cultural factors (Karno & Edgerton, 1969). Among these is the serious barrier that bureaucratic mental health agencies present to the Spanish-speaking client. The embarrassing questions and forced exposure the Spanish-speaking client must confront in seeking assistance frequently causes feelings of vulnerability that can immobilize any initial motivation to engage in therapy. The resulting loss of self-esteem, frequently felt by the Anglo client as well, is greatly heightened for the Spanish-speaking. Other obstacles such as the language barrier, unfamiliarity with the location of agencies, and fear of and hostility toward Anglos can create a state of crisis for the individual and negate any desire for assistance. Whether the problems reside at the interpersonal level, between therapist and client, or at the institutional level, in the formal and informal policies of mental health centers, remains a question. In addition, the question of how acculturation interacts with these levels continues to be neglected. Clearly, any attempts to ameliorate the situation through effective planning and implementation of mental health services to the Spanish-speaking population requires formulating relevant questions and designing studies directed toward answering them.

Conclusions about the Spanish-speaking client entering and remaining in therapy suggest a strong relationship between the ability to identify with middle class values and the underlying goals of psychotherapy. More specifically, the hypothesis to be tested is that Spanish-speaking clients demonstrating both psychological and behavioral identification with the dominant culture are more likely to seek and remain in psychotherapy. In contrast, Spanish-speaking clients exhibiting greater cultural boundedness are likely to express less interest.

Method

DESIGN OF STUDY

In order to study the relationship between clients' level of acculturation and length of stay in psychotherapy, two groups of subjects (continuous and discontinuous clients) were identified on the basis of the number of therapy sessions they attended. The continuous group consisted of women who attended five or more therapy sessions after the initial interview. The discontinuous group consisted of women attending no more than two sessions after the intake interview.

The subjects were obtained from the case files of two community mental health centers and a large county-operated medical center with a university affiliation. All three facilities are located in the East Los Angeles area where approximately 76% of the population is of Mexican descent.

All subjects included in the study were individually interviewed. Questions about their perception of the therapy experience and various measures of acculturation were administered. In all cases, the interviewers were bilingual-bicultural and each client was offered the option of being interviewed in English or Spanish.

Analysis of the data consisted of comparing the responses of the subjects as either continuous or discontinuous. Data about the level of psychological and behavioral acculturation and the perception of the benefit of therapy were analyzed to compare the two groups on relevant socioeconomic variables. To control for the interactive effect of the therapist's ethnicity, only subjects who saw a bilingual-bicultural therapist were selected for study.

SAMPLE

Case records of adult Mexican-American women (aged 21-55) who sought mental health services between January 1973 and December 1975 at the three centers were examined for possible inclusion in the study. Only clients who were continuous (five or more therapy visits) or discontinuous (two or fewer visits) and saw a bilingual-bicultural therapist were placed in the eligible sample population. This produced a total population of 246 clients (87 continuous and 159 discontinuous). From this population, 60 subjects (30 continuous and 30 discontinuous) were randomly selected. A randomly selected replacement list was developed for each group in case some originally selected subjects could not be located or refused to participate.

Extensive data were collected for each subject in the following areas: (*a*) number of therapy appointments attended, (*b*) initial assessment of subject's problems, (*c*) sex of therapist, (*d*) professional status of therapist, and (*e*) the subject's background variables of marital status, educational level, gross monthly income, and generational level such as place of birth, place of parents' birth, and place of grandparents' birth.

MEASUREMENTS

Previous acculturation studies (Thompson, 1948; Rapaport, 1954; Jessor, Graves, Hanson, & Jessor, 1968) strongly indicated the need to obtain psychological measures of acculturation in addition to the usual measures of behavioral adaptation. Failure to obtain some indices of psychological change seriously reduces the validity of the construct inferences one can make in studying the relationship of acculturation levels to other sociopsychological variables. In order to deal with this potential problem, the present study employed a procedure developed by Graves (1967b) to measure acculturation at both the psychological and behavioral levels.

PSYCHOLOGICAL ACCULTURATION

Among the many aspects of psychological acculturation that distinguish the various cultural groups, three have particular theoretical relevancy to the present study: (*a*) interpersonal behavior, (*b*) feelings of personal control, and (*c*) future time perspective. These correspond roughly to Kluckhohn's "value orientations" with respect to man's relation to man, man's relation to his wider environment, and man's relation to time (Kluckhohn & Strodtbeck, 1961).

Measurement of interpersonal behavior was obtained through use of an 18-item anomie scale developed by Jessor *et al.* (1968). The theoretical basis of the scale is derived from an overall community interaction system in which members of the community (irrespective of ethnic identification) participate. The normative structure guiding conduct in this community interaction system tends to be the normative structure of the Anglo majority group. In other words, members of the minority group (in this case, Mexican-Americans) are under pressure to learn the normative expectations of the Anglo group in everyday situations. Consequently, the operational definition of "psychological acculturation" for any subgroup is its degree of consensus with empirically defined norms of the majority group. Low psychological acculturation, thus, will be defined as a relative lack of consensus about the standards of appropriate behavior in common community roles as these standards are defined by the Anglo group.

Measurement of the feeling of personal control was obtained through a 15-item scale gauging the concept of belief in internal versus external control (I-E). The I-E concept refers to a dimension running from a belief that one has control over and can influence the consequences of one's behavior (internal control) to the belief that what happens to one is governed largely by fate, luck, chance, or powerful external forces (external control). The scale is a modification of the forced choice I-E inventory constructed by Liverant (1958). The test format involves pairing one statement expressing a belief in personal control against another expressing a belief in external control, with both items equated for social desirability. The I-E inventory is scored so that the higher the score, the greater the belief in external control.

A modified version of the Wallace (1965) life space scale was used as the measure of future time perspective. Theoretically, the scale attempts to determine the degree to which individuals think about and are concerned with various past implications and future consequences of their actions. In terms of test format, subjects were asked to look ahead and identify five things they think they will do or might happen. Following the identification of the five events, the subjects were asked to estimate how long it would take for each to occur. The assumption underlying this technique is that a legitimate inference can be drawn from this sample of future events to the temporal extension of the subject's psychological field as a whole. Operationally, future time perspective is defined as the median time from the present to the five future expected events.

BEHAVIORAL MEASURE OF ACCULTURATION

The level of behavioral acculturation refers to the availability of legitimate access to the valued goods of the dominant culture. For such access to occur, at least three conditions are required: adequate *exposure* to the beliefs and behavior of the dominant group; *identification* with the dominant culture as a new reference group; and *access* to the valued resources or goals of the dominant society (Chance, 1965).

Following the model developed by Graves (1967b), three measures of these overt aspects of behavioral acculturation were employed. The first simply measures the amount of formal education each respondent had received (exposure). The measurement consists of a seven-point scale ranging from no schooling to completion of college.

The second measure consisted of a nine-item acculturation index (identification). These nine items indicate voluntary association with the dominant community and adoption of its symbols rather than simple minimal accommodation to the requirements of the contact situation. Representative items are: "I have lived in a town rather than the countryside" and "English is spoken as the main language in my present home." These items require yes or no responses, and affirmative responses are scored one, yielding a possible range of zero to nine.

The third measure consisted of looking at the subject's listed occupation (access). The rationale behind this measure is the belief that economic position is perhaps the most sensitive indicator available in gauging command over the reward and resources of the dominant society. Each subject's present occupation was classified along a seven-point scale, ranging from unemployment through professional work.

PROBLEM IDENTIFICATION

An open-ended question about the client's reason for seeking psychotherapy was asked of each of the subjects. They were encouraged to provide as much detail as possible. The responses were categorized into one of three categories: (*a*) a problem attributed entirely to some outside source such as husband's alcoholism or occupational difficulties; (*b*) a mixture of external and interpersonal factors such as an inability to get along with one's mate because of personality problems on both sides; and (*c*) a problem attributed entirely to intrapersonal difficulties such as unexplainable depression or nervousness, where the individual does not feel that the environment is a factor.

THERAPEUTIC PROCESS QUESTIONNAIRE

An open-ended questionnaire, designed to measure client perception of the therapeutic process, was developed. Basically, it focused on such factors as (*a*) therapist effectiveness and concern, (*b*) therapeutic techniques utilized, (*c*) institutional factors that facilitate or impede service delivery, (*d*) personal expectations of what therapy was going to provide, (*e*) personal assessment of gain (as well as why or why not gain occurred), and (*f*) overall evaluation of effectiveness of psychotherapy for Mexican-Americans.

ADMINISTRATION OF THE INTERVIEW

Trained bilingual-bicultural interviewers were responsible for conducting the interviews. Intensive training in interviewing involving lectures, role playing, and independent practice was provided. All subjects were interviewed in their homes unless an alternative was preferred. The interviews were conducted in either Spanish or English. Each interview was completed within an hour.

Results

DEMOGRAPHIC VARIABLES

A comparison of means and standard deviations (or percentages where appropriate) for the continuous and discontinuous groups on selected background characteristics may be found in Table 1. With the exception of generational level, none of the demographic variables differed significantly between the two groups. In terms of the generational level, 78% ($N = 23$) of the discontinuous group were born in Mexico and 23% ($N = 7$) of the continuous. Among married subjects, 65% ($N = 13$) of the discontinuous subjects were married to men of Mexican' birth, and 33.3% ($N = 6$) of the continuous. The comparability in generational status for married subjects and their husbands, irrespective of group status, contributes to the observation that the two groups fall at significantly different points along the acculturation dimension.

TABLE 1
Therapy Group Differences on Demographic Variables

Demographic variables	Therapy group		Level of significance
	Continuous group ($N = 30$)	Discontinuous group ($N = 30$)	
Age	M 31.6	34.7	$t = 1.00$
	SD (7.4)	(9.7)	$p > .05$
Family size	M 2.1	2.8	$t = 1.25$
	SD (1.4)	(1.7)	$p > .05$
Educational level[a]	M 3.8	3.3	$t = 0.77$
	SD (1.5)	(1.1)	$p > .05$
Occupational level[a]	M 2.9	2.4	$t = 0.77$
	SD (1.6)	(1.9)	$p > .05$
Marital status (percentage married)	M 66.7%	60.0%	$\chi^2 = .14$ $p > .05$
Generation level (percentage born in Mexico)	78%	23%	$\chi^2 = 8.53$ $p < .01$

[a]Based on 7-point scale, 1 being lowest level and 7 highest.

LEVEL OF PSYCHOLOGICAL ACCULTURATION

Table 2 presents the continuous and discontinuous group means and standard deviations on each of the three measures of psychological acculturation, as well as t-tests for the significance of group differences. On both the interpersonal behavior and the personal control scales, continuous subjects demonstrated significantly higher levels of acculturation. There was no statistically significant difference between the two groups on the future time perspective scale.

TABLE 2
Therapy Group Differences on the Psychological Acculturation Scales

Measures of psychological acculturation	Therapy group		Level of significance
	Continuous group (N = 30)	Discontinuous group (N = 30)	
Interpersonal	M	15.2	11.5	t = 6.17
behavior	SD	(1.8)	(1.5)	p < .001
Personal	M	8.4	5.7	t = 2.08
control	SD	(3.6)	(3.3)	p < .05
Future time	M	1.3	1.1	t = 0.24
	SD	(2.2)	(2.4)	p > .05

The fact that the continuous subjects demonstrated higher acculturation scores on the interpersonal behavior scale indicates that they are inclined to subscribe to the "individualistic equalitarian" ethic, reflective of the value orientation of the dominant society. Considering that most forms of psychotherapy demonstrate a middle class value orientation (Goldstein, 1973), higher scores on this acculturation scale seem compatible with the tendency to remain in a therapeutic relationship. The lower levels of acculturation in this area demonstrated by the discontinuous subjects may represent a value clash that precipitates the tendency to terminate therapy prematurely.

As for the significant difference on personal growth between the two groups, continuous subjects tend to perceive that the development of their lives is directly contingent upon their own actions. The lower scores on this scale demonstrated by the discontinuous subjects are indicative of the belief that outside forces, such as powerful others, luck, or fate are responsible for the quality of one's life.

Since most forms of therapy assume that the client is primarily responsible for developing the therapeutic relationship, an unusually difficult situation is created for clients who believe that the therapist carries primary responsibility for behavioral change. The tendency to accept responsibility for behavioral outcomes shown by the continuous subjects clearly facilitates their ability to remain in therapy.

The insignificant difference between the two groups on the future time perspective scale suggests that the tendency to think in terms of long-range goals does not distinguish one therapy group from the other. It appears that both groups of subjects are sufficiently able to work toward future behavioral changes, but the way these long-range goals are being accomplished is incompatible with the expectations of the discontinuous group. [1]

[1] Comparison of the means of both the continuous group (M = 1.3) and the discontinuous group (M = 1.4) with an Anglo sample (M = 1.4) reported by Graves (1967) reflect no significant differences among the three groups.

LEVEL OF BEHAVIORAL ACCULTURATION

Table 3 presents means and standard deviations for each of the three measures of behavioral acculturation, as well as *t*-tests for the significance of group differences. While neither occupational nor education levels differed significantly

TABLE 3
Therapy Group Differences on the Behavioral Acculturation Scales

Behavioral measures of acculturation	Therapy groups				Level of significance
	Continuous group ($N = 30$)		Discontinuous group ($N = 30$)		
Education level	M	3.8	3.3		$t = 1.06$
	SD	(1.5)	(1.1)		$p > .05$
Acculturation index	M	5.6	3.1		$t = 5.28$
	SD	(1.8)	(0.9)		$p < .001$
Occupation level	M	2.9	2.4		$t = .78$
	SD	(1.6)	(1.9)		$p > .05$

between the two groups, there was a tendency for the continuous subjects to indicate higher levels of education and occupational ratings.[2]

The lack of a significant difference between the two groups on the educational and occupational variable indicates that the tendency to continue in therapy cannot be attributed to socioeconomic status (SES). SES is generally considered (Blenker, 1954) to be one of the major explanatory variables for high dropout rates in psychotherapy. The fact that there were no SES differences between the two groups strengthens the argument that level of acculturation is a major contributing variable in explaining differential therapy continuance patterns.

The significant difference between the two groups on the acculturation index suggests that the continuous subjects were willing both to associate voluntarily with the dominant community and to adopt their symbols such as membership in clubs or organizations.

The discontinuous subjects reflected a minimal interaction with the dominant culture. Analysis of their response patterns to the nine-item acculturation index generally presented an individual reared in a rural setting who had little contact with Anglos in employment settings, watched Spanish-language programs on television, had few or no Anglo friends, preferred to speak Spanish, and continued to identify with Mexican culture.

An item-by-item analysis of the continuous subjects' responses to the acculturation index profiled an individual reared in an urban setting who worked a minimum of 2 years in employment settings dominated by Anglos, dated Anglos and indicated a willingness to continue to do so, preferred to speak English, had a number of close Anglo friends, and identified with the American culture.

[2]For subjects who were married but not working, the husband's occupation was recorded.

The willingness of the continuous subjects to accept the dominant culture and its values placed them at a relatively high level of behavioral acculturation. Their greater familiarity with the Anglo value set or world view due to frequent interaction with the dominant population may explain their increased willingness to react positively (or perhaps only patiently) to the existing mental health delivery system.

PROBLEM IDENTIFICATION

Table 4 presents percentages and frequencies of reasons for seeking therapy for the two groups. As discussed in the section on *methods*, responses to an open-ended questionnaire about why the subjects sought treatment were analyzed and categorized into one of three problem areas. It is surprising to note that the discontinuous subjects attributed most of their problems to intrapersonal difficulties such as personality deficits and chronic depression rather than external factors such as poor employment situation or a disturbed child or husband. The continuous subjects, on the other hand, tended to perceive external factors as significant.

TABLE 4
Therapy Group Differences on Reasons for Seeking Help

Group identification	Problem			Level of significance
	Externally oriented	Mixture of external and internal	Internally oriented	
Continuous group (N = 30)	4 (13.2%)	23 (76.6%)	3 (10.1%)	χ^2 = 10.30 p = < .01
Discontinuous group (N = 30)	14 (46.7%)	11 (36.7%)	5 (16.6%)	

This finding is unexpected in the light of current literature on psychotherapy, which suggests that premature dropouts in psychotherapy generally manifest concrete or externally oriented problems (Goldstein, 1973) rather than abstract, intrapersonal concerns. The fact that 76.6% of the discontinuous subjects complained of problems basically psychoneurotic in nature whereas only 36.7% of the continuous subjects reported such complaints reflects the severe identity problems experienced during the early phases of the acculturation process. Considering that the continuous group demonstrated a relatively high level of both psychological and behavioral acculturation, their concerns may be less focused on identity issues and more directed toward improved interpersonal relationships.

An alternative explanation may stem from the differential psychological mindedness of the two groups. It is quite possible that highly acculturated Mexican-Americans may be more willing to seek therapeutic assistance with interpersonal problems as a result of their greater knowledge of the various available modalities such as family therapy, premarital counseling, and group therapy. Unacculturated individuals, on the other hand, may feel that psychotherapy is basically a treatment process for the insane or that it has little or no relationship to everyday problems. Learning how to deal with one's husband, children, neighbors, or employer may be considered a personal responsibility that each individual should learn to handle individually. Professional intervention at that level may not strike them as particularly relevant. Needless to say, this explanation is highly speculative and requires considerably more research before it can be accepted.

Discussion

In general, the results support the major hypothesis:

Mexican-American women electing to remain in psychotherapy for a minimum of five sessions demonstrated higher levels of psychological and behavioral acculturation relative to Mexican-American women prematurely terminating therapy.

This finding is consistent with the belief that identification with the major value orientations of the dominant Anglo culture facilitates the ability to develop and maintain a psychotherapeutic relationship.

Whereas previous studies (Bakelund & Lundwall, 1975) generally considered the variable of low socioeconomic status as a major explanatory factor in high premature dropout rates, the present study found that neither level of education nor occupational status significantly were related to continuance in therapy. This result provides support for the contention that differential cultural expectations rather than socioeconomic status frequently underlie the inability of the Spanish-speaking to utilize traditional mental health services successfully (Goldstein, 1973; Edgerton & Karno, 1971; Philipus, 1970). Failure to develop a positive communication system incorporating mutually consistent therapeutic expectations frequently creates a cultural impasse that prevents the development of an effective therapist-client relationship. Focusing on the client's limitations, such as low SES, rather than on the limitations inherent in therapy itself can create serious problems in formulating effective treatment approaches for the Spanish-speaking.

The development of an effective client-therapist relationship requires the dual ability of understanding the clients' cultural situation and the mental processes associated with it. Lack of familiarity with the white middle class medical model and its conceptualization of emotional disorder negatively affects the treatment of unacculturated clients. The greatest therapeutic gain generally occurs in an atmosphere where cultural and societal variables are consistent with a client's sense of self-worth. A situation where clients cannot actualize their cultural needs and at the same time are forced to discuss emotional problems in an unfamiliar manner precipitates feelings of personal inadequacy and eventual termination of therapy. Thus, it can readily be understood why this population experiences unusually high dropout rates.

Client-therapist cultural similarity is frequently discussed in the literature (for review see Lorion, 1974) as a necessary condition for therapeutic success.

This contention has lead some agencies to employ both professional and parapro-fessional personnel with cultural backgrounds similar to the clientele they serve. Although there can be no doubt that familiarity with the values and cultural identity of one's clients is a necessary condition for therapeutic success, the con-tention that it alone is sufficient is directly challenged by the results of the pre-sent study.

All of the subjects interviewed were seen by bilingual-bicultural therapists. Thus the opportunity to communicate in either Spanish or English was avail-able to them. In spite of this apparent matching of therapist and client cultural characteristics, the clients who prematurely dropped out of therapy exhibited lower levels of acculturation than the clients who maintained a continuing relationship. Apparently the availability of a bilingual-bicultural therapist did not change the therapeutic environment strongly enough to meet the needs of the unacculturated client.

If there is any significance in this outcome, it must lead to questioning the belief that a bilingual-bicultural background is a *sufficient* prerequisite for success-ful therapeutic work with bilingual-bicultural clients. Conducting psychotherapy in Spanish does not assure that the therapist will adapt therapeutic techniques to the value orientation of the client. Because most, if not all, bilingual-bicultural therapists are trained in a traditional educational setting, they find it exceedingly difficult to develop appropriate bicultural therapeutic skills. With little else to fall back on, they depend on traditional modalities. The cultural gap bridged by match-ing client and therapist background variables is opened again by the differential expectations of the therapeutic process.

RECOMMENDATIONS

Analysis of both the theoretical and empirical data leads us to conclude that *impaired communication* between client and therapist and inappropriate handling of clients' expectancies seriously contribute to the lack of success in psychotherapy with Spanish-speaking clients. It is therefore proposed that effective psychothera-peutic intervention with the Spanish-speaking must effectively deal with client-therapist communication.

Most clinicians agree that the *client-therapist relationship* provides the basis for successful psychotherapy. The establishment of a sense of rapport and freedom of communication with the Spanish-speaking client is the goal in this initial phase. The relaxation of inhibitions and a growing sense of confidence in the relationship frequently lead to increased self-expression by the Spanish-speaking client. In addi-tion, using culture variables that emphasize client-therapist similarity and other factors that work to foster increased affinity helps greatly to establish the client's favorable expectancies and deter premature dropout.

The basis for the eventual success of the treatment is perhaps greatest in this initial phase since so much of it is directly attributable to the skills of the therapist. The therapist must accept the responsibility for becoming sufficiently acquainted with clients, in terms of personality, cultural background, and communication style, to perceive them from a holistic point of view. The therapist must attempt to mobilize the client's favorable expectancies and assist the client to gain increasing responsibility for the direction of the therapeutic outcome. Accepting the premise that all therapeutic relationships are an integrated part of the culture in which they occur requires that attention be directed toward understanding the significant interrelationships between cultural variables and the implementation of effective therapeutic intervention.

Continued insensitivity to the high dropout rate by agencies providing mental health services in Spanish-speaking areas calls for serious questioning of their future existence. The 1963 Mental Health Centers Construction Act mandated that services be provided to all residents within a center's catchment area. Failure to adhere to this mandate by selectively providing services in a manner that excludes certain segments of the population constitutes racist and irresponsible behavior. Efforts to correct this situation call for the development of research programs attempting to identify the cultural variables that require special consideration in the delivery of effective mental health services to neglected populations.

REFERENCES

Bakelund, F., & Lundwall, L. Dropping out of treatment: A critical review. *Psychological Bulletin*, 1975, *82*, 738-783.

Blenker, M. Predictive factors in the initial interview in family casework. *Social Service Review*, 1954, *28*, 65-73.

Broom, L., & Kitsuse, J.I. The validation of acculturation: A condition to ethnic assimilation. *American Anthropologist*, 1955, *57*, 44-48.

Chance, N.A. Acculturation, self-identification, and personality adjustment. *American Anthropologist*, 1965, *67*, 372-393.

Edgerton, R.B., & Karno, M. Mexican American bilingualism and the perception of mental illness. *Archives of General Psychiatry*, 1971, *24*, 286-290.

Goldstein, A.P. *Structure learning therapy: Toward a psychotherapy for the poor.* Academic Press: New York, 1973.

Graves, T.D. Acculturation, access, and alcohol in a tri-ethnic community. *American Anthropologist*, 1967, *69*, 306-321. (a)

Graves, T.D. Psychological acculturation in a tri-ethnic community. *Southwestern Journal of Anthropology*, 1967, *23*, 337-350. (b)

Jessor, R., Graves, T.D., Hanson, R., & Jessor, S. *Society, personality and deviant behavior: A socio-psychological study of a tri-ethnic community.* New York: Holt, Rinehart, and Winston, 1968.

Karno, M., & Edgerton, R.B. Perception of mental illness in a Mexican American community. *Archives of General Psychiatry*, 1969, *20*, 233-238.

Kluckhohn, F.R., & Strodtbeck, F.L. *Variations in value orientations.* Illinois: Row, Peterson & Co., 1961.

Liverant, S. The use of Rottner's social learning theory in developing a personality inventory. *Psychological Monographs*, 1958, *72*, (Whole No. 455).

Lorion, R.P. Patient and therapist variables in the treatment of low-income patients. *Psychological Bulletin*, 1974, *81*, 344-354.

Philipus, M.J. Successful and unsuccessful approaches to mental health services for an urban Hispano American population. *American Journal of Public Health*, 1970, *61*, 820-830.

Rapaport, R. Changing Navaho religious values. *Peebody Museum Papers*, 1954, *41* (2).

Ruesch, J., Jacobson, A., & Loeb, M.B. Acculturation and illness. *Psychological Monographs*, 1948, *62*, 1-40.

Spiro, M.E. The acculturation of American ethnic groups. *American Anthropologist*, 1955, *57*, 1240-1254.

Sue, S., McKinney, H., Allen, D., & Hall, J. Delivery of community mental health services to black and white clients. *Journal of Consulting and Clinical Psychology*, 1974, *42*, 794-801.

Thompson, L. Attitudes and acculturation. *American Anthropologist*, 1948, *50*, 200-215.

Wallace, M. Future time perspective in schizophrenia. *Journal of Abnormal and Social Psychology*, 1965, *52*, 240-245.

CHAPTER 17

CLINICAL STEREOTYPES OF THE MEXICAN-AMERICAN

STEVEN LOPEZ[1]

La Frontera Mental Health Center

The underutilization of mental health facilities by Mexican-Americans is substantially documented (Jaco, 1959; Karno & Edgerton, 1969; Padilla & Ruiz, 1973; Padilla, Ruiz, & Alvarez, 1975).[2] It has been suggested that mental health practitioners themselves may contribute to this low rate of usage (Karno & Edgerton, 1969; Torrey, 1973) because they are insensitive to Mexican-American culture (Padilla & Ruiz, 1973; Phillipus, 1971). This notion intuitively appears to be valid although it has little empirical support. Bloombaum, Yamamoto, and James (1968) is the only empirical study to date that suggests clinicians may be insensitive to Mexican-American culture.

Bloombaum *et al.* (1968) examined clinicians' attitudes toward Mexican-Americans and other ethnic groups. A 10-item stereotype questionnaire was administered to 16 psychotherapists from a hospital psychiatric setting. The results indicated that 22.6% of all responses were "culturally stereotypic in terms of superstitiousness, changeability in impulse, grasp of abstract ideas, and distinction between illusion and facts." Moreover, Mexican-Americans were most frequently stereotyped. It is unclear, however, which clinical stereotypes specifically related to Mexican-Americans.

[1]Present address: Spanish Speaking Mental Health Research Center, University of California, Los Angeles, Los Angeles, California.
[2]This study is based on a thesis submitted to the Department of Psychology, Claremont Men's College. The author would like to express appreciation to the following people for their assistance in obtaining the necessary subjects: Elisa Riesgo, La Frontera Center, Tucson, Arizona; Judy Johnson, Tucson East CMHC, Tucson, Arizona; Dolores Garcia-Wright, Pomona Valley CMHC, Pomona, CA.; Ramon Santos, El Centro, East Los Angeles, CA.; Michael Ward, Los Angeles County General Hospital, Los Angeles, CA. Also, special thanks are given to John Snortum, Claremont Men's College; Dale Berger, Claremont Graduate School; Esteban Olmedo, UCLA; and Leticia Cuecuecha-Lopez, UC Irvine.

Since Bloombaum *et al.* (1968) is the only study investigating clinicians' attitudes toward Chicanos, the present study attempts to corroborate their results. First, the notion that therapists have stereotypic views of Mexican-Americans was tested using a larger sample group. In addition, an attempt was made to identify whatever specific clinical stereotypes of Chicanos may exist.

Padilla (1976) suggested that prejudice against Mexican-American culture implies that its traits are negatively valued by others, particularly members of the dominant culture. It would follow that stereotypes of the Mexican-American based on cultural traits are also negatively valued. Thus, for the purpose of this study, stereotypes are defined as characteristics judged to pertain to an ethnic group that differ from the characteristics judged to represent the ideal notion of mental health. In other words, positively valued traits may represent the ideal concept of mental health and negatively valued traits (stereotypes) may differ from this notion.

To investigate clinicians' stereotypes of Mexican-Americans, the basic research design of Broverman, Broverman, Clarkson, Rosenkrantz, and Vogel (1970) was utilized. Clinicians were asked to rate a normal, healthy Mexican-American, Anglo-American, or normal adult on five different scales. These scales were (*a*) emotionality, (*b*) dominance, (*c*) responsibility, (*d*) religiosity, and (*e*) stereotypic characteristics. It was expected that the normal, healthy Anglo-American would be rated more positively by the clinicians than the normal, healthy Mexican-American. Moreover, it was thought that the normal Anglo-American would be rated more like the normal, healthy adult than the normal Mexican-American.

The investigation also explored therapist variables that might be related to greater cultural sensitivity toward Chicanos. This was accomplished by examining the following groups of therapists: Anglo, Chicano, male, female, Spanish-speaking, and English-speaking. It was also determined whether or not the therapists had experience with Chicano clientele and what percentage of their clientele were Mexican-American. Chicano therapists were expected to have less stereotypic ideas about Mexican-Americans. Bilingual clinicians were also expected to differ from English-speaking clinicians in their ratings of Mexican-Americans (Marcos, Alpert, Urcuyo, & Kesselman, 1976).

Method

SUBJECTS

Questionnaires were delivered or mailed to mental health centers, counseling clinics, and independent clinicians of Tucson, Pomona, East Los Angeles, and Los Angeles. The clinics and clinicians were selected from the yellow pages and from names provided by educators and other clinicians. Of the 82 questionnaires returned only 59 pertained to actively functioning clinicians who had both Mexican-American and Anglo-American clientele. This sample included 7 psychia-

TABLE 1

Clinicians by City and Ethnicity

Degree	Tucson (n = 33)			Los Angeles Area (n = 17)				Pomona (n = 9)	
	Mexican-American	Anglo-American	Latin American	Other[a]	Mexican American[b]	Anglo-American[c]	Latin American[b]	Mexican-American	Anglo-American
M.D.	*	4	2	1	*	*	*	*	*
Clinical Ph.D.	*	5	*	1	*	2	*	*	3
Counseling Ph.D.	*	1	*	*	*	*	*	*	*
M.S.	*	*	*	*	*	*	*	1	*
M.S.W.	4	11	*	*	7	*	*	1	1
M.A.Ψ	*	1	1	1	1	*	*	3	*
M.S.N.	*	1	*	*	*	*	*	*	*
M.S.W. Interns	*	*	*	*	6	*	1	*	*
Total	*4*	*23*	*3*	*3*	*14*	*2*	*1*	*5*	*4*

[a]Two Italian American (M.D. & Ph.D.) and one Australian (M.A.Ψ)
[b]From East Los Angeles
[c]From Los Angeles

trists, 11 clinical psychologists (Ph.D.), 1 counselor (Ph.D.), 7 psychologists (M.A.), 1 counselor (M.S.), 1 psychiatric nurse (M.S.N.), 24 social workers (M.S.W.) and 7 interns (M.S.W.). Table 1 further identifies the clinicians by ethnicity, city, and professional degree.

Development of the Questionnaire

Most of the items for the questionnaire were developed from current literature on the nature of the Chicano (Cabrera, 1963; Goodman & Beman, 1971; Humphrey, 1945; Kagan & Madsen, 1971; Murillo, 1976; Peck & Diaz-Guerrero, 1967; Saunders, 1954; Simmons, 1971; Ulibarri, 1971). In addition, 18 items from the Broverman *et al.* study (1970) that suggested a cultural differentiation were included. The final questionnaire contained 53 items. Through an analysis of the items, five scales were derived: emotionality, dominance, responsibility, religiosity, and (from the remaining items) a stereotypic characteristics scale. There were 10, 14, 13, 3, and 13 items respectively.

All items were bipolar: On a seven-point Likert scale, one pole represented high emotionality, dominance, responsibility, and religiosity; the other pole represented low emotionality, dominance, and so on. The stereotypic characteristics scale was arranged so that the low pole reflected the supposed personality characteristics and behavior of Mexican-Americans and the high pole those of Anglo-Americans (see Table 2). Both items and polarity were randomly ordered on the questionnaire.

TABLE 2
Cultural Stereotype Scale

Low	Emotionality	High
Not at all emotional		Very emotional
Not at all excitable in a minor crisis		Very excitable in a minor crisis
Feelings not easily hurt		Feelings easily hurt
Not at all aware of feelings of others		Very aware of feelings of others
Does not express tender feeling at all		Easily expresses tender feelings
Hides emotions		Expresses emotions
Not at all festive		Very festive
Very insensitive		Very sensitive
Insensitive to the environment		Very sensitive to the environment
Easily able to separate feelings from ideas		Unable to separate feelings from ideas
	Dominance	
Very easily influenced		Not at all easily influenced
Very passive		Active
Not at all adventurous		Very adventurous
Almost never acts as a leader		Almost always acts as a leader
Not at all ambitious		Very ambitious
Very fatalistic		Not at all fatalistic

(Continued)

TABLE 2 (Continued)

Low	Dominance	High
Very submissive		Very dominant
Not at all independent		Very independent
Very conforming		Not at all conforming
Not at all aggressive		Very aggressive
Not at all competitive		Very competitive
Very uncomfortable about being aggressive		Not at all uncomfortable about being aggressive
Very pessimistic		Very optimistic
Very quiet		Very loud

	Responsibility	
Not at all family oriented		Very family oriented
Not educationally oriented		Very educationally oriented
No respect for authority		Great respect for authority
Low orientation towards helping others		High orientation towards helping others
Always tardy		Very punctual
No initiative		Strong initiative
Very impractical		Very practical
Not at all industrious		Very industrious
Not at all thrifty		Very thrifty
No self-control		High degree of self-control
Very unorganized		Highly organized
Does not know way of world		Knows the way of the world
Has difficulty making decisions		Can make decisions easily

	Religiosity	
Not at all religious		Very religious
Not at all spiritually inclined		Spiritually inclined
Not at all superstitious		Very superstitious

	Stereotypic Characteristics	
Mexican-American		Anglo-American
Present time oriented		Future time oriented
Not at all materialistic		Very materialistic
Very tactful		Very blunt
Very generous		Not at all generous
Very polite		Very impolite
Very subjective		Very objective
Very illogical		Very logical
Very sneaky		Very direct
Not at all self-confident		Very self-confident
Very gentle		Very rough
Very neat in habits		Very sloppy in habits
Very strong need for security		Very little need for security
Enjoys art and literature very much		Does not enjoy art and literature at all

TABLE 3

Clinical Groups by Concept of Health Asked to Judge

Concept	Ethnicity				Spanish-speaking		Percentage of Mexican-American clientele [a]		Professional experience with Mexican-Americans [a]		Sex	
	Mexican-American	Anglo-American	Latin American	Other	Yes	No	Greater than 40%	Less than 40%	Greater than 8 years	Less than 8 years	Male	Female
Mexican-American	5	12	1	*	9	9	7	11	7	10	10	8
Normal Adult	7	12	*	1	9	11	9	11	4	16	12	8
Anglo-American	8	8	3	2	15	6	12	8	3	18	15	6
Totals	20	32	4	3	33	26	28	30	14	44	37	22

[a]Missing data for one therapist who failed to respond to the question.

Following the questionnaire items were questions concerning the therapist's city, sex, and professional title. Also included were questions that estimated familiarity with Mexican-American culture including ethnicity of the clinician (Mexican-American or Anglo-American), use of Spanish in talking with clients, professional experience with Chicanos (greater or less than eight years), and percentage of Mexican-American clientele (greater or less than 40%).

INSTRUCTIONS

As in the Broverman *et al.* study (1970), all subjects were given the questionnaire and randomly assigned to one of three sets of instructions. Twenty clinicians were given the "adult" instructions: "Think of normal adults. Then, please indicate on the one to seven scale of each item the degree to which a mature, healthy, socially competent adult person would be." Instructions to describe "a mature, healthy, socially competent Anglo-American adult" went to 21 therapists; and 18 clinicians received the same instructions for a Mexican-American rather than Anglo-American. Table 3 indicates the distribution of the three sets of instructions to the clinicians by sex and by the cultural familiarity variables of ethnicity, professional experience with Chicano clientele, Spanish-speaking ability, and percentage of Chicano clientele.

Results

Multivariate analysis of variance (MANOVA) was performed on the clinicians' ratings of mental health for the three concepts, Mexican-American, Anglo-American, and normal adult. The results of the analysis indicate significant main effects on the concept of mental health for all scales: emotionality ($F(20, 88) = 2.08, p < .01$), dominance ($F(28, 80) = 1.72, p < .031$), responsibility ($F(26, 82) = 2.01, p < .009$), religiosity ($F(28, 80) = 5.09, p < .001$) and stereotypic characteristics ($F(26, 82) = 2.09, p < .006$). There were no significant main effects for sex or for the cultural familiarity variables of ethnicity, professional experience, percentage of Chicano clientele, and Spanish-speaking ability. The final analysis indicated no significant interactions for the three concepts by sex, or by cultural familiarity variables.

To understand the nature of the concept differences, it is necessary to examine those items in each scale that contributed to the significant main effect. Included in Table 4 are the five scales with each of the 17 items that has a significant ($p < .05$) univariate *F*-ratio. The concept means of the significant scale items are included in Table 4 to illustrate how the concepts differed. Only these scale items are analyzed further. The univariate *F*-ratio shows reliable concept differences when each item is considered alone. This ratio, however, does not determine if each Mexican-American concept is significantly different from each Anglo-American concept, nor does it provide information on the similarity between the ideal notion of mental health and the concepts of health judged for the two ethnic groups.

TABLE 4

Mean Values of Clinical Judgments of Health for Scale Items with Significant Univariate F-Ratios (p < .05)

	Means			
Scale and items	Mexican-American (n = 18)	Normal adult (n = 20)	Anglo-American (n = 21)	Univariate F-ratios (2, 56)
Emotionality				
Expresses emotions	4.00	5.00	3.76	4.88
Very emotional	4.61	4.55	3.62	10.78
Very sensitive	4.67	4.80	4.00	3.69
Dominance				
Very aggressive	4.33	4.40	4.95	6.53
Very dominant	4.33	4.20	4.95	10.16
Not at all conforming	4.16	3.85	4.71	4.67
Very independent	4.39	4.60	5.19	4.35
Almost always acts as a leader	3.94	4.45	4.60	3.88
Responsibility				
Family oriented	5.61	4.33	4.65	7.65
Very practical	4.44	4.50	5.19	3.46
Very punctual	4.06	4.60	4.91	3.39
Religiosity				
Spiritually inclined	4.89	4.10	3.86	5.27
Very superstitious	4.12	3.15	2.57	8.12
Stereotypic characteristics				
Not at all materialistic	4.39	4.05	3.05	12.44
Very tactful	4.50	4.50	3.67	4.07
Very gentle	4.44	4.80	4.05	3.35
Very polite	5.11	4.50	4.14	3.41

JUDGMENTS OF MENTAL HEALTH FOR MEXICAN-AMERICANS AND ANGLO-AMERICANS

To determine if there were significant differences between the concepts of mental health for the Mexican-American and the Anglo-American, the Honestly Significant Difference (HSD) statistical test (Kirk, 1968) was performed on each of the 17 significant scale items. As illustrated in Table 5, the results indicated statistically significant differences within the dominance scale (4 items), responsibility scale (3 items), religiosity scale (2 items), stereotypic characteristics scale (3 items) and emotionality scale (1 item). The polar direction of the differences is consistent within all scales except responsibility. The Mexican-American is judged to be less responsible than the Anglo-American in two areas, punctuality (q = .79, df 2/56, $p < .05$) and practicality (q = .75, df 2/56, $p < .05$), and more responsible with regard to the family (q = .82, df 2/56, $p < .01$).

TABLE 5

Mean Differences and Honestly Significant Difference (HSD) Q Values for Clinically Judged Concepts of Health

Scale and items	Mean Differences			HSD Q Values	
	AA-MA[a]	MA-NA[b]	AA-NA[c]		
Emotionality					
Expresses emotions	.24	1.00	1.24*	1.03	1.30
Very emotional	.99**	.06	.93	.59	.74
Very sensitive	.67	.13	.80*	.77	.98
Dominance					
Very aggressive	.62**	.07	.55*	.46	.58
Very dominant	.62*	.13	.75**	.51	.64
Not at all conforming	.55	.31	.86*	.69	.88
Very independent	.80*	.21	.59	.68	.86
Almost always acts as					
a leader	.66*	.51	.15	.60	.76
Responsibility					
Family oriented	.96*	1.28**	.32	.82	1.03
Very practical	.75*	.06	.69	.75	.95
Very punctual	.85*	.54	.31	.79	1.00
Religiosity					
Spiritually inclined	1.03**	.79*	.24	.79	.99
Very superstitious	1.55**	.97*	.58	.93	1.17
Stereotypic Characteristics					
Not at all materialistic	1.34**	.34	1.00**	.69	.87
Very tactful	.83*	.00	.83*	.82	1.04
Very gentle	.39	.36	.75*	.72	.90
Very polite	.97*	.61	.36	.90	1.13

[a]Anglo-American — Mexican-American

[b]Mexican-American — Normal Adult

[c]Anglo-American — Normal Adult

 * $p < .05$.

** $p < .01$.

NORMAL ADULT COMPARISONS

Statistical comparisons using the HSD test (Kirk, 1968) were also made of the normal adult and the two ethnic groups. The results showed that the Anglo-American was viewed as significantly different from the ideal notion of health on nine scale items, three within each of the following scales: emotionality, stereotypic characteristics and dominance (see Table 5). In comparison, the judgments about the Mexican-American are shown to deviate significantly from the normal adult on three scale items, two in the religiosity scale and one in the responsibility scale.

Discussion

The differences between Mexican-Americans and Anglo-Americans judged by clinicians seem to be consistent with the Mexican-American stereotypes reported in the literature. Padilla (1976) suggested that Mexican-Americans have been stereotyped as uncompetitive and neither achievement oriented nor ambitious. Similarly, the sample therapists judge them to be less aggressive, less independent, less leadership oriented, and more submissive than Anglo-Americans. In the area of religiosity, clinicians seem to agree with those authors who suggested that Mexican-Americans rely on folk medicine (Madsen, 1964; Kiev, 1968). The therapists judged Mexican-Americans to be considerably more spiritually inclined and superstitious than Anglo-Americans. Hernandez, Haug, and Wagner (1976, p. 124) suggested that (like women) Mexican-Americans may be seen as very emotional. It appears that clinicians agreed with this notion; they rated Mexican-Americans much more emotional than Anglo-Americans. Simmons (1971) suggested that Anglo-Americans tend to reinforce images that Mexican-Americans are "child-like and irresponsible." Clinical judgments seem to be consistent with this view; Mexican-Americans are rated less practical and less punctual than Anglo-Americans. Finally, clinicians appear to have consistently viewed the Mexican-Americans as more quiet (Humphrey, 1945), more polite (Cabrera, 1963), more tactful, and less materialistic (Murillo, 1976) than Anglo-Americans.

Because of the stereotypic differences between Mexican-Americans and Anglo-Americans reported in the literature, it was expected that the traits attributed to the former would be valued negatively and those attributed to the latter would be positively valued. The results, however, contradicted this expectation. As Table 5 illustrates, therapists rated the Anglo-American to differ significantly from the standard of mental health on 9 of the 17 significant scale items. In contrast, the Mexican-American was judged to vary from this standard on only three of the items. Thus, on the basis of the 17 items, the results suggest that clinicians view the healthy Mexican-American as closer to the notion of mental health more than the healthy Anglo-American.

The judgments of the therapists seem to be consistent with Kagan (Note 1) who stated:

> In some respects, Chicanos have been uniquely able to resist the pressure of the urban melting pot and are preserving and creating more prosocial and adaptive values in contrast to the unmitigated press for competition and achievement in urban centers.

The present investigation provides empirical evidence that clinicians view some of these "prosocial and adaptive values" to be in the areas of emotionality and dominance. Kagan (Note 1) demonstrated that the relatively noncompetitive nature of the Mexican-American may in fact be an asset to the general group, as well as to the individual. Further empirical investigations are needed to identify the specific strengths in the personalities of Mexican-Americans. The knowledge of these strengths could be extremely helpful in providing quality mental health care to the Mexican-American community.

Even though clinicians may judge Mexican-Americans to resemble the notion of mental health more than Anglo-Americans, evidence indicates that Mexican-Americans are not free from clinical stereotypes. Therapists judged the Mexican-American to be significantly more family oriented, spiritually inclined, and superstitious than the standard of mental health. These findings seem to be consistent with stereotypic notions reported in the literature; Mexican-American childrearing practices are believed to strongly reinforce compliant and dependent behaviors (Padilla, 1976), and Mexican-Americans are thought to rely heavily on folk medicine and religious beliefs (Kiev, 1968).

The work of Bloombaum *et al.* (1968) does not describe how Mexican-Americans were scored by therapists on the "imputations of superstitiousness" item. Thus it is not known if this part of their results is similar to the present study's finding. Despite this, the present investigation corroborates the general finding by Bloombaum *et al.* that clinicians have stereotypic notions of Mexican-Americans. Additional evidence is thus provided that therapists may lack some degree of sensitivity to Mexican-American culture. Further research is needed, however, to determine if and possibly how these stereotypes interfere with therapy. Only then can it be conclusively determined whether psychotherapists themselves contribute to the underutilization of mental health facilities by Mexican-Americans.

The last finding of the study, that the different groups of sampled therapists (see Table 3) do not significantly differ in their views of the healthy Mexican-American, Anglo-American and adult, suggests that all therapist groups stereotype Mexican-Americans equally. This is particularly surprising, since bicultural therapists (Karno & Morales, 1971) and bilingual therapists (Marcos *et al.*, 1976) are thought to have a greater cultural sensitivity toward the Spanish speaking or Mexican-American. One interpretation of this inconsistency may be that clinicians in general have adopted an equivalent perspective of mental health. For example, even though therapists judged Mexican-Americans to be highly superstitious, they may believe a normal adult should not be *as* superstitious, based on middle class values. The adoption of this middle class perspective may be the result of strong assimilation factors in graduate school and within the mental health profession, and of the "overwhelming" middle class orientation of professional training (Gordon, 1965). A second explanation of these negative findings may be that the subgroup samples were small (see Table 3) and may not be truly representative. Thus, the negative findings of no within group differences may be tenuous because of the small sample; however one cannot prove the null hypothesis. Further investigations are needed to determine how Mexican-American and/or bilingual therapists differ from other therapists in their perceptions of the Mexican-American. This may provide objective data to substantiate further the need for bilingual-bicultural therapists.

There are four general limitations to the present investigation. As noted, the sample group was relatively small, particularly for determining within-group differences. Second, the instrument used in measuring cultural stereotypes was limited in significant mental health items, and of possible differences between Anglo-Americans and Mexican-Americans. Third, the study investigated clinical views of the Mexican-American, Anglo-American and normal adult as though each group were homogeneous although there is great diversity within the groups. The final limitation is inherent in any attitude survey; an attitude may not be consistent with an individual's actual behavior.

REFERENCE NOTE

1. Kagan, S. Competition, assertiveness and cognitive styles of Chicano and Anglo children. Paper presented at the First Symposium on Chicano Psychology, Irvine, CA, May, 1976.

REFERENCES

Bloombaum, M., Yamamato, J., & James, Q. Cultural stereotyping among psychotherapists. *Journal of Consulting and Clinical Psychology*, 1968, *32*, 99.

Broverman, I.K., Broverman, D.M., Clarkson, F.E., Rosenkrantz, P.S., & Vogel, S.R. Sex role stereotypes and clinical judgments of mental health. *Journal of Consulting and Clinical Psychology*, 1970, *34*, 1-7.

Cabrera, Y.A. *A study of American and Mexican-American culture values and their significance in education.* (Doctoral dissertation. University of Colorado, 1963). *Dissertation Abstracts*, 1964, *25*, 3774A. (University Microfilms No. 64-4348).

Goodman, M.E., & Beman, A. Child's-eye-view of life in an urban barrio. In N.N. Wagner and M.J. Haug (Eds.), *Chicanos: Social and psychological perspectives*. St. Louis: C.V. Mosby, 1971.

Gordon, J. Project cause: The federal anti-poverty program and some implications of subprofessional training. *American Psychologist*, 1965, *29*, 333-343.

Hernandez, C.A., Haug, M.J., & Wagner, N.N. (Eds.), *Chicanos: Social and psychological perspectives* (2nd Ed.). St. Louis: C.V. Mosby, 1976.

Humphrey, N.D. The stereotype and the social types of Mexican American youths. *Journal of Social Psychology*, 1945, *22*, 69-78.

Jaco, G.E. Mental health of the Spanish American in Texas. In M.K. Opler (Ed.), *Culture and mental health: Crosscultural studies*. New York: Macmillan, 1959, 467-485.

Kagan, S., & Madsen, M.C. Cooperation and competition of Mexican, Mexican-American, and Anglo-American children of two ages under four instructional sets. *Developmental Psychology*, 1971, *5*, 32-39.

Karno, M., & Edgerton, R.B. Perception of mental illness in a Mexican-American community. *Archives of General Psychiatry*, 1969, *20*, 233-238.

Karno, M., & Morales, A. A community mental health service for Mexican Americans in a metropolis. *Comprehensive Psychiatry*, 1971, *12*, 116-121.

Kiev, Ari. *Curanderismo: Mexican American folk psychiatry*. New York: The Free Press, 1968.

Kirk, R.E. *Experimental design: Procedures for the behavioral sciences*. Belmont, Calif.: Wadsworth Publishing Company, 1968.

Madsen, W. Value conflicts and folk psychiatry in South Texas. In A. Kiev (Ed.), *Magic, faith and healing*. New York: The Free Press, 1964, 420-440.

Marcos, L.R., Alpert, M., Urcuyo, L., & Kesselman, M. The effect of interview language on the evaluation of psychopathology in Spanish-American schizophrenic patients. In C.A. Hernandez, M.J. Haug and N.N. Wagner (Eds.), *Chicanos: Social and psychological perspectives* (2nd ed.). St. Louis: C.V. Mosby, 1976, 223-229.

Murillo, N. The Mexican American family. In C.A. Hernandez, M.J. Haug and N.N. Wagner (Eds.), *Chicanos: Social and psychological perspectives* (2nd ed.). St. Louis: C.V. Mosby, 1976, 15-25.

Padilla, A.M. Psychological research and the Mexican American. In C.A. Hernandez, M.J. Haug and N.N. Wagner (Eds.), *Chicanos: Social and psychological perspectives* (2nd ed.). St. Louis: C.V. Mosby, 1976, 152-159.

Padilla, A.M., & Ruiz, R.A. *Latino mental health*. (National Institute of Mental Health DHEW Publication No. ISM 73-9143). Washington, D.C.: U.S. Government Printing Office, 1973.

Padilla, A.M., Ruiz, R.A., & Alvarez, R. Community mental health services for the Spanish speaking/ Spanish surnamed. *American Psychologist*, 1975, *30*, 892-905.

Peck, R.F., & Diaz-Guerrero, R. Two core culture patterns and the diffusion of values across their border. *International Journal of Psychology*, 1967, *2*, 275-282.

Phillipus, M.J. Successful and unsuccessful approaches to mental health services for an urban Hispano-American population. *Journal of Public Health*, 1971, *61*, 820-830.

Saunders, L. *Cultural difference and medical care: The case of the Spanish-speaking people of the Southwest*. New York: Russell Sage Foundation, 1954.

Simmons, O.G. The mutual images and expectations of Anglo-Americans and Mexican-Americans. In N.N. Wagner and M.J. Haug (Eds.), *Chicanos: Social and psychological perspectives*. St. Louis: C.V. Mosby, 1971, 62-71.

Torrey, E.F. *The mind game: Witch doctors and psychiatrists*. New York: Bantam, 1973.

Ulibarri, H. Social and attitudinal characteristics of Spanish-speaking migrant and ex-migrant workers in the Southwest. In N.N. Wagner and M.J. Haug (Eds.), *Chicanos: Social and psychological perspectives*. St. Louis: C.V. Mosby, 1971, 164-170.

PART V
Foundations for a Chicano Psychology

CHAPTER 18

FIELD DEPENDENCE-INDEPENDENCE AND MEXICAN-AMERICAN CULTURE AND EDUCATION

SPENCER KAGAN AND RAYMOND BURIEL

University of California, Riverside

Introduction

This chapter discusses the theory and research on field dependence-independence as it relates to Mexican-American culture and formal educational attainment among Mexican-Americans.[1] The chapter contains four main sections. The first is an overview of previous theory and research that has attempted to explain school achievement among Mexican-Americans. The second section contains a brief history of the field dependence-independence (FDI) construct, including a discussion of the methods commonly used to measure FDI, the areas of psychological functioning that have been found to relate to FDI, and some problems with FDI as a construct. In the third section, a review of the theory and research that has related FDI to Mexican and Mexican-American cultural background is presented. The fourth section contains a review of theoretical and empirical relations between FDI and education among Mexican-Americans. The conclusion notes some implications for research in attempting to understand school achievement and the nature of cultural differences in cognitive styles. Implications for further research and for those using FDI in applied settings are also discussed.

[1] The authors are grateful to Harold Gerard, Jann Gumbiner, Chris Hoppe, George Knight, William Nelson, Manuel Ramirez, Clarence Romero, Mary Sanders, James Scholz, and G. Lawrence Zahn for their permission to describe unpublished data. George Knight, William Nelson, and G. Lawrence Zahn carried out some statistical analyses especially for this chapter. The authors are especially grateful to Curt Hoffman for his helpful comments on the first draft and to Ildiko Bartnicki-Garcia for her willingness to set other work aside to create the illustrations. This research was partially funded by Social Ecology Training Grant no. MH 13060 from the National Institute of Mental Health.

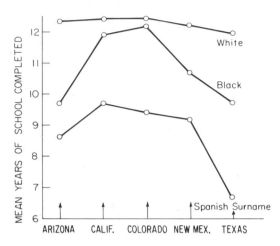

FIGURE 1. Mean years of school completed (according to the U.S. Census of 1970) by white, black, and Spanish surnamed persons in the five southwestern states. White includes Spanish surnamed people, and persons of Mexican descent.

Educational Attainment among Mexican-Americans: The Problem and Previous Explanations

The relatively low educational attainment of Mexican-Americans stands out as perhaps the most important social problem facing members of this ethnic and cultural group. As of 1970, Mexican-Americans 25 years and over throughout the Southwest had completed far fewer years of school than both Anglo-Americans and blacks, as pictured in Figure 1. (It is important to note that Anglo-American education is underestimated by the figures for white in Figure 1, for that group includes Spanish surnamed individuals.) Certainly, the lower formal educational attainment of Mexican-Americans pictured in Figure 1 is in part a result of the inclusion of Mexican-Americans who grew up in Mexico, where the average number of years of school completed is considerably lower than in the United States. Nevertheless, Mexican-Americans growing up in the United States also drop out of school sooner and, on the whole, have a higher school attrition rate before high school graduation than either Anglo-Americans or blacks. It is estimated, for example, that by the time of high school graduation only 60% of Mexican-Americans are still in school as compared to about 67% of blacks and 86% of Anglo-Americans (U.S. Commission on Civil Rights, 1971).

The academic performance of those Mexican-Americans remaining in school falls considerably below that of the dominant population. A nationwide educational survey by Coleman, Campbell, Hobson, McPortland, Mood, Weinfeld, and York (1966) observed that the verbal, reading, and math achievement of Mexican-Americans at grades 3, 6, 9, and 12 was substantially lower than that of their Anglo-American classmates. Further analyses of the Coleman *et al.* data by Okada (1968) revealed a widening of the achievement gap with each succeeding school year.

Numerous explanations of the lower educational attainment of Mexican-Americans have been offered. Some evidence relating to each of the most important of these explanations is summarized in the remainder of this section. In general this review indicates that explanations to date are inadequate.

Economic Class

A number of investigators have related the educational underattainment of Mexican-Americans to their generally lower socioeconomic status (Anderson & Johnson, 1968; Coleman *et al.*, 1966; Sheldon, 1961). Other studies, however, reported little or no relationship between this variable and scholastic performance (Rieber & Womack, 1968; Schwartz, 1969; Singer, Gerard, & Redfearn, 1975). The latter evidence is frequently interpreted to support the notion that there are inherent ethnic or cultural differences in intellectual ability. However, the life experiences of middle class Chicanos are different from those of middle class Anglos, and equating groups on economic class does not equate them on numerous other variables, including exposure to prejudice and realistic perception of limited economic or educational opportunities.

Bilingualism

The issue of bilingualism has attracted considerable attention as a probable cause of Mexican-Americans' low academic achievement. In a series of early papers, Caldwell and Mowry (1933, 1934, 1935) cited bilingualism as an important negative influence on the academic achievement of Mexican-American students. The conclusions of numerous subsequent studies by various researchers have echoed similar concerns (see the review by Padilla & Ruiz, 1973). However, the results of many studies of bilingualism are highly questionable because of inadequacies in the way bilingualism was operationally defined. In many of these studies, Mexican-Americans were classified as bilingual strictly on the basis of self-reports or teacher evaluations. These gross assessment procedures often failed to give sufficient consideration to important variables such as language dominance, fluency, or level of bilingualism. Recently, a growing body of research using more appropriate measures of language skill has shown that, contrary to previous results, bilinguals may actually manifest higher levels of intellectual performance than monolinguals (see Lambert & Anisfeld, 1969, and Cummins, Note 1, for a review). In sum, it is not clearly established that bilingualism accounts for the lower scholastic performance of Mexican-Americans.

Self-Concept

A negative or lower self-concept is often given to explain the academic underattainment of Mexican-Americans. Studies by Coleman *et al.* (1966) and Schwartz (1969) found both the self-concepts and scholastic achievement of Mexican-Americans to be lower than those of their Anglo-American classmates. Palomares and Johnson (1966) also reported that Mexican-American students tended to view themselves unfavorably, both emotionally and socially.

A consistent finding in more recent studies, however, is that there is no difference in the self-concepts of Mexican-American and Anglo-American children (Anderson & Johnson, 1971; Carter, 1968; DeBlassie & Healy, 1970). Furthermore, the fact that the earlier studies by Coleman *et al.* (1966) and Schwartz (1969) found lower self-concepts among Mexican-Americans does not necessarily mean that self-concept explains the lower achievement of these children. Close inspection of the Coleman *et al.* data revealed that, on the whole, self-concept accounted for approximately 7% of the school achievement variance for Anglo-Americans, but only about 1% of the variance for Mexican-Americans. The results of the Schwartz data indicated that self-concept accounted for less than 1% of the school achievement variance for both Anglo-Americans and Mexican-Americans.

The available evidence does not suggest that Mexican-Americans have a lower self-concept than Anglo-Americans. What does seem certain, however, is that at least for Mexican-Americans, self-concept bears practically no relationship to school achievement.

Attitude toward School

A study by Demos (1960) is often cited to support the notion that Mexican-Americans have a negative attitude toward education. On the basis of students' responses to a 29-item questionnaire, Demos concluded that Mexican-Americans had a less desirable attitude toward education than Anglo-Americans. Demos' conclusion is questionable, however, because of the specific content of items which in many cases appear to measure students' perceptions of how they were treated by teachers and administrators, and since this treatment is often less favorable, the more negative responses of Mexican-American students may reflect their realistic perception of an institution unresponsive to their needs rather than their attitudes toward the value of education. Ramirez, Taylor, and Peterson (1971) also found Mexican-American junior and senior high school students to express an unfavorable attitude toward education. Since these researchers used Demos' scale to measure attitudes toward education, their results are equally questionable.

A study by Gordon, Schwartz, and Nasatir (1968) involving junior and senior high school students in Los Angeles found that Mexican-Americans had lower educational aspirations than Anglo-Americans. It is noteworthy, however, that only 1% of the 1551 Mexican-American students sampled expressed a desire to quit school as soon as possible, and 31% of these students intended to undertake some type of formal education after high school. Although these percentages were lower for Mexican-Americans than for Anglo-Americans in the same areas, they nevertheless indicated a more positive attitude toward education than one would expect on the basis of prevalent stereotypes. Gordon also collected information on students' expectations for achieving their educational goals and observed that the expectations of Mexican-Americans were unexpectedly high.

Juarez (1968) also observed high educational aspirations among tenth-grade Mexican-American and Anglo-American boys. Anglo-Americans, however, had higher expectations of achieving their educational goals than Mexican-Americans.

On the other hand, studies by Anderson and Johnson (1971) and Jessor, Graves, Hanson, and Jessor (1968) found Mexican-American adolescents to be significantly more educationally motivated than their Anglo-American peers. In addition, there were no significant differences in the educational expectations of Mexican-Americans and Anglo-Americans in either study. Finally, Johnson (1970) found no difference in the educational motivation of Mexican-American and Anglo-American eighth-grade students.

The available evidence does not support the conclusion that Mexican-Americans are generally less academically motivated than Anglo-Americans. However, the confidence of Mexican-Americans in achieving their stated educational goals remains uncertain.

Intelligence

The issues involved in measuring intelligence cross-culturally are extremely complex. Critical discussions of IQ testing are available elsewhere (Cole & Bruner, 1971; Padilla & Ruiz, 1973; Price-Williams, 1975). Although Mexican-Americans generally score lower on IQ tests than Anglo-Americans, studies generally fail to control for socioeconomic, linguistic, and cultural differences. Mercer (1973) addressed these problems directly and identified sociocultural variables that account for the difference in IQ scores. She found that when Mexican-Americans and Anglo-Americans were roughly equated on parent job type, family size, urban family background, and parental generation level, there were no differences in IQ scores between the groups. She indicated that IQ tests to a significant extent measure familiarity with Anglo-American culture.

The use of IQ tests with Mexican-Americans may be criticized because the individual IQ test items reflect Anglo-American middle class values and life experiences and therefore unfairly penalize minority children who come from different cultural backgrounds. For example, a question on the general comprehension subtest of the Wechsler intelligence scale for children (WISC) asks why it is better to pay bills by check than by cash. Not only does this question ask children for a value judgment about an issue on which different cultural groups hold different values, but it also places many Mexican-American children from lower socioeconomic backgrounds at an unfair disadvantage because they are less familiar with the meaning and use of checks. To some extent then, a high IQ is a measure of subscription to Anglo-American middle class values and experiences.

The use of IQ tests with Mexican-Americans can be criticized for an even more important reason — their lack of predictive validity. Traditionally, IQ tests have been used to predict school achievement, and the correlation between IQ tests and school achievement measures for Anglo-Americans is substantial (Sattler, 1974). Nevertheless, Mexican-American and Anglo-American children matched on school achievement differ in IQ (Killian, 1971), a finding that may indicate that the lower IQ scores of Mexican-American children are not necessarily associated with lower academic potential or achievement. Consistent with this interpretation is the finding that IQ scores of Mexican-American primary-grade children are practically unrelated ($r = .12$) to their academic GPA (Goldman & Hartig, 1976).

It is not certain exactly what IQ tests measure among Mexican-Americans, but there is evidence that whatever is measured is not necessarily important for school achievement.

Prejudice

Prejudice against Mexican-Americans in the educational sphere today still takes many forms, ranging from overt, unwarranted physical abuse of students by teachers to subtle instructional practices that communicate lower teacher expectations. An example of the former is the familiar case of Mexican-Americans being punished for speaking Spanish in school (U.S. Commission on Civil Rights, 1968). Also, racially motivated attacks by teachers against Mexican-American students exist even today (Daily News, 1976).

Less overt, but equally damaging forms of prejudice against Mexican-Americans take place daily in the classroom. Using observational methods, the United States Commission on Civil Rights (1973) sampled 429 classrooms in California, New Mexico, and Texas in order to study the verbal interaction between teachers and students. After making the necessary corrections for class size and ratio of Anglo-American to Mexican-American students, the commission obtained the following statistically significant differences: Anglo-Americans were praised by their teachers 36% more often than Mexican-Americans; teachers used or built upon their ideas 40% more often; teachers responded, overall, more positively by a margin of 40%; teachers directed questions to Anglo-Americans 21% more often; and Mexican-Americans received 35% less attention. In light of these findings, it is not surprising that Mexican-Americans' verbal participation in class was about 40% lower. From their observations the commission concluded that, in the classroom, "Mexican American students are ignored compared to their Anglo counterparts [p. 43]." The detrimental effects of the greater attention teachers give Anglo-American students may explain why teachers have a greater effect on the academic achievement of Mexican-Americans (Coleman *et al.*, 1966).

Some have argued that teachers tend to react less favorably to low achieving students, and so the negative attitude of teachers is not a result of prejudice but a response to the lower academic ability of Mexican-Americans. However, Johnson, Gerard, and Miller (1975) showed that the achievement level of high achieving Mexican-Americans in classrooms with "high discrimination" teachers drops significantly in comparison with that of other high achieving Mexican-Americans with "low discrimination" teachers. In sum, the role of prejudice in the United States schools must be given serious consideration in attempting to explain the lower educational attainment of Mexican-Americans.

Not all prejudice in educational systems is a result of discrimination by teachers. Institutionalized prejudice may be built into curriculums if they are more responsive to the needs, values and cognitive styles of some cultural groups than others. As will be seen, the claim has been made that United States public schools are insensitive to the cognitive styles of Mexican-American children.

The empirical research reviewed elsewhere in this chapter was designed in part to determine if Mexican-American children have identifiably different cognitive styles than Anglo-American children and if children with certain cognitive styles perform better in the United States schools. To date, the notion of FDI has been the focus of research attempting to relate cognitive styles to Mexican-American culture and school achievement. Extensive research using FDI measures has been conducted, and a number of meanings have been attached to the FDI construct. Nevertheless, the validity of FDI is still open to question. For this reason, the next section of this paper will briefly review the history of FDI and point out some of its major weaknesses as a psychological construct.

The Field Dependence-Independence Construct (F D I)

Witkin and his co-workers (Witkin & Berry, 1975; Witkin, Dyk, Faterson, Goodenough, & Karp, 1962; Witkin, Lewis, Hertzman, Machover, Meissner, & Wapner, 1954) attached a great deal of meaning to performance in several rather simple situations that involved aligning a rod to the vertical while ignoring a frame, producing a predetermined set of patterns with a set of blocks, finding some simple figures in more complex designs, and drawing human figures. In fact, using these simple behavioral measures, they claimed to be able to determine important aspects of an individual's psychological functioning in the perceptual, intellectual, social, personality, and intrapsychic domains. Persons who perform these simple tasks in one way are described as field independent, those who perform in another are field dependent.

In contrast to field-dependent individuals, field-independent persons are thought to be superior in solving intellectual and perceptual problems which demand that some critical element be taken out of the context in which it is presented, to have a more articulated body concept, a greater sense of separate identity, a greater independence from some forms of social influence, and a more specialized defense system. Field independence is thought to be the end product of socialization practices that encourage separation of the child from the mother and internalized regulation of impulses. Field-independent individuals, in short, are thought to be better able to see not only aspects of the field apart from their context, but also themselves apart from others. They are thought to have more complex and analytic cognitive structures, that is, to be more differentiated.

For several reasons, the FDI construct is potentially attractive. It promises to integrate individual differences in the cognitive, perceptual, interpersonal, and intrapsychic realms and to explain them in terms of antecedent socialization practices. Further, the socialization practices thought to foster or inhibit FDI parallel cross-cultural differences in socialization practices. For these reasons, together with the simplicity of the behavioral measures of FDI, the FDI construct has received a great deal of attention by cross-cultural researchers (Witkin 1967; Witkin & Berry, 1975).

The various meanings that have come to be attached to the FDI measures are best understood in a historical context. Following a brief presentation of the history of the FDI measures and the psychological constructs associated with them, a number of problems with the FDI construct will be explored.

HISTORY OF THE FIELD DEPENDENCE-INDEPENDENCE CONSTRUCT

The historical roots of FDI measures and the FDI construct may be found in the Gestalt school of psychology. As early as 1912, Wertheimer used a rod and frame to determine influences on the perception of the vertical. The embedded figures tests may be traced to Gottschaldt (1950). It remained, however, for Herman Witkin and his co-workers to develop a theory of psychological functioning based on the results of the experiments with these tasks. The history of the FDI construct is that of meanings attached to performance of individuals faced with these measures. At first, the measures were thought to be indicators of perceptual abilities; later, they were thought to be indicators of cognition and personality; and yet later they were thought to indicate the degree of development on a psychological dimension called differentiation. The field dependence-independence construct is continuing to evolve, for even recently Witkin and Goodenough have begun to reformulate it. Thus four stages may be distinguished in its development.

Simple Perception

The earliest studies using FDI measures investigated perceptual processes. Witkin, together with his co-workers at Brooklyn College, were concerned, in part, with the question of why some pilots flying with zero visibility lost their sense of the upright and flew upside down or sideways. They attempted to determine the relative importance of bodily and visual stimuli in the perception of the upright, using a variety of tasks that varied information from the visual and kinesthetic senses.

The tilting room-tilting chair test, a part of which is now known as the body adjustment test (BAT), was among the early test situations developed to study the relative influence of gravitational and visual factors in the perception of the upright. The test apparatus consisted of a boxlike room 70 inches high by 71 inches wide by 69 inches deep, suspended on pivots so that it could be tilted to the right or left of true vertical. White tape along the corners of the room provided horizontal and vertical visual information. Inside the room a chair (for the subject) could also be tilted right or left, independent of the room. Subjects were seated in the chair, and both room and chair were tilted by set amounts. The subjects were directed by the experimenter to move the chair until it was upright while the room remained in a tilted position. The closer subjects moved the chair to the true upright, the greater their presumed reliance on internal cues for determining the perception of body position. On the other hand, the perception of body position was presumed to be primarily influenced by the external visual field whenever the subject left the chair tilted from true vertical in the direction of the tilted room.

In another task called the rod-and-frame test (RFT), a subject was seated erect in a completely darkened room facing a luminous rod enclosed by a luminous frame. The rod and frame could be tilted independently of each other. The subject was presented with the rod and frame in tilted positions and asked to adjust the rod to the true upright while the frame remained tilted. Subjects who perceived the rod as straight when in fact it was tipped in the direction of the tilting frame were assumed to depend on information from the visual field in making judgments concerning the upright. Conversely, subjects who adjusted the rod close to true vertical were assumed to make their determination of the upright independently of information in the visual field and to rely instead on internal bodily cues.

Comparison of subjects' performance on the two perceptual orientation tests revealed a significant correlation between the two measures. Subjects who adjusted the rod close to the true upright in the rod-and-frame test tended to orient their bodies to the true vertical in the tilting room-tilting chair test. On the other hand, subjects who tended to align the rod with the tilted frame also tended to perceive their bodies as straight when they were actually tilted in the direction of the tilting room.

Witkin and his co-workers hypothesized that the correlation between these perceptual tasks was caused by individual differences in the tendency to perceive the environment in an analytic or global fashion. It was thought that individuals differed in their ability to separate items from their embedding contexts. To test this hypothesis, various embedded figures tests were developed in which subjects were shown a simple geometric figure, such as a triangle, and asked to find the figure when it was hidden within a larger, complex geometric figure or drawing. The embedded figures test (EFT), though in no way involving body position or orientation, did resemble the orientation tests in requiring the separation of an item from its background. On the basis of positive correlations between ability to find hidden figures in the EFT and ability to set the rod or one's body upright in the RFT and BAT tests, it was concluded that individuals were either "field dependent" or "field independent." Field independent individuals were thought to perceive themselves and objects independent of the surrounding field, and field dependent individuals were thought to perceive themselves and objects in relation to the surrounding field and therefore to have more difficulty in separating an item from its background.

Personality through Perception

After establishing that individuals showed some consistency with the FDI measures, Witkin and his co-workers used the thematic apperception test, the Rorschach inkblot test, the draw-a-person test, and various ingenious tests of their own design to test the relation of FDI to personality variables (Witkin *et al.*, 1954). They concluded that field dependent and field independent persons differed on three broad dimensions of personality functioning: (*a*) the relationship of the individual to the environment, including the social environment — field independent persons were seen being active and manipulatory whereas field dependent persons were supposed to accept things as they are and manifest an absence of initiating activity; (*b*) management of impulses and strivings — field independent persons were thought to display an awareness of inner life, accepting and integrating hostile and sexual impulses, while field dependent individuals are marked by a poverty of inner life, with poor acceptance or control of impulses; and (*c*) self-concept — field independent individuals were thought to manifest a positive self-evaluation, whereas field dependent persons have low self-evaluation.

Thus, in their earliest attempts to conceptualize the relationship between personality and perception, Witkin *et al.* (1954) appeared to equate a field dependent mode of perception with passivity and a field independent mode with assertiveness. They stated:

> We have found that the extent of activity in dealing with one's environment is the characteristic that most effectively discriminates among people with different modes of perception. The attitudes and behavior involved represent two more-or-less opposite trends: one, passivity, is associated with field dependent perceptual performance; the other, activity, is associated with independent or analytical perceptual performance. Passivity signifies inability to function independently of environmental support, or absence of initiating activity, and a readiness to submit to forces of authority [p. 467].

The Differentiation Hypothesis

The FDI construct underwent a major revision as a result of an extensive research program with young boys (Witkin *et al.*, 1962). It was claimed that performance on FDI measures provided information about individuals' problem-solving behavior, body image, sense of separate identity, and major psychological defenses. Thus, Witkin *et al.* (1962) noted that field independent children excelled on those parts of intelligence tests, such as the block design, picture completion, and object assembly, that require analytic (disembedding) and restructuring abilities similar to those necessary for successful performance on perceptual orientation tests. They also had (*a*) an articulated body image suggesting experience of the self as segregated and structured, (*b*) a clearly defined sense of separate identity indicating a greater awareness of their individual needs, feelings, and attributes as their own and distinct from those of others, and (*c*) a tendency to use specialized defenses such as intellectualization and isolation that "extracted' them, psychologically speaking, from threatening situations. Field dependent children, on the other hand, did best on those parts of intelligence tests having to do with vocabulary, information, and comprehension and poorest on those parts requiring analytic and restructuring abilities. They had (*a*) a less clearly defined body image, suggesting a more diffused and unstructured experience of the self, (*b*) a more limited sense of separate identity, indicating a relative inability to distinguish feelings, needs, and attributes as separate from those of others, greater likelihood of using nonspecialized defenses such as repression and denial.

The findings that emerged from these diverse areas of psychological functioning were taken as support for a theory of psychological differentiation. The term *differentiation* referred to the level of complexity and capacity for segregation or specialized functioning found throughout a broad range of an individual's psychological activities. Thus, whether a person was field independent or field dependent in perceptual style was indicative of greater or lesser differentiation in other areas of psychological functioning. In describing the relationship of field dependence-independence to differentiation, Witkin *et al.* (1962) stated:

> The fact that field-dependent perception is associated with earlier stages of development implied that it may be more rudimentary. Conversely, field-independent perception appeared to represent a developmentally more advanced level of functioning. Placing mode of perception in a developmental context suggested that children who persist in an ontogenetically earlier way of perceiving may have made less progress in some general aspect of their psychological development. At the same time, other evidence suggested that the aspect involved might be extent of differentiation. . . .Such discriminating attributes as extent of definition of self-concept, articulateness of body image, and method of impulse regulation formed an interrelated cluster which is apt to be considered in evaluating people as more differentiated or less differentiated [p. 8].

The reconceptualization of the FDI measures as indicators of the level of psychological differentiation indicated a significant shift in the meaning attached to FDI instruments. Originally, a tendency toward an active or passive relationship to the environment was the dimension most central to the FDI construct. The differentiation hypothesis, however, took on a more organismic character that stressed individual self-consistency in the development of both the cognitive and affective aspects of a person's psychological functioning. Furthermore, the differentiation hypothesis emphasized field independence as an end point of development toward which an organism strives, an achievement that provides individuals with richer, more diverse resources:

> A developing system is endowed with a given potential. The diverse end-points of the growth of an individual developing system are broadly predictable. On the quite specific basis that it represents "fulfillment of its fate," development which brings the system close to the achievement of these potential end-points is apt to be assigned positive value. Differentiated structure is one of these end-points and therefore likely to be valued. This seems justified since, other things being equal, the differentiated person has richer, more diversified resources for coping than the less differentiated person [Witkin *et al.*, 1962, p. 21].

At the time, therefore, Witkin's theory of psychological differentiation assumed that field dependence represented a more rudimentary stage of development. Field dependence was thought to be the result of inhibited development.

The presumed socialization antecedents of a field dependent cognitive style, called by Witkin and his co-workers the "field-dependence socialization cluster," were described by Dyk (1969), Dyk and Witkin (1965), and Witkin (1969). The research that "established" these socialization antecedents employed global rating scales to assess the behavior of mothers on those variables thought to either facilitate or inhibit the development of differentiation. Mothers of field dependent children were thought to discourage separation of their children from themselves by giving care inappropriate to a child's age, limiting the activities of the children because of fears and anxieties about the child, regarding the child as in need of special attention or protection, not accepting a masculine role for boys, limiting curiosity, and stressing conformity. Mothers of field dependent children were further thought to be either submissive or indulgent toward children, administer discipline arbitrarily, use irrational threats to control aggression, waver between indulgent and coercive behavior, and be unable to set limits for their children. Finally, mothers of field dependent children were thought to lack assurance in themselves, which hampered their children's abilities to define their own role as separate persons.

A Recent Reconceptualization

Since the publication of Witkin's *Psychological Differentiation* (1962), there has been an enormous accumulation of research findings on the correlates of field dependence-independence. (For comprehensive bibliographies containing over 2500 references, see Witkin, Cox, & Friedman, 1976; Witkin, Cox, Friedman, Hrishikesan, & Siegal, 1974; Witkin, Oltman, Cox, Ehrlichman, Hamm, & Ringler, 1973.) In response to this new information, Witkin and his co-workers have begun yet another reformulation of the FDI construct. They have begun to emphasize the value neutrality of the FDI construct – that there are advantages and disadvantages to both cognitive styles. They have asserted that the FDI dimension is a bipolar, stylistic dimension, not a unipolar ability dimension. No longer is field independence described as the end point of psychological development. In asserting this interpretation, Witkin and his co-workers (Witkin & Berry, 1975; Witkin & Goodenough, 1976a, b) relied heavily on two lines of evidence: (a) the findings from cross-cultural research which indicate that cultural groups are relatively either field independent or field dependent as a function of their ecological environment and associated socialization practices; and (b) studies that indicate that field dependent individuals may have superior social skills.

Although Witkin earlier emphasized the possibility that sex differences in field dependence-independence might be biological, cross-cultural research tended to show that males are not relatively more field independent than females in mobile, hunting societies which emphasize greater independence among females (Witkin & Berry, 1975). Further, in sedentary, agricultural societies, the sex differences are marked, and males and females are generally more field dependent. These findings have been related to the greater sex-role differentiation in traditional agricultural settings and indicate that field dependence or field independence might be an adaptive adjustment to ecological variation (Witkin & Berry, 1975). To maintain that the field independent cognitive style is superior in the face of such data would be to deny cultural relativism and assert the superiority of certain cultural norms.

The second body of research that led Witkin and his co-workers to assume a more value-neutral stance was the finding of greater social orientation among field dependent individuals. This work was summarized by Witkin and Goodenough (1976a). Evidence exists that field dependent persons literally look more at the faces of others, presumably as a source of information about what others are feeling and thinking, attend more to verbal messages with social content, and prefer to be physically closer to others. There is also some indication that field dependent people are more popular with others.

In contrast to the "other-centered" orientation of field dependent people, field independent people were described as having a more impersonal or self-centered orientation. Thus, for example, in real life settings, field independent children spent greater amounts of time in solitary play than in play with other children. Field independent people were also described as "cold and distant with others," "unaware of their social stimulus value," "individualistic," less self disclosing, and interested in the abstract and theoretical.

Witkin and Goodenough (1976b) interpreted the stronger social orientation of field dependent individuals as related to less differentiation. Compared to field dependent persons, field independent individuals are thought to have greater "self-nonself segregation," that is, greater awareness of the distinction between their own characteristics, desires, and emotions and those of others. This self-nonself segregation presumably leads to reduced reliance on external sources of support and more autonomous functioning.

PROBLEMS WITH THE FIELD DEPENDENCE-INDEPENDENCE CONSTRUCT

A full critique of the FDI construct is beyond the scope of this chapter and will be presented elsewhere (Hoffman & Kagan, Note 2). Nevertheless, there are four problems with the FDI construct that merit consideration: (*a*) It contains a confusion of fact and value; (*b*) it is operationalized by ambiguous measures; (*c*) the FDI construct lacks essential forms of validity; and (*d*) support for the FDI theory is overstated.

Disguised Value Judgments

In a number of ways, the FDI literature contains a confusion of facts and values. Especially in the early work, empirical findings were presented in a way that attached negative value judgments to field dependence. For example, field dependent persons were said to have "poor" impulse control. This description made an unsupported leap from some behavioral observation to a statement of value concerning the behavior. What may be described by some as poor impulse control might be described by others as freedom from repressive puritanical values. Similarly, field dependent individuals were described as "passive," and the mothers of field dependent children were described as generally overprotective and arbitrary. Again, what was considered passive by some might be considered a healthy absence of an obsessive competitive achievement orientation by others. The discipline by a mother from one culture might appear arbitrary only to someone unfamiliar with the values of that culture.

It is clear that Witkin and his co-workers have begun to take a more value-neutral stance, but even their most recent description of field dependence was essentially negatively tinged. The greater social orientation of field dependent individuals was described as a derivative of their lack of restructuring abilities, that is, because internal referents are less available to field dependent individuals, in situations of ambiguity they rely more on social referents and develop social skills (Witkin & Goodenough, 1976a). Thus, in part the social abilities of field dependent individuals are seen as compensation for lack of ability to structure situations on their own. This deficit-and-compensation model is hardly value neutral. It would be possible to look at the same data and indicate that the more intense task and nonsocial orientation of field independent individuals is a compensation for their failure in interpersonal relations. Neither view is supported by the data, merely an interpretation of the data; an interpretation perhaps based in part on the value placed on field independence.

In general, Witkin and his co-workers have emphasized the positive consequences of the development of analytic abilities associated with field independence but have not recognized that the development of those abilities represents a cultural value not shared by all cultures. Vernon (1965) presented evidence that the field dependence-independence measures load quite heavily on "g" factors, but was quick to recognize that "the group of skills which we refer to as intelligence is a European and American middle-class invention: something which seems to be intimately bound up with puritanical values, with repression of instinctual responses." Vernon went on to indicate that those types of intelligence were perhaps better suited for control and exploitation of the physical world and for carrying out materialistic objectives but less successful than other types of intelligence for providing harmonious personal adjustment.

An examination of the nature of what individuals are asked to do in some typical intelligence and field independence tests reveals the value-laden nature of these tests. In the block design test, for example, individuals are asked to copy an abstract form by quickly manipulating colored blocks; they are scored on how quickly and accurately they make the blocks conform to a predetermined pattern. They get a high score if they quickly and actively manipulate their environment to meet an external standard of excellence. If they stop to enjoy the experience, muse over the novel colored blocks, or try to determine what the examiner is feeling or thinking, they get a lower score. To some extent, a field independent score on the block design test clearly indicates conformity to a certain set of values.

The issue of values merits considerable attention because the value judgments inherent in the FDI construct are potentially damaging for Mexican-Americans, who tend to be relatively field dependent on some FDI measures. For example, even in their recent reconceptualization of the FDI construct, Witkin and Goodenough (1976a) seem to indicate that the development of a social orientation among field dependent individuals is a compensation for a lack of inner resources.

Mexican-Americans do have a more social orientation than Anglo-Americans (Kagan, 1977; Ramirez & Castañeda, 1974) but social orientation probably represents an autonomous cultural value, not a compensation for lack of other skills.

Ambiguous Measurement Instruments

Although the FDI construct has undergone some rather dramatic changes, the measures on which the construct is based have remained relatively constant. Today, three main measures are used: the rod-and-frame test (RFT), the embedded figures test (EFT), and the block design (BD). Draw-a-figure tests have also been used to assess degree of differentiation, but they do not play as central a role in the FDI construct.

The most obvious problem with the FDI measures is that they confound ability and style. In each of the three main tasks, subjects are scored as field independent if they succeed (aligning the rod the way they are instructed to, making the correct block design, finding the correct embedded figure) and they are scored field dependent if they fail. Thus a field-independent score results from the presence of analytic abilities, whether or not accompanied by a preference for analytic modes of perception; a field dependent score may result from the absence of analytic abilities or a preference for global modes of perception. The basic ambiguity of whether field dependence represents a style or a lack of ability has not been resolved and has allowed those formulating the FDI construct sometimes to speak of field independence as a reflection of a value-neutral cognitive style and at other times as a positive, development-linked ability. The most disturbing aspect of this ambiguity is that a field dependent score may represent a lack of ability for some groups and yet a perfectly valid cognitive style for others. Serpell (1976) argues that FDI probably measures different degrees of style and ability for different groups.

There are yet further ambiguities inherent in the FDI measures. On any of the measures, a field dependent score could result from lack of motivation to perform well on the tasks, carelessness, cultural irrelevance of psychological tasks, or lack of familiarity with the requirements of psychological tests. Further, for each of the individual FDI measures, there are many ways in which an individual can obtain a field dependent score. For example, in the RFT, an individual who does not fully understand the notion of the upright may be scored field dependent (Lester, 1968), as may someone who does not agree with the experimenter on the subjective direction of the tilt of the frame (Fine & Danforth, 1975), or someone unfamiliar with or hesitant to manipulate mechanical instruments. In the block design test and embedded figures test, lack of familiarity with printed materials, hesitancy to manipulate the blocks, lack of sense of urgency needed to perform well on the timed test, or even a different sense of time could result in a score supposedly reflecting field dependence. In general "field dependence" has been uncritically inferred from low scores on tests, but many alternative explanations are possible.

Lack of Validity

For a psychological construct to demonstrate acceptable validity, it must demonstrate both convergent and discriminant validity (Campbell & Fiske, 1959). That is, the various measures of the construct must correlate highly with each other, and more highly with each other than with other variables assumed to be unrelated to the construct. Although no absolute levels for sizes of correlations were ever established, for reliable measures like those used to operationalize the FDI construct, a correlation of .70 or higher (which indicates that the measures share at least half their variance in common) seems acceptable. The convergent validity of the measures is especially critical for the FDI construct, for Witkin and Berry (1975, p. 11) essentially cast the differentiation hypothesis in terms of convergent validity. They state that ". . . any manifestation of differentiation may be used to identify an individual's overall level of psychological differentiation." Thus, if the FDI measures fail to correlate highly, an essential requirement of the FDI theory is not met.

From the start, however, the FDI measures have demonstrated only weak convergent validity. Witkin *et al.* (1954, p. 85) reported that the rod-and-frame and embedded figures tests correlated relatively well for males (.43 to .76), but those same measures did not correlate well for females (.03 to .26). Further work also failed to confirm a consistently high correlation between the two measures (Arbuthnot, 1972; Cabe, 1968; Gruen, 1955), and, as will be seen, Buriel (Note 3) demonstrated that the measures show only a small intercorrelation for Mexican-American children. The low convergent validity for the FDI measures fails to support the central propositions of the differentiation hypothesis and the FDI construct.

Low convergent validity implies that if a variable correlates with one FDI measure it may not correlate with another. In general, the implications of this problem have not been realized, and investigators have treated the various tests as if they were equivalent. Correlations between a single FDI measure and some other variable are generally reported as correlations of that variable and "field independence" or "field dependence," rather than as correlations of the variable with the rod-and-frame behavior or embedded-figures behavior. Thus there has been a confusion of the tests with the construct, as discussed by Wachtel (1972), and this confusion produced inflated estimates of the correlates of FDI as a construct.

With regard to the second type of validity, discriminant validity, the field dependence-independence construct is open to equally damaging criticism. Zigler (1963a, b) suggested that many of the correlates of the FDI measures, as well as their correlation with each other, could be accounted for by general intelligence as measured by IQ tests. Crandall and Sinkeldam (1964) found EFT to correlate .70 with the Wechsler intelligence scale for children (WISC) for some children, indicating that to a considerable extent the EFT measures whatever is measured by IQ tests. Further the EFT lacks discriminant validity since it did not correlate more highly with object assembly, a measure of analytic ability, than it did with vocabulary, comprehension, or information. Vernon (1972) has shown that the FDI measures have a high loading on the "*g*" factor and that, in fact, much of their shared variance is accounted for by that loading. Further, Dubois and Cohen (1970) found that the EFT did not correlate any higher with the RFT than it did with math ability. This lack of discriminant validity was apparent since it correlated with all abilities in a battery including English, social studies, art, and music. Because the FDI measures lack discriminant validity, the basis of their correlation with other variables is suspect. For example, Witkin and his co-workers indicated that the more global responses of field dependent persons to the Rorschach inkblot test is a function of personality organization as measured by the field dependence-independence measures. Weisz, O'Neil, and O'Neil (1975), however, have shown that the correlation is best accounted for by mental age. In this regard, it should be emphasized that although FDI measures correlate highly with IQ test scores, the meaning of both IQ and FDI test scores, especially with respect to Mexican-American populations, as noted earlier, is open to question.

Overstated Support

In important areas, empirical support for the FDI theory has been overstated or misrepresented. For example, it is often claimed in the FDI literature that field dependent individuals are superior in their memory for faces. A review of the relevant literature and recent data, however, indicate the opposite (Hoffman & Kagan, 1977). Perhaps the most important overstatement of the empirical support for the FDI theory occurred in regard to the socialization antecedents of field dependence. If the presumed field dependence socialization cluster were true, it would almost certainly lead to a passive and dependent child. Extensive observation of free play among children, however, has not indicated a greater passivity or dependency among field dependent children (Crandall & Sinkeldam, 1964). The presumed field dependence socialization cluster was inferred from global ratings of maternal behavior, not actual quantification of observable behaviors. Further, as will be seen in the subsequent review of the literature, the presumed field dependence socialization antecedents consistently failed to receive support from empirical investigation. Nevertheless, Witkin and his co-workers have continued to describe the field dependence socialization cluster as if it had been established (Witkin & Berry, 1975).

Field Dependence-Independence and Mexican-American Culture

Discussions of the relation of FDI to cross-cultural research have been presented elsewhere (Berry, 1971; Serpell, 1976; Witkin, 1967; Witkin & Berry, 1975). Two recent books devoted considerable attention to the relation of the FDI construct to Mexican and Mexican-American cultural background (Holtzman, Diaz-Guerrero, & Swartz, 1975; Ramirez & Castañeda, 1974). In these presentations it was generally asserted that traditional, sedentary, and agricultural cultures maintain socialization practices that emphasize strong family ties and respect for and obedience to elders, practices that are thought to lead to a relatively field dependent cognitive style. In contrast, modern, mobile, and hunting societies have socialization practices that emphasize individuation and autonomous functioning, practices that presumably lead to a relatively field independent cognitive style. Further, Mexican and Mexican-American cultural groups are described as traditional, with strong emphasis on family ties and parental authority, and parallels are drawn between the socialization practices presumed to be common among Mexicans and Mexican-Americans and those presumed to lead to a field dependent cognitive style.

Ramirez and Castañeda (1974) emphasized the positive qualities of a field dependent cognitive style and preferred to call it a field sensitive cognitive style. They indicated that a relatively field sensitive cognitive style is found among Mexican-Americans because traditional Mexican-American cultural values maintain socialization practices that produce a field sensitive cognitive style. They indicated four aspects of cognitive style that distinguish Mexican-Americans: learning styles, incentive-motivational styles, human-relational styles, and communication styles. The greater cooperativeness, affiliativeness, and sensitivity of Mexican-Americans in interpersonal relations was attributed to their field sensitive cognitive style, and research was cited that indicates field dependence is related to a more social orientation.

The model presented by Ramirez and Castañeda (1974) differed somewhat from that presented by Berry (1971). Berry emphasized ecology and asserted that ecological factors associated with agricultural societies (in contrast with hunting societies) lead to distinct cultural, socialization, nutritional, and genetic factors, that in turn determine individual differences in perception and cognitive styles. The difference between the model presented by Berry and that presented by Ramirez and Castañeda is that in the Berry model, cultural factors and socialization factors are separate, each having independent influences on cognitive styles. In the Ramirez and Castañeda model, the effect of cultural values is mediated by socialization practices, so that socialization practices explain the observed cultural differences in cognitive styles. Both models, however, assume that socialization practices play a large role in determining cultural differences in FDI, with field dependence as a result of traditional socialization practices and emphasis on obedience and conformity to family and cultural norms and roles.

MEXICAN CULTURAL BACKGROUND

Four major studies have compared performance of Mexican children with that of United States children (or norms) on the FDI measures (Holtzman *et al.*, 1975; Kagan, 1974; Mebane & Johnson, 1970; Witkin, Price-Williams, Bertini, Christiansen, Oltman, Ramirez, & Van Meel, 1974). These studies all predicted and found greater field dependence among Mexican children. The studies as a group, however, did not support the presumed socialization antecedents of field dependence and indicated serious problems with the FDI construct.

In the first study to apply the FDI construct to understanding cultural differences between Mexico and the United States, Mebane and Johnson (1970) administered the children's embedded figures test (CEFT) and the draw-a-person test (DAP) to Mexican boys and girls attending school in a working-class neighborhood in Monterrey, Mexico. The school was strictly divided by sex. Girls were taught by female teachers in a building separate from boys.

The results partially supported the predicted relations: Mexican girls were significantly more field dependent than United States norms for girls on the CEFT, and were significantly more field dependent than Mexican boys. Norms for Mexican boys did not differ significantly from United States norms for boys on the CEFT. Contrary to predictions, Mexican boys and girls did not differ significantly on the DAP. Modest correlations between the CEFT and DAP were reported for boys ($r = .42, p < .05$) and girls ($r = .43, p < .05$).

To determine the relationship of socialization practices to FDI, Mebane and Johnson had children fill out a questionnaire developed by Devereux, Bronfenbrenner, and Suci (1962) to measure nine dimensions of parental behavior: nurturance, instrumental companionship, principled discipline, prescription of responsibility, power, physical punishment, achievement pressure, deprivation of privileges, and expressive rejection. In comparison with Mexican girls, Mexican boys were found to describe their fathers as more nurturant, more ready to be a companion, and more principled in their use of discipline and saw their mothers as more depriving of privileges. Contrary to FDI theory, however, CEFT performance was unrelated to the socialization variables on which boys and girls differed.

There were some relations between the child-rearing variables and the FDI measures, but these were in the expected direction only for males. For boys, instrumental companionship and principled discipline from the mother were positively correlated with CEFT performance. None of these relations proved significant for girls, and in some cases the correlations were in the opposite direction. Furthermore, for boys, in no case did a socialization variable that proved to relate significantly to CEFT performance also relate significantly to DAP performance. This pattern of results did not support a relationship between socialization and the FDI construct.

For girls, experience variables tended to correlate with performance on the FDI measures. That is, girls who indicated greater independence in housework, creative play, and total independence scored higher on field independence. Mebane and Johnson concluded that child-rearing and experience variables that govern performance on cognitive tasks may be different for boys and girls.

In the second study to use a FDI measure to compare Mexican and United States children, Kagan (1974) compared the performance of rural Mexican and urban Anglo-American children on the man-in-the-frame test (MIFT) which is similar to the portable rod and frame test (PRFT). The 7 to 9-year-old rural Mexican children averaged approximately twice as many degrees deviation from the true upright per trial (mean = 11.1) as their Anglo-American counterparts (mean = 5.8). This difference was statistically significant. Only a small number of children in each culture (16) were compared, however, and among those small groups no significant sex differences emerged. Kagan noted that the meaning of the cultural differences in behavior was questionable. The usual interpretation of field dependence as indicating greater reliance on the tilting frame was essentially an environmental *press* interpretation. Kagan suggested that the observed differences might instead be explained by an individualistic *need* interpretation. That is, cultural groups may differ on the value they place on moving a tilting rod to the upright in an artificial experimental situation. As will be discussed, Sanders, Scholz, and Kagan (in press) confirmed a small but significant correlation of field independence with need for achievement as measured by traditional *n* Ach tests. Ramirez and Price-Williams (1976) noted that such tests may indicate how much an individual values achievement for the self in contrast to achievement for the group or family. If the rod-and-frame tasks are seen as an individualistic achievement situation, and if Mexican and Mexican-American children are more motivated toward achievement for the group, the rod-and-frame tasks may be less culturally relevant for those groups.

Holtzman *et al.* (1975) confirmed that Mexican children score in a more field dependent direction than Anglo-American children. In a large, longitudinal developmental study comparing both working and middle class United States and Mexican children, they found that Mexican children were more field dependent than United States children at all ages sampled (6-15 years) on the embedded figures test, the block design, and the Harris-Goodenough human figure drawing test. The performance of children on the embedded figures test was analyzed in detail and indicated that Mexican children took longer to find the figures, found fewer figures, and reexamined the figures more than did United States children. This was true at all ages tested for both socioeconomic status groups. With increasing age, all children became far more proficient on the embedded figures test, and the cultural differences diminished. The sex differences were appreciably greater among Mexican children; by 14 years of age, Mexican boys performed as quickly as United States children; only the Mexican girls continued to take longer to find the embedded figures.

The Holtzman *et al.* (1975) study provided partial support for the convergent validity of the FDI construct. The correlations of the embedded figures test with the block design were substantial and significant for both Mexican and United States children, ranging from .41 to .78. The correlation of the embedded figures test and the human figures drawing test, though lower, were significant, ranging from .20 to .48. The correlations between the block design and the human figures drawing test, while mostly significant, were the lowest of the three comparisons, ranging from .12 to .49.

The correlations between the three field dependence measures might indicate some convergent validity for the FDI construct, but those results must be interpreted within the total correlational pattern observed. For the FDI construct to obtain discriminant as well as convergent validity, the measures should correlate with each other better than with other ability measures. The results, however, indicated the FDI measures had substantial correlations with a number of ability variables, including information, arithmetic, and vocabulary. For example, vocabulary correlated well with the embedded figures test (range = .15 to .43) and the block design (.13 to .51). The discriminant validity of the FDI construct was also not supported by the results of a factor analysis. For the Mexican 9-year-olds, the embedded figures and block design tests had significant loadings only on a factor that included information, arithmetic, vocabulary, picture completion, and object assembly. As Holtzman *et al.* (1975) indicated, such a factor resembles general intelligence. It is interesting to note that the human figure drawing test did not load on the same factor, but rather on another factor on which the embedded figures and block design tests had no significant loadings. Not all the factor analyses were similarly unsupportive of the FDI construct, but that such a picture emerges for any group indicates, at the very least, that the FDI construct may have no discriminant validity for some groups.

In spite of the relative lack of discriminant validity for the FDI construct in their results, Holtzman *et al.* (1975) interpreted the greater field dependence of Mexican compared to United States children as related to the close resemblance of Mexican attitudes, values, family lifestyle, and socialization practices to the field dependence socialization cluster. They listed 14 parallels between what they described as Mexican socialization practices and those likely to foster field dependence, including authoritarianism, passivity of mothers, noninvolvement of fathers, intrusiveness of parents, emphasis on obedience and social conformity, and inhibition of initiative and independence among children. It was pointed out, however, that no empirical relationships were established between the parent socialization scores and scores on the FDI measures. Thus, although the Mexican groups were higher on the socialization variables presumed to foster field dependence and were, in fact, more field dependent, the data were consistent with the conclusion that the variables presumed to foster field dependence are, in fact, unrelated to field dependence.

There are a large number of alternative explanations for the greater field dependence of the Mexican children. As Holtzman *et al.* noted, United States parents completed more years of school, took their children on more trips, subscribed to more newspapers and magazines, read to their children more often, and had higher educational aspirations for their daughters. Furthermore, it was estimated that United States children generally spent more time reading and engaged in solitary activities than Mexican children, pursuits that perhaps promoted a field independent test performance quite apart from the presumed authoritarianism and intrusiveness attributed to Mexican parents.

In the remaining study in Mexico, Witkin and his co-workers (1974) conducted a large cross-cultural study explicitly designed to test the cross-cultural validity of the FDI construct and the presumed field dependence socialization cluster. The results of the study have been presented in various forms (Witkin *et al.*, 1974;

Irving, 1970; Ramirez & Price-Williams, 1974a). The study compared children from two villages in each of three countries, Mexico, Holland, and Italy. In each country, the villages were chosen to differ in aspects of socialization that would either foster or hinder the development of differentiation. Children received a battery of FDI measures (PRFT, CEFT, BD, and HFDT), and their mothers were administered socialization questionnaires designed to assess the field dependence socialization cluster.

The results were somewhat supportive of the FDI theory, in that children from villages in which social conformity was stressed obtained significantly greater field dependence scores on every measure than did children from the comparison village in each country. Nevertheless, a detailed analysis of the results by Irving (1970) indicated that, contrary to the Witkin *et al.* (1974) presentation of findings, the results were not generally supportive of either the FDI construct or the presumed socialization antecedents of field dependence. Irving's analysis thus merits careful consideration.

In Mexico, one community was characterized as having traditional Mexican values and the supposed field dependence socialization cluster, and the other was less identified with such values and practices. The more traditional community was characterized as having strict emphasis on respect for authority and social convention, strong family ties, strict sex-role differentiation, and a Mexican Catholic ideology. The less traditional community is located near the Mexican-United States border and was characterized by a higher prevalence of father absences, maternal mobility, independence and mobility among children, decreased sex-role differentiation, and less identification with Mexican Catholic ideology.

For both groups, the convergent validity of the FDI measures was not acceptable, indicating serious limitations to the validity of the FDI construct. In the more traditional community, the correlations between the rod-and-frame and the children's embedded figures test ranged from -.24 to .15, and none were statistically significant. The DAP and CEFT did correlate significantly in the right direction in all cases, but the DAP and RFT were not significantly correlated in three of the four age and sex groups studied. Finally, in the less traditional community, RFT and CEFT correlated significantly in the right direction for only two of the four groups compared.

Further, the presumed field dependence socialization antecedents were not upheld. To test the relation of the field dependence socialization cluster to actual field dependence among children, their mothers were administered 50 questions designed to assess self-assurance, self-realization, overprotectiveness, acceptance of masculine roles, and stress on individual assertiveness versus conformity. Although the children in the less traditional community scored in a more field independent direction than those in the more traditional community on the FDI measures, the results of the socialization questionnaire revealed no consistent relationship between the socialization questionnaire and the FDI measures. In the more traditional community, mothers who answered the socialization questionnaire in ways presumed to foster field dependence tended to have more *field independent* children in four of the eight comparisons made. In the less traditional community, half of the correlations were in the predicted direction and half were in the opposite direction, and all were relatively low.

Subsequent factor analyses for each community did not support the presumed socialization antecedents of field dependence. Six factors were identified in the more traditional community. All of the field dependence items loaded on one factor, but only three of the 50 socialization items loaded significantly on that factor, indicating a relative independence of the socialization items and the FDI tests. In the less traditional community, six factors were also identified. Three factors contained only the socialization items, and one factor contained age. Another factor contained the CEFT and a number of socialization items but not RFT. Still another contained RFT and a number of socialization items, but not CEFT. Finally, one factor did contain both RFT and CEFT and a number of socialization items. Only one of the three socialization items that loaded on the field dependence factor in the traditional community, however, also loaded on the field dependence factor in the less traditional community. This pattern of results indicates that field dependence is probably associated with different socialization practices in different settings, and that the relation of the different FDI measures is considerably different in different communities, even within one country.

MEXICAN-AMERICAN CULTURAL BACKGROUND

Rod-and-Frame Measures

In the first publication to assert that Mexican-American children are more field dependent than Anglo-American children, Ramirez (1973) summarized two main bodies of evidence: (*a*) the results of a Houston study (to be described in more detail later by Ramirez & Price-Williams, 1974b) that compared 60 Anglo-American and 60 Mexican-American fourth-grade children on the portable rod-and-frame, and (*b*) the results of the Riverside desegregation study that compared 596 Mexican-American and 571 Anglo-American children from grades K through 6 on the man-in-the-frame. The results of both studies demonstrated significantly more field dependent performance among Mexican-American than Anglo-American children.

In the Houston study, Mexican-American children as a group were significantly more field dependent than Anglo-American children, and females were significantly more field dependent than males among both Anglo-American and Mexican-American children. An indicator of economic class indicated that the differences were not attributable to that variable. In the Riverside desegregation study, similar results were obtained. Mexican-American children and females were significantly more field dependent than Anglo-American and male children. Furthermore, all children became significantly more field independent as they grew older as can be seen in Figure 2.

Subsequent research confirmed that Mexican-American children are more field dependent than Anglo-American children, at least as indicated by rod-and-

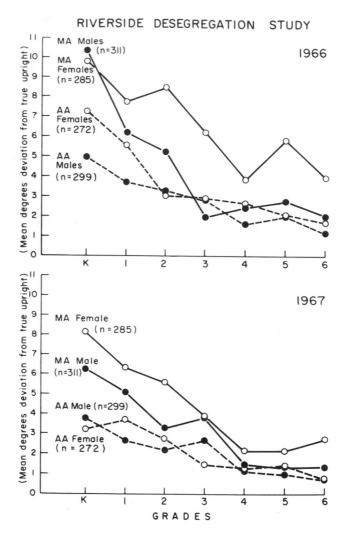

FIGURE 2. Mean degrees deviation from the true upright on the man-in-the-frame test in the Riverside desegregation study (Culture x Sex x Age, trials collapsed).

frame type measures. Figure 3 presents some of the results from four studies using rod-and-frame FDI measures to compare the behavior of Anglo-American and Mexican-American male and female children. Two studies used the portable rod-and-frame test (PRFT) (Oltman, 1968); and two used the man-in-the-frame test (MIFT) (Gerard, Note 4). Furthermore, two studies were conducted in relatively traditional communities (in which Spanish was the dominant language, many parents were born in Mexico, and there was strong identification with Mexican and Catholic values and ideology) and two were conducted in more dualistic

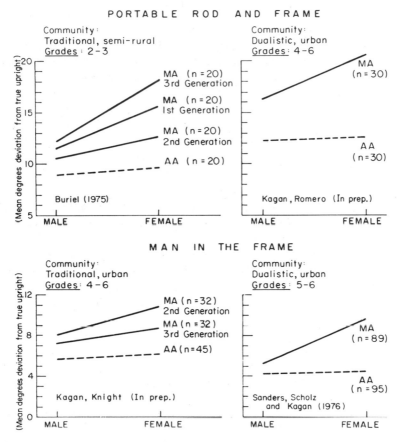

FIGURE 3. Mean degrees deviation from the true upright on four rod-and-frame type field dependence-independence studies (Culture x Sex, community characteristics, and grades noted).

communities (in which English was the dominant language, more parents were born in the United States, and there was weaker identification with Mexican and Catholic values and ideology). As will be noted, however, differences among the methodologies in the studies limit the conclusions that can be drawn from comparisons among them.

In the first study (Buriel, 1975) the PRFT was administered to second- and third-grade Mexican-American and Anglo-American children living in a very traditional semirural Mexican-American community. The Mexican-American children were either first, second, or third generation. The results indicated that none of the Mexican-American groups differed significantly from each other; only the third-generation Mexican-Americans were significantly more field dependent than the Anglo-American control group. Buriel interpreted the trend toward greater field dependence of the third generation group as a possible result of "acculturation to the barrio." That is, the traditional, semirural barrio where the children lived resembled traditional settings where children tended to be more field dependent in a number of respects. Buriel speculated that relatively field independent Mexicans may leave their homeland for the United States, but after settling in a traditional rural setting, their children become more field dependent from the second to the third generation.

In the second study (Kagan & Romero, Note 5) the portable rod-and-frame test was administered to fourth- through sixth-grade Anglo-American and Mexican-American children in a more dualistic community. A significant cultural difference in PRFT behavior was found. Although both the Buriel (1975) and Kagan and Romero (Note 5) studies used the PRFT, they were not designed for purposes of comparison, and subtle differences in methodology might account for differences between the findings of the two studies. Buriel slightly altered the construction of the PRFT by placing a slim figure on the rod to insure that children would understand the notion of the upright. Furthermore, he took considerable time with the instructions, which were given in English and Spanish. In contrast, Kagan and Romero used standard operating instructions. Thus, although a between-study comparison indicates a trend for greater field dependence among children in the dualistic community (see Figure 3), differences in instructions might account for that trend.

In the third study, Kagan and Knight (Note 6) contrasted the behavior of second- and third-generation Mexican-American children with that of Anglo-American children on the MIFT. Both Mexican-American groups tended to score more field dependent than the Anglo-American group, but, as in the Buriel (1975) study, there was no significant difference between the generations among Mexican-American children. Unlike the Buriel (1975) study, however, there was a tendency for second-generation children to be more field dependent.

In the fourth study presented in Figure 1 (Sanders *et al.*, 1976), the MIFT was administered to fifth- and sixth-grade Anglo-American and Mexican-American children in three schools in dualistic communities, using the same methodology as Kagan and Knight (Note 6). The results indicated that Mexican-American children were significantly more field dependent than Anglo-American children. There was a slight tendency for children in the dualistic communities sampled by Sanders *et al.* (1976) to score more field independent on the MIFT than children in the traditional community sampled by Kagan and Knight (Note 6). The slight tendency in that direction, however, could be accounted for by the slight differences in the ages of the children sampled (Grades 4-6 versus 5-6), since older children are more field independent.

As a group, the four studies are remarkably consistent. In all four studies, Mexican-American children were more field dependent. Consistent with the FDI theory, there was a tendency for sex differences to be greater among Mexican-American than Anglo-American children in all four studies, but in no case was there a significant culture by sex interaction. The cultural difference was robust in that it occurred across four communities and two measurement instruments. As a group, the four studies do not support any consistent generalizations with regard to differences due to community characteristics or generation level. As a group, however, the four studies were not designed to systematically vary generation level of community characteristics, and conclusions about those variables based on post hoc comparisons must be considered tentative.

The four studies do support a generalization with regard to the differences between the MIFT and PRFT measures because children made considerably fewer errors on the MIFT than on the PRFT (degrees off the true vertical). This finding is almost certainly in part a result of the more compelling three-dimensional frame in the PRFT compared to the two-dimensional frame in the MIFT. The pattern of results indicates that compared to the MIFT, the PRFT in some respects is a superior measurement instrument. It is less likely to be influenced by a "basement" effect as children approach the sixth grade. Nevertheless, for children of the elementary school level both instruments appear to indicate the same pattern of results.

Nonsignificant CEFT Comparisons

Three studies compared Mexican-American and Anglo-American children on the children's embedded figures test (CEFT), and, in contrast to the studies using rod-and-frame type measures, the cultural groups do not differ significantly in all three samples (Buriel, Note 3; Kagan, Zahn, & Gealy, 1977; Knudson & Kagan, in press). This different pattern of results observed with the CEFT could be attributed to any combination of three explanations: sample characteristics, age differences, or method differences.

It is possible that the studies using the CEFT have by chance sampled populations of Mexican-American and Anglo-American children that do not differ along the FDI dimension. Such an explanation gains some support from the finding of no difference on the PRFT in one of the studies using the CEFT (Buriel, Note 3). Nevertheless, since almost all of the eight studies to include rod-and-frame type measures have found significant differences and none of the three studies to include the CEFT found significant differences, it seems unlikely that random sampling differences could account for the difference between the two methods.

The second explanation of the absence of differences on the CEFT involves age. Unlike the rod-and-frame measures, the CEFT is designed for use with very young children, and the studies that included the CEFT sampled kindergarten through second-grade children in contrast to studies using the rod-and-frame type measures which included mainly fourth- through sixth-grade children. Therefore, if the cultural difference increased with age, the rod-and-frame studies would be more likely to show significant cultural differences than the CEFT studies. The support for this interpretation, however, is relatively weak. Three studies examined the influence on age on the size of the cultural difference. In the Buriel (Note 3) and Kagan and Zahn (1975) studies, four FDI measures were used. In spite of trends for increasing cultural differences with age, the culture by age interaction was not significant in three of the four comparisons, as shown in Figure 4. Only in the block design did the culture by age interaction reach significance, indicating

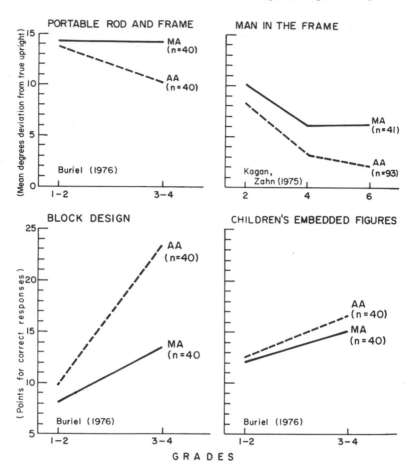

FIGURE 4. Development of field dependence-independence on four measures.

differences at the older age. In contrast, however, the Riverside desegregation study (Figure 2) and the Holtzman *et al.* (1975) study, both found that
differences tended to *decrease* with age. In sum, attributing the failure to
find cultural differences on the CEFT to the younger age of the children sampled
in the CEFT studies is not consistently supported.

The remaining explanation of the absence of cultural differences on the
CEFT is the most parsimonious. Unlike the PRFT, the CEFT may measure variables
on which Mexican-American and Anglo-American children do not differ. This
explanation, of course, is based on a possible lack of convergent validity between
the two measures. The rod-and-frame measures may tap a different set of abilities
or styles than those measured by the CEFT, and the cultural groups may differ
on one set but not the other. Such an explanation is supported by research indicating a lack of convergent validity between these measures for young Mexican-
American and Anglo-American children.

Lack of Convergent Validity

Buriel (Note 3) explicitly tested the convergent validity of the PRFT, CEFT, and BD among first- through fourth-grade Mexican-American and Anglo-American children. Partial correlations between the three FDI measures controlling for grade and sex were computed separately for Anglo-American and Mexican-American children. As presented in Table 1, the results indicated that the three measures were only modestly intercorrelated with each other for both groups. On the average, the measures shared less than 10% of their variance in common for both cultural groups, indicating that the three FDI measures tap primarily different variables. The construct validity of the FDI dimension thus failed to receive support, at least for the young children sampled. The relative independence of the three measures indicated that Mexican-American and Anglo-American children could very well differ on the PRFT but not on the CEFT. There may be a general cultural difference in one of the FDI measures, but not necessarily in FDI as a construct.

TABLE 1

Second-Order Partial Correlations between the Three Field Dependence Measures for Mexican-American (above Diagonal) and Anglo-American (below Diagonal) Children (Partial with Respect to Sex and Grade)

	Mexican-American (n = 40)		
	PRFT	CEFT	BD
PRFT	- - - - -	.41**	.17
CEFT	.30	- - - - -	.33*
BD	.29	.31	- - - - -
		Anglo-American (n = 40)	

* $p < .05$.
** $p < .01$.

Socialization

As indicated, the comparisons of the studies presented in Figure 3 did not support a consistent generalization with regard to the effects of community characteristics on FDI. Conclusions based on comparisons between studies, however, must remain extremely tentative. Ramirez, Castañeda, and Herold (1974) conducted a study to test directly the hypothesis that field dependence among Mexican-American children was partially a function of maintenance of Mexican cultural values and socialization practices associated with life in traditional communities. They tested 541 Mexican-American first-, fourth-, and sixth-grade elementary school children and their mothers. The children were about equally divided by sex and by middle and lower socioeconomic classes. The children came from three communities: (a) traditional, in which Mexican-Americans made up about 90% of the population, Spanish was spoken in the community, family ties were close, and residents identified with Mexican Catholicism and the Mexican culture; (b) dualistic, in which Mexican-Americans made up about half of the community population, English was the primary language, family ties were not as close, and identification with Mexican Catholicism and culture was weaker; (c) atraditional, in which there was greater contact with Anglo-Americans, English was dominant, assimilation pressures were strong, and there was little identification with Mexican Catholicism or culture.

The children were administered the PRFT; mothers were administered a draw-a-person test (DAP), a field dependence socialization questionnaire, and a Mexican-American family values questionnaire. The results indicated that children from the traditional community scored significantly more field dependent on the PRFT (mean = 17.18) than children from the dualistic (14.69) and atraditional (13.26) communities, which did not differ significantly from each other. Females and younger children were more field dependent than males and older children in all three groups; socioeconomic class did not account for a significant portion of the variance.

Compared to mothers in the other communities, mothers in the traditional community scored more field dependent on the DAP as well as expressing more agreement with the field dependence socialization questionnaire and Mexican cultural value questionnaire. Unfortunately, the empirical relations between the socialization and values questionnaires and the field dependence scores of mothers and children were not presented. The study thus offers no empirical support for the hypothesis that the socialization practices or values common among Mexican-Americans in traditional communities were responsible for the great field dependence on the PRFT of children from those communities. As demonstrated by the results of Holtzman *et al.* (1975), it was possible for parents of a Mexican cultural background to have more of the presumed field dependence socialization practices but for there to be no significant relationship between those socialization practices and the relatively greater field dependence of their children. The lack of a strong relationship between the values and socialization practices of the mothers and the field dependence of their children was suggested also by the pattern of results obtained by Ramirez, Castañeda, and Herold (1974). On the values and socialization questionnaires, there was little difference between scores of the traditional and dualistic mothers, but there was a relatively large difference in the scores of their children on the PRFT. Furthermore, on the PRFT there was little difference between the scores of children from the dualistic and atraditional communities, but there was a relatively large difference in the scores of their mothers on the socialization and cultural values questionnaires.

In a quite different approach to testing the possible relationship between Mexican-American socialization practices and field dependence, Hoppe, Kagan, and Zahn (in press) had Mexican-American and Anglo-American mothers and children role play three situations designed to provoke conflicts over maternal authority versus children's independence. The children from each cultural group were chosen for their extreme field dependence or extreme field independence, a procedure designed to increase the likelihood of finding differences associated with the FDI dimension.

The verbal responses of the mothers and children were recorded, transcribed, and factor analyzed. The results indicated that Mexican-American mothers were significantly higher on a factor that included more simple dissent, will assertions, will justifications, and fewer questions of fact. In brief, it appeared that Mexican-American mothers said more of what they wanted and why than did Anglo-American mothers, who asked more questions of their children. These cultural differences, however, were unrelated to the field dependence of the children. Children's FDI was related to a maternal factor that included length of utterances, will justifications, pronouns of various types, and questions of permission. The factor was somewhat ambiguous, but may indicate that mothers of field-independent children provide a more differentiated verbal environment for their children. It is important to note, however, that Mexican-American and Anglo-American mothers did not differ significantly on that factor. In sum, the Hoppe *et al.* (in press) results, like those of Holtzman *et al.* (1975), indicated that mothers with a Mexican cultural background in fact differ from Anglo-American mothers, but those differences are not empirically related to FDI measures of their children.

Assertiveness

The Hoppe *et al.* (in press) results also tended not to confirm the early conceptualization of field independence as related to passivity. One factor included primarily assertive behaviors (asking questions of one's mother, disagreeing, not agreeing, making more utterances), but that factor was not generally associated with greater field independence. In fact, a field dependence by sex interaction indicated that field independent boys and field dependent girls were higher on the assertiveness factor. Mexican-American children appeared to give more deference or respect to their mothers; they were significantly lower on a factor that included various forms of dissent, contradictions, lack of agreements, and will justifications. It is important to note, however, that field dependence was not significantly associated with that factor. Thus, again, although Mexican-American and Anglo-American children differed on variables presumed to be related to the FDI dimension, an analysis revealed that the cultural difference between children was not empirically related to FDI.

Recent research has not confirmed a relation of FDI to another form of assertiveness. Kagan and Romero (in press) recently demonstrated that in some situations Mexican-Americans are less nonadaptively assertive than Anglo-Americans. Anglo-American children repeatedly pulled an "assertiveness pull scale" so hard that they failed to obtain valued rewards more often than did Mexican-American children. In subsequent work, Kagan and Romero (Note 5) found no significant relationship between the extreme assertiveness of Anglo-American children measured by the assertiveness pull scale and their greater field independence. Compared to Anglo-Americans, Mexican-American children were significantly more field dependent and significantly more often adaptively modified their assertiveness, but again the lack of correlation between these variables indicated they were manifestations of two distinct cultural differences.

Social Orientation

Recent conceptualizations of the FDI construct have emphasized that field dependence is related to a more social orientation, but recent work has failed to confirm that the generally more prosocial orientation of Mexican-American children is related to their greater field dependence. Kagan *et al.* (in press) found Mexican-American children more cooperative in their choices when faced with two-person outcome-interdependence choice cards, and further, they were more field dependent on the MIFT, but there was no consistent relation of field dependence to cooperation. Similarly, Sanders *et al.* (1976) found Mexican-American children to be more field dependent on the MIFT and more affiliative, as measured by projective measures of need for affiliation, but again field dependence was not correlated with *n* Aff. The study further demonstrated a significant correlation between field independence and need for achievement, *n* Ach, which emphasizes achievement for oneself. That correlation, however, was relatively low ($r = .21$, $p < .05$). Furthermore, findings in the Riverside desegregation study (Canavan, Note 7) indicated that the presumed relation of field dependence to sensitivity to social stimuli in some situations may be quite low. Field dependence was found to relate significantly to sensitivity to peer pressure, but the size of the correlation ($r = .11$) indicated little common variance between the two variables. In general, this pattern of results does not support the hypothesis that field dependence is related to the relatively more social orientation of Mexican-American children.

SUMMARY OF THE EMPIRICAL LITERATURE

One or more FDI measures have been included in more than a dozen empirical studies of Mexican-Americans. A review of those studies indicates that Mexican-American children generally score more field dependent than Anglo-American children on rod-and-frame type measures, but that the groups do not differ significantly on the CEFT. Furthermore, these two presumed FDI measures share little variance in common. Thus, it is not meaningful to describe Mexican-American children as generally more field dependent than Anglo-American, at least on the basis of data to date. The very existence of a field dependence-independence dimension underlying the behavior in the FDI measures is called into question by the low intercorrelation between the presumed FDI measures.

Furthermore, the FDI theory, which indicates that field dependence is associated with socialization practices like those common in Mexican cultural groups, does not receive support from the existing literature. Mexican cultural groups do differ from Anglo-American groups on various socialization practices, but an empirical relation between those socialization practices and the behavior of Mexican and Mexican-American children on FDI measures has not been confirmed, despite interpretations to the contrary.

Finally, the assertion that the relatively more prosocial orientation of Mexican-American children is related to their field dependent cognitive style has not been demonstrated. The results indicate that, contrary to various conceptualizations of the FDI construct, field dependence is not necessarily related to a more social orientation or passivity, at least in the studies conducted among Mexican-American children to date. Not only are Mexican-American children not more field dependent in the broad sense of that term as denoted in the FDI construct, but the broad connotations of the meaning of field dependence have not been confirmed in studies including Mexican-American children. Field dependent children do not necessarily have the presumed socialization experiences, or the presumed social and personality characteristics indicated by the FDI theory.

The results of the studies to date with Mexican-American children do indicate a rather general cultural difference between Mexican-American and Anglo-American children in rod-and-frame behavior, with Mexican-American children, especially females, being more field dependent. Ambiguity in the meaning of rod-and-frame scores, and the lack of high correlations between rod-and-frame behavior and other presumed indicators of field dependence, bring into question the extent to which cultural differences in rod-and-frame scores are caused by "field dependence." What has been established is a rather reliable cultural difference. Alternative explanations of cultural differences merit consideration, such as (a) the extent to which early development of certain kinds of rather specific spatial or analytic skills are emphasized; (b) preference for specific kinds of global or relational modes of perception without the general connotations of global "cognitive style"; (c) familiarity with and willingness to manipulate mechanical objects; and (d) motivation to achieve the correct response in a situation resembling an impersonal individualistic achievement test.

Field Dependence-Independence and Mexican-American Education

Fundamentally, two opposing stances can be taken with regard to the relation of field dependence-independence and Mexican-American education. The first was exemplified by Witkin, who in 1967 called for schools to train children to be more field independent, stating, "it is a challenge to future social action research to translate into forms appropriate to the school and other social settings, the processes which. . .have been found to foster development of an articulated cognitive style and self-differentiation [Witkin, 1967, p. 249] ."

Ramirez (1973) outlined the opposite stance. He noted that teachers tend to have a field independent cognitive style in contrast to Mexican-American children, who are generally more field dependent. He stated,

> I am hypothesizing that the primary reason for failure of educational institutions to fulfill the needs of the majority of Mexican Americans, and others in this country, is that they are not sensitive to the cognitive styles of these people. That is, these institutions are oriented toward serving the person who is relatively more field independent [Ramirez, 1973, p. 903].

Clearly Witkin in 1967 was calling for schools to train children to be more field independent, but Ramirez was indicating that schools should accept the field dependent cognitive style of minority students and design educational programs more responsive to them. Witkin treated field dependence as a deficit; Ramirez treated it as a valid cognitive style. Ironically, it appears that Witkin is now beginning to emphasize the stylistic aspects of the FDI dimension (Witkin & Goodenough, 1976a, b), but the nature of the FDI measures remains ambiguous.

Two main questions arise for those who would attempt to approach this social issue empirically. First, to what extent is a field dependent score in the FDI measures related to lower school achievement? Second, what is the basis of that relationship?

At present, there are enough data to provide a fairly solid answer to the first question, but the second is only beginning to be answered empirically. This section will first present the evidence about the empirical relation between FDI measures and school achievement among Mexican-American children and then will discuss possible bases for that relation, presenting the little evidence available. Finally, a cognitive style approach to Mexican-American education will be described.

FIELD DEPENDENCE-INDEPENDENCE AND
SCHOOL ACHIEVEMENT

A number of studies have been conducted by researchers at the University of California, Riverside that establish the nature of the relationship between FDI measures and school achievement among Mexican-American and Anglo-American children. The results of those studies are summarized in Table 2.

It should be emphasized that most of the studies are still in preparation and that they were not designed primarily to analyze the basis for the relationship between FDI measures and school achievement. Nevertheless, the data are available, and a post hoc general conclusion about the empirical relation of FDI test scores to school achievement is possible.

The correlation of the FDI tests to measures of school achievement given in Table 2 is presented separately as well as combined for Mexican-American and Anglo-American children. Partial correlations, controlling for grade and sex, are also presented for studies involving more than one grade level. Signs for correlations involving the PRFT and MIFT have been reversed so that positive correlations reflect a positive relationship of field independence to achievement for all measures.

In all of the studies using rod-and-frame type measures, the data were analyzed in two ways: (*a*) using total degrees error from the true upright, and (*b*) using a log transform of the total degrees error from the true upright. The log transform analysis was included because the extremely field dependent scores of

TABLE 2

Correlation of Field Independence with Reading and Math Achievement among Anglo-American and Mexican-American Children

Study	Measure	Grade	Ethnicity[a]	(n)	Reading achievement Raw	Reading achievement Partial[b]	Math achievement Raw	Math achievement Partial[b]
Canavan (Note 7)	Man in Frame	3	A-A and M-A	(214)	- -		.18**	.18**
Sanders and Scholz (Note 8)	Man in Frame[c]	6	A-A and M-A	(161)	.20**		.19**	.19**
		6	A-A and M-A	(126)	.31***		.22**	.22**
			A-A	(63)	.21*		.10	
			M-A	(82)	.38***		.34***	.34***
Kagan and Zahn (1975)	Man in Frame[c]	2-6	A-A and M-A	(132)	.43***	.29**	.49***	.38***
			A-A	(93)	.45***	.26*	.52***	.34**
			M-A	(41)	.42**	.29†	.48***	.42**
Nelson, Kagan, Knight, and Gumbiner (Note 9)	Man in Frame	4-6	A-A and M-A	(168)	.21*	.27***	.15*	.18**
			A-A	(44)	.26	.23	.19	.15
			M-A	(124)	.18	.34***	.11	.24**
Kagan and Romero (Note 5)	PRFT[c]	4-6	A-A and M-A	(60)	.32**	.30**	.30**	.28*
			A-A	(30)	.30*	.20	.37*	.22
			M-A	(30)	.22	.22	.18	.21
Buriel (Note 3)	PRFT	14	A-A	(40)	.26†	.18	.23	.13
			M-A	(40)	.01	.11	.16	.18
	BD	14	A-A	(40)	.42***	.13	.55***	.35**
			M-A	(40)	.32	.11	.39**	.25
	CEFT	14	A-A	(40)	.41**	.21	.47***	.31†
			M-A	(40)	.24	.05	.47***	.40**
Kagan, Zahn, and Gealy (1977)	CEFT	K	A-A and M-A	(48)	.41***		.38***	
		2	A-A and M-A	(24)	.00		.08	

† = $p < .10$.
* = $p < .05$.
** = $p < .01$.
*** = $p < .001$.

[a]AA = Anglo-American
 MA = Mexican-American
[b]Partial with respect to grade and sex.
[c]Correlations based on log transformed scores.

some individuals create skewed distributions and correlations with raw scores give inordinate weight to extreme scores. Kagan and Zahn (1975) reported slightly improved predictions using the log transform scores. Inspection of the differences between correlations based on natural and log transformed scores did not reveal large differences in any study. Table 2 presents the best predictor for each study, but the general size of the correlations and the conclusions based on both natural and log transformed data remain essentially the same.

Inspection of Table 2 indicates that the FDI measures reliably relate to school achievement, with positive correlations ranging from .00 to .55. The partial correlations are somewhat lower than the raw correlations (mean r: reading, raw = .28; reading, partial = .21; math, raw = .30; math, partial = .27). This indicates that the predictive capacity of the FDI measures is inflated somewhat because both school achievement and the FDI measures are developmental variables. The relation of the FDI measures to standardized school achievement measures, although reliable, is not large, accounting on the average for approximately 5 to 10% of the variance in school achievement. Further, the contribution of the FDI measures may be inflated somewhat because studies have not controlled within-grade age differences, and because older children tend to be more field independent and obtain higher achievement scores, age may act to enhance the correlations. In sum, the FDI measures, while reliably related to school achievement, explain only a relatively small proportion of the variance in school achievement.

In general, inspection of Table 2 reveals that the FDI measures predict school achievement about equally well for Mexican-American and Anglo-American children. Furthermore, no clear superiority emerges for any of the four FDI measures as a predictor of school achievement. It is perhaps worth noting that the FDI measures have particularly low correlations for younger children, with the exception of the CEFT correlations with achievement readiness in grade K.

Although the amount of variance in school achievement accounted for by FDI measures is not extremely high, in some schools it may account for the school achievement difference between Anglo-American and Mexican-American. For example, Kagan and Zahn (1975) found that all of the school achievement gap between Anglo-American and Mexican-American children in math and about half of the achievement gap in reading could be accounted for by the greater field dependence of Mexican-American children. Nevertheless, they noted that, contrary to the field dependence theory, the greatest school achievement gap occurred in reading, not math, and indicated that the pattern of findings did not support field dependence and its presumed associated socialization practices as an adequate explanation of the general school achievement gap between Anglo-American and Mexican-American children.

Although field dependence in no way fully explains school achievement among Mexican-American children, it does appear to contribute to that explanation. The question then becomes, "What is the basis for the correlation of the FDI measures to school achievement?"

POSSIBLE BASES FOR SCHOOL ACHIEVEMENT – FIELD
INDEPENDENCE RELATION

Given the positive correlation of field independence and school achievement,
four possible explanations of that relationship merit consideration. First, field
independence may cause school achievement. That is, field independent scores
may result partially from basic cognitive abilities necessary for the acquisition of
reading, math, and other school achievement variables. Supporting this interpretation is the evidence indicating that field independence relates to abilities measured
by standard IQ tests. The ambiguity of what is measured by IQ tests and the un-
established correlation of standard IQ tests with school achievement for Mexican-
American children, however, leave such an interpretation questionable. Second,
school achievement may cause field independence. A field independent score may
be a reflection of analytic abilities that result from successful experiences in school.
In support of this interpretation is evidence that embedded-figures test scores are
higher for Africans who attend school than for those who do not (Wober, 1967).
Third, school achievement tests and field independence tests may share common
variance because they are similar in format and administration. As similar test
experiences, they may tap common motivations. For example, the correlation
of field independence with *n* Ach could indicate that some children score higher
on field independence tests because they try harder in certain types of tests, including achievement tests. Fourth, field dependent children may be discriminated
against by teachers and curriculums unresponsive to their cognitive styles. This last
possibility will be considered in full in the remainder of this section.

Two types of discrimination are possible. First, the curriculum materials
presently used could be structured to favor success by those who score field independent on FDI measures whereas other materials might be better suited to those
who score field dependent. This first possibility emphasizes the content of curriculum materials. The second type of discrimination might be caused by the interpersonal process between teachers and students. It may be that teachers are insensitive to the needs and expectations of field dependent children and therefore fail
to create an optimum atmosphere for learning. These two possible forms of discrimination, content and process, will be discussed in more detail before relevant
data are presented.

Field Dependence-Independence and Educational Content

Curriculum materials and tests, to a greater or lesser extent, may be structured so that analytic abilities are necessary for their successful completion. For
example, in teaching early reading, curriculum materials and teaching styles that
emphasize phonemic instruction may demand that children visually identify discrete vowels and syllables within the framework of a larger, more complex word.
Similar disembedding requirements may also be emphasized in carrying out math

computations to the extent that such operations require the child to conceptually break numbers into their components in order to arrive at new relations.

Cohen (1969) presented evidence indicating that traditional measures of school achievement are heavily slanted in favor of field independent children and unfairly penalize field dependent children. She claims that field independent children process by a parts-specific approach; parts or attributes of a stimulus have meaning in themselves. On the other hand, field dependent children presumably process information in a more global manner such that attributes of a stimulus have significance in reference to some total context. Her analysis of various IQ and achievement tests suggested that the item solution requirements of these tests focus heavily on the use of analytic rule sets. Hence, even though both field dependent and field independent children may be equally familiar with the content of test items, the rule sets built into these items which must be followed in order to demonstrate knowledge may heavily favor a parts-specific rather than a relational problem-solving approach.

Field Dependence-Independence and Educational Process

The role of field dependence-independence as a process variable in education has been discussed in detail by Ramirez and Castañeda (1974) and Witkin, Moore, Goodenough, and Cox (in press). Central to this view is that the field independence of teachers may lead to an interpersonal process unfavorable to field dependent children. Field independent teachers may not only favor curriculum materials that emphasize analytic styles, they may also fail to include sufficient social or human content in their style of presenting the curriculum, thus leaving field dependent children without familiar referents. Teachers may also use reinforcements that are more or less effective with children with different cognitive styles. Field dependent children may be more motivated by social reinforcements (hugs, expressions of endearment) whereas field independent children may be more motivated by impersonal types of rewards (gold stars, candy). Konstadt and Forman (1965) have shown that the use of criticism or lack of encouragement depresses the learning performance of field dependent children more severely than that of field independent children. The way in which teachers structure learning tasks may also provide an advantage to either a field dependent or field independent child. Situations requiring a hypothesis-testing or trial-and-error approach may favor field independent children in contrast to situations requiring a successive approximation approach that may favor field dependent children (Nebelkopf & Dreyer, 1973).

Match-Mismatch

Ramirez (1973) argued that teachers may not be sensitive to the needs of field dependent children, in part because of their own field independence. There has been some support for the notion that a cognitive style match will produce more rapport between teachers and students than a mismatch. DiStefano (1970) observed that teachers and students of similar cognitive styles evaluate each other in more positive terms, while those with dissimilar styles describe each other in more negative terms. Sanders and Scholz (Note 8) presented the initial results of a study which examined the school achievement of Anglo-American and Mexican-American children as a function of student characteristics, teacher characteristics, and the interaction of these variables. Although the study encompassed social motives and attribution of responsibility as well as FDI, as measured by the MIFT, only preliminary results are available.

The subjects of the study were sixth-grade children and their teachers in eight classrooms from three schools in dualistic communities near Riverside, California. The children and teachers were given the MIFT. Children also filled out a classroom climate questionnaire used to assess their perception of the teacher and his or her classroom climate with regard to amount of responsibility, warmth, reward, clarity of organization, standards, morale, and discipline provided.

It was expected that field dependent and Mexican-American children would make relatively more school achievement gains over the school year with field dependent teachers. In contrast, it was expected that field independent and Anglo-American children would make relatively more school achievement gains over the year with field independent teachers. It was further expected that children matched with teachers closer to them in cognitive style would have more positive and fruitful school experiences.

The results were contrary to expectations in a number of ways. As pictured in Figure 5, students with field independent teachers gained more than one grade equivalent during the school year; students with field dependent teachers gained less than one grade over the year. Furthermore, field dependent children were most influenced by teacher field dependence-independence. When placed with a field independent teacher they gained far more than when placed with a field dependent teacher; field independent students were not influenced as much by teacher FDI.

Thus, contrary to expectations the results indicated that a cognitive style mismatch, at least as determined by a rod-and-frame type apparatus, was beneficial for field dependent children. These initial results must be viewed with some caution, for only the most field independent and field dependent teachers were inclu-

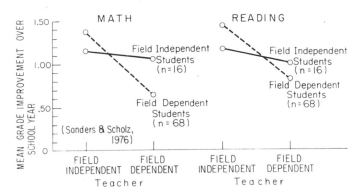

FIGURE 5. Teacher-student field dependence-independence match-mismatch and school achievement gains in reading and math.

ded, reducing the numbers of children studied. Analysis of a larger sample is presently in progress.

With regard to how children viewed the teachers, all children, field independent and dependent, Mexican-American and Anglo-American, tended to rate the field independent teachers higher in all categories except discipline. The differences, however, were significant in only three categories: Field independent teachers were rated as significantly warmer, more (and more fairly) rewarding, and more giving of responsibility.

Several cultural differences merit note. Although both Anglo-Americans and Mexican-Americans rated field independent teachers higher than field dependent teachers, a significant interaction indicated that Mexican-American children rated field dependent teachers higher than did Anglo-American children, and Anglo-American children rated field independent teachers higher than did Mexican-American children. Further, the field dependent teachers were rated higher overall on discipline, and that variable was significantly related to superior math achievement for Mexican-American ($r = .28, p < .05$) but not Anglo-American children ($r = .01, p > .05$). Thus, the preliminary results provided some support for the contention that Mexican-American children might gain more from teachers who place greater emphasis on certain types of interpersonal interaction. For the most part, however, Anglo-American and Mexican-American children were similar in how they perceived field dependent and field independent teachers; both groups tended to rate the field independent teachers more favorably and to gain more from them in school achievement.

The findings that field independent teachers were experienced by all children as significantly warmer and more rewarding than field dependent teachers contradict the common contention that field dependent individuals are superior in their interpersonal skills. The perceived warmth of field independent teachers was most clearly related to gains in math achievement. The correlations between teacher warmth and math gains were significant for Mexican-American ($r = .25, p < .05$), but not Anglo-American children ($r = .23, p > .05$) and for field dependent ($r = .28, p < .05$) but not field independent ($r = .17, p > .05$) children.

Competition and Assertiveness

McClintock (1974, p. 353) noted that Mexican-American children were less competitive than Anglo-American children and suggested that "given the strong likelihood that American primary schools both shape and use competitive motives to promote and reward academic achievement and performance, one can ask whether Mexican-American children may not be ontogenetically out of phase with the educational system of the majority culture."

It could be argued that the field dependence of Mexican-American children is associated with a less competitive orientation that places them at a disadvantage in the competitive school system. Results of the Kagan *et al.* (in press) study, however, indicated that the more prosocial orientation of Mexican-American children does not place them at a disadvantage in school and that their relatively higher field dependence scores on the MIFT is not related to lower competitiveness. Similarly, the lack of relationship between FDI scores and behavior on the assertiveness pull scale (Kagan & Romero, Note 5) argues against the notion that field dependence is associated with a general passivity that produces lower school achievement.

A COGNITIVE-STYLES APPROACH TO MEXICAN–AMERICAN EDUCATION

Ramirez and Castañeda (1974) proposed a cognitive-styles approach for implementing culturally democratic bilingual-bicultural educational programs. In suggesting such an approach, these researchers redefined the meaning of field dependence-independence in a number of important ways. First, they substituted the term *field sensitive* for field dependent in order to convey more clearly the greater sensitivity of field dependent people to the social and physical environment. Second, they argued that field independence and field sensitivity are actually two distinct cognitive styles, each reflecting the predominant norms and value orientation of the person's home and community. Since field independence and field sensitivity are viewed as separate cognitive styles, the potential for growth in both styles is believed to exist within each individual. Third, cognitive styles are presumed to encompass four broad areas of behavior relating to (*a*) the way people perceive, assimilate, and organize information about the environment (learning styles), (*b*) the way people seek support and recognition from their environment (incentive-motivational styles), (*c*) the way people relate to others (human-relational styles), and (*d*) the preferred language for communicating with others (communication styles). Finally, they developed observational methods for assessing cognitive styles in both teachers and students. Hence, for these researchers, field independent and field sensitive cognitive styles are defined by specific sets of observable behaviors rather than by scores on one of the various perceptual orientation tests. The concepts of field independence and field dependence (sensitivity) as defined by Ramirez and Castañeda differ considerably from the way they have been conceptualized and described previously.

Determination of whether a child or teacher is field independent or field sensitive is made on the basis of classroom behavioral observations that do not necessarily relate to traditional FDI measures. For children, the behavioral criteria are as follows: (*a*) *relationship to peers* (field sensitive children like to work with others to achieve a common goal, in contrast to field independent children who prefer to work alone); (*b*) *personal relationship to teacher* (field sensitive children more openly express positive feelings for their teachers and are interested in their teachers' personal experiences, whereas field independent children seek less physical contact with teachers and limit their interactions to tasks at hand); (*c*) *instructional relationship to teachers* (field independent children like to try new tasks without their teachers' help and seek nonsocial rewards, whereas field sensitive children model teacher behavior and seek rewards that strengthen relationships with their teachers); (*d*) *characteristics of curriculum that facilitate learning* (field independent children prefer curriculums that stress details about facts and tasks that involve working from the specific to the whole, in contrast to field sensitive children who perform best when concepts are presented in a humanized format, are related to their personal interests and experiences, and require working from the whole to specifics). Two separate student behavioral rating forms, one focusing on field independent behaviors and the other on field sensitive behaviors, are used to identify the child's preferred cognitive style and then again periodically throughout the school year to measure the student's growth in each cognitive style.

Determination of a teacher's cognitive style is made on the basis of the following behavioral criteria related to teaching strategies: (*a*) *personal behaviors* (field sensitive teachers express more approval and warmth and use personalized rewards, in contrast to field independent teachers who maintain a more formal relationship to students and focus heavily on instructional objectives); (*b*) *instructional behaviors* (field sensitive teachers encourage more learning by modeling, provide more guidance, and encourage group achievement by students, whereas field independent teachers encourage more trial and error learning, adopt a consultant role with students, and encourage individual student achievement); (*c*) *curriculum-related behaviors* (field sensitive teachers humanize and personalize curriculums, and emphasize global aspects of concepts, in contrast to field independent teachers who focus on facts and principles and rely more on impersonal curriculums such as graphs and formulas). A teacher's preferred instructional mode or cognitive style is assessed through the use of separate field independence and field sensitivity teacher observation scales. These scales are also used to evaluate teacher progress in using both field independent and field sensitive teaching strategies.

Ramirez and Castañeda (1974) argued that a field independent cognitive style is reflected in the teaching strategies and curriculums of most classroom environments, thus making them inappropriate for Mexican-American children who are generally field sensitive in their cognitive style. Ramirez and Castañeda referred to such classroom environments as culturally undemocratic since the values and norms of Mexican-American children, and hence their cognitive styles, are not represented in the educational process. The exclusion of a field sensitive cognitive style means that Mexican-American children cannot use their preferred learning style, incentive-motivational style, human-relational style, and communication style for functioning in the classroom, and thus their educational opportunities and chances for success in comparison to field independent children are severely restricted.

To correct this disadvantageous situation for Mexican-Americans and other children who are field sensitive in their cognitive styles, Ramirez and Castañeda (1974) proposed the implementation of culturally democratic learning environments to replace traditional classroom environments. This involves the rearrangement of all phases of the classroom environment to reflect both field sensitive and field independent styles. Field sensitivity is treated as a valid cognitive style with qualities worth developing and using to teach children the skills necessary for scholastic success.

The implementation of culturally democratic learning environments follows a prescribed number of steps. First, teachers' preferred cognitive styles are determined using the teacher observational rating scales. Teachers then receive training designed to develop fully their preferred teaching styles. They are trained in the use of the opposite style so that eventually they can work effectively with all children by adapting their teaching strategies to fit each child's learning style, whether field independent or field sensitive. Curriculum materials are developed for field sensitive children that emphasize the relationship of educational concepts to the experiences and interests of students and include human and social content. Most commercial curriculums are appropriate for field independent children. Heritage units are developed and used to reinforce the cultural identity of students, both Mexican-American and Anglo-American, and to introduce children to different cultural forms while maintaining an identity with their own group. Spanish and English are given equal status in the classroom as mediums for communication and instruction. Early in the school year, children's preferred cognitive styles are determined using the children's observational scales, and they are then placed in classrooms with other children of the same cognitive style. These groups of field independent or field sensitive children receive instruction from teachers using teaching strategies and curriculum materials appropriate to them. After children have mastered educational concepts and skills using their preferred style, they are gradually introduced to using the unfamiliar cognitive style. The proposed outcome of this educational program is to develop both the field independent and field sensitive styles in children so that they can function "bicognitively," that is, in one or the other cognitive style as the situation demands. Paralleling children's bicognitive development is the development of a bicultural identity fostered by the inclusion of both Mexican-American and Anglo-American heritages, as well as both Spanish and English, as integral parts of the educational process. The program is designed, in part, to allow children the opportunity to identify with Mexican-American as well as mainstream Anglo-American cultural values.

It is apparent that the implementation of culturally democratic learning environments, as proposed by Ramirez and Castañeda (1974), goes far beyond the limits of what is traditionally considered the area of cognitive styles. It entails fundamental changes in the sociocultural orientation of the educational process to make it more representative and thus responsive to the entire community of people served by the school.

Ongoing research in a predominantly Mexican-American elementary school, using the educational techniques and philosophy described by Ramirez and Castañeda, has produced favorable results. They report that the academic performance of children in their experimental program is better than that of children in control classrooms (Ramirez & Castañeda, 1974). Recent evidence (Ramirez, personal communication) also indicates positive long-term effects from participation in this educational program. Reading and math grade-equivalent scores for a small group of children participating in this program between the first and third grades were higher at each grade level compared to those for a control group of children matched on socioeconomic status and proportions of English or Spanish monolingual and bilingual students. At the end of grade one, the average grade-equivalent scores for the experimental group for total reading and total math were 1.8 and 2.0, respectively, and 1.1 and 1.5 for the control group. At the end of grade three, the average grade-equivalent scores for the experimental group for total reading, math problem solving, and total math were 3.2, 3.8, and 3.6, respectively, and, 3.0, 3.0, and 3.2 for the control group. The higher overall performance of the experimental group is especially impressive because some children were referred to the experimental group by school administrators because of their underachievement in traditional classrooms.

Conclusion

A review of the theoretical and empirical literature relating the FDI construct to Mexican-American culture and education has some implications for the understanding of cultural differences, cognitive styles, and school achievement. It appears that Mexican-American children rather reliably differ from Anglo-American children on rod-and-frame type FDI measures, but contrary to the literature, a general cultural difference in cognitive style cannot be supported on the basis of the empirical studies conducted to date. Not only do Mexican-American children not differ significantly from Anglo-American on the CEFT, but, more important, those two presumed measures (rod-and-frame and CEFT) of field dependence fail to correlate to a sufficient degree to meet the basic convergent validity requirements of a psychological construct. Investigations using the FDI measures to study the cognitive styles of Mexican and Mexican-American groups have revealed sufficient problems both with the FDI construct and its measures to render their contribution to our understanding of culture questionable. Not only do the FDI measures fail to meet the requirements of a valid psychological construct, they fail to correlate with socialization practices and social behaviors in ways indicated by the FDI theory. The FDI measures are sufficiently ambiguous that they cannot clarify the nature of cultural differences in cognitive styles. The cross-cultural study of cognitive styles would benefit from new measures that do not confound ability and preference, that is, pure cognitive-style measures.

In recent years, there has been increased interest in the use of cognitive-style tests, including FDI measures, to predict childrens' achievement-related abilities (White, Day, Freeman, Hartman, & Messenger, 1973). The use of FDI measures for that purpose rests to some extent on the assumption that there is one underlying dimension called *field dependence-independence*, which has been validated as a psychological construct. The evidence, at least with regard to studies that have included Mexican-American children, does not support that assumption. Furthermore, although the FDI measures reliably correlate with school achievement, the proportion of variance in school achievement explained by the FDI measures is small and the basis of the relationship between the FDI measures and school achievement remains unexplained.

Since the most common practice is to use only a single test to measure level of field dependence, educators and researchers should be aware that the results they obtain may be more functions of the particular tests they use than reflection of actual differences in the trait they presume to be measuring. Failure to realize the limitations of these tests in educational settings can lead to an inaccurate assessment of children's academic potential and, in turn, to unrealistic teacher expectations. Children misclassified by FDI tests as having high academic potential who subsequently perform below expectation may be punished by their teachers for supposedly not trying hard enough. On the other hand, students misclassified as low achievers may fail to receive sufficient attention from their teachers to stimulate an active interest in school, thus, fulfilling teachers' expectations for them. In either case, the ultimate result may manifest itself in both a lessening of students' motivation to achieve and a loss in self-image.

In view of the limits of the FDI measures and construct, the design of educational institutions more responsive to the needs of Mexican-American and other students might well proceed more efficiently if the needs of those students were directly assessed and addressed rather than inferred from presumed differences in field dependence as traditionally defined.

REFERENCE NOTES

1. Cummins, J.P. Bilingual cognition: A reply to Neufeld. Paper presented to the Ontario Institute for Studies in Education, 1974.
2. Hoffman, C., & Kagan, S. Untitled Manuscript, in preparation.
3. Buriel, R. Relationship of three field dependence measures to reading and math achievement of Anglo American and Mexican American children. Paper presented at the Western Psychological Association Meetings, Los Angeles, April, 1976.
4. Gerard, H.B. *Factors contributing to adjustment and achievement in racially desegregated public schools*. Progress Report Grant No. PHS HO-02863, Department of Psychology, University of California, Los Angeles, 1969.
5. Kagan, S., & Romero, C. Assertiveness, field dependence and school achievement of Mexican-American and Anglo-American children. In preparation.
6. Kagan, S., & Knight, G. Untitled manuscript, University of California, Riverside. In preparation.
7. Canavan, D. Field dependence in children as a function of grade, sex, and ethnic group membership. Paper read at the American Psychological Association Meeting, Washington, D.C., 1969.
8. Sanders, M., & Scholz, J.P. Field Independence match-mismatch and school achievement gains of Anglo-American and Mexican-American children. Paper presented at the Western Psychological Association Meetings, Los Angeles, April, 1976.
9. Nelson, W., Gumbiner, J., Knight, G., & Kagan, S. Untitled manuscript. University of California, Riverside. In preparation.

REFERENCES

Anderson, J.G., & Johnson, W.M. *Sociocultural determinants of achievement among Mexican-American students*. New Mexico: Educational Resources Information Center, New Mexico State University, 1968.

Anderson, J.G., & Johnson, W.H. Stability and change among three generations of Mexican-Americans: Factors affecting achievement. *American Educational Research Journal*, 1971, *8*, 285-309.

Arbuthnot, J. Cautionary note on measurement of field independence. *Perceptual and Motor Skills*, 1972, *35*, 479-488.

Berry, J.W. Ecological and cultural factors in spatial perceptual development. *Canadian Journal of Behavioral Science*, 1971, *3*, 324-336.

Buriel, R. Cognitive styles among three generations of Mexican-American children. *Journal of Cross-Cultural Psychology*, 1975, *6*, 417-429.

Cabe, P.A. The relation between the rod-and-frame test and Witkin's embedded figures test. *Educational and Psychological Measurement*, 1968, *28*, 1243-1245.

Caldwell, F.F., & Mowry, M.D. The essay versus the objective examination as measures of achievement of bilingual children. *Journal of Educational Psychology*, 1933, *24*, 696-702.

Caldwell, F.F., & Mowry, M.D. Teachers' grades as criteria of achievement of bilingual children. *Journal of Applied Psychology*, 1934, *18*, 288-292.

Caldwell, F.F., & Mowry, M.D. Sex differences in school achievement among Spanish-American and Anglo-American children. *Journal of Educational Sociology*, 1935, *8*, 168-173.

Campbell, D.T., & Fiske, D.W. Convergent and discriminant validation by the multitrait-multimethod matrix. *Psychological Bulletin*, 1959, *56*, 81-105.

Carter, T.P. Negative self-concept of Mexican American students. *School and Society*, 1968, *96*, 217-219.

Cohen, R.A. Conceptual styles, culture conflict, and nonverbal tests of intelligence. *American Anthropologist*, 1969, *71*, 828-856.

Cole, M., & Bruner, J.S. Cultural differences and inferences about psychological processes. *American Psychologist*, 1971, *26*, 867-876.

Coleman, J.S., Campbell, E.Q., Hobson, C.J., McPortland, J., Mood, A.M., Weinfeld, F.D., & York, R.L. *Equality of Educational Opportunity*. Washington, D.C.: U.S. Department of Health, Education and Welfare, Office of Education, U.S. Government Printing Office, 1966.

Crandall, V.J., & Sinkeldam, C. Children's dependent and achievement behaviors in social situations and their perceptual field dependence. *Journal of Personality*, 1964, *32*, 1-22.

Daily News: Coachella Valley Unified School District Eyes Possible Action Against Teachers. Thermal, California, April 9, 1976.

DeBlassie, R.R., & Healy, G.W. *Self-concept: A comparison of Spanish-American, Negro, and Anglo adolescents across ethnic, sex, and socioeconomic variables*. Las Cruces, N. Mex.: ERIC, 1970, ED. 037287.

Demos, G.A. Attitudes or Mexican and Anglo American groups toward education. *Journal of Social Psychology*, 1960, *57*, 249-256.

Devereux, E.C., Bronfenbrenner, V., & Suci, G.N. Patterns of parent behavior in the United States of America and the Federal Republic of Germany: A cross-national comparison. *International Social Science Journal*, 1962, *14*, 488-506.

DiStefano, J.J. *Interpersonal perceptions of field independent and dependent teachers and students*. Working Paper Series No. 23, London, Ontario: University of Western Ontario, 1970.

Dubois, T.E., & Cohen, W. Relationship between measures of psychological differentiation and intellectual ability. *Perceptual and Motor Skills*, 1970, *31*, 411-416.

Dyk, R.B. An exploratory study of mother-child interaction in infancy as related to the development of differentiation. *Journal of the American Academy of Child Psychiatry*, 1969, *8*, 657-691.

Dyk, R.B., & Witkin, H.A. Family experiences related to the development of differentiation in children. *Child Development*, 1965, *30*, 21-55.

Fine, B.J., & Danforth, A.V. Field-dependence, extroversion and perception of the vertical: Empirical and theoretical perspectives of the rod-and-frame test. *Perceptual and Motor Skills*, 1975, *40*, 683-693.

Goldman, R.D., & Hartig, L.K. The WISC may not be a valid predictor of school performance for primary-grade minority children. *American Journal of Mental Deficiency*, 1976, *80*, 583-587.

Gordon, C.W., Schwartz, R.W., & Nasatir, D. *Educational achievement and aspirations of Mexican-American youth in a metropolitan context.* Report No. 36, Center for the Study of Evaluation, Graduate School of Education, University of California, Los Angeles, 1968.

Gottschaldt, K. Gestalt factors and repetition. In W.D. Ellis (Ed.), *A source book of Gestalt psychology*. London: Routledge and Kegan Paul, 1950.

Gruen, A. The relation of dancing experience and personality to perception. *Psychological Monographs: General and Applied*, 1955, *69*, 1-16.

Hoffman, C., & Kagan, S. Field dependence and facial recognition. *Perceptual and Motor Skills*, 1977, *44*, 119-124.

Holtzman, H.W., Diaz-Guerrero, R., & Swartz, S.D. *Personality development in two cultures.* Austin: University of Texas Press, 1975.

Hoppe, C.M., Kagan, S.M., & Zahn, G.L. Conflict resolution among field independent and field dependent Anglo-American and Mexican-American children and their mothers. *Developmental Psychology*, in press.

Irving, D. The field dependence hypothesis in cross-cultural perspective (Doctoral dissertation, Rice University, 1970). *Dissertation Abstracts International*, 1970, *31*(6), 3691-B. (University Microfilms No. 70-23, 529).

Jessor, R., Graves, T.D., Hanson, R.C., & Jessor, S.L. *Society, personality, and deviant behavior: A study of a tri-ethnic community.* New York: Holt, Rinehart, and Winston, 1968.

Johnson, P.B., Gerard, H.B., & Miller, N. Teacher influences in the desegregated classroom. Factors mediating the school desegregation experience. In H.B. Gerard and N. Miller (Eds.), *School Desegregation*. New York: Plenum, 1975.

Johnson, H.S. Motivation and the Mexican-American. In H.S. Johnson and W.J. Hernandez, (Eds.), *Educating the Mexican American*, Valley Forge, Penn.: Judson Press, 1970.

Juarez, R.Z. *Educational status orientations of Mexican-American and Anglo-American youth in selected low-income counties of Texas.* Washington, D.C.: United States Department of Agriculture, 1968.

Kagan, S. Field dependence and conformity in rural Mexican and urban Anglo American children. *Child Development*, 1974, *45*, 765-771.

Kagan, S. Social motives and behaviors of Mexican-American and Anglo-American children. In J.L. Martinez (Ed.), *Chicano Psychology*, New York: Academic Press, 1977, 45-86.

Kagan, S., & Romero, C. Non-adaptive assertiveness of Anglo-American and Mexican-American children of two ages. *Interamerican Journal of Psychology*. In press.

Kagan, S., & Zahn, G.L. Field dependence and the school acheivement gap between Anglo-American and Mexican-American children. *Journal of Educational Psychology*, 1975, *67*, 643-650.

Kagan, S., Zahn, G.L., & Gealy, J. Competition and school achievement among Anglo- American and Mexican-American children. *Journal of Educational Psychology*, 1977, *69*(4), 432-441.

Killian, L.R. WISC, Illinois test of psycholinguistic abilities, and Bender visual-motor Gestalt test performance of Spanish-American kindergarten and first-grade school children. *Journal of Consulting and Clinical Psychology*, 1971, *37*, 38-43.

Knudsen, K.H.M., & Kagan, S. Visual perspective role-taking and field-independence among Anglo-American and Mexican-American children of two ages. *Journal of Genetic Psychology*, 1977. In press.

Konstadt, N., & Forman, E. Field dependence and external directedness. *Journal of Personality and Social Psychology*, 1965, *1*, 490-493.

Lambert, W.E., & Anisfeld, E. A note in the relationship of bilingualism and intelligence. *Canadian Journal of Behavioral Sciences*, 1969, *1*(2).

Lester, G. The rod-and-frame test: Some comments on methodolgoy. *Perceptual and Motor Skills*, 1968, *26*, 1307-1314.

McClintock, C.G. Development of social motives in Anglo-American and Mexican-American children. *Journal of Personality and Social Psychology*, 1974, *29*, 348-354.

Mebane, D., & Johnson, D.L. A comparison of the performance of Mexican boys and girls on Witkin's cognitive tasks. *Interamerican Journal of Psychology*, 1970, *4*, 227-239.

Mercer, J.R. *Labeling the mentally retarded*. Berkeley: University of California Press, 1973.

Nebelkopf, E.B., & Dreyer, A.S. Continuous-discontinuous concept attainment as a function of individual differences in cognitive style. *Perceptual and Motor Skills*, 1973, *36*, 655-662.

Okada, T. *Dynamics of achievement: A study of differential growth of achievement over time*. Technical Note No. 53, National Center for Educational Statistics, Office of Education, U.S. Dept. of Health, Education, and Welfare, Washington, D.C.: U.S. Government Printing Office, 1968.

Oltman, P.K. A portable rod-and-frame apparatus. *Perceptual and Motor Skills*, 1968, *26*, 503-506.

Padilla, A.M., & Ruiz, R.A. *Latino mental health: A review of literature*. National Institute of Mental Health, Washington, D.C.: U.S. Government Printing Office, 1973.

Palomares, U.H., & Johnson, L.C. Evaluation of Mexican-American pupils for EMR classes. *California Education*, 1966, *3*, 27-29.

Price-Williams, D.R. *Explorations in cross-cultural psychology*. San Francisco: Chandler & Sharp Publishers, Inc., 1975.

Ramirez, M. Cognitive styles and cultural democracy in education. *Social Science Quarterly*, 1973, *53*, 895-904.

Ramirez, M., & Castañeda, A. *Cultural democracy, bicognitive development, and education*. New York: Academic Press, 1974.

Ramirez, M., Castañeda, A., & Herold, P.L. The relationship of acculturation to cognitive style among Mexican Americans. *Journal of Cross-Cultural Psychology*, 1974, *5*, 425-433.

Ramirez, M., & Price-Williams, D. Cognitive styles in children: Two Mexican communities. *Interamerican Journal of Psychology*, 1974, *8*, 93-100. (a)

Ramirez, M., & Price-Williams, D. Cognitive styles of children of three ethnic groups in the United States. *Journal of Cross-Cultural Psychology*, 1974, *5*, 212-219. (b)

Ramirez, M., & Price-Williams, D.R. Achievement motivation in children of three ethnic groups in the United States. *Journal of Cross-Cultural Psychology*, 1976, *7*, 49-60.

Ramirez, M., Taylor, C., & Peterson, B. Mexican American cultural membership and adjustment to school. *Developmental Psychology*, 1971, *4*, 141-148.

Rieber, M., & Womack, M. The intelligence of pre-school children as related to ethnic and demographic variables. *Exceptional Children*, 1968, *34*, 609-614.

Sanders, M., Scholz, J.P., & Kagan, S. Three social motives and field-independence-dependence in Anglo American and Mexican American children. *Journal of Cross-Cultural Psychology*, 1976, *7*(4), 451-462.

Sattler, J.M. *Assessment of children's intelligence*. Philadelphia: W.B. Saunders Company, 1974.

Schwartz, A.J. *Comparative values and achievement of Mexican-American and Anglo pupils.* Los Angeles, Calif.: Center for the Study of Evaluation, UCLA Graduate School of Education, 1969.

Serpell, R. *Culture's influence on behaviour*. London: Methuen and Co. Ltd., 1976.

Sheldon, P. Mexican-Americans in urban public schools – An exploration of the drop-out problem. *California Journal of Educational Research*, 1961, *12*, 21-26.

Singer, H., Gerard, H.B., & Redfearn, D. Desegregation and achievement of Anglo, Black and Mexican-American pupils. In H.B. Gerard and N. Miller (Eds.), *School desegregation*. New York: Plenum, 1975.

United States Bureau of the Census. *Census of Population: 1970, Vol. I.* Characteristics of the population - parts 4, 6, 7, 33 and 45. Washington, D.C.: U.S. Government Printing Office, 1973.

United States Commission on Civil Rights: Hearings held in San Antonio, Texas, December 9-14, 1968. Washington, D.C.: U.S. Government Printing Office, 1968.

United States Commission on Civil Rights. *The unfinished / education (Report II: Mexican-American education study)*. Washington, D.C.: U.S. Government Printing Office, 1971.

United States Commission on Civil Rights. *Teachers and students (Report V: Mexican American education study: Differences in teacher interaction with Mexican American and Anglo American students)*. Washington, D.C.: U.S. Government Printing Office, 1973.

Vernon, P.E. Ability factors and environmental influences. *American Psychologist*, 1965, *20*, 723-733.

Vernon, P.E. The distinctiveness of field independence. *Journal of Personality*, 1972, *40*, 366-391.

Wachtel, P.L. Field independence and psychological differentiation: Re-examination. *Perceptual and Motor Skills*, 1972, *35*, 179-189.

Weisz, J.R., P., & O'Neil, P.C. Field dependence-independence on the children's embedded figures test: Cognitive style or cognitive level? *Developmental Psychology*, 1975, *11*, 539-540.

Wertheimer, M. Experimentelle Studien uber das Sehen von Bewegung. *Zeitschrift Psychologie*, 61, *161-265*.

White, S.H., Day, M.C., Freeman, P.K., Hartman, S.A., & Messenger, K.P. *Federal programs for young children: Review and recommendations (Vol. I. Goals and standards of public programs for children)*. Publication No. (OS) 74-101, Washington, D.C.. U.S. Department of Health, Education, and Welfare, U.S. Government Printing Office, 1973.

Witkin, H.A. A cognitive style approach to cross-cultural research. *International Journal of Psychology*, 2, 233-250. 1967.

Witkin, H.A. Social influences in the development of cognitive style. In D.A. Goslin (Ed.), *Handbook of socialization theory and research*. New York: Rand, McNally, 1969, 687-706.

Witkin, H.A., & Berry, J.W. Psychological differentiation in cross-cultural perspective. *Journal of Cross-Cultural Psychology*, 1975, *6*, 4-87.

Witkin, H.A., Cox, P.W., Friedman, F., Hrishikesan, A.G., & Siegal, K.N. *Supplement No. 1, Field dependence-independence and psychological differentiation: Bibliography with index* (ETS RB 74-42). Princeton, NJ: Educational Testing Service, 1974.

Witkin, H.A., Cox, P.W., & Friedman, F. *Supplement No. 2, Field dependence-independence and psychological differentiation: Bibliography with index*. Princeton, NJ: Educational Testing Service, 1976.

Witkin, H.A., Dyk, R.B., Faterson, D.R., Goodenough, D.R., & Karp, S.A. *Psychological differentiation*. New York: Wiley, 1962.

Witkin, H.A., & Goodenough, D.R. *Field dependence and interpersonal behavior* (ETS RB 76-12). Princeton, NJ: Educational Testing Service, 1976. (a)

Witkin, H.A., & Goodenough, D.R. *Field dependence revisited.* Research Bulletin, *Princeton,* NJ: Educational Testing Service, 1976. (b)

Witkin, H.A., Lewis, H.B., Hertzman, M., Machover, K., Meissner, & Wapner, S. *Personality through perception.* New York: Harper & Brothers Publishers, 1954.

Witkin, H.A., Moore, C.A., Goodenough, D.R., & Cox, P.W. Field-dependent and field-independent cognitive styles and their educational implications. *Review of Educational Research,* in press.

Witkin, H.A., Oltman, P.K., Cox, P.W., Ehrlichmann, E., Hamm, R.M., & Ringler, R.W. *Field dependence-independence and psychological differentiations: A bibliography through 1972 with index* (ETS RB 73-62). Princeton, NJ: Educational Testing Service, 1973.

Witkin, H.A., Oltman, P.K., Raskin, E., & Karp, S.A. *Manual for embedded figures test, children's embedded figures tests, and group embedded figures test.* Palo Alto, Calif.: Consulting Psychologists Press, Inc. 1971.

Witkin, H.A., Price-Williams, D., Bertini, M., Christiansen, B., Oltman, P.K., Ramirez, M., & Van Meel, J. Social conformity and psychological differentiation. *International Journal of Psychology,* 1974, *9,* 11-29.

Zigler, E. A measure in search of a theory? *Contemporary Psychology,* 1963, *8,* 133-135.(a)

Zigler, E. Zigler stands firm. *Contemporary Psychology,* 1963, *8,* 459-461. (b)

CHAPTER 19

PSYCHOLOGY OF THE CHICANA

MARIA NIETO SENOUR

San Diego State University

Psychological literature relating directly to the Chicana (Mexican-American woman) is extremely limited. This undoubtedly reflects the lack of interest, on the part of social scientists, in both Mexican-Americans and women until recent years. The scant data on Chicanas that do exist are generally to be found within studies focusing on other issues. Moreover, the validity of these data is not beyond question. However, the purpose of this chapter is not to present a definitive Chicana psychology, but rather to initiate an exploration of the topic by reviewing the literature on the psychology of women, Mexican and Mexican-American cultures and experience, a limited amount of research on Chicanos, and some recent studies on the relationship between sex roles and ethnicity.

Traditional Mexican-American Culture

The Mexican family is purportedly founded on the supremacy of the father and the corresponding total self-sacrifice of the mother (Diaz-Guerrero, 1955). Literature on the Mexican family indicates that the wife must devote herself to the satisfaction of everyone else's needs by the complete denial of her own. As a child, she is groomed for her destiny at home and school by encouragement to acquire the appropriate feminine skills. Generally, any attempt to achieve academically or professionally is seen as unfeminine and is discouraged.

If this is indeed an accurate reflection of the Mexican woman's role in the family, there must also be rewards for the woman in this system, such as the devotion of her children. However, in terms of her mental health, there may be a price as well. Diaz-Guerrero (1975) estimated that 44% of the female population of

Mexico City over 18 years of age is "neurotic." This neurosis is manifested mostly in self-belittlement and depression.

Three studies by Mexican psychoanalysts indicate the existence of conflict between Mexican males and females (Aramoni, 1961; Gonzalez, 1961; Ramirez, 1959). Men are shown to assert their dominance by wielding economic power over their women or by using even cruder means such as physical abuse. They are described as demonstrating little tenderness or affection for their wives. Women are described as feeling exploited, as experiencing pressure to respond lovingly to men who treat them like personal property. These perceptions of their status leave Mexican women feeling vengeful so that they deliberately undermine the father's relationship with his children. They are said to frequently raise boys who doubt their masculinity and are compulsively *machos* while attempting to mask feelings of dependence on the mother and fears of impotence. Their daughters are raised to be distrustful of all men and consequently unable to love men genuinely. While this Freudian image of punishing men and passively resistant women can by no means be considered the norm in Mexican families, Aramoni, Gonzalez, and Ramirez report the existence of such traits in numerous individuals seeking therapy.

In a continent-wide study of sex roles, San Martin (1975) found notions of the inferiority of women and superiority of men alive and well throughout Latin America. Women are expected to be gentle, mild, sentimental, emotional, intuitive, impulsive, fragile, submissive, docile, dependent, and timid. Men are hard, rough, cold, intellectual, rational, farsighted, profound, strong, authoritarian, independent, and brave.

The literature indicates that within the Mexican-American family are also found clearly defined sex roles to govern behavior. The older have authority over the younger, and the men have authority over the women (Madsen, 1969). Women, in traditional Mexican-American culture, are said to devote themselves totally to their families, allowing their entire lives to revolve around husband and children. They are the primary source of nurturance and maintain a close relationship with their children throughout life. Traditional Chicanas have few contacts with individuals outside the family, so their affectional ties with those in the family, especially with other females, are very strong (Murillo, 1971). In comparison with people of other cultures in the United States, Chicanos are said to dominate their wives, overprotect their daughters, and expect passive compliance in return (Padilla & Ruiz, 1973). Derbyshire (1968) suggested that this male dominance exists only because females choose to play a subordinate role. He finds Chicanas attempting to bolster a *machismo* at home that is threatened by the Chicano's lack of status in the dominant culture.

Other writers have attacked these portrayals of Chicano males and females as stereotyped. Inappropriate research tools, methodologies, and examiner bias are accused of perpetuating destructive myths about the Chicano family which need to be disproved by adequate research (Cotera, 1976). Nevertheless, Jaco (1957) found that Spanish-surnamed women in Texas exhibit higher incidences of manic-depressive, involutional, and schizophrenic psychoses than men. In Fabrega, Rubel, and Wallace's (1967) study of Mexican-American outpatients, women reported a greater number of psychiatric symptoms than men.

The authors attributed their finding to notions of masculinity and femininity in Mexican-American culture. In a recent study on Chicano acculturation, Go (Note 1) found females between the ages of 13 and 18 reporting significantly higher anxiety levels than men on the manifest anxiety scale.

Psychology of Women of the Dominant Culture

The Chicana is a product of two cultures; traditional Mexican-American culture, which she experiences at home, although frequently in diluted forms, and dominant American culture, which she experiences almost everywhere else, especially at school.

Therefore, a look at recent research in the psychology of American women will give information on the other half of the Chicana's feminine experience.

Since most of these data were gathered on American, white, middle class undergraduates, their applicability to Mexican-American women must be viewed with caution. It is also appropriate to remember that while these studies emphasize the differences between men and women, there are many more similarities than differences between the sexes and the differences that do exist are not absolute; there is a distribution of all traits within both sexes. Finally, it should be noted that the dominant culture is not without its contradictions regarding sex roles and contains more than one model of behavior.

Keeping these things in mind, it can nevertheless be said that real psychological differences exist between men and women of the dominant culture. These differences are reflected in lifestyles, ego organization, personality qualities, motives, and goals. The sources of these differences include (*a*) infant differences in gross activity level and sensitivity to stimuli, (*b*) parental responses that are sex linked, (*c*) social pressures to identify with appropriate models of the same sex, (*d*) the physiology of the mature reproductive system, and (*e*) the internalized concepts of masculinity and femininity by which individuals evaluate themselves (Bardwick, 1971).

The main personality characteristics that Bardwick (1971) says separate women from men are passivity, dependence, and lack of self-esteem. Some of these differences are apparent at birth. Female infants are less active and more introverted, more sensitive to stimuli, and more responsive to greater numbers of stimuli than male infants. At 13 months, females show a greater preference for high complexity stimuli and demonstrate earlier language development and greater field dependence than males.

Middle class girls of the majority culture, unlike traditionally raised Mexican-American girls, are encouraged to achieve, especially in academic and affiliative areas. They frequently develop motives to achieve and self-concepts rooted in successful achievement while remaining dependent on the reactions of others and pursuing popularity. After puberty, the stress on social success decreases the need for academic success as a means of acquiring self-esteem. This trend continues until academic-vocational success is perceived as a threat to success as a woman. Because the dominant culture applies masculine criteria to the evaluation of the performance of females as well as of males, the greatest esteem is given to women who distinguish themselves professionally. Yet such women also run the risk of being perceived failures as women. Hence, the development of fear of success in career-oriented women and a selection of such nurturing fields as nursing, teaching, and counseling for those who pursue a career. It seems, then, that the Chicana receives many more ambivalent messages regarding sex-role expectations from the dominant culture than she does from traditional Mexican-American culture. Rewards for conformity with cultural expectations are also more uncertain from the dominant culture.

Biological Influences

Female biology is one aspect of the Chicana's life experience identical to that of her Anglo counterpart. Strong evidence exists that regular, predictable changes in the personalities of sexually mature women correlate with their menstrual cycles. The degree to which a woman is affected varies with individuals, but low levels of negative affect and high self-esteem are commonly reported during ovulation while anxiety, depression, and low self-esteem are reported during the low estrogen, low progesterone premenstrual and menstrual days (Coppen & Kessal, 1963; Frank, 1931; Ivey & Bardwick, 1968; Shainess, 1961; Sutherland & Stewart, 1965). Studies indicate that during pregnancy, when estrogen and progesterone levels are high, psychologically healthy women experience increased integration of the ego (Hamblen, 1962). Research on the effects of oral contraceptives finds that hormone content of different products produces corresponding mood changes (Paige, Note 2). Finally, menopause, with its decline of estrogen levels, produces a variety of negative symptoms in 50 to 85% of women (Bardwick, 1971).

Some cautions in the interpretation of these data seem in order. Findings indicate that only some women are seriously affected by changing hormone levels. There is also a lack of evidence that they have a detrimental effect on a woman's performance of her daily responsibilities. In addition, despite documentation of emotional changes accompanying menstrual cycles, women have not generally been shown to be more emotionally unstable than men (Sherman, 1971). There is a final point to consider. The way women respond to the experience of menstruation is influenced by cultural conditioning. Studies need to be conducted using Chicanas as subjects in order to see how the cultures in which Chicanas are reared affect their responses to hormone shifts.

Acculturation

• The Chicana is influenced by two cultures and appears to be in transition between the two. Some social scientists see Mexican-Americans as an insulated group which continues Mexican customs despite residence of several generations in the United States (Kiev, 1972). Others say that Mexican-American cultural isolation is on the wane because of a decline in educational segregation, exposure to military service, changes in housing patterns, employment, and political movements. As a result, these social scientists predict that traditional sex roles are changing and will continue to change (Padilla & Ruiz, 1973).

Murillo (1971) believes in the existence of a good deal of conflict among Chicanos regarding the Chicana's role. He maintains that fewer women are accepting the traditional role. Many are struggling for greater equality and a greater range of personal and vocational choice within both the dominant society and Mexican-American culture.

The effect of acculturation on Chicanas is not fully understood. Some data suggest that individuals who either retain their cultural values or wholly ascribe to the value system of the majority culture manifest less psychopathology than those in the midst of assimilation (Wallace & Fabrega, 1968; Fabrega, Swartz, & Wallace, 1968a, b).

Demographic data on the Chicana indicate that she is not isolated from the institutions of the dominant culture. There are currently over 3 million Chicanas in America. Of these, 85% live in the Southwest; the remainder reside throughout the country; and 85% are urban dwellers. Their median age is 19.6 years, 10 years younger than the median age of all American women (Cotera, 1976). Census data (U.S. Bureau of the Census, 1973) for 1970 reveal that 87.2% of Spanish-surnamed women in the five Southwestern states between the ages of 14 and 17 are enrolled in school, and 21.9% of Chicanas over the age of 16 are high school graduates (as opposed to 31.5% of Chicanos). They have attained a median educational level of 9.1 years, which is 3 years below that of the entire female population in the United States but only .3 years behind the 9.4 year level of Mexican-American males. Of Chicanas over the age of 16, 36.7% are currently employed, including 29% of married Chicanas. In contrast, 39% of all married women in the United States work. Chicanas earn a mean income of $2515; only 1% earn $10,000 a year or more (77.2% of Chicanos are employed, and their mean income is $5424; 10% earn $10,000 a year or more).

The effects of these contacts of Mexican-American women with the dominant society are not altogether clear. Kiev (1972) stated that women, old people, and adolescents experience particular difficulty during such transitions because new economic demands and employment opportunities conflict with the traditional values that require women to remain in the home. According to Derbyshire (1968), Mexican-American adolescent girls experience less conflict over their own identities and social roles than boys. He found girls identifying more closely with Anglo females and their maternal roles, while boys identify more closely with *machismo* and the husband roles of the traditional Mexican culture. In a comparison of Anglo and Chicano responses to sex-role related verbal stimuli, Martinez, Martinez, Olmedo, and Goldman (1976) found that Chicana responses resembled those of Anglos while Chicano males differed from other groups. In a study on Mexican-American acculturation, Go (Note 1) arrived at findings that appear to conflict with those of Derbyshire. She found adolescent Chicanas under 18 years of age to report higher levels of anxiety than young Chicanos. She also found that highly acculturated Chicanas reported higher anxiety than highly acculturated Chicanos. The more acculturated Chicanas became, the greater the anxiety they reported. This was not true for Chicanos. While these studies on acculturation yield somewhat contradictory results, they seem to indicate that acculturation pressures are experienced differently by Mexican-American males and females.

Male-Female Differences

In addition to apparent dissimilarities in response to acculturation, research indicates a number of other psychological differences between Chicano males and females, but studies that look at sex differences are extremely limited. They are also scattered over a variety of topics with findings which, at times, appear contradictory. Therefore, it is difficult to compose either a clear or a consistent psychological profile of the Chicana from empirical data.

PERSONALITY CHARACTERISTICS

In 1969, Hishiki found Mexican-American sixth-grade girls to possess lower self-concepts than Anglo-American girls of the same grade level. In a multiethnic study 3 years later, Larkin (1972) found that girls from homes that gave boys higher status had lower self-esteem than their brothers. Thus, Chicanas had lower self-esteem than Chicanos.

A second dissimilarity between the sexes has been found in the area of field dependence and field independence, concepts proposed by Dyk and Witkin in 1965. Briefly, field dependence-independence refers to an individual's response to external versus internal cues in forming a perceptual judgment.

Ramirez and Price-Williams (1974) found girls to be more field dependent or field "sensitive" than boys in a study of black, Anglo-American, and Mexican-American school children. This study was a followup of earlier research in which Castañeda, Ramirez, and Herold (Note 3) found Mexican-American students to be more field dependent than Anglo-Americans.

In a study of settled and migrant Mexican-Americans, Gecas (1973) found that Mexican-American girls expressed greater awareness of their physical selves and their body images than Mexican-American boys. This awareness of their physical selves, however, may be accompanied by a tendency on the part of Chicanas to possess more diffuse and less defined psychic selves.

Brenneis, Brooks, and Roll (1975) conducted a study of ego modalities in the manifest dreams of male and female Chicanos in which they discovered striking dissimilarities. Males tended to organize their internal psychic world around a highly visible, well demarcated self which was seen as robust, randomly active, and engaged in contentious interactions with unfamiliar characters. Chicanas reported a less sharply defined, less active, and less contentious self that engaged in a greater range of interactions with more familiar characters. These dream selves also appeared to place less emphasis on boundaries, to possess greater predictability, and to engage in more goal-directed locomotion. It therefore seems that while Chicanas may have less well defined psychic selves, these psychic selves are more peaceful and aware of others in their lives.

Further indication of Chicanas' awareness of their physical selves is found in another dream study by Roll and Brenneis (1975). In this study, they found Mexican-American females to have a higher incidence of dreams of death than Mexican-American males, who did not differ from Anglo-American males and females. The researchers explain these findings as the results of a greater tendency of Chicano women to carry the influences of the traditional culture.

Besides experiencing more death dreams, Chicanas were also found to report a greater incidence of depression than Chicanos, who exhibit more aggression (Stoker & Meadow, 1974). These findings were the result of a study of Mexican-American and Anglo-American children brought for treatment to child guidance clinics, and this sample did not come from a normal population. Nevertheless, Stoker and Meadow explain their results as related to culturally determined aspects of family structure, role conflicts, and personality. It appears, then, that Mexican-American males suffering from psychological stress are more likely to direct it outward while females are more likely to turn it inward.

Although Mexican-American girls are not as likely to act out their psychological conflicts as are boys, a study by Littlefield (1974) showed them to be more self-disclosing. When black, Anglo, and Chicano ninth graders were given Rivenbark's revision of Jourard's self-disclosure scale, females reported more self-disclosure than males, across ethnic groups. Mexican-American females indicated a preference for a same-sex friend as the target of self-disclosure. Mothers were ranked second, opposite-sex friends third, and fathers last as confidantes.

SOCIAL DIMENSIONS

A 1968 study by Werner and Evans of perceptions of prejudice in Mexican-American 4- and 5-year-olds found that school accelerated children's ability to discriminate and evaluate color differences. While both girls and boys attributed goodness to white dolls and badness to dark dolls, the boys had a greater tendency to perceive the white adult male dolls as larger than dark ones of the same size. Also, girls did not reject the dark dolls with vehemence, as did boys.

While Chicanas did not reject the dark skinned dolls as much as Chicanos in the Werner and Evans study, another study indicated that they do not choose other Chicanos as frequently as boys. Padilla, Ruiz, and Rice (Note 4) asked a sample of black, Anglo, and Chicano school children to react to photographs of unknown children. Each subject was presented with photographs of six children of his or her own sex, representing the three ethnic groups studied. Among other directions they were given, they were asked to identify the photograph of the child they would "most like to be" and the child they would most like to have as a friend. Only the Chicano children displayed a strong preference for their own ethnic group which is interpreted to reflect pride in group, heritage, and self. However, 81% of the Chicano boys wanted to be like the photographed Chicanos, but only 58% of the Chicano girls chose other Chicanas. Again, in choosing a friend, 75% of the Chicano boys chose Chicanos, while only 53% of the Chicanas did so. As previously stated, there is an apparent contradiction between these findings and those of the previous study.

In terms of cooperative versus competitive behavior, the available research again appears to be somewhat contradictory. Madsen and Shapira (1970) conducted three experiments measuring cooperative and competitive behavior of black, Anglo, and Chicano 7- to 9-year-olds. In the first experiment, Mexican-American boys were less competitive than Mexican-American girls. In the two subsequent experiments, all groups were equally competitive. Kagan and his colleagues (Note 5) have found inconsistent results when comparing the behavior of Chicano boys and girls. Although they found Chicanos to be consistently more cooperative than Anglos, their comparisons of Chicano boys and girls are inconclusive. However, in their most recent studies (Note 6) they have discovered Chicana girls to be significantly less competitive than Chicano boys. It should be noted that a similar sex difference has emerged between Anglos, girls being less competitive than boys.

Kagan thought (personal communication) this difference may be caused by a shift in experimental methodology. Previously children participated in the experiments in pairs, while in the two most recent studies, they were tested individually. When two children are involved in a competitive endeavor, it appears that the pace is set by the more competitive member of the dyad. Therefore, the individual's behavior, without the influence of another individual, probably reflects more accurately his or her own base level of competitive drive. Under these circumstances, Mexican-American girls appear to be more "prosocial," as Kagan terms such behavior, than are boys.

ACADEMIC ACHIEVEMENT

The competitiveness required for success in American schools and the lack of cooperative learning methods in our public schools appear to place Chicanas at a serious disadvantage. This may be one of the reasons for the low academic achievement of Mexican-American females. In successive studies, Mason (1967, 1969) administered the California psychological inventory (C.P.I.) to American Indian, Chicano, and Anglo students. The C.P.I. measures attitudes toward self, so-called "social maturity" and achievement motivation. In the 1967 study, Mason found that Mexican-American females' responses across the 18 subtests were the most consistently negative of all groups. This parallels the findings of Ramirez, Taylor, and Peterson (1971) who found that Mexican-American females differed from males in their responses to the school situations picture stories test which is scored for power, achievement, affiliation, and rejection. On power and affiliation, differences between the scores of males and females were slight; however, females scored lower on achievement and higher on rejection than males.

From these data, the emerging picture of the Chicana's academic performance appears to be negative; but other studies introduce a more positive note. Mason's second study (1969) of American Indian, Anglo, and Chicano students showed a change in the scores of Chicano males and females, females scoring higher than in the first study (Mason, 1967) and males relatively lower. A 1974 study by Fisher of nonintellectual attributes of children in first-grade bilingual-bicultural programs also showed gains on the part of Chicanas. In this study, the Anglo and Chicano children were tested on the Piers-Harris children's self-concept scale and the Howard maze test in order to assess self-concept, self-description, and stimulus-seeking activity. The results indicated that the bilingual-bicultural program significantly enhanced the self-concepts of Chicano girls, but not of Chicano boys. While boys remained unchanged, girls were found to be happier and more satisfied and expressed feelings that their behavior at school had improved. Mexican-American girls also increased their stimulus-seeking activity, that is, they became more open to environmental stimuli, while boys showed no significant change.

SUMMARY OF RESEARCH

A summary of the psychological differences between Mexican-American males and females appears to indicate that Mexican-American females are suffering more from oppression. With respect to personality characteristics, Chicanas show: (*a*) lower self-esteem; (*b*) more field dependence; (*c*) greater identity with families and homes that tend to give males more status; (*d*) more concern about their physical selves; (*e*) less well defined psychic selves, (*f*) more death dreams, and (*g*) more depression. With respect to social dimensions, Chicanas appear not to reject dark skin as much as Chicanos, yet choose Mexican-Americans socially less frequently than do boys. Chicanas also appear to be more prosocial and less competitive than Chicano males. In school, Chicano girls show less achievement and a more generalized negative reaction than boys.

Despite a fairly consistent picture of the effects of oppression, it appears that Chicanas are also more responsive to positive intervention. They appear to benefit more from supportive programs than do males. They also tend to be more self-disclosing, a characteristic that makes them better candidates for traditional therapeutic intervention.

The only conclusion to be drawn from this survey of psychological research on Mexican-Americans is that the data are insufficient. There is a pressing need for carefully conducted studies using Mexican-American females as subjects and for the wide dissemination of the information resulting from these studies. Most important, one must be very cautious in drawing conclusions about Chicanas on the basis of psychological tests and techniques that clearly suffer from Anglocentric bias and were not designed to assess the psychological state of the Chicana.

Androgyny

As was previously noted, the increasing contact of Mexican-Americans with the dominant culture and the resulting acculturation is rapidly modifying sex-role attitudes. Meanwhile, concepts regarding sex role identification in the dominant culture are also being altered. In both the field of psychology and society at large, masculinity and femininity have traditionally been dichotomized, so that an individual was considered feminine or masculine, but not both. It has been proposed that individuals might be psychologically androgynous, therefore possessing masculine *and* feminine characteristics and that androgynous people may be more psychologically healthy than sex-typed individuals (Bem, 1974).

In a study of black, Asian-American, Mexican-American and Anglo-American high school women, Hawley (Note 7) found a correlation between ethnicity and sex-role orientation. Anglo females were the most androgynous, while black females and Chicanas were more sex-typed in their responses. She found, however, that IQ scores were a better predictor of sex-role orientation than ethnic identity, with high IQ girls more likely to be androgynous in orientation than low IQ girls across all ethnic groups studied.

Senour and Warren (Note 8) used the Bem sex-role inventory (BRSI) to assess ethnic differences in masculinity, femininity, and androgyny among Anglos, blacks, and Chicanos. The inventory was administered to community college students: 60 black males, 64 black females, 83 Chicanos, 97 Chicanas, 106 Anglo males, and 144 Anglo females. A two-way analysis of variance (sex by race) was used to analyze the results separately for masculinity, femininity, social desirability, and androgyny.

As expected, significant sex differences were found, females scoring higher on femininity and lower on masculinity than males. Androgyny scores also differed, females scoring in the feminine direction and males in the masculine direction on androgyny.

An interesting finding was that, as a group, blacks scored in the masculine direction on androgyny, while both Anglos and Chicanos scored in the feminine direction, F (2, 548) = 3.33, $p < .036$. The androgyny score is a reflection of the relative strength of a masculine and feminine orientation in a person's self-description. The greater the absolute value of a person's androgyny score, the more the person is sex typed or sex reversed. High positive scores indicate an endorsement of feminine items over masculine items, while high negative scores indicate an endorsement of masculine items over feminine items. The closer the score is to zero, the greater the extent of agreement between the individual's endorsement of masculine and feminine items.

Figure 1 illustrates the differences found among the groups on androgyny. As can be seen, Chicano males scored -.80 while Chicanos scored 1.29. Anglo

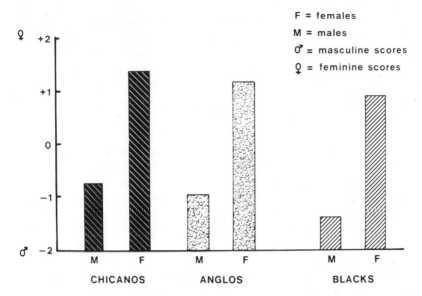

FIGURE 1. The *y* axis represents the mean androgyny *t*-ratio for each ethnic group. This is a bipolar scale with a positive score indicating a higher endorsement of feminine items and a negative score indicating a higher endorsement of masculine items. Note the differences between ethnic groups with Chicanos as a group describing themselves in the most feminine sex-typed terms and blacks as a group describing themselves in the most masculine sex-typed terms.

males scored -1.00 while females scored 1.09. Black males scored -1.43 while females scored .88. Of the three ethnic groups, Chicanos, then, demonstrated the greatest tendency to endorse feminine items over masculine items and Chicano women did so more than did any other category of respondents.

There were, however, no significant sex by race interactions in any of the analyses. Chicanos did not emerge as super masculine in comparison to black or Anglo males, and Chicanas were found to be no more feminine than their black and Anglo counterparts, although there was a tendency in this direction.

It should be noted, however, that the BSRI is an Anglocentric measure and that the black and Chicano subjects used in this study were presumably moderately to highly acculturated. Perhaps future research on ethnicity and sex roles can control these factors and thereby clarify the role of ethnicity in sex-role development and orientation.

Summary

Prior to terminating this chapter, it seems appropriate to reiterate that it would be incautious to accept at face value the profile of the Chicana that has emerged from the work cited. The use of Freudian analysis in examining the Mexican family, the absence of empirical support for much of the work describing Chicano sex roles, the lack of research by Mexican-American women on Mexican-American women, and the insufficiency of current research tools and methodologies should be kept in mind. In addition, this work does not give information on the numerous Chicanas that do not conform to the general norms. On the other hand, it would be equally incautious to simply dismiss the existing literature and research. Careful analysis of each study, article, and book should first be conducted.

It appears that traditionally, the Mexican-American woman has accepted the roles of mother, wife, and homemaker where she has functioned as the pillar of family life. Subservience to her father and later to her husband has long been accepted in silence. It is, however, becoming increasingly apparent that the Chicana is affected by a dominant culture which is in the midst of a sex-role revolution. Although at a different pace than her Anglo counterpart, the Chicana is also changing her traditional sex roles. Since culture is dynamic, this is inevitable.

It seems important that social science research be conducted on the emerging Chicana. Such studies would be useful not only for purposes of developing a psychology of the Chicana but also a means of feedback on the effects sex-role changes will have on Mexican-American culture. It is imperative that the Chicana achieve her full human potential, for she possesses a wealth of human resources that remains untapped by her *raza* (race) and her country. Both for the sake of her fulfillment and for her contribution to society, barriers to her full participation in whatever aspects of life she chooses to involve herself must be eliminated. It seems equally imperative, however, that this struggle be conducted in a manner that avoids polarization from the Chicano, for the Mexican-American woman is only half of the people in need of liberation.

REFERENCE NOTES

1. Go, O. *Mexican American acculturation: Its relation to self-report anxiety and attitudes toward counseling and psychotherapy*. Unpublished master's thesis. California State College San Bernardino, 1975.
2. Paige, K.E. *The effects of oral contraceptives on affective fluctuations associated with the menstrual cycle*. Unpublished doctoral thesis.
3. Castañeda, A., Ramirez, M., & Herold, L. *Culturally democratic learning environments: A cognitive styles approach*. Prepared for the Multi-Lingual Assessment Project. Riverside Component, 1972.
4. Padilla, A.M., Ruiz, R.A., & Rice, A. *Perception of self and future achievement among children of different ethnic backgrounds*. Unpublished manuscript, 1973.
5. Kagan, S., Zahn, G.L., & Gealy, J. *Competition and school achievement among Anglo-American and Mexican-American children*. Unpublished manuscript. University of California at Riverside.
6. Knight, B., & Kagan, S. *Development of altruism, equality, relative gains and rivalry in Anglo-American and Mexican-American children*. Unpublished manuscript. University of California at Riverside.

7. Hawley, P. *The state of the art of counseling high school girls.* (Project Report No. 0675 P). The Ford Foundation Faculty Fellowship for Research on Women's Roles in Society, June 1975.
8. Senour, M.N., & Warren, L.W. *Sex and ethnic difference in masculinity, femininity, and androgyny.* Paper presented at the meeting of the Western Psychological Association, Los Angeles, April 1976.

REFERENCES

Aramoni, A. *Psicoanalsis de la dinamica de un pueblo.* Mexico, D.F.: Universidad Nacional Autonoma de Mexico, 1961.

Brenneis, C., Brooks, & Roll, Samuel. Ego modalities in the manifest dreams of male and female Chicanos. *Psychiatry*, 1975, *38*, 172-185.

Bardwick, J.M. *Psychology of women: A study of biocultural conflicts.* New York: Harper & Row, 1971.

Bem, S.L. The measurement of psychological androgyny. *Journal of Consulting and Clinical Psychology*, 1974, *42*, 155-162.

Coppen, A., & Kessel, N. Menstruation and personality. *British Journal of Psychiatry*, 1963, *109*, 711-721.

Cotera, M. *Profile on the Mexican American woman.* Austin, Tex.: National Educational Laboratory, 1976.

Derbyshire, R.L. Adolescent identity crisis in urban Mexican-Americans in East Los Angeles. In E.B. Brody (Ed.), *Minority group adolescents in the United States.* Baltimore: The Williams and Wilkins Co., 1968.

Diaz-Guerrero, R. Neurosis and the Mexican family structure. *American Journal of Psychiatry*, 1955, *112*, 411-417.

Diaz-Guerrero, R. *Psychology of the Mexican: Culture and personality.* Austin, Tex.: University of Texas Press, 1975.

Dyk, R.B., & Witkin, H.A. Family experiences related to the development of differentiation in children. *Child Development*, 1965, *36*, 21-55.

Fabrega, H.J., Rubel, A., & Wallace, C.A. Working class Mexican psychiatric outpatients: Some social and cultural features. *Archives of General Psychiatry*, 1967, *16*, 704-711.

Fabrega, H., Swartz, J.D., & Wallace, C.A. Ethnic differences in psychopathology. I. Clinical correlates under varying conditions. *Archives of General Psychiatry*, 1968, *19*, 218-266. (a)

Fabrega, H., Swartz, J.D., & Wallace, C.A. Ethnic differences in psychopathology. II. Specific differences with emphasis on the Mexican American group. *Psychiatric Research*, 1968, *6*, 221-235. (b)

Fabrega, H., & Wallace, C.A. Value identification and psychiatric disability: An analysis involving Americans of Mexican descent. *Behavioral Science*, 1968, *13*, 362-371.

Fisher, R.I. A study of non-intellectual attributes of children in first grade bilingual-bicultural programs. Journal of Educational Research, *67*, 323-328.

Frank, R.T. The hormonal causes of premenstrual tension. *Archives of Neurology and Psychiatry*, 1931, *26*, 1053.

Gecas, V. Self conceptions of migrant and settled Mexican-Americans. *Social Science Quarterly*, 1973, *54*, 579-595.

Gonzalez, F. *El Mexicano, psicologia de su destructividad.* Mexico, D.F.: Editorial Pax-Mexico, S.A., 1959.

Hamblen, E.C. Benefits of steroid-induced pseudopregnancy. *Consultant*, February, 1962, p. 4.

Hernandez, C.A., Haug, M.J., & N.N. Wagner (Eds.), *Chicanos: Social and psychological perspectives.* St. Louis, Mo: C.V. Mosby, 1971.

Hishiki, P.C. Self concepts of sixth grade girls of Mexican-American descent. *California Journal of Educational Research, 20*, 56-62, 1969.

Ivey, M.E., & Bardwick, J.M. Patterns of affective fluctuation in the menstrual cycle. *Psychosomatic Medicine*, 1968, *30*.

Jaco, E.G. Social factors in mental disorders in Texas. *Social Problems*, 1957, *4*, 322-328.

Kiev, A. *Transcultural psychiatry*. New York: The Free Press, 1972.

Larkin, R.W. Class, race, sex and preadolescent attitudes. *California Journal of Educational Research*, 1972, *23*, 213-223.

Littlefield, R.P. Self-disclosure among some Negro, White, Mexican American adolescents. *Journal of Counseling Psychology*, 1974, *2*, 133-136.

Madsen, W. Mexican-Americans and Anglo-Americans: A comparative study of mental health in Texas. In S.C. Plog and R.B. Edgerton (Eds.), *Changing perspectives in mental health*. New York: Holt, Rinehart, & Winston, 1969.

Madsen, M.C., & Shapira, A. Cooperative and competitive behavior of urban Afro-Americans, Anglo-Americans, Mexican-Americans, and Mexican village children. *Developmental Psychology*, 1970, *3*, 16-20.

Martinez, J.L. Jr., Martinez, S.R. Olmedo, E.L., & Golman, R.D. The Semantic Differential Technique: A comparison of Chicano and Anglo high school students, *Journal of Cross-Cultural Psychology*, 1976, *7*, 325-333.

Mason, E.P. Comparison of personality characteristics of junior high students from American Indian, Mexican and Caucasian ethnic backgrounds. *Journal of Social Psychology*, 1967, *73*, 145-155.

Mason, E.P. Cross-validation study of personality characteristics of junior high students from American Indian, Mexican, and Caucasian ethnic backgrounds. *Journal of Social Psychology*, 1969, *77*, 15-24.

Murillo, N. The Mexican American family. In C.A. Hernandez, M.J. Haug, and N.N. Wagner (Eds.), *Chicanos: Social and psychological perspectives*. St. Louis: C.V. Mosby, 1971.

Padilla, A.M., & Ruiz, R.A. *Latino mental health: A review of literature*. National Institute of Mental Health, Washington, D.C.: U.S. Government Printing Office, 1973.

Ramirez, M., & Price-Williams, D.R. Cognitive styles of children of three ethnic groups in the U.S. *Journal of Cross-Cultural Psychology*, June 1974, *5*, 212-219.

Ramirez, M., Taylor, C., & Petersen, B. Mexican-American cultural membership and adjustment to school. In C.A. Hernandez, M.J. Haug, and N.N. Wagner (Eds.), *Chicanos: Social and Psychological Perspectives*. St. Louis: C.V. Mosby, 1971.

Ramirez, S. *El Mexicano, psicologia de sus motivaciones*. Mexico, D.F.: Editorial Pax-Mexico, S.A., 1959.

Roll, S., & Brenneis, C. Chicano and Anglo dreams of death: A replication. *Journal of Cross-Cultural Psychology*, September 1975, *6*, 377-383.

San Martin, H. Machismo: Latin America's myth-cult of male supremacy. *il por UNESCO Courier*, 1975, *28*, 28-32.

Shainess, N. A re-evaluation of some aspects of femininity through a study of menstruation: A preliminary report. *Comprehensive Psychiatry*, 1961, *2*, 20-26.

Sherman, J.A. *On the psychology of women*. Springfield, Ill: Charles C Thomas, 1971.

Stoker, D.H., & Meadow, A. Cultural differences in child guidance clinic patients. *International Journal of Social Psychiatry*, 1974, *20*, 186-202.

Sutherland, H., & Stewart, I. A critical analysis of the premenstrual syndrome. *Lancet*, 1965, *1*, 1180-1183.

U.S. Bureau of the Census. *1970 Census of population: Subject reports . . . Persons of Spanish surname*. Washington, D.C.: U.S. Government Printing Office, 1973.

Werner, N., & Evans, I.M. Perception of prejudice in Mexican-American preschool children. *Perceptual and Motor Skills*, 1968, *27*, 1039-1046.

CHAPTER 20

RECOGNIZING AND UNDERSTANDING DIVERSITY: MULTICULTURALISM AND THE CHICANO MOVEMENT IN PSYCHOLOGY

MANUEL RAMIREZ III

University of California, Santa Cruz

WE ARE UNIVERSAL MAN,
a spectral rivulet,
multi-hued and beautiful - -

WE ARE LA RAZA

the cradle of civilization
the crucible of human-ness
yesterday, today, & tomorrow

MESTIZO HUMAN-NESS.

From *Canto y Grito Mi Liberacion*
Ricardo Sanchez

The focus of this chapter is a flexibility/synthesis model for conceptualizing certain aspects of multiculturalism, particularly in the areas of personality development and functioning.[1] Chicano psychology is contributing to a changing perception of the multicultural experience. The conflict and replacement theories are being refuted while participation in more than one sociocultural system — or in widely different aspects of a sociocultural system — is being studied in relation to flexibility, synthesis, and expansion. The multicultural orientation of Chicano psy-

[1]The ideas reflected in this paper have emerged from conversations with many colleagues. I am especially grateful to Professor Alfredo Castañeda, Barbara Cox, Professor Les Herold, James Alan Temple, and Alex Gonzalez.

chology has among its origins a Mestizo world view that represents a confluence of Hispano and Indian sociocultural sytems.

Theories and research approaches based on the history, culture, and psychodynamics of Latinos should be developed by Chicano psychologists together with other Latino psychologists in the United States and abroad. Such a Latino psychology could avoid the limitations and mistaken interpretations that have resulted from exclusive use of theories and approaches derived from Anglo-American — Western European world views.

American Social Science and Psychodynamics of Identity in Members of Minority Groups

American social scientists have abstracted a mythical "superculture" from the behaviors and psychodynamics of an American "majority." In comparison with this superculture, all other sociocultural systems have been judged to have less value and status. Within the assimilationist context that this has fostered, members of minority groups have been expected to abandon identification with their native cultures and to strive for identification with the superculture fabrication of the social scientists. Membership in a minority group has been regarded not as a potential source of multicultural functioning but as a developmental disadvantage. In American society, the minority group member has been expected to "overcome" the "obstacles" of this "disadvantage" and to learn to function "appropriately."

In formulating descriptions of the process whereby minority persons develop this identification, the two models most recurrent in American social science literature have been those of replacement and conflict. The former describes the individual's transfer of identification from the ethnic, racial, or religious group to American "mainstream society," and the latter describes what has been considered part of the identification transfer or replacement process — the conflict that has been seen as inevitable when an individual faces a choice between identifying with his own cultural group and identifying with another sociocultural system.

An early model based on conflict-replacement theory was that proposed by Stonequist (1964) who referred to members of minority groups as "marginal." Stonequist's central theme is reflected in the following statement: "The marginal man as conceived in this study is one who is poised in psychological uncertainty between two (or more) social worlds; reflecting in his soul the discords and harmonies, repulsions and attractions of those worlds. . .[1964, p. 329] ."

According to Stonequist, the "life cycle" of marginal man follows three stages: (a) positive feelings toward the host culture; (b) conscious experience of conflict; and (c) responses to the conflict, which may be prolonged and more or less successful in terms of adjustment. Furthermore, the third stage may encourage the individual to adopt one of three roles: (a) nationalism — organization of a collective movement to raise the status of the group: (b) intermediation — bringing the two cultures closer to promote accommodation; and (c) assimilation. Although

Stonequist commented on the possibility that some of these situations or conditions might result in creativity, citing the case of the Jewish people, for the most part his model focused on conflict and implied that the only "healthy" resolution is assimilation into the dominant culture.

Another prominent model of the conflict genre was proposed by psychologist Irving Child (1943) who focused on young adult male second-generation Italian-Americans in New Haven. Child observed that socialization occurred within a dual cultural context, Italian and American. In describing the conflict he observed in his subjects, Child suggested a framework based on three types of conflict reaction: (*a*) the rebel reaction — behaviors indicating desire to achieve complete acceptance by the American majority group and to reject Italian associations; (*b*) the in-group reaction — behaviors indicating an active desire to participate in and identify with the Italian group; and (*c*) the "apathetic reaction" — a retreat from conflict situations and avoidance of strong "rebel" and "in-group" behaviors.

The apathetic reaction, according to Child, could be observed in the individual making a partial approach toward both cultures in an effort to find a compromise as solution to the conflict. It is interesting to note that Child chose to view this attempt at adjustment as "apathetic."

In addition to the central role given to conflict in the Stonequist and Child models, a notion of cultural replacement was implied. Although it is a simplification, the models could be described as viewing the minority group member positioned on a continuum between two cultural poles — a linear model. As the individual becomes more identified with one of the cultures, he moves away from the other culture, replacing values and lifestyles of one with those of the other.

Challenges to the Conflict-Replacement Models

Despite the popularity that the conflict and replacement theories apparently enjoyed, researchers studying different aspects of minority group experience have begun to propose other descriptions of participation in two or more cultures. McFee (1968), for example, working in a Blackfeet reservation, observed that individuals accepted or adopted behaviors of a second culture, expanding their repertoire of behavior potential, without setting aside the first culture. Appropriately, the article is entitled "The 150% Man: A Product of Blackfeet Acculturation."

McFee found that the bicultural reservation community provided a variety of roles and situations for selective use of Indian and white behaviors. To describe the biculturalism of his subjects, McFee developed a two-dimensional matrix. The vertical axis represented Indian orientation (as indicated by knowledge of Blackfoot language, religious beliefs, and lore, participation in ceremonies, dances, and songs), and the horizontal axis represented white orientation (as indicated by behavior indicating knowledge of American mainstream culture). Each subject's participation in the two cultures was then plotted on the matrix to show a scattergram representation of the sample.

Fitzgerald (1971) conducted research with Maori university graduates in New Zealand and provided another model of biculturalism. His investigations focused on the dynamic nature of situations and situational adjustments using a "biographical role" approach. While other researchers interpreted cultural change in Maoris as occurring exclusively in the direction of European culture, Fitzgerald hypothesized that Maori individuals experienced dual acculturation. That is, Maoris are socialized into both Maori culture and New Zealand culture. Fitzgerald concluded that it is possible for an individual to utilize the "norms" of one culture while participating in another. He described the Maori university graduates as having developed a cultural compartmentalization in their lives — the ability to shift from one perspective to another while participating in a succession of transactions in the two cultures.

Fitzgerald concluded that cultural orientation and identification in Maoris operates selectively, depending on situational factors, including interaction and expectation. To a large extent, the social structure regulates which aspects of the two cultures would be available to the individual to ultimately learn or adopt, but, according to Fitzgerald, individual choice becomes highly significant in acculturative settings. Fitzgerald further described Maoris as differentially developing the capacity for flexibility and the ability to "shuttle" between the two cultures (depending on the amount of exposure to situations in the European culture and their own choice).

Basic to Fitzgerald's discussion are the concepts of social and cultural identity. For example, an individual's behavior in a specific situation could reflect a European social identity while the Maori cultural identity would remain unaffected; the individual could function in a European role without that experience causing or reflecting any change in his cultural identity. Fitzgerald's model implies that external or behavioral biculturalism has little effect on the basic personality structure or on cultural identity.

Another interesting discussion of multicultural functioning is that of Peter Adler (1974), who described a fluidity brought about by multicultural experience. Adler's multicultural man is ever in transition — values, beliefs, attitudes, and world views are relevant only to given situations and are continually evolving and being reformulated through experience. Adler's position is in many ways a challenge to the conflict and replacement models. On the other hand, Adler's multicultural man replaces his original cultural identification with a supraculturalism. While the multicultural individual of Adler may not necessarily suffer the conflicts described by Child (1943) or Stonequist (1964), he is susceptible to a "loss of self" or "diffused identity."

Chicano Experience and the Conflict Model

Octavio Paz's (1959) description of the Chicano experiences in Los Angeles in the 1940s supported the conflict-replacement model. Paz concluded that pachucos had no cultural identity, that they were ashamed of their origins, and that they refused to identify with mainstream American culture:

Lo que me parece distinguirlos del resto de la poblacion es su aire furtivo e inquieto, de seres que se disfrazan, de seres que temen la mirada ajena, capaz de desnudarlos y dejarlos en cueros. Cuando se habla con ellos se advierte que su sensibilidad se parece a la del pendulo, un pendulo que ha perdido la razon y que oscila con violencia y sin compas. Este estado de espiritu – o de ausencia de espiritu – ha engendrado lo que se ha dado en llamar el "pachuco" [1959, pp. 12-13].

Paz did not recognize the possibility that pachucos may have been in the process of developing a bicultural identity, neither Mexican nor mainstream American, but an amalgamation of the two sociocultural systems. Like Child (1943), Paz (1959) focused on conflict and more specifically on what Child termed the rebel and apathetic reactions to that conflict. Paz did not recognize that the pachucos' drive to be different may have been part of an attempt to establish a new identity in a hostile environment that made continuation of a strong Mexican culture impossible. Paz criticized pachucos both for being unwilling to assimilate into mainstream culture and for having apparently severed their ties with Mexican culture:

Desprendido de su cultura tradicional, el pachuco se afirma un instante como soledad y reto. Niega a la sociedad de que procede y a la norteamericana. El 'pachuco' se lanza al exterior, pero no para fundirse con lo que lo rodea, sino para retarlo. Gesto suicida, pues el 'pachuco' no afirma nada, no defiende nada, excepto su exasperada voluntad de no-ser. (1959, p. 16).

Conclusions similar to those of Paz were drawn by Madsen (1964) who observed Chicanos in South Texas. Like Paz, Madsen seemed to adopt the conflict-replacement model. He described Chicanos as caught between dissimilar and demanding sociocultural systems and concluded that the difficult choice between cultures results in ambivalence and conflict. Madsen focused on the psychodynamics of those Chicanos whom Child would have identified as "rebels," those who most desired to participate fully in American mainstream culture and deny their Mexican and Chicano heritage. He hypothesized that these people experienced severe feelings of guilt, frequently turning to alcohol for relief, and labeled those who adopted this role "alcoholic agringados."

Nonconflict Models Describing Chicano Biculturalism

Recent research, some of it conducted by Chicano investigators, has indicated that the bicultural experiences of Chicanos may not be entirely negative and may in fact provide the basis for more flexible and sophisticated psychological adjustment. For example, Long and Padilla (Note 1) surveyed successful (Ph.D. recipients) and unsuccessful (dropouts) Chicano graduate students at the University of New Mexico. They found that 94% of the successful students but only 7 to 8% of the unsuccessful students reported being reared in bilingual homes.

A study by Henderson and Merritt (1969) also indicated that biculturalism might give Chicanos an advantage in terms of successful adjustment to educational environments. They tested Chicano preschool children in Tucson to determine their potential for success in school and then interviewed and tested the mothers of these subjects. The results showed that the mothers of the children who showed high potential had participated more in both Chicano and Anglo sociocultural systems and also scored higher on a test of Spanish vocabulary than the mothers of low potential children.

Ramirez and Castañeda (1974) identified bicultural Chicano children using a behavior observation instrument that included willingness to speak Spanish and English, role playing Chicano and non-Chicano characters, friendship patterns, and other factors. These bicultural elementary school children in Southern California demonstrated greater flexibility in their behavior than "monocultural" children. The bicultural children exhibited greater ability to shift learning and social behaviors according to the demands of a situation or the requirements of a task. The flexibility demonstrated by the bicultural Chicano children may be similar to that described by Fitzgerald as occurring among the Maoris in New Zealand.

To conceptualize biculturalism in Chicanos, Ramirez and Castañeda (1974) proposed a model of bicognitive development and functioning. This model assumed that traditional Chicano culture encourages development of personality functioning characteristic of a field sensitive cognitive style, whereas experience with the majority culture encourages a field independent cognitive style. According to this conceptualization, the bicultural develops factors characteristic of either style of functioning and, furthermore, may develop unique behaviors and perceptual modes as a result of merging elements of both styles.

A Flexibility-Synthesis Model of Chicano Biculturalism

To better understand the psychodynamics and developmental process of biculturalism in Chicanos, we are presently conducting research with Chicano college students. College students were chosen as subjects for this endeavor since they are at a stage in personality development where they can examine multicultural experiences consciously and intensively. They are also able to evaluate socialization and life experiences in terms of their relative contribution to the development of a multicultural orientation.

The initial phase of this research project involved a series of life history interviews with some Chicano college students who, judging from behavioral observations over a period of several months and socialization and demographic information obtained from a short questionnaire, appeared to be multicultural in their lifestyles. These life histories provided further information about socialization and other life experiences that served as the focal points for developing item pools for a questionnaire of Chicano multiculturalism. The items developed were then field tested with other college students who had also been identified as multicultural on the criteria listed above and with students who on these same criteria seemed to be monocultural. Items that discriminated best between the multiculturals and monoculturals in the field testing and were also identified as having tapped sources of multicultural experiences were then chosen for inclusion in a Chicano multiculturalism inventory. This questionnaire is presently being administered to Chicano college students in universities and colleges in southern, central, and northern California. Those students who are identified as multicultural will be invited to participate in intensive life history interviews and in testing on a variety of personality variables. From these data, profiles of multicultural Chicano college students will be developed. The profiles should provide some information on which to base a model of multicultural development and functioning.

The information obtained from the pilot life histories and the short questionnaire allowed us to make some preliminary efforts toward evolving a model to describe the development of multiculturalism in Chicanos. We refer to this tentative conceptual framework as the flexibility-synthesis model. The model asserts that as a consequence of meeting the demands of two or more cultures — or of widely different situational demands within the same sociocultural system — the individual can develop a greater variety of areas of personality functioning (flexibility). As a function of a person's experiences in two or more sociocultural systems, values, attitudes, perceptual modes, and coping styles specific to each sociocultural system are developed. Furthermore, under certain conditions, the factors specific to each sociocultural system can be merged with those of another with which the person has had experience (synthesis). This amalgamation in turn results in new values, attitudes, perceptual modes, and coping styles that are multicultural (expansion).

Environmental situations may produce episodes of behavior or personality states based on the stimulation of a set of values, attitudes, perceptual modes, and coping styles that may be linked to a sociocultural premise (Diaz-Guerrero, 1972) of the individual's first culture, another culture that he or she has experienced, or a rearrangement of elements that has resulted from a multicultural experience. The set of values, attitudes, perceptual modes, and coping styles will be called a sociocultural module. The cognitive style reflected in the personality state — field sensitive, field independent, or a combination — therefore, reflects, to a certain degree, the cognitive style associated with the values, attitudes, perceptual modes, and coping styles being stimulated in a given environment.

The socialization and life experiences to which individuals have been exposed determine their potential for becoming multicultural. Socialization and life experiences increase the pool of available values, attitudes, perceptual modes, and coping styles individuals have in their repertoires. The data obtained from the life histories of the multicultural subjects indicated that their parents established friendships with people of different backgrounds and also provided them with opportunities to come into contact with different languages and cultures. In addition, the communities in which these subjects lived and the schools they attended facilitated contact between people of different ethnic groups and peoples of the same ethnic group whose backgrounds and experiences were different. Socialization and life experiences also determine attitudes of individuals, attitudes that are critical in terms of determining potential for multiculturalism. Positive experiences with other cultures and languages facilitated development of multicultural modules.

The synthesis experience, that is, the bringing together of elements of sociocultural modules that developed from socialization and life experiences in different cultures to arrive at a new combination of elements — and at a new philosophy of life based on participation in two or more cultures — makes the individual a functioning multicultural. The life history data indicated that this integration is more likely to occur when the individual is faced with a life dilemma or is attempting to establish life goals. It is possible that this happened because the subjects could recall the dilemma situation and the conscious effort to articulate various personality components. This does not, however, exclude the possibility that this type of integration occurs without conscious analysis by the individual.

The new sociocultural modules that develop from synthesis experiences make it possible for individuals to continue to develop multiculturally. They serve three major functions: (*a*) they give meaning and direction to a person's life (they make up the philosophy of life), (*b*) they make it possible for a person to function meaningfully and effectively in different sociocultural settings or in widely different situations of the same culture, and (*c*) they make it possible for the person to have meaningful interpersonal relationships with people of different backgrounds. The sociocultural modules that result from synthesis are the key to continued multicultural development. These multicultural modules make it possible for individuals to overcome such interpersonal barriers as stereotypes, foreign accents, and physical attributes that often serve to keep people of different sociocultural systems from having meaningful interactions. In overcoming these barriers, individuals are able to establish significant relationships with people whose backgrounds are different from their own, thus learning about other persons' significant life experiences and sociocultural modules that can serve to elaborate and enhance their own modules and even help them to establish new ones.

Multicultural persons can benefit from the life experiences and guiding life philosophies of people of other cultures. In addition, this ability to relate to others exposes them to cognitive styles or aspects of cognitive styles with which they are unfamiliar, thereby stimulating development of bicognitive functioning. These synthesis experiences, and the resultant sociocultural modules, which make it possible for individuals to function bicognitvively and interact meaningfully with people and institutions of other cultures, might result in the creativity and adaptability that Stonequist (1964) and Adler (1974) observed in multicultural people.

From the life histories, we were also able to ascertain that multicultural persons can maintain their identity with the culture or cultures in which they were socialized or had had extensive life experiences. Those modules, based on the sociocultural premises of the cultures with which they have interacted, are part of their repertoires. Nevertheless, the particular philosophies of life that individuals have derived from their multicultural experiences have given them new and personalized perspectives from which to view sociocultural systems. From this multicultural perspective, individuals are able to discern aspects of those cultures that are barriers to individual and collective growth and do not permit individuals to communicate effectively and work together cooperatively. Multicultural persons can thus be effective change agents between members of the cultures with which they have had contact.

The Mestizo World View and Biculturalism-Multiculturalism in Chicanos

Mexican philosophers such as Vasconcelos (1976) and Zea (1974) proposed that the mestizo experience and world view encourage the development of multiculturalism in Latinos. Vasconcelos predicted that a new race of people, *la raza cosmica*, would emerge from a synthesis of the world's four principal races. This confluence of the races would produce a race of *"Totinem"* or "whole men." Latin America, Vasconcelos believed, was fertile ground for development of *la raza cosmica*, because this part of the world had already evolved a *mestizaje*.

Zea (1974), on the other hand, viewed multiculturalism as the vehicle by which oppressed peoples could escape the dependency that had been imposed on them. He saw Latino and black identity struggles as necessary first steps toward understanding the meaning of human experience. Zea concluded that whites attach so much importance to skin color that they are unable to perceive themselves as similar to other peoples; consequently human experience becomes a meaningless abstraction for them. On the other hand, Latinos and blacks see themselves as similar to others because the skin color which makes them different from whites also makes them similar to many other people. This feeling of a bond with others has led Latinos and blacks to a different perspective of the human experience. Furthermore, because of racism and oppression, Latinos and blacks have focused more on their identities, according to Zea, and have learned to accept themselves. As a consequence of this self-acceptance, they are more receptive to the life experiences and the world view of others. Zea, however, warned of dangers in assimilation. The lifestyles of Latinos and blacks should be enriched by incorporating life styles and world views of European and Anglo-American cultures; European and Anglo-American peoples should also learn from the lifestyles and world views of Latino and Black cultures. Zea's words argue for multiculturalism:

> Se trata, no de ser incorporado, asimilado, sino de incorporar y asimilar. Es en esta preocupación que coinciden negritud y mestizaje latinoamericano. El negro no quiere dejar de ser negro para ser blanco, como tampoco el latinoamericano dejar de ser mestizo para ser europeo o anglo-sajón. De lo que se trata es de 'comulgar' la cultura del blanco, la cultura europea u occidental, asi como toda expresión cultural del hombre sin que por ello se deje de ser hombre concreto, negro o latino-americano. El ser negro o el ser latino-americano debe ser enriquecido, ampliado, nunca negado. A su vez, el otro, el blanco, el occidental, cualquier hombre, puede enriquecerse con la experiencia cultural del negro y el latino-

americano. Tal es lo que ofrece la negritud, tal es lo que ofrece el latinoamericano a otras culturas, la experiencia cultural del hombre en otra circunstancia o situación. Experiencias que pueden y deben ser conocidas por hombres de otras latitudes para que reconozcan en ellas otra dimensión del hombre [1974, p. 71].

Zea stresses the importance of multiculturalism while underlining the importance of maintaining cultural identity. This mestizo world view parallels many of the central premises of the flexibility-synthesis model because it has been central to the life experiences of Chicanos and to the philosophy of the Chicano movement. The concept of *la raza*, for example, has figured prominently in the socialization of many Chicanos and has led many to feel that there is a spiritual bond between them and other mestizos. The most prominent symbol of the Chicano movement, la virgin de Guadalupe, is a mestizo symbol.

Conclusion

The diversity of Chicano culture, along with the economic, historical, and political realities of the Chicano experience in the Untied States, has provided a unique opportunity for participation in many sociocultural systems and for synthesis experiences. This ability to share with others and learn from others is what the poet Ricardo Sanchez (1971) called Mestizo human-ness and is at the heart of multiculturalism. This mestizo experience and world view is guiding the Chicano psychology movement toward developing new theoretical and research approaches. Furthermore, together with Mexican and Latino social scientists, Chicano psychologists are beginning to develop a Latino psychology that reflects this mestizo world view and the mestizo multicultural experience. It is to be hoped that this will become a part of a worldwide movement to develop theories and approaches in the social sciences that are based on the history, culture, and traditions of the people involved. One of the most important goals of the Chicano psychology movement, then, is to identify the positive effects of diversity on individuals and societies and to counteract the tendency of traditional social science to be ethnocentric and colonial in its orientation.

REFERENCE NOTE

1. Long, K.K., & Padilla, A.M. An assessment of successful and unsuccessful college students. American Association for the Advancement of Science. Regional meeting, Colorado Springs, Colorado, 1969.

REFERENCES

Adler, P.S. Beyond cultural identity: Reflections on cultural and multicultural man. Richard Brison (Ed.), *Topics in culture learning* (Vol. 2). Hawaii: East-West Culture Learning Institute, 1974.

Child, I.L. *Italian or American? The second generation in conflict.* New Haven: Yale University Press, 1943.

Diaz-Guerrero, R. *Hacia una teoria historico-biopsico-sociocultural del comportamiento humano.* Mexico: Editorial Trillas, 1972.

Fitzgerald, T.K. *Education and identity — A reconsideration of some models of acculturation and identity.* New Zealand Council of Educational Studies, 1971, 45-57.

Henderson, R.W., & Merritt, C.C. Environmental backgrounds of Mexican American children with different potentials for school success. *The Journal of Social Psychology*, 1969, *75*, 101-106.

Madsen, W. The alcoholic agringado. *American Anthropologist*, 1964, *66*, 355-361.

McFee, M. The 150% man, a product of Blackfeet acculturation. *American Anthropologist*, 1968, *70*, 1096-1103.

Paz, O. *El laberinto de la soledad* (2nd Ed.), Mexico, D.F.: Fondo de Cultura Economica, 1959.

Ramirez, M. III, & Castañeda, A. *Cultural democracy, bicognitive development and education.* New York: Academic Press, 1974.

Sanchez, R. *Canto y grito mi liberacion*, El Paso: Mietla Publications, 1971.

Stonequist, E.V. The marginal man: A study in personality and culture conflict. E. Burgess and D. J. Bogue (Eds.), *Contributions to Urban Sociology.* Chicago: University of Chicago Press, 1964.

Vasconcelos, J. *La raza cosmica* (4th ed.). Mexico, D.F.: Espasa-Calpe Mexicana, S.A., 1976.

Zea, L. *Dependencia y liberacion en la cultura latinoamericana.* Mexico, D.F.: Editorial Joaquín Mortiz, S.A., 1974.

CHAPTER 21

TRADITIONALISM, MODERNISM, AND ETHNICITY

ALFREDO CASTAÑEDA

Stanford University

In previous work (Ramirez & Castañeda, 1974) a relationship between ethnicity and "learning styles" was proposed as a means of conceptualizing both interethnic and intraethnic sources of variability.[1] Ethnicity was defined in terms of those values presumed to be characteristic of an ethnic group. Learning style comprises variability in incentive preferences, preferences with regard to modes of relating and communicating as well as modes of cognitive processing. The major factor mediating these relationships is those socialization practices related to the development of specific preferences. As applied to Mexican-American children, variability in learning styles was assumed to be related to the degree to which Mexican rural values, or those of the "mainstream American middle class," or some combination of the two, served as the basis for determining socialization goals and practices. The basic relation is depicted schematically in Figure 1.

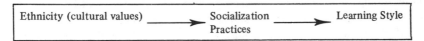

FIGURE 1. Relation between ethnicity and learning style.

Reexamination of the two sets of values suggests that they reflect or are based on two distinguishable sets of comprehensive beliefs concerning the universe,

[1] It is a rare personal pleasure to participate in and contribute the keynote address to the First Symposium on Chicano Psychology. For my contribution I have chosen to share some thoughts which have come not only to influence my teaching but also my efforts to clarify the psychological understanding of that one important concept which, in my own opinion, unites our diverse concerns more than any other, biculturality.

the environment, and humanity's relation to them. These two sets of beliefs have been conventionally referred to as *traditional* versus *modern* beliefs. Indeed, much of recent world history can be described in terms of the conflict between traditionalism and modernism (Nisbet, 1970) that erupted at the end of the nineteenth century, given form by the democratic and industrial revolutions. The conflict has since continued in life and literature, politics and culture, in both macrocosm and microcosm. Each defines a distinctly different perception of reality and may be thought of as the genesis of *dialectically* opposed sets of values and goals, "preferred modes of behavior and end states of existence [Rokeach, 1973]," which, in turn, serve as determinants of socialization goals and practices in different sociocultural systems. Inkeles (1976) has recently suggested that Weber's analysis of the Protestant ethic is the prototype for this mode of analysis, particularly with reference to modernism. The present analysis suggests that the character of both interethnic and intraethnic variability may be strongly influenced by the unique pattern of confluence of traditional and modern beliefs in the history of any ethnic group.

It is estimated that approximately two-thirds of the earth's four billion people live in environments where traditional values prevail (Critchfield, 1976). The politics of the conflict reaches its more poignant heights, however, in those polyethnic societies where traditional and modern beliefs continue to vie for pre-eminence in national policy and in the everyday life of the people. While the dialectical and political dimensions of the conflict between traditional and modern beliefs are relatively more apparent, it is not understood whether the conflict is also based on a *psychological* incompatibility between the two belief systems. For individuals in such societies, accommodation to these two forces may be complicated by the political dimensions of the conflict.

When modernistic beliefs prevail in the institutional life of a given polyethnic society, the acculturation of the various ethnic groups within the society may be gauged by the degree to which the newly acquired "preferred modes of behavior and end-states of existence" (values) reflect modernistic beliefs. In such societies the "successful" assimilation of new immigrant groups appears to take place more rapidly among those groups who have been previously influenced by modernistic beliefs, despite the presence of marked language differences.

If these two belief systems play a significant role in the determination of values, socialization goals, and practices and if the individual *interacts* (Inkeles, 1975a, b) with these two systems, any psychological theory that takes this into account could be of value in fuller understanding the sociopsychological situation not only of Mexican-Americans but also of other ethnic groups. Indeed, the present analysis suggests that in those polyethnic societies where the two belief systems are differentially emphasized, depending on what aspect of life is considered, a major need would be to learn to function competently and effectively in each. This need appears to be most compelling when the individual perceives that each belief system is associated with different but more or less equally important sources of support, such as social versus economic sustenance. Viewed in this manner, such a situation appears to imply some form of biculturality, that is, the individual comes to learn of the need to acquire two different sociocultural competencies in order to meet the need for the two types of support. In some cases, differences between the two belief systems may be associated with ethnic differences such as language; and in other cases, they are not.

Selected Aspects of Traditionalism and Modernism

Selected examples of both traditional and modern beliefs are presented in Table 1. These examples represent but a few of the two types of beliefs described by other writers.

TABLE 1
Type of Belief and Its Focus

Focus of belief	Type of belief	
	Traditional	Modern
Creation of the Universe	Sacred	Rational
Identity	Community	Individual
Social organization	Hierarchical	Egalitarian

CREATION OF THE UNIVERSE

In the traditional mode, accounts and explanations of the beginning (and the end) of the universe, birth, death, the animate and inanimate environment, relations between the sexes, the origin of the group, and the purpose and meaning of existence assume the existence of a supernatural force. In the politics of the conflict between traditionalism and modernism, the sacred account has been and continues to be referred to as both "superstition" and "primitive." Interethnic variability can be reflected in the character and form manifested in religious values and practices. Thus, for example, Mexican Catholicism has evolved selected practices, imagery, and symbolism unique to its history and rendering it distinguishable from Italian or Irish Catholicism.

If the focus of socialization is on moral and ethical behavior in the traditional mode, the diety punishes and rewards accordingly. Internalization of the appropriate symbolism or imagery may lead to some form of manipulation of the self (confession, penance, or sacrifice) as a means of exculpation. That is to say that *blame-acceptance* becomes a "preferred mode of behavior" since it leads to the "preferred end-state existence" without the anguishing pangs of guilt. The continuing politics of the conflict may result in the view from the modern mode stressing, as it does, that reason is the supreme authority in matters of opinion, belief, or conduct and that such behavior is "nonadaptive" or exemplifies "residues of primitive, superstitious ritual." Assuming that psychology, when practiced as a scientifically based discipline, adopts the perceptions of modern belief, it can become susceptible to the politics of the conflict. The modernist's conception, in stressing the *secular*, appears to have resulted in a belief in a search (scientific) for the *universal* in evolving a scheme for moral and ethical conduct. Indeed, the current emphasis on the logical aspects of American developmental psychology, particularly as reflected in the work of Piaget, can be interpreted as consistent with identifying an interest in and developing those attributes necessary for optimal functioning within the modern perception of reality. Thus it is not surprising that more recent approaches to moral and ethical development stressed the rational (reasoning) dimension such that "value clarification" is viewed as an essentially logical process.

IDENTITY

More than any other modern in the Western tradition, Rousseau sculpted the image of the monolithic political (institutional) community into a fortress erected against the tyrannies and injustices presumed to be the product of the traditional sense of community (kinship, region, social stratification, and ethnicity). Thus, the politics of the conflict, from the modern point of view, called for divesting oneself of such forms of loyalty and seeking the development of impartial (to ethnic, regional, social, and kinship loyalties) institutions in order to regulate conduct and resources. Consequently, human identity evolved another option, identification with such institutions rather than with the traditional sense of community. In so doing, according to the modernist view, the individual would become free from traditional loyalties and obligations thought to impede self-fulfillment.

One of the important consequences for values and socialization within the modern conception has been the reordering of priorities of two human motives; that the purpose of individual human endeavor is for the welfare of either the self or the community traditionally defined. Consequently, socialization practices stressing competition as a preferred mode of behavior appear to place greater value on the welfare of the self whereas those stressing cooperation value benefit the community more highly. In this connection, it is of interest to note that in many brands of psychotherapy indigenous to American psychology, of which the methods and philosophy developed by Carl R. Rogers is a prominent example, the general goal is the improvement or fulfillment of some aspect of the self. Interpretations of the source, nature, and amelioration of psychological problems differ between the two belief systems. It is frequently observed that among traditionally oriented individuals, problems involving the family have the highest priority and that the family therapy approach (if the therapeutic goal is clearly the welfare of the family) appears appropriate.

SOCIAL ORGANIZATION

The modernist sense of social organization in the form of democratic ideology and an emphasis upon the positive rights of the individual and antipathy to totalitarian control by governments has supplied a value system defining socialization practices and goals. Behaviors implying independence from totalitarian control (internal locus of control) such as deciding upon and initiating courses of action (self-initiativeness), relying less on authority figures (parents, teachers) for seeking information (preference for the discovery approach to learning) achieved competitive status over prescribed examples. A behavior valued because it reflects the positive rights of individuals is *assertiveness*. Indeed, minority status among several ethnic groups, including Mexican-Americans, is presumed to result from *non*-assertiveness, and recent proposals for assertiveness training programs are based on the assumption that assertive (verbal) behaviors need to be taught and developed. This conception can be contrasted with the traditional view that community cohesiveness, strength, and stability are directly related to the degree to which those in authority (in the kinship form of community these would be parents, grandparents, elder siblings, godparents, and so on) meet these obligations and responsibilities by behavior (decision making, for example) oriented toward the welfare of the community. The traditional view, then, generates or is consistent with respect for authority since it is a source of guidance, wisdom, and vital information. In this connection, it is interesting to note that the Spanish term *malcriado* (ill-bred) implies criticism of those responsible for rearing a child who exhibits *disrespect* in the form of challenge or defiance of parental authority. Such behavior, furthermore, is incompatible with that style of teaching and learning thought to be most consistent with the socialization goal of respect, modeling, and imitation.

Summary and Conclusions

It is my personal belief that the politics of conflict between traditional and modern beliefs have diminished in intensity, at least to the extent that closer examination of the two belief systems may be profitable in suggesting their importance to social and psychological theories of ethnicity and biculturality. This seems most appropriate to theories of ethnicity and biculturality that stress the role of *values*. For these reasons, I have suggested viewing the two belief systems as potential sources of both interethnic and intraethnic variability, a viewpoint which may help to further understanding of acculturation. For example, if acculturation implies the acquisition of preferred modes of behavior and end-states of existence associated with a different belief system, the process of acculturation may be accompanied by greater resistance than if the modes of behavior and end-states are consistent or compatible with the present belief system of the individual. Furthermore, it would appear necessary that the individual's perception of the politics of the conflict be understood, for it may also be an important determinant of the character and form of acculturation. Most important, and perhaps paradoxical, it seems that a democratic society is confronted with the need for impartial attention to the two belief systems in the evolution of public policies and institutions. There is a need for the application of democracy in the domain of cultural differences. Throughout the world, this need is as pressing today as when the American Constitution was created.

REFERENCES

Critchfield, R. Survivors at the fringe. *The bridge: A Journal of Cross-Cultural Affairs*, 1976, 5-6.

Inkeles, A. Becoming modern: Individual change in six developing countries. *Ethos*, 1975, 323-342. (b)

Inkeles, A. Understanding and misunderstanding individual modernity. In L.A. Caser, and O.N. Larsen (Eds.), *The uses of controversy in sociology*. New York: The Free Press, 1976, 103-130. (a)

Nisbet, R.A. *Tradition and revolt*, New York: Vintage Books, 1970.

Ramirez, M., & Castañeda, A. *Cultural democracy, bicognitive development and education*. New York: Academic Press, 1974.

Rokeach, M. *The nature of human values*. New York: The Free Press, 1973.